Understanding Statistics in Education

Understanding Statistics in Education

W. James Popham
University of California, Los Angeles

Kenneth A. Sirotnik
University of Washington

F. E. Peacock Publishers, Inc.   Itasca, Illinois

Cover Painting:
Stuart Davis, *Ready-to-Wear*, 1955
Oil on canvas, 142.9 × 106.7 cm
Gift of Mr. and Mrs. Sigmund Kunstadter
© 1991 The Art Institute of Chicago
All rights reserved

Copyright © 1992
F. E. Peacock Publishers, Inc.
All rights reserved
Library of Congress Catalog Card No. 90–63795
ISBN 0–87581–348–8
Printed in the United States of America
Printing: 10 9 8 7 6 5 4 3 2 1
Year: 96 95 94 93 92

Contents

Tables

Preface

Old wine in new bottles? Why not?...as long as the aging has been kind, the repackaging has not caused damage, and, as a bonus, the product has become more appealing and more accessible to contemporary consumers.

Metaphorically speaking, we believe this applies in important ways to this text. The astute reviewer will find much that it has in common with—indeed, is basically identical to—our earlier text *Educational Statistics: Use and Interpretation,* published in 1973 as a revision of the original 1967 version. The 1973 volume was used for nearly 15 years by teachers and students before it went out of print.

We have revived and repackaged this book on statistics because, in the 1990s as in the 1960s, there is a need in elementary statistics courses for a straightforward, easy-to-read, nontechnical and nonthreatening, hands-on treatment of basic statistical methods. The focus is on the methods students of education are likely to encounter as they review the literature or complete their thesis or dissertation work. We have enjoyed much positive feedback from instructors and teachers regarding the pedagogical usefulness of the preceding versions. It seems to us, therefore, that the book ought to be made available to them and their students at least through the end of this century.

Thanks to Ted Peacock and F. E. Peacock Publishers, this is now possible. We have retained all of the features from preceding editions that made the text unique and were most valued by teachers and students. Paramount among these is our use of companion chapters for the principal statistical techniques; in each case, a chapter on the *conceptual* underpinnings of the method is followed by a chapter on the corresponding *computational* procedures. We believe that when students acquire an intuitive understanding of how a procedure works, they can learn how to do the computations involved in the procedure more easily. We also remain firm believers in the value of computations "by hand" in order to solidify conceptual understanding, as well as to demonstrate the importance of becoming intimately familiar with one's own data.

Nevertheless, we acknowledge that things *have* changed on the way to the 21st century. For statisticians, the foremost change has been the technological explosion and the ready availability to students of electronic calculators and computers to aid in computations. In addition to updating our language and modernizing some of our examples, we have developed a concluding chapter on computer data processing using the popular SPSS statistical computing package as an example. We have augmented our treatment of analysis-of-variance methods by including conceptual and computational discussions of a priori and post hoc comparison procedures. To allow for these needed additions, we have eliminated the rather simplistic chapter on factor analysis that appeared in our earlier text, since such multivariate methods are accessible in many other elementary and advanced statistics texts. We are grateful to the Literary Executor of the late Sir Ronald A. Fisher, F.R.S., to Dr. Frank Yates, F.R.S., and the Longman Group Ltd., London, for permission to reprint Tables III and IV from their book *Statistical Tables for Biological, Agricultural and Medical Research* (6th edition, 1974). Finally, with relevant modifications, we have retained another feature which was positively received—the programmed-learning chapter on selecting statistical techniques. Like paper and pencil, some old ideas still prove useful.

December 1990

W. James Popham
Kenneth A. Sirotnik

Introduction

One mark of the professional practitioner—physicians, attorneys, educators—is a continuing interest in acquiring new knowledge and skills. In medicine, for example, surgeons seek knowledge that will enable them to perform their delicate tasks more effectively. Professionals in education, too, seek new ways to improve their instructional or administrative procedures. But whereas surgeons can consult medical journals to learn of new discoveries regarding human anatomy or operating procedures, school administrators and classroom teachers often must learn a new language to understand reports of educational investigations.

Suppose the teachers in an elementary school learn that evidence regarding the effectiveness of certain films to be used in teaching about North American geography can be found in a recent issue of an educational research journal. To explore the suitability of the films for their school, the teachers should, of course, read the research report. But what if they find that the discussion is centered on the following sentence: "The analysis of covariance yielded an F value of 4.62 which, with 1 and 38 degrees of freedom, is significant beyond the 0.05 level"? How many of them could make sense out of such a statement? Yet this is the language of statistics—the language employed in many educational investigations. Classroom teachers and school administrators who want to benefit from the newer discoveries in their field must be able to comprehend at least the statistical procedures that are most commonly used in describing the results of educational investigations.

The inquiring educator will encounter statistical analyses and terminology at numerous times and in many places. For example, imagine that a team of district-level school administrators is deciding whether to use a standardized achievement test and wishes to know something about the test. Team members read the test manual and find that "the standard deviation of the normative sample was 16.24," "the split-half reliability of the test was 0.89 ($p < 0.01$)," and "subtest intercorrelations ranged from 0.52 to 0.71." Will the team be able to interpret the data properly, or will this be an instance where relevant information is overlooked because of the educators' lack of statistical understanding? Readers who do not have an understanding of the statistical methods commonly employed in educational investigations must "skip over" crucial segments of reports.

This is analogous to fitting together a jigsaw puzzle with one of the important pieces missing. Only through an understanding of essential statistical concepts can school administrators and classroom teachers become professionally literate, that is, able to read and comprehend the sources of new knowledge in their field of specialization.

The possibility always exists that some educational investigator, either unwittingly or through deliberate intellectual dishonesty, will misuse statistical methods. Indeed, it is not necessary to look very far in educational research journals to find rather serious errors in the application of statistical techniques. Just because a research article is in print is no assurance that the statistical analyses are appropriate. Competent educators must be prepared to evaluate the suitability of all of an educational investigator's methods, including the statistical techniques employed.

There are encouraging signs that in evaluating their endeavors, educators are placing increasing emphasis on **empirical information**, which can be obtained through experiment or observation. Instructional specialists, for example, frequently assess the merits of teachers' instructional procedures on the basis of changes in learner behavior rather than their subjective impressions of the teachers' competence. Program evaluators are likely to assemble solid evidence of a program's effectiveness for use in making decisions on educational programs, and more often than not they subject this evidence to statistical analysis. The attention being given to empirical evidence has increased the need for educators to be conversant with the statistical language used in reporting it.

There are important differences between educational *research* studies and *evaluations* of educational programs, but both often require the use of statistical methods. In this text, in fact, we ordinarily use the term **educational investigation** to describe both types of studies. Thus "educational investigator," for example, refers to an educational researcher, an educational evaluator, or some other educator engaged in relevant research or evaluation. A working knowledge of statistical techniques is needed both by those who conduct educational research investigations and by those who carry out program evaluation studies. Moreover, almost all educators—classroom teachers, counselors, school-site administrators, district-office administrators—must be able to understand statistical concepts in order to fulfill their professional responsibilities. It follows that every educator needs to acquire at least a nodding acquaintance with the most important statistical concepts and most widely employed statistical techniques in educational investigations.

A WORD TO STUDENTS

A few words regarding the approach and organization of this text should be helpful to the student. First, the emphasis throughout is on the *common-sense rationale* underlying the statistical methods described. By learning *how* a statistical technique operates, you will often be able to understand the purpose of the technique and the types of educational situations in which it should be used. Further, many examples of appropriate applications for different statistical techniques are supplied so you will be able to see not only *why* a technique can perform certain functions but also *when* it should be used. Whenever possible, statistical concepts are described in a verbal or graphic fashion. Mathematical explanatory techniques are rarely used, and derivations of formulas are not given.

Some statistical techniques, such as correlation, regression, and analysis of variance, necessarily involve considerable computation, however. We discuss such techniques in *companion chapters*, one dealing with the general function of the technique, followed by another describing its computational procedures. Instructors can determine to what extent the computational chapters should be studied. The material in these chapters would be required for an educational statistics course, for example, but not in certain other education courses.

A statistical text also requires you to be able to deal with some statistical symbols and a certain amount of mathematical calculations. Statistical symbols are merely a shorthand method for identifying particular mathematical operations or quantities. The symbols in statistical formulations could be replaced by the verbal explanations of the operations they represent, and such explanations would be easier to read. However, if we did this, the book would have to be almost doubled in size in order to accommodate such elaborations. Because we will deal with only a few symbols at a time, you should be able to master those you need for the statistical techniques used most commonly in educational investigations.

Most chapters end with exercises which may require either verbal, "thinking" responses or a certain amount of arithmetic computation. In either instance, completing these exercises will increase your knowledge of the topic. Answers to all exercises are given at the back of the book.

Two final chapters round out this text. Chapter 20 shows you how to select appropriate statistical techniques when faced with data from educational investigations. This chapter is organized in a manner similar to a branching self-instructional program. Chapter 21 introduces the world of data processing by computer. It demonstrates how a typical statistical software package, SPSS, can be used to analyze the data for most of the statistical techniques described in Chapters 2–19. Although Chapter 21 will not make you an expert in data processing, it will certainly familiarize you with the environment and power of computer-based statistical analysis.

Realistic Expectations

What can you realistically expect if you undertake a serious-minded journey through the 21 chapters of this text? To begin with, you will acquire a set of tangible skills that will enable you to perform many statistical operations, some fairly simple and others quite complex. For example, you should be able to compute a standard deviation, a correlation coefficient, and a *t* test with relative ease. With or without the assistance of a calculator or computer, you will be able to carry out the sorts of statistical analyses that are routinely required in educational investigations.

In addition, when you encounter educational investigations requiring the use of statistics, you will be able to decide what statistical procedures should be employed. This is a particularly important competency; not only will you be able to select suitable statistical analyses for your own purposes, you will also be able to judge whether other investigators have chosen appropriate statistical techniques.

Perhaps most important, when you have finished this text you will be unintimidated by those who claim to be adept at statistical analyses. In too many instances, educators who are competent in other respects allow themselves to be browbeaten by number-juggling statimagicians. Like all those who possess special skills, people with statistical competencies are often believed to possess special wisdom as well, but this is seldom the case. If you become reasonably familiar with the use and interpretation of statistics, there is less likelihood that you will defer to statistical wizards when, more often than not, they should be deferring to you.

A serious-minded perusal of this text, therefore, will give you:

1. Skill in using commonly employed statistical procedures.
2. The ability to determine which statistical procedures should be used for particular data analysis situations.
3. Sufficient confidence in your own understanding of statistical methods so you will not be intimidated by statistical experts.

These are not trivial accomplishments, and they should be possessed by every educational investigator including both school administrators and classroom teachers.

You need not strive to attain a particularly deep or extensive statistical understanding while working through the text. Its purpose is not to transform you into a statistical whizbang who can induce awe by spouting statistical formulas. Rather, it is to help you acquire a general, *intuitive* understanding regarding the workings of statistical procedures used in educational investigations. For instance, anyone can use a telephone without understanding the principles of physics that allow a speaker to transmit sounds as electrical impulses over a telephone wire or through a cellular phone. We all have a somewhat general but reasonably good idea of how telephone messages are sent and received.

It is that sort of general, intuitive understanding of statistical methods that you will acquire by using this text. You may not understand all the nuances about the inner workings of the statistical techniques described, but you will gain a reasonably accurate idea of how each one fundamentally does its job.

The first of the two companion chapters for each of the major statistical techniques presented in this text is intended to promote your intuitive understanding of the technique. The second of these chapters is designed to show you how to compute the statistical procedures introduced in the preceding chapter. If you have finished the first chapter of a companion pair, which describes the general function of a technique, without being reasonably certain about how it works or when it should be used, we suggest that you review that chapter. Studying the second, computation-based chapter will help, but an intuitive understanding is more likely to be found in the first of each pair of chapters. You also may find that rereading the initial chapter in the pair after working through the computations in the second chapter will improve your understanding and knowledge of the technique.

Statistics and Graduate Research Projects

Many masters or doctoral graduate degree programs in education require a final research or evaluation project, designated as a thesis, a dissertation, or in some other way. Often the project requires the degree candidate to carry out some sort of quantitative, empirical investigation. Recently, there has been an increasing trend for graduate degree candidates to hire "statistical consultants" to conceptualize and carry out the substantial analyses that may be required by such projects.

We believe there is nothing wrong with hiring someone to assist in the statistical analyses of data for a degree project. It *is* wrong, however, for the degree candidate to abdicate intellectual control over the project by relinquishing to the hired helper any understanding of the analysis. Far too often, this is what happens in the completion of masters' theses or doctoral dissertations in education.

If a quantitatively oriented investigation is required as part of your degree program, having studied this book will make it easier for you to avoid such intellectual abdication. Although you may, of course, legitimately secure assistance in statistical matters from computer consultants, you will be able to understand, *intuitively,* the services they are providing. The more completely you understand what is taking place in a statistically based empirical investigation (how the data are gathered and analyzed), the better your report of the investigation will be.

The Role of Technology

If you had tackled the topic of educational statistics a generation or so ago, you doubtless would have had to do all the practice exercises "by hand." Now, with handheld calculators and personal computers readily available, you may be tempted to avoid any numerical calculations other than those necessary to determine whether you have enough money to purchase an electronic device to make statistical computations painless.

The authors of this text, having been obliged to do a bit of hand calculating as youths, ask for some actual by-hand calculations as you study these chapters. This is not because we want you to work as hard as we did but because we believe that by calculating certain statistics and statistical tests you will understand them better. A Chinese proverb puts it this way: "Tell me and I'll forget; show me and I'll remember; involve me and I'll understand."

In Chapter 2, for example, you will be asked to calculate some standard deviations by hand. It is true that almost any statistically equipped handheld calculator will pump out standard deviations in the twinkling of an eye. Why, then, should it be necessary to go through all that trouble? After all, the calculator's battery is probably live and ready to make numbers appear on a screen. The answer is that by doing the calculations by hand you will see *how* it is that different sets of data actually yield different sorts of standard deviations. Merely pressing the "standard deviation" button on a calculator gives the value of the statistic, but the likelihood that you will understand its ancestry is small.

We recognize that students are apt to enlist the aid of technology to help them master the content of this text. We will, in fact, provide a final chapter describing the details of processing data by computer. But we will also ask for a certain amount of computation by hand. Be assured that this will help you arrive at a genuine, experience-based understanding of the statistical techniques you will be studying.

THE USES OF STATISTICAL METHODS

In education as in other areas of inquiry, the branch of mathematics known as **statistics** serves two primary purposes: the *description* of data and the *inferences* that can be drawn from data.

The use of statistical techniques to describe **data** is referred to as **descriptive statistics**. Educational investigators choose an appropriate descriptive statistic or statistical technique to summarize sets of numerical data such as pupils' test scores, ages, or years of education. By summarizing, descriptive statistics conserve the time and space necessary to describe *data*—the results of an investigation in numerical terms.

The second purpose of statistics is to allow a researcher or evaluator to draw better inferences as to whether a phenomenon observed in a relatively small number of individuals considered in an investigation (a **sample**) can be legitimately generalized to a larger number of individuals (a **population**). This use of statistical techniques is called **inferential statistics**.

Inferential statistics is concerned with making inferences about relationships among **variables**, i.e., attributes or characteristics that vary among individual beings, objects, or events. Educators attempt to discover relationships between such variables as student achievement and student attitudes, so they can take these effects into consideration in structuring school programs. They might, for example, observe a clear relationship between students' self-esteem and test performance in a relatively small sample of fifth-graders. But the investigators would be far more interested in the presence of the relationship for fifth-grade pupils in general, because the finding could then be used as the basis for decisions regarding other pupils in that category. They would use inferential statistics to determine to what extent the investigators' findings in the sample can be generalized to a larger population of fifth-grade pupils. Inferential statistics is employed to determine the degree of confidence that can be placed in inferences about the generalizability of sample-based relationships.

A particularly important function in the design of educational investigations thus is served by inferential statistics. Studies must be carefully designed so the results—the data they yield—can be analyzed meaningfully. To a considerable degree, the availability of suitable statistical techniques is a crucial factor in the design of a well-conceived educational investigation.

Novice investigators cannot simply turn over their data to a statistician for appropriate analysis, however. Statisticians are not alchemists. Even a highly sophisticated statistical analysis can rarely salvage a poorly designed empirical study in which the investigator has paid scant attention to the data analysis procedures that might be used.

Educators who deal with measurement and evaluation procedures, even in the classroom, particularly need a knowledge of both descriptive and inferential statistics. Developers of nationally standardized tests, for example, use descriptive statistics extensively to summarize the performance of normative groups on a test, for use in evaluating the performance of other individuals. They may use inferential statistics in attempting to generalize to a population on the basis of the performance of a student sample on a predictor test (such as a test of music aptitude) and a predicted measure of performance (such as subsequent musical ability). Test publishers often rely on statistical techniques, both descriptive and inferential, to describe the technical properties of their tests, and classroom teachers and school administrators considering such tests for possible adoption must be able to read and interpret these data.

STATISTICAL RESULTS AND EDUCATIONAL JUDGMENT

There is, unfortunately, no one-to-one relationship between the results of statistical operations and the judgments that should guide educational decision makers. Statistics provides a tool whereby educational data can be efficiently described and analyzed more precisely than by visually "inspecting the scores." The results of these analyses should undoubtedly influence the decisions reached by educators and, in general, make such decisions far more enlightened. Nevertheless, statistical results should not be equated with the final conclusions of educational investigators. For one thing, both statistical questions and research design issues must be considered. It is possible, for example, that the proper statistical procedures have been applied to a poorly designed research study. But even with a skillfully designed study and the judicious use of statistical methods, the wise decision maker must weigh factors in addition to statistical results.

For example, a research study may reveal that a new program for teaching foreign languages yields results that are slightly, but consistently, higher than those produced by conventional programs. A difference favoring the new program has, therefore, been found. Is the educator obliged to adopt the new program? Perhaps the new approach is particularly expensive, or highly demanding of teacher time and energy. If the results favoring the new program, however reliable, are not of great magnitude, the educator may justifiably decide against adopting it.

There is a crucial difference between a statistically significant result and a *practically significant* result. While knowledge of statistics is an invaluable asset to educators, it is the proper responsibility of school administrators and class-room teachers to be *guided* by statistical results, not *led* by them.

More Is Not Magic

The widely accepted maxim that "less is more" applies without question to the field of educational statistics. Some statistical beginners who learn about certain high-powered statistical techniques assume that they should be used in every statistical analysis. That can be like removing a flyspeck with an acetylene torch. More often than not, the statistical analyses needed for a particular situation can be quite elementary. For instance, the most sensible way to present students' test results from program evaluation studies to school board members may be to simply rely on the "average percentage correct" scores of students' pretests and posttests. The sophistication of the statistical techniques to be employed must be consonant with the statistical literacy of those who must use the results of the analyses.

Statisticians who always opt for the most complicated and exotic statistical approach may impress others with their statistical wizardry, but they do not impress others with their good sense. Those who must draw on the results of statistical analyses are likely to be put off by the esoteric and *incomprehensible* nature of the analysis, and its underlying mission will fail to be accomplished. One of the chief tasks for students of educational statistics is to gain an ability to judge the degree to which a certain statistical technique is insufficient, or genuinely warranted, or downright excessive.

TERMS TO KNOW

A working knowledge of the language of statistics and educational investigation requires an understanding of certain terms. From this chapter, you should be able to comprehend the meaning of the terms that are printed in boldface type. These terms are listed below in the order of their appearance in the chapter.

empirical methods
educational investigation
statistics
descriptive statistics
sample
population
inferential statistics
variables

SELECTED READINGS

Pagano, Robert R. *Understanding Statistics in the Behavioral Sciences*. St. Paul, MN: West Publishing Co., 1986, chap. 1.

Shavelson, Richard J. *Statistical Reasoning for the Behavioral Sciences*. Boston: Allyn and Bacon, 1988, chap. 1.

Tukey, John W. "The Future of Data Analysis," *Annals of Mathematical Statistics,* vol. 33, no. 1 (March 1962), p. 1.

Walker, H. M. *Studies in the History of Statistical Method*. Baltimore: Williams & Wilkins, 1929.

Weinberg, George H.; Schumaker, John A.; and Oltman, Debra. *Statistics: An Intuitive Approach*. Monterey, CA: Brooks/Cole, 1981, chap. 1.

Descriptive Techniques

One of the most common uses of statistical methods in education is to provide a technique through which educational data, such as test scores, ratings, and grade marks, can be sensibly communicated. Teachers, counselors, and administrators constantly find it necessary to describe these sorts of data clearly and precisely.

The description of data such as a group of test scores can be handled in several ways. Suppose two teachers want to compare how their classes performed on key examinations. One way would be for the teachers to read aloud all their pupils' test scores—that is, if one teacher could ever hold the attention of another for the necessary time. Alternatively, the two teachers could exchange gradebooks so that each could visually inspect the test scores of the other's pupils. But such descriptive procedures are highly uneconomical in terms of time for both the describer and the listener or reader. Better descriptive methods are needed.

GRAPHIC DESCRIPTIVE TECHNIQUES

One of the techniques teachers can use to describe a set of test scores is to represent the data graphically. This is demonstrated in the set of test scores in

Figure 2–1. The baseline across the bottom of the figure represents the number of items each student in a class answered correctly on a ten-item true-false quiz. Each cross above the numbers represents a student in the class. The five crosses above the score 8, for example, indicate that five students answered eight of the ten true-false items correctly. Similarly, there is only one cross above the number 2, so it can be concluded that one student answered only two questions correctly on the quiz.

This graphic method of describing the performance of a group is satisfactory for certain purposes, but it can be refined further by transforming the cross marks into equivalent squares or rectangles. Then another type of graphic display, an upright **bar graph**, can be constructed. This is shown in Figure 2–2, where the students' test scores originally seen as crosses in Figure 2–1 are now shown as small shaded rectangles. If the horizontal lines were erased, the figure would be a bar graph such as that shown in Figure 2–3. This type of graphic display is sometimes called a **histogram**.

In each of these graphs it is easy to see how the class of students performed on the quiz. Consequently, each serves its descriptive purpose satisfactorily. The horizontal line in such graphs is called the horizontal scale or *X* **axis**, and the vertical line is called the vertical scale or *Y* **axis**. The scales represented by the horizontal and vertical lines must be clearly designated in most cases if the graph is to be meaningfully interpreted. For example, in Figure 2–3, the horizontal scale represents the *number of items* answered correctly, and the vertical scale represents the *frequency* or number of students who attained a given score.

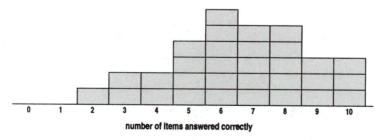
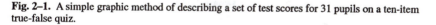

Fig. 2–1. A simple graphic method of describing a set of test scores for 31 pupils on a ten-item true-false quiz.

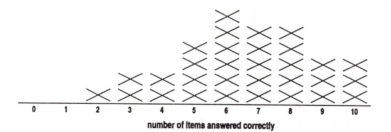
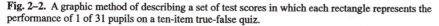

Fig. 2–2. A graphic method of describing a set of test scores in which each rectangle represents the performance of 1 of 31 pupils on a ten-item true-false quiz.

Another method of portraying a set of scores graphically is to use a **frequency polygon**, which is simply a modification of the bar graph. Connecting the midpoints at the upper level of each bar yields a figure like that shown in Figure 2–4. If you contrast the frequency polygon in Figure 2–4 with the bar graph in Figure 2–3, you will see that the shaded *area* beneath the heavy line which forms the frequency polygon is equivalent to the shaded area below the outline of the bar graph.

The frequency polygon can be modified by rounding the sharp corners and developing a curve something like that shown in Figure 2–5. All that has been done in Figure 2–5 is to smooth out the rough edges of the frequency polygon in Figure 2–4.

All of these graphic methods are similar ways of portraying the *distribution* of these particular test scores; that is, how the test scores of 31 pupils are

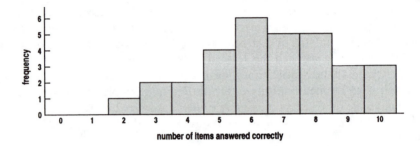

Fig. 2–3. Histogram representing scores of 31 pupils on a ten-item true-false quiz.

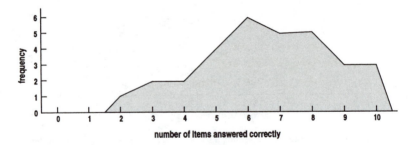

Fig. 2–4. Frequency polygon describing the performance of 31 pupils on a ten-item true-false quiz.

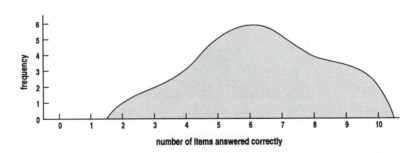

Fig. 2–5. Curve describing the performance of 31 pupils on a ten-item true-false quiz.

distributed over all possible numbers of items answered correctly. Collectively, Figures 2–1 through 2–5 are referred to as **frequency distributions**.

In Figure 2–5, the frequency distribution is depicted by a **distribution curve**. The distribution curve always represents data of some kind, such as scores on the true-false quiz. This representation is in the form of *area*; in Figure 2–5, the **area below the curve** between any two score values is proportional to the number of pupils obtaining scores between these two values. You can think of the distribution curve as being shaped by a series of points representing hypothetical frequencies of test scores that might be obtained for a test with a very large number of students.

In drawing frequency polygons, the assumption of a **continuous distribution** of score values is being made. Scores such as 3.8, 9.107, 5.33, and so on, are assumed to exist in theory, even though only the separate or **discrete values** (0, 1, 2, 3, and so forth) can actually be observed. This assumption is not only theoretically useful but has immense practical value.

Graphic vs. Numerical Techniques

Each of the graphic methods shown in Figures 2–1 through 2–5 is suitable for describing data with visual techniques. However, there is another way to describe educational data that is even more economical. This is the use of statistical formulations to describe data numerically.

Statisticians tend to prefer numerical methods rather than graphic methods of describing data. Since all the information is contained in the numbers, why bother with a picture of this information as well? However, to modify an old adage: A picture can be worth a thousand numbers. The astute educator will find many situations in which graphic descriptive procedures, perhaps used together with numerically oriented descriptive statistics, will be most appropriate. For instance, a teacher trying to communicate the preprogram-to-postprogram test gains of students to a group of parents may find that a clearly constructed and well-presented bar graph gets the best response.

Although numerical descriptive statistics will be featured in this text, this should not be taken to deny the appeal of properly presented graphic descriptors.[1] Indeed, as the use of personal computers has become widespread, numerous software programs that produce excellent graphics at all levels of sophistication have been made available.

STATISTICAL DESCRIPTIVE TECHNIQUES

In describing a set of test scores, educators usually want to convey at least two notions regarding the nature of the scores. First, they want to indicate something about the **central tendency** of the scores, that is, where the scores appear to center, or group together, on the numerical scale being used. Second,

---

1. An excellent source for examples of creative graphical methods for presenting numerical data is Edward R. Tufte, *The Visual Display of Quantitative Information* (Cheshire, CT: Graphics Press, 1983). To study the graphical methods of exploratory data analysis, see John W. Tukey, *Exploratory Data Analysis* (Reading, MA: Addison-Wesley, 1977).

they want to give some notion of the **variability** of scores along that numerical scale, or, to put it another way, an idea of how far the scores spread out from the center of the score distribution.

Assume that Mr. Collins, a high school instructor, has given a 100-item multiple-choice examination to a class of 30 students. He could summarize the performance of the class by indicating what the typical score was—for example, the number of exam questions that most students had answered correctly. He could also describe how the scores were spread out along the 100-point scale—for example, the way students' scores tended to differ, or how they varied from the typical score. The characteristics used by this instructor to describe the test scores represent the two major types of descriptive statistical measures: measures of central tendency in the first instance, and measures of variability in the second. By employing statistical descriptions of a distribution's central tendency and variability, an accurate and economical representation of the data under consideration can usually be conveyed. Because this can be accomplished without the use of graphic methods, both time and effort can be conserved. However, measures of central tendency and variability do not convey *all* the information regarding a distribution of scores. Two distributions of very different shapes could have the same central tendency and variability measures.

Measures of Central Tendency

The statistical measures of central tendency most commonly used in educational investigations are the mean, the median, and the mode.

The Mean.   The measure of central tendency used most often is the **mean**, which is actually the arithmetic average of a set of data. You have probably employed this kind of average to informally describe sets of data. If, for example, you want to determine the average height of a group of students, you would simply find out the height of each individual, perhaps in inches, add all the heights together, and divide this total by the number of individuals in the group. This process would yield an average height called the mean.

The calculations of the mean can be depicted symbolically. In the next few paragraphs, you will be introduced to some of the more common symbols used in statistics. Imagine that you are working with a set of test scores. The symbol X can be used to represent a single raw score on the test. For example, a student who attained a score of 89 items correct on a 100-item test would have a raw score of 89, which would be represented in the following fashion: $X = 89$. Actually, any unit of measurement is referred to as a **raw score** if it is untreated in any way. Thus age, weight, years in school, and so forth, could be considered raw scores.

In dealing with statistics it is frequently necessary to add together sets of scores or, employing a technical phrase, to *sum* them. The statistical symbol representing this summation operation is the capital Greek letter *sigma* (Σ). Whenever this symbol Σ is encountered in statistics, whatever quantity immediately follows it must be *summed*, that is, added together. For example, the notation ΣX indicates that the raw scores under consideration must be added together. In a class of 30 students, each student's score on an examination is represented by the symbol X; to signify that these 30 scores are to be added together, the expression ΣX is used.

Another symbol frequently used in statistics is the Latin letter N, which represents the number of measurements in the group under consideration. To illustrate, if there were 30 students' scores to be described, N in this instance would equal 30. If there were 150 students, N would equal 150.

With these three symbols (X, Σ, N), a formula for the calculation of the mean can be presented. The mean is represented in many statistical texts by the lowercase Greek letter *mu* (μ). Using this symbol, the formula for the mean would be:

$$\mu = \frac{\Sigma X}{N} \tag{2.1}$$

When interpreted, this formula would indicate that the mean is computed by summing all of the raw scores and dividing that summed quantity by the number of scores in the group.

A simple illustration of the use of this formula is presented below. With seven scores, 1, 2, 3, 4, 5, 6, and 7, $\Sigma X = 28$:

$$\mu = \frac{28}{7}$$
$$= 4$$

A mean for any set of data may be computed in this fashion.

The Median.   Another measure of central tendency employed in statistics is the median. By definition, the **median** is the midpoint in a set of ranked scores. Suppose all the scores of students who have taken a test are ranked (say, highest to lowest). Then a point is selected at which the number of scores above it and below it are the same. That point would be the median. The median provides another kind of information about the central tendency of a distribution of scores and is of considerable value in describing data.

The calculation of the median is very simple in many instances. For example, examine the set of scores below:

7, 9, 11, 12, 13, 13, 15

In observing these seven scores you will see that the middle score is 12, and both above and below this point there are three scores. The score 12, then, is the median for this set of scores. When working with an odd number of scores, it is often quite easy to determine the median point, particularly if there is only one score value in the center of the distribution.

A slightly different problem is presented when encountering an even number of scores, such as the eight scores below:

5, 6, 7, 9, 11, 12, 12, 14

In this instance, the lower half of the distribution and the upper half of the distribution are easily discerned, but no existing score can be used to divide the distribution of scores. However, the uppermost score in the lower half (four lower scores) of the distribution is 9, and the lowermost score in the upper half (four higher scores) of the distribution is 11. Therefore an artificially inserted, or **interpolated,** point of 10 is used as the median for the distribution, *even though in reality no such score was attained by anyone.*

In general, this interpolated value is found by computing the mean of the two observed scores (9 and 11 in the above example) on either side of the midpoint. This procedure demonstrates that the median is not a score but a *point* that divides a distribution into two equal halves. For instance, the median for a set of final exam papers might be 28.4, even though every student obtained a whole-number score with no decimal. Suppose you were working with the following four scores: 10, 11, 12, 13. The median for those four scores would be 11.5. Of course, the point dividing the distribution in two equal halves *could* be an actual score, as in the following set of scores: 3, 4, 6, 8, 9. Here, the median clearly is 6.

For more complicated situations in which the median must be determined, there are formulas that can be used to calculate the precise midpoint of a set of scores.[2] Because the exact computation of the median is not necessary for most practical purposes, however, these formulas will not be treated here.

The Mode.   Another index of central tendency which is less frequently used is called the mode. The **mode** is the score that occurs most frequently in a distribution. For example, the mode in Figure 2–2 is 6. Usually the mode is located near the center of the distribution of scores, but this need not be the case. In some distributions, two or more modes are present. These are described as bimodal or even trimodal distributions.

Which to Use: Mean, Median, or Mode?   Educators may be perplexed as to whether to use the mean, the median, or the mode to describe the central tendency of a set of data. Of these three, only the mean uses all of the information available in a set of data. That is, every score in the distribution is used in computing the mean (arithmetic average), whereas much less information is required to compute the median or the mode. Ordinarily, then, use of the mean will provide a more sensitive index of central tendency. Statistically, the mean is also more stable than the median or mode, but sometimes there are *disadvantages* in using every score in the distribution.

Suppose Mrs. Benzel, a school superintendent, wishes to discover the "average" income of wage earners in the school district. She knows that among the 5,000 families, there are two with a household income of over $10,000,000 a year. Would the mean (arithmetic average) provide her with a meaningful estimate of the typical income in the district? Of course not, for the two enormous incomes would inflate the mean income of the district's wage earners unrealistically. In such cases the median would be a better choice as a measure of central tendency, because it is not influenced by extreme scores.

The median is also a good index of central tendency for unusually shaped distributions of data, as when there is a particularly large proportion of very

---

2. For these formulas, see Robert B. McCall, *Fundamental Statistics for Behavioral Sciences* (San Diego, CA: Harcourt Brace Jovanovich, 1986), p. 52.

high scores and an extremely small proportion of very low scores. Another case where the median is useful is in describing sets of data that have been cut off or *truncated* at one or both ends, as when the lower scores for a group of pupils are collectively described as "65 and below."

Since the mode is an easily located measure of central tendency, you might use it if you were in a hurry and wanted to roughly describe a set of scores. In some cases, the mode is the only reasonable kind of central tendency measure to use. For a shoe manufacturer, for example, the highest sales would be realized by producing the most shoes in sizes that are near the modal value of shoe sizes, or the sizes that most customers are able to wear. The manufacturer's focus therefore would be on the mode.

The type of answers needed from the data must be analyzed before choosing to use the mean, the median, or the mode as a measure of central tendency. Most of the time, the choice will be the mean.[3]

Measures of Variability

In addition to measures of central tendency, educational investigators often need statistical measures that reflect the way in which data are dispersed in either direction from the center of the distribution. Measures of variability commonly used in educational statistics include the range, the standard deviation, and the variance.

The Range. The most easily calculated index of variability is undoubtedly the **range**. This measure is obtained by subtracting the lowest score value from the highest, as shown in Formula 2.2:

$$\text{Range} = X_h - X_l \qquad (2.2)$$

where:

X_h = the highest score in the distribution
X_l = the lowest score in the distribution

For instance, you might have a distribution of scores such as:

$$20, 25, 26, 27, 28, 29, 29, 30$$

The range for this distribution would be $X_h - X_l$ = range, or $30 - 20 = 10$. Only two scores are involved in the calculation of this measure of variability. If these two scores are greatly divergent from the general variability of the distribution, the range may yield a misleading notion of the nature of that variability. For example, if in a class of 32 pupils, 30 test scores are located very close to the mean but there is one extremely high score and one extremely low score, the range for the class might reflect a much larger spread of scores than actually exists.

The Standard Deviation. The most widely used statistical index of variability is the standard deviation, which typically is used to describe variability

---

3. See D. Huff, *How to Lie with Statistics* (Norton, 1954) for a good discussion of the misuses of measures of central tendency and other statistics in general.

when the mean is used to describe central tendency. Actually, the standard deviation is somewhat analogous to the mean; the mean is an average of the scores in a set, and the **standard deviation** is a sort of *average* of how far removed the individual scores in a distribution are from the mean.

To obtain the standard deviation, considerable use is made of the *distance* of scores from the mean along the **baseline**, or horizontal scale, of a graphically represented distribution. The symbol *x*, which is called a **deviation from the mean**, is obtained by subtracting the mean from a raw score. This is expressed in Formula 2.3 as:

$$x = X - \mu \qquad (2.3)$$

where:

x = a deviation from the mean
X = the original raw score
μ = the mean

Computing the standard deviation is illustrated with the data in Figure 2–6, which is a hypothetical distribution of 18 test scores in a blocked-out bar graph, with each rectangle representing a single raw score. These scores are also summarized in Table 2.1, where convenient operations are performed on the raw scores (column 1), such as deriving the *x* deviations (column 2) and squaring these deviations (column 3).

To obtain the deviations, the mean must first be calculated. In this case,

$$\mu = \frac{180}{18} = 10$$

The mean is then subtracted from each raw score to obtain the *x* scores in column 2. Column 3 is obtained by squaring each of the deviations. (Remember that a minus times a minus equals a plus.) As we have previously suggested, the standard deviation is analogous to an average of variability. To see how this measure is actually calculated, examine Formula 2.4 for the standard deviation:

$$\sigma = \sqrt{\frac{\Sigma x^2}{N}} \qquad (2.4)$$

where:

σ = the standard deviation of a set of scores, symbolized by the Greek lowercase letter *sigma*
Σx^2 = the sum of the squared deviations from the mean
N = the number of cases in the distribution

An inspection of the formula reveals that, aside from the number of cases, the critical quantity upon which the size of the standard deviation depends is Σx^2. This quantity, which is frequently referred to as the **sum of squares,** is often encountered in statistical work, so you must be thoroughly familiar with the process by which it is obtained. First, the deviations from the mean are found by subtracting the mean from each raw score. Note from Figure 2–6 that the further the original score is removed from the mean, the

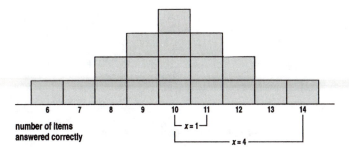

number of items
answered correctly

Fig. 2–6. Blocked-out bar graph representing 18 hypothetical test scores.

greater will be the value of x. A score of 11 minus the mean would yield a deviation of only 1. Generalizing to scores on either side of the mean, a -4 has a greater *absolute* magnitude (disregarding the sign) than a -1 while a $+4$ would have a greater magnitude than a $+1$.

It would seem possible to sum all of these deviations and divide by the number of cases to provide an average of dispersion. However, as can be seen in Table 2.1, the sum of the deviations, Σx, is zero. To get around the difficulty of dealing with a zero quantity, all negative deviations can be transformed into positive quantities by squaring the deviations. Then, by summing the squares and dividing this new total (Σx^2) by N, a measure of variability is obtained. Taking the positive square root of this figure returns to the original scale of measurement. This process yields a sort of *average* of dispersion which, as can be seen from an analysis of the formula, becomes larger as the variability or dispersion of the distribution increases. Note the similarities of the formulas

Table 2.1   **Eighteen Hypothetical Scores, Their Squares, Deviations, and Squared Deviations**

(1) Scores X	(2) Deviations x	(3) Squared Deviations x^2	(4) (Raw Scores)^2 X^2
14	4	16	196
13	3	9	169
12	2	4	144
12	2	4	144
11	1	1	121
11	1	1	121
11	1	1	121
10	0	0	100
10	0	0	100
10	0	0	100
10	0	0	100
9	-1	1	81
9	-1	1	81
9	-1	1	81
8	-2	4	64
8	-2	4	64
7	-3	9	49
6	-4	16	36
$\Sigma X = 180$	$\Sigma x - \mu = 0$	$\Sigma x^2 = 72$	$\Sigma X^2 = 1,872$

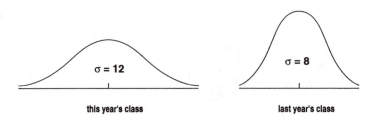

Fig. 2–7. Hypothetical class distributions with different standard deviations.

for the mean (2.1) and for the standard deviation (2.4). Both are basically averages.

Suppose an educator reports that the standard deviation of scores for this year's class on the final exam for a course was 12, while the standard deviation for last year's class was only 8. The mental image of this situation you might form would be something like Figure 2–7.

As with most statistical concepts, the standard deviation becomes more meaningful when you actually calculate a few of these statistics, particularly if you attempt to note *the contributions made by the raw scores* to the statistical quantities involved. The standard deviation for the set of scores in Table 2.1 can be calculated as follows:

$$\sigma = \sqrt{\frac{72}{18}}$$

$$= \sqrt{4}$$

$$= 2$$

In computing this standard deviation, note how much difference the addition of new raw scores, for example, scores of 20 and 0, would have made in the size of σ. The deviation value for these two new scores ($x = \pm 10$), when squared, actually exceeds the entire contribution of the 18 scores already present. The result would be:

$$\Sigma x^2 = 72 + 100 + 100 = 272$$

$$\sigma = \sqrt{\frac{272}{20}} = 3.7$$

Such is the sensitivity of the standard deviation.

Aside from its value in serving as a general indication of the dispersion in a set of measurements, the standard deviation can also be used as a unit of measurement along the baseline of a distribution of scores. For instance, in a normally distributed set of test scores, approximately 68 percent of the scores fall within an area plus and minus 1 standard deviation from the mean. Such applications of normally distributed test scores in terms of standard deviation units will be described in the next chapter.

In order to determine a standard deviation for a set of scores, you could follow the procedure used previously. However, to save time, you can employ a faster and easier method for obtaining Σx^2. It can be demonstrated that the sum of squares can be obtained without ever reducing the data to actual deviations. The way to accomplish this is by employing Formula 2.5, the raw-score formula for the sum of squares:

$$\Sigma x^2 = \Sigma X^2 - \frac{(\Sigma X)^2}{N} \qquad (2.5)$$

where:

$\Sigma x^2 =$ the sum of squared deviations
$\Sigma X^2 =$ the sum of squared raw scores
$\Sigma X =$ the sum of raw scores
$N =$ the number of cases

Without going into algebraic equivalences, it can easily be shown that this raw-score formula yields a quantity identical with that obtained from summing the individually squared derivations. This can be done by computing Σx^2 for the data in Table 2.1, in which the sum of squares equals 72. For the raw-score formula, ΣX^2 is obtained by adding together the squared raw scores in column 4. The sum of these squares is 1,872. Thus,

$$\Sigma x^2 = 1,872 - \frac{(180)^2}{18}$$
$$= 1,872 - \frac{32,400}{18}$$
$$= 1,872 - 1,800$$
$$= 72$$

The 72 obtained by the raw-score formula for the sum of squares is, of course, the same as the 72 obtained by the original method. This raw-score formula is particularly valuable when you have access to a calculator that can yield both ΣX and ΣX^2 by a relatively simple operation.

The Variance. Suppose, in the calculation of the standard deviation, that the computation had not been completed, that is, the square root of $\Sigma x^2/N$ had not been taken. Then another widely used but less easily understood measure of dispersion known as the variance would have been available. Formula 2.6 is the formula for the variance:

$$\sigma = \frac{\Sigma x^2}{N} \qquad (2.6)$$

where:

$\sigma^2 =$ the variance of a set of scores
$\Sigma x^2 =$ the sum of the squared deviations from the mean
$N =$ the number of cases

Because the **variance** is merely the square of the standard deviation (or, conversely, the standard deviation is the square root of the variance), the same logic applies to this measure of variability as to the standard deviation. Again, it is a kind of average that reflects the distance of the individual scores from the mean of the distribution. The larger the variance, the greater the variability; that is, the greater the distance of scores from the mean. The smaller the variance, the less the variability. Because variances are squared standard deviations, they are, of course, much larger than standard deviations (unless the standard deviation is less than 1). For the data in Table 2.1, the variance would be 4. If the standard deviation were 12, however, the variance would rise to 144.

Thus, whereas the standard deviation is a *linear* measure of variability, expressed in the original units of measurement, the variance is given in terms of *squared* units of measurement. As a measure of variability, the variance can be likened to the *area* of a surface, say a rectangle. Just as the area of a rectangle can be divided into two or more sections, so can the variance be partitioned into sources, each associated with some characteristic accounting for variability in the data. This ability to analyze the variance forms the basis of more advanced statistical techniques, which will be described later.

DESCRIPTIVE STATISTICS AND THE EDUCATOR

What value do concepts such as the mean and standard deviation have for the practicing educator? It might be easy to see the need researchers and evaluators would have for such descriptive tools, but it is harder to see how classroom teachers and school administrators could use them. Imagine that a teacher who has used the same final examination for several semesters discovers that while the mean performance of the most recent groups exceeds that of earlier classes, the standard deviation is becoming smaller. What does this indicate?

The situation might be graphically represented as in Figure 2–8. Student achievement apparently is improving, as evidenced by the increased mean performance. Perhaps this is attributable to constantly improved instructional techniques. Perhaps, because the same exam has been used for several semesters, more and more students have had access to a "missing" copy of the test. In any case, the increasingly smaller standard deviations indicate the reduced variance of the groups. It may be that the teacher's methods are actually developing more homogeneous student achievement. Another explanation might be that, with improved mean performance, the upper limit of the test is acting as a "ceiling" that has reduced the possible range of high scores and produced smaller standard deviations.

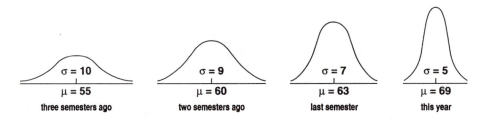

Fig. 2–8. Four hypothetical final-examination distributions.

Classroom teachers and administrators have many occasions to use measures such as the mean, median, and standard deviation to describe educational data economically. These descriptive statistics also can sharpen educators' perceptions of educational situations and help them reach more insightful decisions in instructional matters. Knowledge of statistical measures such as those discussed in this chapter is especially valuable in interpreting test manuals for commercially distributed standardized tests, many of which are literally laden with descriptive statistics.

■   ■   ■

REVIEW

This chapter introduces graphic and statistical methods of describing data. There are various techniques for graphically portraying sets of data, such as bar graphs, histograms, and frequency polygons. In the distribution curves frequently employed in educational statistics, data are represented by the area below the curve in a graphic display.

Statistical descriptive techniques include measures of central tendency and measures of variability. The three most commonly used measures of central tendency are the mean, the median, and the mode. Because the mean is an arithmetic average, it is used most frequently.

Measures of variability often employed in educational statistics are the range, standard deviation, and variance. The standard deviation is a sort of average of the distance of the raw scores from the mean of a distribution of scores. A large standard deviation reflects considerable dispersion or spread in a set of scores; a small standard deviation reflects a less variable set of scores.

TERMS TO KNOW

Listed in order of presentation in chapter:

bar graph
histogram
X **axis**
Y **axis**
frequency polygon
frequency distribution
distribution curve
area below the curve
continuous distribution
discrete values
central tendency
variability
mean
raw score
median
interpolated
mode
range
standard deviation
baseline
deviation from the mean
sum of squares
variance

EXERCISES

1. A class of 25 tenth-grade pupils obtained the following scores on a midterm examination. Determine the mean of the distribution.

49	42	40	38	34
48	41	39	37	30
48	40	39	36	29
47	40	38	36	28
42	40	38	35	26

2. What is the mean score of the following set of ability scores?

120	118	114	110	100
119	115	112	106	94

3. Find the median for each of the following samples. Locate the median by counting and, if necessary, interpolating.

(a) 106, 104, 100, 99, 96, 95
(b) 14, 13, 11, 9, 8, 7, 6, 2, 2
(c) 28, 27, 27, 26, 26, 25, 24, 22, 22, 20

4. Determine the mean for each of the following distributions.

   (a) 10, 10, 9, 9, 9, 8, 8, 7, 7, 7, 6, 6, 5, 4, 2, 2
   (b) 29, 28, 28, 27, 27, 27, 27, 21
   (c) 49, 48, 48, 48, 48, 47, 46, 43

5. Find the range and the mode of the following set of aptitude scores.

   120, 119, 118, 118, 118, 117, 117, 115, 114, 111, 98, 92

6. Compute the standard deviation of the ten quiz scores given below.

20	18	17	15	14
19	18	16	14	10

7. Compute the variance and the standard deviation of the set of achievement-test scores presented below.

78	73	71	68	62
76	73	70	68	60
74	72	69	66	58
74	72	69	65	57

8. Two first-grade classes are given reading aptitude tests. Their scores are presented below.

Group A			Group B		
62	56	50	69	64	56
60	55	50	68	63	56
60	55	48	68	62	54
59	54	47	67	61	54
58	53	40	65	60	51
57	52	37	64	58	50
57	51	32	64	58	48

   (a) Find the mean, median, standard deviation, and range for each group.
   (b) Which group could you predict would perform better in first-grade reading assignments?
   (c) Which group has the more variable or heterogeneous scores on the reading aptitude test?
   (d) If other factors are equal, which group would you expect to perform most homogeneously in first-grade reading tasks?

(Continued next page)

9. Should the mean or the median be used as an index of central tendency for the set of scores listed below?

Score	Frequency
10 and above	4
9	6
8	14
7	10
6	7
5 and below	4

10. Is someone who refers to "the average income of the Canadian citizen" referring to "mean citizen," "median citizen," or "modal citizen"?

11. A teacher described the final examination performance of two history classes as follows: "Period 2 class had a mean of 76.4 and a standard deviation of 6.3, while period 4 class had a mean of 69.8 and a standard deviation of 11.6."

    (a) Which class achieved a better overall performance in the final examination?
    (b) Which class performed more homogeneously?
    (c) If you had access to no additional information, in which class would you guess the highest and lowest scores were made?

SELECTED READINGS

Edwards, Allen L. *Statistical Analysis*. New York: Holt, Rinehart & Winston, 1969, chaps. 3–5.

Freeman, David; Pisani, Robert; and Purves, Roger. *Statistics*. New York: W. W. Norton, 1978, chaps. 3–7.

Guilford, J. P., and Fruchter, Benjamin. *Fundamental Statistics in Psychology and Education*. New York: McGraw-Hill, 1978, chaps. 4, 5.

Kirk, Roger E. *Elementary Statistics*. Monterey, CA: Brooks/Cole, 1984, chaps. 1–4.

McCall, Robert B. *Fundamental Statistics for Behavioral Sciences*. San Diego, CA: Harcourt Brace Jovanovich, 1986, chaps. 1–4.

Tufte, Edward R. *The Visual Display of Quantitative Information*. Cheshire, CT: Graphics Press, 1983.

Tukey, John W. *Exploratory Data Analysis*. Reading, MA: Addison-Wesley, 1977.

The Normal Curve

A theoretical distribution called the normal curve is central to the use of statistical techniques and analyses. The **normal curve** is a symmetrical, bell-shaped distribution curve in which most of the measurements are located in the center and very few are at the extremes (see Figure 3-1). As you saw in Chapter 2, the area under the curve in a graphic representation of the distribution of a set of scores is proportional to the number of students who earned scores between any two values on the baseline.

Behavioral scientists have found that many of the characteristics of a population that are studied and measured by educators, such as aptitude or ac-

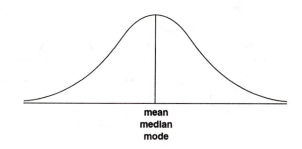

mean
median
mode

Fig. 3-1. A normal distribution curve.

ademic achievement, are distributed among the sample in approximately a normal fashion. If, for instance, the measures of musical abilities of a large number of individuals were graphically represented by a distribution curve, most scores would be located near the mean. A smaller number of scores would fall at the extremes or ends of the curve, representing individuals with either very much or very little musical ability. The graphic portrayal of the distribution of this particular attribute in a sample would look much like the curve in Figure 3–1. For many variables in education that are believed to be normally distributed, relatively large samples are required in order to generate a distribution curve that approaches normality.

NORMAL DISTRIBUTIONS

The normal distribution curve has several distinctive features that make it a valuable tool for the statistician. For one thing, the mean (average), median (midpoint), and mode (most frequent score) are identical in a normal curve. For another, the normal curve is extremely useful with respect to the determination of the *probabilities* associated with certain events. Probability, an important concept in inferential statistics, will be discussed later in this chapter in reference to the normal curve and treated more extensively in Chapter 4.

One of the most interesting features of the normal curve is that when the baseline of the curve is considered *in terms of standard deviation units*, certain proportions of the distribution can be isolated by erecting **ordinates** (vertical lines) at the baseline. (The ordinate at the mean is shown in Figure 3–1.) As you saw in Chapter 2, the baseline, or horizontal scale, of a graphically represented distribution of scores indicates the scale on which the measurements in the distribution were taken, for example, correct answers on a test, age, or scores on an attitude inventory.

Each distribution of measurements has a mean and a standard deviation. The standard deviation, usually thought of as an index of variability, can also be employed as a *unit of measurement* that can be used along the baseline of a distribution curve. This standard deviation unit is employed in much the same way a foot ruler is used to measure distances. If the standard deviation of a distribution is 6.25, for example, the standard deviation "foot ruler," or unit of measurement, for that set of scores is 6.25, and this can be used to measure distances along the baseline of the distribution curve. When such standard deviation units of measurement are applied to a normal curve, it is possible to identify the proportion of the area under the curve that is occupied by a particular segment of the distribution.

Standard deviation units to the right of the mean are positive values and are said to be *above* the mean; those to the left of the mean are negative values and are said to be *below* the mean. Erecting ordinates at the mean (μ) and at +1 standard deviation (σ) in any normal distribution always isolates 34.13 percent of the area in the curve above the mean (see Figure 3–2). If, in a normally distributed set of test scores, for example, the mean were a test score of 70 and the standard deviation were 10, then 34.13 percent of the measurements would fall between test scores of 70 and 80. Similarly, 34.13 percent of the scores in a normal distribution always fall between the mean and −1 standard deviation.

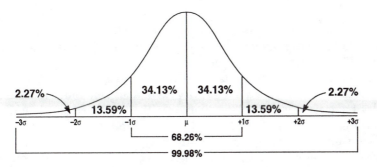

Fig. 3–2. Percentages of the normal distribution enclosed by ordinates erected at standard deviation points.

In the test-score example ($\mu = 70$; $\sigma = 10$), 34.13 percent of the measurements below the mean would fall between test scores of 60 and 70.

Therefore, as shown in Figure 3–2, over two-thirds (68.26 percent) of the area under a normal curve is contained within an area plus and minus 1 standard deviation from the mean. Moreover, virtually 100 percent of the total area under a normal curve always is included within 6 standard deviations from the mean (-3σ to $+3\sigma$). Because the distributions of many educational variables approach normality, the normal curve is of considerable value to educators in converting raw scores into standard deviation units.

Some useful quantities associated with the normal distribution curve are given in Table A in the Appendix. This table lists the proportions of the normal curve between the ordinate at the mean and ordinates erected at various points along the baseline. A point can indicate either a whole or a fractional standard deviation unit. The following example shows how to use Table A to ascertain what proportion of the normal curve is found between ordinates erected at the mean and at $+1.15$ standard deviations.

First, locate 1.15 in column 1. Then look in column 2 to determine the proportion of the total area under the curve that is included between the mean and the standard deviation point. In this case, 0.3749 (or 37.49 percent) of the total area under the distribution curve is contained between an ordinate erected at the mean and one erected at $+1.15$ standard deviation units.

In column 3 you will find the area in the *larger* portion of the total distribution. This area 0.8749, is obtained by adding 50 percent (the half of the normal distribution located below, or to the left of, the mean) to the value found in column 1; 50 percent added to 37.49 percent yields a total of 87.49 percent. Column 4 gives the area in the *smaller* portion of the distribution, in this instance 0.1251, or 12.51 percent. This proportion would be found in the small area of the curve that is located above (to the right) of the ordinate located at $+1.15$ standard deviation units. Column 5 gives the proportional *height* of an ordinate erected at various points along the baseline. These heights are used in the calculation of a few statistical techniques which will be described later.

NONNORMAL DISTRIBUTIONS

Many sets of data encountered in educational situations are not normally distributed or even symmetrically distributed. Various descriptive terms are used to identify such distributions. A **skewed distribution**, for example, has a disproportionately large number of scores at one extreme or end, so a sort of **distribution tail** is formed at the other end.

A distribution in which the tail extends toward the left, or the lower scores in a distribution, is called a **negatively skewed distribution**. Figure 3–3 is an example of a negatively skewed distribution with the relative positions of the mean and median indicated. The mode would correspond to the point on the baseline that is under the highest point of the curve. Such a distribution might result when a very simple test is given to a class, so most pupils would score well and only those few who did not pay any attention would score poorly.

A **positively skewed distribution** is one in which the tail extends toward the right, or the higher scores in the distribution. Figure 3–4 is an example of a positively skewed distribution which indicates the relative positions of the mean and median. A positively skewed curve might result if an extremely difficult test were given to a class, so only a few students would attain high scores and most of them would receive low scores.

The type of skew, positive or negative, thus depends on the direction of the *tail* of the curve. Skewed curves with a tail going toward the right, or positive direction, are positively skewed; those with tails going toward the left, or negative direction, are negatively skewed. In relation to the median, the mean is closer to the tail or the direction of skewness in the distribution.

If you compare the normal distribution in Figure 3–2 with the skewed distributions in Figures 3–3 and 3–4, it should be clear that the notions of area associated with the normal curve and standard deviation units do not apply to a distribution that is markedly skewed. In fact, these notions do not apply if the distribution departs greatly from normality in any fashion. Only when a curve is *perfectly normal* can it be asserted that *precisely* 34.13 percent of the distribution will fall between ordinates erected at the mean and at +1.0 standard deviation. With *approximately* normal distributions it is possible to designate

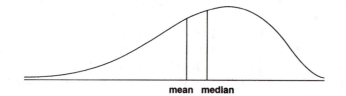

mean   median

Fig. 3–3. A negatively skewed distribution showing relative positions of mean and median.

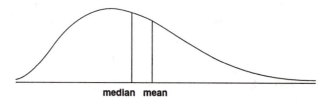

median   mean

Fig. 3–4. A positively skewed distribution showing relative positions of mean and median.

approximate proportions of the distribution in terms of standard deviation units. In order to employ normal-curve notions with nonnormal distributions, the data must be treated in such a way as to artificially "normalize" the scores. This technique will be discussed later in the chapter.

PERCENTILES

Educators are interested not only in describing groups of scores but also in describing the scores of particular group members in relation to the scores of others in the group. For example, a teacher might want to describe one student's score in relation to the scores of classmates on the same exam. Merely asserting that a student obtained a score of 76 on an achievement examination, for example, gives relatively little information. A raw score of 76, without some type of reference base, could be good or bad, high or low.

One helpful method of describing individual scores is to employ percentiles. A **percentile** indicates the position of a particular measurement in a group in terms of the percentage of measurements that fall *below* it. For example, a student who scored at the 25th percentile on a nationally standardized test would have exceeded the performance of 25 percent of the students included in the national group. A student scoring at the 95th percentile would have exceeded the scores of 95 percent, or scored below only 5 percent, of the group. The 50th percentile, then, is equivalent to the median because it divides the group into two equal segments. Percentiles that divide the group into quarters are called **quartiles**; the 25th percentile is referred to as the *first quartile* and the 75th percentile is referred to as the *third quartile*. Like the median, quartiles are *points*—not areas or proportions of the distribution. It would be wrong for an educator to state, for example, that "Maria scored *in* the first quartile." Maria can score *above* the first quartile, *below* the first quartile, or *at* the first quartile. She cannot score *in* the first quartile because this is only a point, not an area under a curve. Points such as quartiles need not be actual scores, only positions along the baseline of a distribution which divide it into specified proportions.

Percentiles may vary depending on the reference group or norm being used. For example, *local* school norms for nationally standardized examinations are developed over a period of years and typically do not coincide with the national norms. A raw score of 85 items correct on a mathematics achievement test therefore might be equivalent to a percentile of 65 in local norms, but national normative figures would place that score at a percentile of only 57. The norm group being used should always be specified when employing percentiles.

One difficulty in using percentiles as a technique for describing relative position can be illustrated with distributions that are fairly normal. A great many scores are centered near the mean of the group, so a difference between the 40th and 60th percentiles, for example, may take up only a few points along the baseline. But at the outer edges of the baseline, the same *distance* in score points might involve only a small proportion of the cases in the group. The distance along the baseline between the 50th and 55th percentiles, for example, is much smaller than the baseline distance between the 90th and 95th percentiles.

In using percentiles, therefore, you must be alert to the fact that differences between percentiles, based as they are on a *cumulative percentage of scores*, usually do not yield comparable differences in score points on a baseline measurement scale.

Percentiles are easily communicated measures of an individual's position in a group. Teachers and school administrators often find that percentiles are useful in interpreting student performance on both standardized and locally developed tests.

STANDARD SCORES

Another method for expressing relative positions of scores takes into account the distance of a score from the mean *in terms of standard deviation units*. This technique involves measures known as **standard scores**. The data in Table A in the Appendix, introduced earlier in this chapter, are given in terms of standard scores.

Though teachers and administrators frequently use percentiles to describe pupils' test performance, statisticians more often use standard scores. Certain types of standard scores also are now being used by test publishers to describe students' scores on standardized tests. Standard scores provide useful methods of describing the position of a raw score in a distribution by expressing the score's *distance above or below the mean*.

One kind of standard score, referred to as z, is defined by Formula 3.1:

$$z = \frac{X - \mu}{\sigma} \tag{3.1}$$

By examining Formula 3.1, you will see that in order to determine the standard score for an individual measurement, you must first calculate the mean and the standard deviation of the group. Then you would subtract the group mean from the raw score and divide the difference by the standard deviation to obtain z. For example, assume that a pupil obtained a score of 45 on a test in which the mean was 38 and the standard deviation was 3.0. In this case z would be calculated as follows:

$$z = \frac{45 - 38}{3.0} = 2.33$$

This z indicates that the pupil obtained a raw score that is 2.33 *standard deviation units* above the mean of the group.

Consider another example. Suppose John weighs 110 pounds, but the national mean weight for his age group is 125 pounds and the standard deviation is 10 pounds. His standard score for weight would be calculated as follows:

$$z = \frac{110 - 125}{10} = -1.5$$

The z of -1.5 indicates that John is 1.5 standard deviation units *below* (note the minus sign) the mean weight for his age group.

Table 3.1   Comparison of X Scores and z Scores for Two Students on Four Quizzes

Quiz	Mean (μ)	Standard Deviation (σ)	Joan's X	Mary's X	Joan's z	Mary's z
1	130	22	152	141	1.00	0.50
2	75	10	70	60	−0.50	−1.50
3	38	7	59	38	3.00	0
4	200	60	140	320	−1.00	2.00
Mean Score			105.25	139.75	2.50	1.00

If all raw scores of any distribution were transformed into z scores, the resulting distribution of z scores would have a mean of zero and a standard deviation of 1. Such z scores can be used to *average* students' scores on different tests because they have a common mean and a common standard deviation. This is done in order to obtain a more representative estimate of a student's total performance relative to that of other students than could be gained by merely summing raw-score points.

The advantage of standard scores is illustrated in Table 3.1, which compares the scores of two girls on four quizzes, on the basis of both raw scores (X) and standard scores (z). Whereas Mary has obtained more total points from the four tests, Joan has the higher z-score total. This disparity results from the greater contribution to Mary's total score of points on the fourth quiz. On the other three tests, Joan's scores exceed Mary's by marked differences based on standard deviation units, that is, according to the quality of the relative performance of the two girls on three individual tests. The use of average-standard-score estimates of performance produces a more representative picture of student academic attainment than can be obtained by the use of total points.

When adding together several examination performances, it is also possible to ascribe varying degrees of importance to different examinations by simply multiplying (weighting) the standard score for a given exam by 2, 3, and so forth. If Mr. Graves, a classroom teacher, believes that one quiz is worth three times more than another, because of the importance of the content covered on that quiz, he could weight (multiply) the standard score for student performance on that quiz by 3. Similarly, if he considers one quiz less important than another, Mr. Graves can multiply students' z scores for that quiz by 0.5. This would cut the contribution of the less important quiz to the z-score total by half.

STANDARD SCORES, PERCENTILES, AND THE NORMAL DISTRIBUTION

Both percentiles and z scores describe the position of a score in a distribution, but they convey different kinds of information. For example, it is not unusual to find two different distributions with a given score at the same percentile in both distributions but different z scores in each one. Consider two distributions, each of which contains only three test scores. In the first distribution the scores are 0, 10, and 11, and the mean for this set of scores is 7. In the second distribution the scores are 9, 10, and 14, and the mean is 11. In both of these distributions, the score 10 is the median, or the 50th percentile. But whereas in the first distribution 10 is above the mean, so it has a positive z score, in the second distribution 10 is below the mean, so it has a negative z score. Neither measure of location, then, tells the whole story.

The relationship between z scores and percentiles cannot be determined unless the distribution of scores is completely defined. If the distribution curve is normal, Table A can be used to determine this exact relationship, so you can infer a percentile location from a z-score location, or vice versa.

To illustrate this point, refer back to Figure 3–2. You will see that there is a one-to-one correspondence between the distance of a score from the mean (in standard deviation units) and the percentage of area under the normal curve between ordinates erected at the mean and the score. The z score is, in fact, the distance of the raw score from the mean in standard deviation units. Thus, knowing a z score tells you how many standard deviations the raw score equivalent to that particular z score is from the *mean. If the scores are normally distributed* and the z score for some raw score (X) is 1.5, then the raw score is 1.5 standard deviations above the mean. By looking in column 2 of Table A, you will see that approximately 43 percent of the area under the curve lies between this point and the mean. Thus you can interpret the percentage of area between ordinates under a distribution curve by thinking of the area as a percentage of scores. In this case, you can say that 43 percent of all scores in the distribution occur between ordinates erected at the mean and the X score equivalent to a z score of 1.5.

Furthermore, because 50 percent of the scores always fall below the mean in a normal distribution, the sum of 50 percent and 43 percent, that is, 93 percent, of all the scores fall below the X score with a z score of 1.5. That is, the raw-score equivalent of a z score of 1.5 is at the 93rd percentile. Thus, if you know that *the original raw-score distribution was normal*, you are able to find the percentile for any raw score by computing its z score and using Table A.

As a further example, consider a normal distribution with a mean of 25 and a standard deviation of 3. Suppose you want to find the percentile of a raw score of 30. First, compute the z score corresponding to $X = 30$ by using Formula 3.1; that is, $z = (30 - 25)/3 = 1.67$. Then enter $z = 1.67$ into Table A. You will find that approximately 45 percent of the area lies between a z score of 1.67, that is, a raw score of 30, and the mean. Thus the raw score of 30 is equal to a percentile of $50 + 45$, or 95.

Using the same distribution, that is, a mean of 25 and a standard deviation of 3, try one more example. If the raw score is 23, which is below the mean, the standard score will be negative: $z = -0.67$. Table A gives the approximate proportion of the area between ordinates erected at 23 and the mean as 0.25. Hence the raw score of 23 would be at the 50th percentile *minus* 25 percent, that is, the 25th percentile. In working problems of this nature, you will usually find it helps to draw a simple diagram of a normal curve and keep track of the proportion of area at each stage of the computation. Figure 3–5 illustrates the diagram you might draw for the preceding problems.

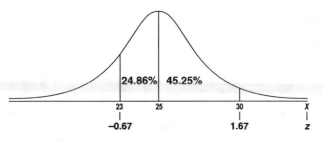

Fig. 3–5. Typical diagram for use in relating percentages of area under the normal curve to raw scores (*X*) and corresponding standard scores (*z*).

Probability and the Normal Curve

The proportion of area under a distribution curve can also be directly interpreted as a probability. In the example above, you might want to know what the probability is of obtaining a raw score of 30 or less. In fact, this question has already been answered: The probability is equal to the proportion of area *below* the raw score of 30. Thus the probability of obtaining a score of 30 or less is 0.95. Likewise, the probability of obtaining a score of 23 *or more* is $0.25 + 0.50$, that is, 0.75. The probability of obtaining a score *between* 25 (the mean) and 30 is 0.45. We will have much more to say about probability in the next chapter.

TRANSFORMED STANDARD SCORES

Because of the way standard scores are computed, *z* scores can result in decimals and negative numbers, such as $z = 2.14$ or $z = -1.38$. **Transformed standard scores** provide methods of avoiding decimals and negatives.

One modified standard score, known as *Z*, has been developed to transform the values obtained in computing *z* scores by multiplying *z* by 10 and adding 50, as in Formula 3.2:

$$Z = 10z + 50 = \frac{10(X - \mu)}{\sigma} + 50 \qquad (3.2)$$

Using this method creates a transformed distribution of scores with a mean of 50 and a standard deviation of 10. A *Z* score of 40, for example, is equal to a *z* of -1.0 and indicates that the *z* score (and the raw score to which it is equivalent) is 1 standard deviation unit below the mean.

The following example shows how a *Z* score would be computed for a raw score of 56, drawn from a distribution with a mean of 48 and standard deviation of 6.0:

$$Z = \frac{10(56 - 48)}{6} + 50$$
$$= 10(1.33) + 50$$
$$= 63.3$$

Note that as a first step, the *z* value of 1.33 is calculated, using Formula 3.1.

With a large number of individuals, as in most distributions of scores, the Z-score distribution might range approximately 6 standard deviation units, from −3.00 to +3.00. The z-score distribution for the same set of scores, using a mean of 50 and a standard deviation of 10, would range from 20 to 80.

In certain widely used standardized tests, different sorts of transformations are employed to eliminate decimals and negative numbers. For example, some nationally standardized admissions tests use means of 500 and standard deviations of 100 instead of 50 and 10. Others use different means and standard deviations. Classroom teachers and administrators therefore should not assume that all transformed standardized scores have been transformed by multiplying a z score by 10 and adding 50 to the result. Decidedly different species of standard scores are found in the educational terrain.

The transformed standard Z score is sometimes referred to as a *T* score in other textbooks. In this text, however, we give *T* scores a considerably different kind of meaning, as explained in the next section.

NORMALIZED STANDARD SCORES

When educational investigators are faced with sets of data that are not normally distributed, they may want to normalize the scores artificially in order to make it easier to work with them. They can do this by transforming all of the scores to **normalized standard scores** (*T*) or **normal curve equivalents** (*NCE*).

Although it takes a certain amount of calculation effort to compute a normalized standard score, it is nothing more than a score which is comparable in appearance to a Z score and which would be equivalent to the raw score *if the distribution had been perfectly normal*. To calculate normalized standard scores, the raw scores are first converted to percentiles based on the actual distribution of raw scores. The Z scores that would be equivalent to these percentiles *in a perfectly normal distribution* then are determined.

An example of how the process of normalizing standard scores works will help you understand this idea. Suppose one of the higher raw scores in a test-score distribution is 76 items correct, and the proportion of the scores in the distribution actually falling below the raw score is found to be 0.89. In other words, in the actual distribution of scores, the raw score is equal to the 89th percentile. You would then turn to Table A for the normal curve to select the z score that represents the 89th percentile. This is found in column 3, which gives the area in the larger portion of the normal curve. The z score corresponding to the area of 0.8907, or the 89th percentile, is 1.23. This z of 1.23 is then transformed to a *T* score (or *NCE*) by the same process used in deriving Z scores, that is, multiplying by 10 and adding 50. This process yields a *T* score of 62.3. In essence, this *T* score of 62.3 is the standard-score equivalent of the original raw score of 76 if the actual distribution had been perfectly normal.

For an additional example, suppose a student scores at the 16th percentile in a group. What is the student's *T* score? From Table A you can see that when 16 percent (0.1587) is in the smaller part of the distribution, the z value is 1.0. Because 16 percent is less than 50 percent, the z value is negative, that is, -1.0.[1] Transforming the z of -1.0 (multiplying by 10 and adding 50) yields a T score of 40.

If you were to follow this procedure for all the scores in a distribution, the scores would be artificially regrouped into a normal shape—*on the basis of their equivalence to Z scores in a normal distribution.*

As in the case of Z scores, a T-score distribution has a mean of 50 and a standard deviation of 10. But the shape of the original distribution is distorted by the process of converting raw scores into T scores, while the shape is not altered by changing raw scores into z and Z scores.

Educators may need to use *NCE* or T scores because they must compare scores on two or more tests that do not have the same number of items or identical means or standard deviations. Although there are some perils in doing so, scores on several tests can be converted to *NCE*s so performance on these tests can be aggregated and then compared on the basis of *NCE* or T scores. For such comparisons to be meaningful, however, the distributions of scores being compared must satisfy certain assumptions that, in the real world of education, may be difficult to satisfy.[2]

■　　■　　■

REVIEW

Properties of the normal curve include the proportions of the curve bounded by ordinates erected at given points along the baseline. Approximately two-thirds of a normal distribution is contained within an area plus and minus 1 standard deviation unit from the mean. Table A in the Appendix provides useful data for working with the normal curve.

Nonnormal distributions include positively and negatively skewed curves. Normal-curve distribution proportions do not apply to such distributions.

Percentiles and standard scores provide techniques for describing an individual's relative position in a group. While percentiles are based on the percentage of scores falling below a given score, standard scores are based on an individual score's distance above or below the mean, in terms of standard deviation units. The relationship between z scores and percentiles in the normal distribution can be determined with the help of Table A.

To avoid decimals and negative numbers in z scores, z scores can be transformed into Z scores. A distribution of z standard scores has a mean of zero and a standard deviation of 1.0, whereas a distribution of Z scores has a mean of 50 and a standard deviation of 10. Normalized standard scores, that is, T or *NCE* scores, can be used to transform a nonnormal set of data into a normalized distribution.

---

1. Until you are familiar with the use of Table A, you may find it helpful to sketch a normal curve so you can see whether the "smaller portion" or the "larger portion" results in a positive or negative z value.

2. These and other related issues are discussed in detail in measurement texts. See, for example, Gilbert Sax, *Principles of Educational and Psychological Measurement and Evaluation* (Belmont, CA: Wadsworth, 1989).

TERMS TO KNOW

Listed in order of presentation in chapter:

normal curve
ordinates
skewed distribution
distribution tail
negatively skewed distribution
positively skewed distribution
percentile
quartile
standard scores (z)
transformed standard scores (Z)
normalized standard scores (T)
normalized curve equivalents (NCE)

EXERCISES

1. If scores on a final examination are distributed in an approximately normal fashion, what percentage of classmates scored below a student whose examination score was 1 standard deviation below the mean?
2. If a distribution of scores departs from normality in such a way that there are a great many low scores and a few extremely high scores, how could you describe the distribution?
3. Assuming that a set of scores is distributed in the shape of a normal curve, match the z scores in the right-hand column with the percentiles in the left-hand column.

Percentiles	z Scores (to be matched)
84th	-1.0
50th	2.0
16th	-2.0
98th	0.0
2nd	1.0

4. In a distribution with a mean of 80 and a standard deviation of 3.5, find the z scores for the following raw scores:

   (a) 87.0   (b) 76.5   (c) 83.5   (d) 73.0

5. In a distribution with a mean of 71.8 and a standard deviation of 6.4, find the z scores for the following raw scores:

   (a) 62.9   (c) 64.9   (e) 79.0
   (b) 71.9   (d) 78.6   (f) 74.1

6. Scores on the first exam in an educational statistics course were normally distributed with a mean of 12 and a variance of 4. The professor decides to grade "on a curve," such that the following z-score intervals get the following grades:

Above 1.5	A
0.5 to 1.5	B
-0.5 to 0.5	C
-1.5 to -0.5	D
Below -1.5	F

(a) of the 30 students in the class, how many will receive each of the five letter grades?

(b) What are the four test-score cutoff points for the grading system?

7. For each of the raw scores in exercise 5, compute the Z scores.

8. If scores are distributed normally in a sample, what will the approximate percentiles be for the following Z scores?

(a) 50   (b) 60   (c) 73   (d) 40

9. If a researcher wishes to match pairs of high-school sophomores according to achievement-test scores but finds that the potential subjects have one of three different types of test scores, each with a different mean and standard deviation, what could the researcher do in order to match the students?

10. If a distribution of scores is not approximately normal, what can you say regarding the percentage of scores exceeded by a Z score of 60?

11. Using the table of the normal curve, convert the following T (NCE) scores into percentiles.

(a) 54.4   (b) 58.4   (c) 68.8   (d) 39.2

12. Convert the following raw scores (with the percentiles for each already indicated) into T (NCE) scores.

(a) 62.3 (70th percentile)   (c) 41.4 (31st percentile)
(b) 74.0 (97th percentile)   (d) 52.2 (50th percentile)

SELECTED READINGS

Blalock, Hubert M., Jr. *Social Statistics.* New York: McGraw-Hill, 1979, chap. 7.

Edwards, Allen L. *Statistical Analysis.* New York: Holt, Rinehart & Winston, 1969, chap. 10.

Freeman, David; Pisani, Robert; and Purves, Roger. *Statistics.* New York: W. W. Norton, 1978, chaps. 5, 16-18.

Guilford, J. P., and Fruchter, Benjamin. *Fundamental Statistics in Psychology and Education.* New York: McGraw-Hill, 1978, chap. 7.

Kirk, Roger E. *Elementary Statistics.* Monterey, CA: Brooks/Cole, 1984, chap. 10.

Spence, Janet T., et al. *Elementary Statistics.* Englewood Cliffs, NJ: Prentice-Hall, 1983, chap. 8.

Inferential Statistics

* *hypothesis testing and estimation*

When educators use descriptive statistics, they are describing data they already have. When they use inferential statistics, they are working with data they do not have but wish they did. While inferential and descriptive statistics serve different purposes, inferential statistics often makes use of descriptive measures such as the mean and the standard deviation. Inferential techniques usually are more complex than descriptive techniques are, however, and they are used more often by educational researchers than by classroom teachers, school administrators, and educational evaluators. Nevertheless, any educator may have occasion to understand or make use of the results of research investigations, so all of them need to be familiar with the basic inferential procedures that will be discussed in this chapter.

The statistical concepts addressed in this chapter are seldom instantly understood, so do not be surprised if you need to reread a few paragraphs or pages. As you complete each section of the chapter, ask yourself, "Do I understand these ideas well enough to explain them to a friend—without making the friend an enemy?" If the answer is no, take time for some thoughtful rereading and rethinking before going on to the next section. The ideas and terminology are apt to be new to you, and it is important that you become familiar with them as a basis for understanding the language and method of statistical analysis.

As you learned in Chapter 1, inferential techniques make it possible to draw inferences from sample data that can be generalized to a wider population. But this use should be considered in light of the purpose of educational research, which is to develop a science of behavior for educational situations. This science of behavior should consist of systematically organized statements of verified relationships among educational variables. Once the nature of the relationship between two or more educational variables has been discovered, meaningful predictions can be made regarding related educational situations. Clearly, classroom teachers and school administrators have an advantage if they can propose and defend, on a statistical basis, the predictions they make about the likely consequences of their decisions.

For example, teachers frequently must decide which instructional technique will work best with a given group of students. Suppose Miss Gustafson must choose between method X and method Y for her class of below-average readers. She might just guess at which method is better and then hope for the best. However, she might learn that several researchers, in relatively small experiments, have shown that method Y is clearly superior with students who have difficulty reading. Then she can base her decision as to which method to use on the *inference* that the researchers' discoveries will also apply to her class. Essentially, inferential statistics permits educators to determine the degree of confidence they can place in the generalizability of research findings to the decision options they are considering.

This should take nothing from the desirability of using descriptive statistics in educational decision making. Investigating educational phenomena on a descriptive basis is a perfectly legitimate and often necessary first step in understanding them. Unfortunately, a certain aura of respectability is often associated with the detection of *statistically significant differences* resulting from applications of inferential procedures, unwarranted as such procedures may be by the nature of the data. Strictly speaking, inferential procedures are only appropriate when two conditions are both present:

1. There is a target population to which an inference can be made.
2. Appropriate random sampling and/or sample assignment procedures have been employed, so the sample being studied is truly representative of the population from which it is drawn and about which the inference will be made.

Educators often have available only a "convenient" sample—that is, a nonrandom sample from some target population that is "like" the population on the basis of certain important variables. In such cases, inferential techniques can be used as long as the investigator makes it clear that any inferences drawn are "extra-statistical" in nature. Such inferences cannot be considered statistically valid, but they may prove illuminating to educational decision makers.

EDUCATIONAL VARIABLES

At the heart of most educational investigation is a quest for knowledge regarding relationships among variables, a term introduced in Chapter 1. We have defined a variable as an attribute or characteristic in regard to which individual beings, objects, or events differ among themselves. For example, individual people, animals, or objects possess certain attributes, such as size or skills, which are called variables if they vary among the individual entities. Variables may be attributes that are quite concrete, such as height, length of hair, or amount of money. They may also be nebulous attributes such as self-efficacy, social sensitivity, or amount of tact in dealing with others.

A distinction can also be made between variables that are quantitative and those that are qualitative. A **quantitative variable** denotes differences in amount, degree, or frequency. Examples of a quantitative variable are the number of pupils in a school, scores on an examination, or frequency of student absences. Quantitative variables such as these can be rank ordered because successively larger numerical designations are assigned to indicate greater quantities or frequencies of pupils, scores, or absences. For example, with a quantitative variable such as number of students entering college, there is a natural ordering of categories which can commence with 0, 1, 2, 3, 4, and so on. When the variable is quantitative in nature, order is essentially present.

A **qualitative variable** denotes differences in kind, such as make of automobile, nationality, religion, and type of books read. Such variables have no inherent ordering system, as do quantitative variables. For example, major in college, a qualitative variable, includes categories such as history, English, or mathematics, which are not intrinsically ordered according to quantity or frequency. In fact, any order imposed on qualitative variables is strictly arbitrary.

The extent to which intrinsic order is present in particular variables is one reason measuring scales used in statistical analysis have been classified according to their mathematical properties. Different levels of measurement commonly used in educational research and evaluation will be described in Chapter 18.

An attribute that constitutes a variable for one group of beings, objects, or events may be an invariable, or a **constant,** for another group. To illustrate, some entities are living (plants or animals), whereas other entities are not (minerals). For *all* such entities the attribute of life is a variable. However, this attribute is a constant rather than a variable for human beings, all of whom possess life. Similarly, knowledge of chemistry would be considered a variable for people in general. But if knowledge of chemistry were measured by administering a particular test, then it might be considered a constant for all those who scored above a defined standard of achievement.

Elusive attributes such as attitudes or achievement are often assessed with various measuring instruments such as a test or inventory that provides an index of the variable being considered. In educational investigations, the variable being affected by the relationship may be operationally defined as performance on a particular measuring instrument. For example, student self-esteem might be operationally defined as the students' scores on inventory X.

The concepts of criterion and predictor variables and dependent and independent variables will be defined in Chapter 5. Further consideration of the nature of variables and how they are treated statistically is beyond the scope of this text. You will find this intriguing topic treated extensively in most introductory and advanced educational measurement books.

POPULATIONS AND SAMPLES

In attempting to establish the precise nature of the relationships among educational variables, educational investigators usually must rely on relatively small samples of the appropriate population. For example, Miss Jackson, a high school counselor, may wish to study the relationship between students' academic performance in secondary school programs and their subsequent achievement in college. To investigate this relationship, she could select a *sample* of college students, then collect data regarding these students' college academic achievement and certain aspects of their academic performance in secondary school. Miss Jackson is not interested only in this sample of students, however. Rather, she seeks to discover the nature of the relationship between the two variables, so it can be usefully generalized to the entire *population* or *universe* from which the sample was drawn.

We have defined the purpose of inferential statistics as making it possible to draw sample-based inferences regarding phenomena that can be generalized to a larger population. The kinds of samples educational investigators study in order to make these inferences vary considerably. It is not difficult to see how a group of kindergarten children, perhaps several thousand of them, drawn from various classes throughout Canada, Mexico, and the United States would constitute a sample of the population of North American kindergarten pupils. But imagine another situation in which a totally new method of teaching physics is being employed with a group of 200 senior high school physics students. The population this sample of 200 students represents is less obvious than in the preceding example. This sample represents the population of all senior high school physics students *who would be taught by the new instructional method*, even though no such group exists at the moment. Thus samples may be studied with a view to generalizing notions about relationships between variables in populations that may not even exist. The educational investigator usually works with small samples of individuals, such as school children who have been exposed to differential treatment conditions in the form of modified instructional techniques. Generalizations from the results of the sample-based investigation then are made to similar populations of students.

Actually, any sample can be considered to represent an infinity of populations. For instance, a sample of 100 high school juniors in a large city might *conceptually* be used to represent all similar pupils in the city, the county, the state, the nation, or the world. However, with most kinds of data, it is hazardous to draw inferences about populations that are considerably removed from the sample. You might confidently generalize about the latency of the eye-blink reaction from a sample of students in Indiana and Manitoba to similar students throughout the United States and Canada. But it would be unwise to consider the attitudes of Indiana parents toward high school basketball, or the attitudes of Manitoba parents toward high school hockey, as representative of parental attitudes in other parts of the United States and Canada.

Behavioral scientists encounter similar problems when they attempt to generalize to human behavior from the behavior of animals in the laboratory. The degree to which inferences drawn from sample data hold true for populations is in large measure a function of the *equivalence* between the sample and the particular population to which the inference is to be applied. Thus if you

Table 4.1   Symbols Used for Sample Statistics and Population Parameters

Sample Statistic Symbol	Data Measure	Population Parameter Symbol
$\overline{X}$	Mean	μ
s	Standard deviation	σ
s^2	Variance	σ^2

decide to conduct your investigation exclusively in an animal laboratory, but you also want to generalize the findings to human behavior, your subjects should be primates, who resemble humans in some respects, rather than lizards, who have no human characteristics.

The term **statistic** (in the singular) can technically be defined as a measure based on a sample. For example, a standard deviation computed from sample data is called a sample statistic. A measure based on a population rather than a sample is called a population **parameter.** If it were possible to determine statistically the standard deviation of mathematics skills scores for all sixth-grade pupils in the world, for example, that standard deviation would be called a parameter. Another way of thinking of inferential statistics, then, is as a way of making *estimates* based on sample statistics about the nature of the parameters, or "real values," in populations.

Lowercase Greek letters are usually employed to represent parameters, whereas lowercase Latin letters are usually used to represent sample statistics. The Greek letter σ used to represent the standard deviation in Chapters 2 and 3, for example, would be a population parameter, and the letter s would represent the standard deviation as a sample statistic. The symbol for this measure and the other measures with population parameters that we have introduced, along with the corresponding symbols for sample statistics used to estimate these parameters, are presented in Table 4.1. The data discussed in preceding chapters were treated as constituting a population rather than a sample because inferences were not being made and the data were being summarized for descriptive purposes only. Knowing the meaning of these symbols is essential to an understanding of the language of inferential statistics.

Educational investigators rarely have access to the values of parameters in their investigations because it is typically too difficult to obtain data from an entire population. Moreover, in most cases it would be extremely wasteful of time and energy to obtain parameters directly. With large samples, most parameters can be estimated quite accurately.

Ensuring a Representative Sample

In order to draw legitimate inferences about a population from a sample, the sample must be chosen in such a way that it really represents the population. It would be impossible to generalize from a sample that has been drawn from a population in a *biased* manner, so it is not typical of the population it represents. For instance, if only very able children were chosen to participate in a study regarding new teaching materials, the results would say little about the effectiveness of these materials with youngsters of average or low ability. Even with the best intentions and most careful research designs, however, it is seldom possible to draw a sample that *exactly* reflects the population it represents. The degree of difference between the characteristics of a sample and the characteristics of the population from which it was drawn is called **sampling error.**

One way to minimize sampling error in an investigation is to randomly assign members of the population to the sample. Such **random sampling** is one of the two necessary conditions for the use of inferential statistics that were given earlier in this chapter. In theory, then, samples *must* be constituted by a random-sampling method if valid inferences are to be drawn. But even though random sampling is theoretically required, educators can probably draw meaningful inferences from sample data that have not been randomly drawn, provided there is evidence that precautions were taken so the sample selection was not biased by undue factors.

Using a Table of Random Numbers.   A simple but time-consuming method of drawing a sample randomly is to assign a number to each member of an entire population, enter the numbers on disks, place the disks in a container, and draw out one at a time. When the desired number of disks representing a selected proportion of the population has been drawn from the container, the individuals whose numbers coincide with these disks can be considered a randomly selected sample. Each individual in the population has an equal chance of being selected for the sample.

A more efficient method of random sampling from a population is to employ a table of random numbers such as Table B in the Appendix. Tables of random numbers consist of rows and columns of numbers arranged at random. They can be entered at any point and read in any direction, right or left, up or down. To illustrate the use of Table B, imagine that you want to select five students at random from a group of ten students. First you must assign numbers to the ten students, as follows: 01, 02, 03, 04, 05, 06, 07, 08, 09, 10. It is necessary to insert the zero before all the single-digit numbers because 10 is a two-digit number, and the number of digits for all members of the population to be studied must be the same in using a random-number table.

Now turn to the second page of Table B (labeled "2nd Thousand") and arbitrarily enter the table in the upper right-hand corner (any point in the table would do as well). This portion of the table is reproduced below:

9	5	0	4	5		9	5	9	4	7
0	7	3	4	8		2	3	3	2	8
•	•	•	•	•		•	•	•	•	•

Then, for this example, read *left* and *down,* using the upper two rows. The first *two-digit* number you encounter is 78, then 42, 93, 53, 92, 58, and 44. The first seven two-digit numbers are all larger then the numbers of the ten students, so skip them. But the next number, 03, is a number for one of the students, so this is the first number of your sample of five. Then return to the table and continue reading to the left; you will find no more of the ten numbers in the upper two rows, all the way to the left edge of the table. Now you might drop down to the next two rows and read to the right, so the first number is 76. The second number, 10, should also be drawn for the sample. In a similar manner, you proceed until five of the ten numbers have been selected. If you encounter the same numbers twice before five subjects have been selected, simply pass over those that you have already selected.

Other Sampling Methods.   In addition to random-sampling methods, there are other ways of securing a representative sample of the population. A population composed of subgroups which may respond differently to the experimental variables can be represented better by drawing a **stratified sample,** or one that represents such subgroups proportionately. For instance, if school neighborhood is related to performance on a personality test, the investigator would want to be sure to include individuals from different neighborhoods in the same proportions that exist in the total population. Or, if sex is a relevant variable in an educational experiment, then a proportionate number of boys and girls should be included in the sample, in order to match the proportion of boys and girls in the population under consideration.

Once the proportions of subgroups to be represented in the sample have been determined, the investigator can randomly draw each subgroup sample. This makes the total sample a *stratified random sample,* which is a particularly good representation of the population. Other, more complicated sampling techniques are described in advanced texts dealing with problems of research design.

HYPOTHESIS TESTING

Hypothesis testing starts with an idea, or a proposition, about the existence of a particular relationship between two or more variables. Once the investigator is satisfied that a representative sample to test this idea has been drawn from the population, the next step is to operationally define the variables and state the proposition in the form of a **hypothesis** which can be tested statistically. In educational studies, hypotheses concern the existence of relationships among educationally relevant variables, such as class size and scores on a test. An educational investigator might focus, for example, on the nature of the relationship between instructional learning time and the degree of student achievement.

By applying statistical tests to hypotheses in regard to such relationships, educational investigators can discover valuable information even if they fail to establish the hypothesized relationship between the variables. For example, suppose the hypothesis is that a relationship exists between students' academic attainment and their degree of anxiety. If, in testing the hypothesis with operationally defined variables, the investigator discovers that the hypothesis that there *is* such a relationship cannot be supported, the results of the investigation could suggest that no meaningful relationship is present between students' academic attainment and their degree of anxiety. A science of behavior in education encompasses notions regarding variables that are *unrelated* as hypothesized, as well as those for which the relationship exists. The tested hypothesis therefore may yield important information, regardless of the outcome of the test.

While hypothesis testing is primarily concerned with testing for *relation-*

ships, not *differences,* among variables, there are situations in which the investigator wants to find out if the performances of the groups under consideration differ. Perhaps this apparent contradiction can be clarified by pointing out that *when different groups are used in research situations, these groups, taken together, usually represent a particular research variable.* For example, when investigators test for group differences between two groups with respect to a particular criterion measure, they are really assessing the nature of the *relationship* between (*a*) the variable represented by the criterion measure and (*b*) the variable represented by whatever characterizes the main difference between the two groups.

To illustrate, suppose Mr. Knutson, a high school mathematics instructor, wants to test his idea (hypothesis) that boys will outperform girls on certain tests of geometric skills he plans to administer. He might divide a sample of students into a group of boys and a group of girls, administer a geometry skills test, and see if the two groups do perform differently on the test. Now, although it may appear that he is looking for a difference between the groups, if you think about it you will see that he really is attempting to see if there is a *relationship* between the *variable* of sex (or gender), on the one hand, and the *variable* of geometry skills, on the other. Ultimately, almost all hypotheses in educational research are suppositions about relationships between two or more variables.

Even though this is true, it is often helpful to think of inferential statistical procedures according to whether they focus on differences, as in testing differences between means of two or more groups, or they focus on the existence of relationships, as in correlation (which will be treated in the next chapter). Because a number of different types of inferential statistics are described in the pages to follow, you may find it helpful to consider each one in light of the following question: Is this a *difference-testing* technique or a *relationship-testing* technique?

Probability and Statistical Significance

Educational investigations that test well-conceived hypotheses produce evidence that can be of considerable importance to educational decision makers. In stating results, the basic issue is to accept as tenable, i.e., not reject those hypotheses that are true and to reject as untenable those that are false. But how does an investigator decide which hypotheses to reject and which not to reject? The decision is seldom so obvious that anyone can merely "inspect" the data and reach a proper conclusion. Deciding whether an observed relationship between variables is probably genuine or merely a fluke is at the heart of inferential statistics.

Probability of Results.   The notion of **probability** is central to the rationale underlying inferential statistics. In order to generalize the results of an investigation from a sample to a population, the investigator must be fairly certain that what is observed in the sample is not a function of mere chance alone.

It is possible to determine statistically, with considerable precision, if a sample outcome is attributable to chance. This can be illustrated by probability statements associated with sets of coin tosses. It is known that the chance a coin will land heads up when tossed is 1 out of 2, and the likelihood that a tossed coin will come up heads two times in a row is only 1 out of 4. The chance of obtaining three heads in three coin tosses is 1 out of 8. The probability of getting ten heads out of ten coin tosses is only 1 in 1,024. All of these probabilities can be determined by using a distribution of statistical events, similar to the way the normal curve can be used. In the case of coin tosses, the statistical probability distribution used is based on two events (heads or tails). Using such curves makes it possible to determine what the probability is that an observed set of events (or a more extreme set of such events) can be attributed to chance alone.

Suppose Joe and June are betting for cups of coffee on the basis of a tossed coin, with the loser buying. Joe does all the coin flipping, and June decides to call tails every time, figuring to win approximately half of the cups of coffee. If the coin turns up heads ten times in a row, June would have to buy more than her share of coffee. And, since the probability of getting ten consecutive heads is 1/1,024, she might begin to suspect that there is something suspicious about the coin—or the person flipping it!

In a similar fashion, the statistician determines the probability that an observed research outcome, or one that is more extreme, is attributable to chance alone. If the probability is rare, for example, only 1 in 100, then the outcome is usually attributed to something *other* than chance—frequently, one of the variables under investigation. For instance, suppose two groups of students have been formed on the basis of whether they have siblings or are the only children in their families (a "sibling group" versus a "no-sibling group"). Then suppose that the performance of the two groups on an achievement test was so substantially different that it would rarely happen by chance alone. The *unusualness* of one variable (the students' performance on the achievement test) would then be considered to be related to the other variable (presence or absence of siblings). It is the educational investigator, incidentally, who decides what is a "rare" event in any given investigation.

Statistical Significance of Results.   When a statistical test reveals that the probability is rare that a set of observed sample data is attributable to chance alone, the result is said to be statistically significant. For example, if the means of the test scores of two groups are so different that such a difference would be found by chance alone only 1 time in 1,000, the difference would be statistically significant. **Statistically significant** means that the observed phenomenon represents a significant departure from what might be expected by chance alone.

An example utilizing the normal curve will help clarify the notion of statistical significance. With certain statistical tests, the chance probability of the value yielded can be interpreted from the baseline and area of the normal distribution. For example, suppose a statistical model for testing differences in means yields a z value of $+2.70$. From the section on probability and the normal curve in Chapter 3, you should know that you can use a table of the normal curve to determine that such a z value will occur *by chance alone* in a normal distribution less than 1 percent of the time. This outcome is illustrated in Figure 4–1, where only 0.35 percent of the distribution is cut off in the tail at the right of the curve by an ordinate erected at $+2.70$ standard deviation units.

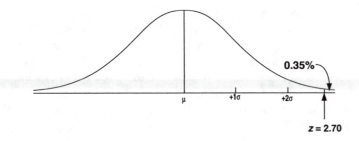

Fig. 4-1. A z value of +2.70 represented on a normal distribution.

Such a z value is statistically significant, that is, a significant departure from what might be expected by chance alone. Under such circumstances, therefore, an observed mean difference would be attributed to something other than chance. Often this "something other" is the relationship between the variables under investigation.

In addition to the normal curve, other probability distributions are used to interpret the results of statistical significance tests. For example, statisticians use the t, F, and χ^2 distributions (to be introduced in later chapters) as often as the normal curve for such purposes. The same general approach is used with these other probability distributions as that employed in the example with the normal curve. A value yielded by a statistical significance test is interpreted along the baseline of a probability distribution to determine what the probability is that the data under study (or more extreme data) could have been produced by chance alone.

The Null Hypothesis

The logic of statistical significance testing is accomplished through the use of the null hypothesis. The **null hypothesis** (often symbolized H_0) postulates that there is *no* (null) relationship in the population between the variables under study. For example, the null hypothesis applied to a test of mean differences between two groups would be: "There is *no* difference between the mean performance of the populations represented by the two groups."

Typically, however, the investigator is concerned with the exact opposite of this hypothesis, namely: "There *is* a difference between the mean performance of the populations represented by the two groups." This hypothesis is designated as the **alternative hypothesis** (symbolized H_1), or the **research hypothesis** of interest to the investigator. Why, then, does the investigator use the null hypothesis?

The null hypothesis is postulated for the sake of argument, using the logic of indirect proof. That is, the investigator, who hopes to accept H_1 as tenable, first assumes that H_0 is true. Then, if warranted by the empirical results, the investigator rejects H_0 at a suitable level of probability. Rejecting H_0 is the logical equivalent of accepting the likelihood of H_1. The null hypothesis, therefore, is merely a convenient statistical and logical device. The mathematics of statistical inference is logically oriented around rejecting or failing to reject H_0. But *failing to reject* H_0 *is not the logical equivalent of "accepting"* H_0.

You may find this discussion to be somewhat abstract—probably because it is. It will make much more sense once you have read further in this text and have a working knowledge of a few actual tests of statistical significance. It is enough to note here that each such test, in its own way, yields a statistic that can be interpreted along the baseline of some statistical probability distribution (like the normal curve in Figure 4–1), *on the assumption that the null hypothesis is true.* Then if the probability of the obtained statistical outcome (a particular mean difference, for example) is highly unlikely (say, only 1 chance out of 100), the investigator may have cause to question the assumption that the null hypothesis is indeed true. If the mathematical theory, arithmetic computations, and the design and conduct of the study have all been adequate, the only remaining assumption to be challenged is the truth of H_0.

This challenge is based on a level of probability that the investigator judges to be so unlikely that the null hypothesis can be reasonably rejected. Suppose the level the investigator chooses is 1 chance in 1,000 (or 0.001). In rejecting H_0 at this level, the investigator could still be wrong! For example, the observed mean difference could actually be that 1 in 1,000 fluke (that chance probability of 0.001) that the null hypothesis is actually true.

Statistical testing of the null hypothesis hinges, therefore, on the selected levels of significance (or probability) and the possibility of error resulting from the investigator's final decision.

Levels of Significance

The **level of significance** in a statistical test is the level of probability at which the null hypothesis can be rejected and the alternative hypothesis can be accepted. The investigator adopts, sometimes rather arbitrarily, a particular level of significance as the criterion for rejecting the null hypothesis. If the sample result is at or below that level of significance, H_0 is rejected and H_1 is accepted.

Levels of significance are expressed in statistical language. When the chance probability that a particular event or a more extreme event will occur is 5 in 100, the observed event is said to be statistically significant at the 0.05, or 5 percent, level (or statistically significant *beyond* the 0.05, or 5 percent, level). The same reasoning holds for probability or significance levels of 0.10, 0.01, and 0.001 and, in fact, for any such level. Sometimes the symbol p is used in such statements; $p < 0.05$, for example, indicates that the probability of the event's occurrence by chance is less than $(<)$ 0.05. Conversely, $p > 0.05$ would indicate that the probability is greater than 0.05. The probability of obtaining a z value of $+2.70$ in the example described earlier is less than 1 in 100. Thus the probability level is $p < 0.01$, and the z value is significant beyond the 0.01 level.

There are several schools of thought regarding the question of what significance levels should be used in rejecting null hypotheses. It has been conventional in behavioral science research to use the 0.05 and 0.01 levels of significance. (Of course, if a statistical test yields a result that is significant at the 0.01 level, it is also significant at the 0.05 level.) These are the significance levels that are usually reported in the research literature. Some contend that these conventional levels should be maintained, because otherwise researchers, for their own purposes, might be inclined to reject null hypotheses with 0.06,

0.09, 0.10, 0.12, or various other significance levels, a practice that could lead to chaos in the interpretation of results—a researcher might "stretch" a probability level in order to support a favored research hypothesis.

Others argue that the level of significance should be a function of the hypothesis tested. They claim that in certain instances a particularly stringent level of significance, such as 0.001, should be employed, while in other situations lower levels of significance, perhaps 0.25, would be acceptable. Consider an example in which a method of placing preschoolers in reading readiness groups is being tested with an experimental group versus a control group. The experimental group, diagnosed and placed by the new method, attains a mean performance in reading at the end of the first grade that is better than that of the control group, but only at the 0.30 level of significance. Proponents of less conventional significance levels would contend that an 0.30 level of significance is entirely acceptable, in the absence of any other method for placing the prereaders; in other words, using a relationship based on 70:30 odds is better than guessing blindly. In other situations, according to this view, the level of significance might be set as low as 0.0001. For example, if a great deal of money is to be spent on new educational equipment, the efficiency of the equipment should be demonstrated so there is even less than 1 chance in 10,000 that the results are accidental.

Educational investigators of both schools of thought tend to agree that the level of significance should be set *prior to* gathering and testing the data. Ex post facto decisions regarding significance levels offer too much opportunity for investigators, perhaps unknowingly, to let their biases color their judgment. Even though this maxim is widely endorsed, however, few educational investigators actually practice it.

Type I and Type II Errors

Significance levels are also related to the probability that the investigator will make errors in judging the tenability of the null hypothesis. These errors are of two types. A **Type I error** is made if the null hypothesis is actually true (that is, the hypothesized relationship between the variables under study does not exist), but the null hypothesis is rejected on the basis of the significance test. A **Type II error** is made if the null hypothesis is actually false but, on the basis of the significance test, H_0 is *not* rejected. The meaning of these two types of error is clarified in Figure 4–2.

The probability of making a Type I error, that is, rejecting a true null hypothesis, can be decreased merely by lowering the level of significance. For example, a true null hypothesis is less likely to be rejected (so a Type I error is committed) at the 0.01 level than at the 0.05 level. Unfortunately, as the probability of making a Type I error decreases, the probability of making a Type II error *increases*. If the significance level is moved from 0.01 to 0.05, a null hypothesis is more likely not to be rejected. When a more stringent significance level is set, however, it becomes increasingly difficult to reject certain null hypotheses that *should* be rejected. For instance, if the significance level is moved from 0.05 to 0.01, then research data that yield a 0.03 significance level would not allow the investigator to reject the null hypothesis. In view of the decisions that might be made on the basis of educational investigations, it is extremely

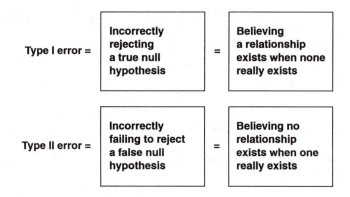

Fig. 4-2. Explanation of differences between Type I and Type II errors.

important for the investigator to decide *which type of error would be more serious*. The significance level should then be set accordingly.

The Power of the Statistical Test

The selection of the statistical test to be used in hypothesis testing is also related to the rejection of null hypotheses that should be rejected. Some inferential tests are more apt to reject a false null hypothesis than are other statistical tests designed to serve the same general statistical purposes. Tests that are more likely to reject false null hypotheses are considered to be more powerful tests. The exact **power of a test** can be determined with some accuracy, but it is a rather technical process.[1] The important point here is that statistical tests that are designed to serve the same purpose (for example, testing differences between the central tendencies of two groups) may not prove equally effective in rejecting null hypotheses. Less powerful statistical tests are often used in research studies where large samples are available, since any deficiencies in the power of a statistical test can be remedied by adequately increasing the number of cases treated.

The concept of Type I and Type II errors and the power of a statistical test can be clarified by inspecting the four combinations possible when either rejecting or not rejecting an either true or false null hypothesis. These possibilities are presented in Table 4.2. The probability of committing a Type I error is denoted by the Greek letter *alpha* (α); the probability of committing a Type II error is denoted by the Greek letter *beta* (β). Many researchers refer to the Type I error as an α error, the size of the significance level being equal to α. For example, a researcher working at the 5 percent or 1 percent significance levels would set $\alpha = 0.05$ or $\alpha = 0.01$, respectively. Because the probability of not rejecting a false H_0 is β, then $1 - \beta$ is the probability of rejecting a false H_0 (mak-

---

1. For a more thorough discussion of the power of a test, see Wilfrid J. Dixon and Frank J. Massey, *Introduction to Statistical Analysis* (New York: McGraw-Hill, 1969), chap. 14; Sidney Siegel and N. John Castellan, *Nonparametric Statistics* (New York: McGraw-Hill, 1988), pp. 10-11; and Janet T. Spence et al., *Elementary Statistics* (Englewood Cliffs, NJ: Prentice-Hall, 1983), pp. 178-81.

Table 4.2 **Consequences of Statistical Decisions Regarding the Null Hypothesis, When H_0 Is Either True or False**

Statistical Decision	Null Hypothesis	
	H_0 true	H_0 false
No Rejection	OK	Type II error Probability $= \beta$
Rejection	Type I error Probability $= \alpha$	OK Power $= 1 - \beta$

ing the correct decision), which is the power of the test of significance. Thus power is dependent on the size of the Type II error, which is dependent on the size of the Type I error as well as other research considerations.

One-Tailed and Two-Tailed Tests

In a well-conceived investigation, a prediction can often be made as to the precise type of relationship that will be observed. These predictions are usually based on either prior research related to the hypothesis under analysis or some type of theoretical rationale. For example, an investigator contrasting the performance of two groups might test the alternative hypothesis that group A's performance will be *superior* to group B's. Stated in the form of a null hypothesis, the proposition would be that group A's performance will be equal to or less than that of group B. Symbolically, using mean performance (μ) as the statistic, this null hypothesis would be expressed as $\mu_a \leq \mu_b$.

An investigator who does *not* make such a prediction must allow for the possibility of a statistical result that may be either positive or negative. In the discussion of statistical significance earlier in the chapter, a z value of $+2.70$ was interpreted as significant beyond the 0.01 level, and in Figure 4–1 it was shown that this z value falls in the right tail of the normal curve distribution. Similarly, a z value of -2.70 is significant beyond the 0.01 level, though it falls in the left tail rather than the right one. When the result may be either a positive or a negative value, that is, $+z$ or $-z$, the investigator must use a **two-tailed test** to interpret the result, as in Figure 4–3.

An investigator who does make a directional (positive or negative) prediction regarding the outcome of an investigation may use a **one-tailed test** of significance such as those depicted in Figure 4–4. When one-tailed tests are used, a null hypothesis will be rejected more often if the direction of the difference or relationship is the same as that predicted by the investigator. Because all of the rejection area is in one tail, the value yielded by the significance test need not be as large, that is, as far from the mean, in order to be considered statistically significant. For example, in the case of the normal curve, a z value must be at least as large as ± 1.96 to be significant at the 0.05 level, using a two-tailed test. If the investigator makes a directional hypothesis (for example, predicts a *positive* z value), then the z value need only be $+1.65$ in order to reject the null hypothesis when $p < 0.05$. This difference is illustrated in Figure 4–5.

Strictly speaking, one-tailed tests do not have a logical statistical basis. Only specific null hypotheses such as those of "no difference" or "x amount of

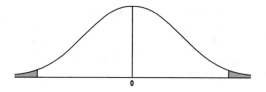

Fig. 4–3. Two-tailed test of significance, in which the value yielded by the significance test must fall in either of the tails (the shaded areas) in order for the null hypothesis to be rejected.

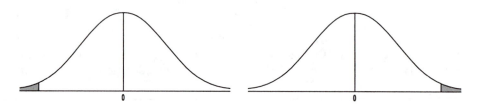

Fig. 4–4. One-tailed tests of significance, in which the value yielded by the significance test must fall in the shaded area in order for the null hypothesis to be rejected.

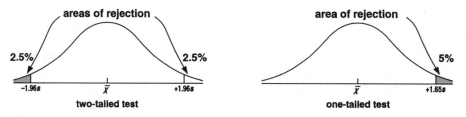

Fig. 4–5. Areas of null hypothesis rejection on a normal curve contrasted for a two-tailed test and a positive-direction, one-tailed test at the 0.05 level.

difference" can be rigorously tested; nonspecific hypotheses involving "less than" or "greater than" cannot be. However, it is possible to perform statistical analyses that are not mathematically rigorous in the strict sense, as long as this leads to empirically useful results. Thus one-tailed tests can be employed *when they are thoroughly justified* by some empirical evidence or theoretical rationale.

However, it takes more than a mere hunch to justify the use of one-tailed tests. To take an extreme case, once the directional hypothesis is posited, even if the significance test yielded a fantastically improbable result *in the opposite direction,* the investigator cannot ethically reject the null hypothesis. Such an unusual occurrence would certainly offer grounds for replicating the research study or the investigation—this time using a two-tailed significance test.

ESTIMATION

Hypothesis testing allows the investigator to consider whether the observed phenomenon (the result) is likely to be attributable to chance or there is a probability that nonchance factors are operating. In other words, it provides an answer to the question of whether the results of statistical tests can be considered significant. The answer to this question may not be sufficient for the educational investigator, however.

Most educational decisions that are based on assumed relationships between variables, such as whether method A or method B yields greater achievement, require notions of *how strong* the variable relationship actually is. It is often not enough to know merely that method A is better than method B, even on the basis of statistical significance. Educational decision makers need to have an idea of *how much better* method A really is.

Because of the complexities of studying behavioral science relationships, precise answers to such questions are not readily forthcoming. However, techniques are available which make it possible to estimate such statistical measures as the population mean or the magnitude of differences between two population means. This section considers estimation approaches in statistical methodology.

To many research methodologists, the testing of null hypotheses represents a relatively primitive level of inference, whereas estimation approaches reflect research sophistication of a markedly higher order. Proponents of this viewpoint argue that little knowledge is really produced by merely locating statistical "significance," because statistical significance is often only a function of the number of individuals in the sample. For example, a seemingly trivial mean difference between two groups often turns out to be statistically significant if the samples involved are large enough. Many years ago, Richard Savage, in making this point, asserted, "Null hypotheses of no difference are usually known to be false before the data are collected; when they are, their rejection or acceptance simply reflects the size of the sample and the power of the test, and is not a contribution to science."[2]

Some investigators have shown that the emphasis on null hypothesis tests of significance has actually led them to overlook the importance of estimation. From the educator's point of view, these arguments make considerable sense, because in educational investigations the concern is far more frequently with questions of the *magnitude* of relationships among variables rather than the mere *existence* of such relationships.

Basically, hypothesis-testing procedures and estimation procedures are designed to answer two different types of questions. Tests of hypotheses provide answers only to the question of whether or not there is a relationship (difference) between the variables examined. Estimation procedures can be used to answer the questions, "How great is the difference?" or "How strong is the relationship?" Answers to both of these different types of questions are needed by educational decision makers.

This should not be interpreted as an attempt to disparage hypothesis testing in educational investigation. To the contrary, sound hypothesis testing is one of the fundamental operations in developing understandings about educational phenomena. But it is only *one* fundamental operation; another that is at least equally important is estimation.

---

2. Richard J. Savage, "Nonparametric Statistics," *Journal of the American Statistical Association,* vol 52 (1957), pp. 332-33.

Point Estimation

A technique is available for determining the "best" estimate of a population parameter using a sample statistic. With this technique, known as **point estimation,** a statistic based on a sample can be used to supply the best estimate of such population values as means and standard deviations. Statisticians have an explicit set of criteria in mind when they refer to an estimate as being "best." The most important is the criterion of an **unbiased estimate.** When the mean of the sampling distribution of a statistic equals that of the population parameter that the statistic is estimating the estimate is said to be unbiased.

Point Estimates of the Population Mean.   The sample mean ($\overline{X}$) is an unbiased estimate of the population mean (μ) (see Table 4.1). The formula for the sample mean is just like the formula for the population mean (see Formula 2.1 in Chapter 2), except that n is used to denote the size of the sample drawn from the population of size N. The formula for the sample mean is shown in Formula 4.1:

$$\overline{X} = \frac{\Sigma X}{n} \tag{4.1}$$

Here, ΣX refers to the sum of the scores in the *sample* rather than the sum of the scores in the *population*.

Suppose you have a large population of scores in a distribution that has a mean of 50. You draw a random sample of 30 scores from the population and use these scores to compute an estimate of the population mean, using Formula 4.1. Then suppose you replace the 30 scores in the population and again draw a random sample of 30 scores and compute a new estimate of the population mean. You now have two estimates of μ. If you repeat the process 1,000 times you would have 1,000 estimates of μ. These estimates are merely numbers, so you can construct the distribution curve representing the 1,000 estimates. This curve is called the **sampling distribution of the mean.** It turns out that the more samples you draw, the closer the sampling distribution of the mean is approximated by the normal curve, such that the mean of the sampling distribution equals the mean of the population. That is, if you computed the mean of the 1,000 estimates, you would get a value very close to 50. This property, known as the **central limit theorem** for the mean, forms the basis of the statistical inference procedures discussed previously. It is the property which enabled us to portray Figures 4–1 through 4–4 using the normal curve. When the mean of the sampling distribution of a statistic equals the population parameter the statistic is estimating, we say that the estimate is *unbiased*. Thus, because of the central limit theorem, the sample mean is an unbiased estimate of μ.

Point Estimates of the Population Variance and Standard Deviation.   Unlike the case with the sample mean, a sample variance (s^2), computed according to Formula 2.6 for the population variance (σ^2) in Chapter 2, would *not* be an unbiased estimate of the population variance. However, an unbiased estimate of the population variance can be obtained if, in computing the sample variance, the sum of squared deviations (or, as it is also called, the sum of squares) is divided by 1 less than the number of cases in the sample, symbolized $n-1$. This is shown in Formula 4.2 for the sample variance:

$$s^2 = \frac{\Sigma(X-\overline{X})^2}{n-1} = \frac{\Sigma x^2}{n-1} \qquad (4.2)$$

In this formula the sum of squared deviations (or sum of squares), Σx^2, is computed in exactly the same manner as indicated in Chapter 2. An unbiased estimate of the population standard deviation (σ) is obtained similarly, by taking the square root of the variance estimate. This is shown in Formula 4.3 for the sample standard deviation:

$$s = \sqrt{\frac{\Sigma(X-\overline{X})^2}{n-1}} = \sqrt{\frac{\Sigma x^2}{n-1}} \qquad (4.3)$$

Degrees of Freedom

The reason for dividing by $n-1$ in the formulas for the sample variance and sample standard deviation is based on the concept of degrees of freedom, symbolized df. Degrees of freedom is one of the more difficult concepts to grasp in beginning statistical inference. We will deal with the use of df in chapters to follow; here we only introduce the role of this concept in estimation.

Whenever it is necessary to estimate population parameters, a sample of data is taken from the population. For example, in estimating μ, sample data are used to compute $\overline{X}$. All the information about the population is contained in the sample. The total number of independent "pieces of information" is, loosely speaking, the **degrees of freedom,** or the number of values that are "free" to vary.

Suppose you have the following sample of five scores: 1, 2, 3, 4, 5. You have five independent pieces of information, or 5 df. In general, in a sample of n scores, there is n df to start with. When the mean is estimated, one of these degrees of freedom is used up. This is because if you know the sample mean ($\overline{X}$), you automatically know the value of any one score in the sample, given the values of the remaining $(n-1)$ scores. Knowing (from Chapter 2) that the sum of deviations about the mean always equals zero, and knowing that $\overline{X}=3$, you can deduce the value of the remaining score if you know, say, scores 1, 2, 3, and 5.

To take a meaningful (unbiased) arithmetic average, it is necessary to divide by the number of df present in the quantities being averaged. In Formula 4.2 for the sample variance and the estimated population variance, the quantities being averaged are deviations about the sample mean. Because the mean must first be determined in order to calculate such deviations, 1 degree of freedom has been used up. And, because the deviations are based on $n-1$ df, the average sum of squared deviations must be obtained by dividing by $n-1$.

Interval Estimation

Although point estimation is a first step in hypothesis testing, point estimates have little intrinsic utility in practical situations unless their possible error limits are taken into account. A second, more important form of estimation is known as interval estimation. An **interval estimation** procedure makes it possible to determine a range or **confidence interval** within which the parameter in question could be expected to be included a specified percentage of the time if the procedure were to be repeated. For example, from sample data it is possible to determine a 95 percent confidence interval for the population mean. Only 5 percent of the time, using this process, would confidence intervals be obtained that did *not* include the population-mean parameter.

It is tempting but inaccurate to assert that with a certain probability, such as a 99 percent confidence interval, it is 99 percent certain that the population mean is included in the interval. Actually, once an interval has been calculated from sample data, the parameter either falls inside or outside the interval, so that probability is either 1 or 0. All that can be said is that the *process* by which the interval is obtained will yield intervals that will contain the parameter 99 times in 100.

Confidence Intervals for the Population Mean. In order to construct a confidence interval for the population mean, it is first necessary to obtain some notion of the sampling error that results from using the sample statistic $\overline{X}$ as an estimate of μ. In the section on point estimates of the population mean, the example involved 1,000-sample estimates and the resulting sampling distribution of the mean. The fact that these estimates are not all equal—in other words, that the sampling distribution has *variability*—indicates the existence of error in estimation. An estimate of this sampling error is obtained by computing the standard deviation of the sampling distribution, often referred to as the **standard error of the mean** (symbolized $s_{\overline{x}}$). The term *error* is used instead of *deviation* to indicate the extent to which a deviation from the mean is a "mistake" due to sampling.

To get the standard error of the mean for the 1,000 scores (which happen to be sample means), you would compute the standard deviation, using Formula 4.3. Clearly, however, you would have an enormous task if you had to compute 1,000 means every time you wanted to estimate $s_{\overline{x}}$ for some population of interest. Fortunately, the central limit theorem for the mean provides a mathematical way to estimate the standard error by dividing the sample standard deviation by the square root of the sample size. This is shown in Formula 4.4 for the standard error of the mean:

$$s_{\overline{x}} = \frac{s}{\sqrt{n}} \tag{4.4}$$

For example, in the sample of scores you worked with earlier for purposes of illustration, 1, 2, 3, 4, and 5, $s = 1.6$; the standard error of the mean, $s_{\overline{x}}$, is then equal to $1.6/\sqrt{5}$, or 0.73.

Because the sampling distribution of the mean is normally distributed, Table A in the Appendix can be used to determine the z-score cutoff points that would include, say, 99 percent of the area in the sampling distribution. These z values indicate how many standard errors (deviations) of the mean are needed in order to construct intervals expected to contain the population mean 99 times out of 100. For example, the z values for the 99 percent confidence interval are -2.57 and $+2.57$ (often denoted ± 2.57 for simplicity). Ordinates erected at these z values contain 99 percent of the area in the normal-curve distribution, half of the 99 percent being above the mean and the other half being below the mean. With the sample data of five scores, where $s_{\bar{x}} = 0.73$, 99 percent of the area in the sampling distribution of the mean lies between the baseline values that are $(2.57)(0.73)$, or 1.88, units above and below the mean. Because the sample mean $\overline{X} = 3$ is the best estimate of what the population mean is, the best estimate of these boundary points is 3 minus $(2.57)(0.73)$, or 1.12, and 3 plus $(2.57)(0.73)$, or 4.88. In general, the boundary points for any 99 percent confidence interval can be given by $\overline{X} \pm 2.57(s_{\bar{x}})$.

The 95 percent confidence interval can be constructed in the same way. At this level, Table A gives z values of 1.96, leaving 2.5 percent of the area in either tail of the normal distribution. The formula $\overline{X} \pm 1.96 \,(s_{\bar{x}})$ would then provide the boundary points for the 95 percent confidence interval. As an example involving a 95 percent confidence interval, consider a sample of 100 achievement-test scores that have a mean of 50.20 and a standard deviation of 6.00. In this case, 6.00 would be divided by 10, the square root of 100, to obtain a standard error of the mean equal to 0.60. This 0.60 is then multiplied by the plus and minus normal-curve z values associated with 95 percent, the probability figure desired for the interval. Since the z values that limit 95 percent of the normal curve are -1.96 and $+1.96$, $(0.60)(-1.96) = -1.18$, and $(0.60)(1.96) = 1.18$. These values are both added to the sample mean of 50.20 to obtain the confidence limits of 49.02 and 51.38. If the process were repeated, 95 percent of the time the population mean would fall between such confidence limits.

Procedures for developing confidence intervals for the more commonly used statistical operations will be described in subsequent chapters.

Use of Interval Estimation by Educators.   Confidence intervals apply not only to individual statistics but also in the areas of difference and relationship statistics. For example, from a given difference between two sample means, a confidence interval can be calculated for the difference between the two population means. Clearly, such estimates can be of great assistance to the educational decision maker who must choose whether or not to adopt new instructional techniques. Educational evaluators, for example, often find that presenting a confidence interval of mean differences based on a "new-versus-old" instructional program can help policymakers decide whether or not to adopt the new program.

Usually a 95 percent or 99 percent confidence interval is used in this type of estimation, and sometimes both. Intervals having greater or lesser probabilities can also be determined. The arguments in favor of more or less stringent probability levels for confidence intervals are much the same as those for setting different sorts of significance levels when testing null hypotheses.

Although more frequent use of interval estimation is urged by most writers on statistical methods, relatively few instances of its use are found in the reports of educational research studies and program evaluations. The sequence of statistics-related activities for educational investigators could reasonably be: (1) description, (2) tests of hypotheses, (3) interval estimation, and (4) decision making. By short-circuiting the interval-estimation operation, educational investigators make their subsequent decision making more difficult.

■   ■   ■

REVIEW

The central task of educational research or investigation is to discover the nature of relationships among educational variables. Inferential statistical procedures make it possible to determine the mathematical probability that relationships discovered in a sample actually exist in the total population being considered.

Typically, the investigator tests a hypothesis (often stated in *no* relationship terms as the null hypothesis) regarding the nature of a relationship between at least two variables. Data reflecting these variables are gathered from a sample representing a broader population. On the basis of the sample data, rejection of the null hypothesis, or the plausibility of the alternative hypothesis, is determined and, if possible, results are generalized to the population from which the sample was drawn.

An event or outcome that cannot be readily attributed to mere chance is termed statistically significant, indicating that it departs significantly from what might be expected by chance alone. Often the design of the investigation or study makes it possible for the investigator to identify relationships among variables that are not likely to be a function of chance. With the use of inferential statistics, hypotheses can be tested within precise probability limits.

The conventionally accepted levels of probability used in rejecting null hypotheses are 0.05 and 0.01. Different significance levels can be used, however, and they can be employed with either one-tailed or two-tailed significance tests, the latter being more stringent.

A population parameter can be estimated in two ways: according to its probable value (point estimation) or according to the probable numerical boundaries containing its value (interval estimation). When the point estimation process is conceptualized to occur a great many times, a distribution of the resulting estimates, called the sampling distribution, is created. The standard deviation of this distribution, called the standard error, is an index of the error made in the estimation process. The central limit theorem states that the sampling distribution of $\overline{X}$ (the estimate of μ) is normally distributed. A formula is available to compute the standard error ($s_{\overline{x}}$) of this distribution, which can then be used to construct confidence intervals for the estimation of μ.

The importance of estimation procedures has been emphasized by many research methodologists and statisticians. Interval estimation operations can provide answers to different kinds of questions from those addressed by hypothesis-testing operations. Hypothesis tests tell whether or not a relationship exists; interval estimation procedures indicate how strong the relationship is. An estimation procedure we recommend is reporting confidence intervals that indicate, at particular levels of probability, the magnitude of the relationship between variables under investigation.

TERMS TO KNOW

Listed in order of presentation in chapter:

quantitative variable
qualitative variable
constant
statistic
parameter
sampling error
random sampling
stratified sample
hypothesis testing
hypothesis
probability
statistically significant
null hypothesis
alternative hypothesis
level of significance
Type I error
Type II error
power of a test
two-tailed test
one-tailed test
point estimation
unbiased estimate
sampling distribution of the mean
central limit theorem
degrees of freedom
interval estimation
confidence interval
standard error of the mean

EXERCISES

1. In testing a null hypothesis regarding the relationship between two variables, you discover that the relationship observed in the sample is so strong that it or a stronger relationship would have occurred by chance alone only 1 time in 10,000. Should you reject the null hypothesis?
2. You test for differences between the means of two samples and find, through the statistical test you employ, that the mean difference is so small it would occur by chance alone 90 percent of the time. What should your action be regarding the null hypothesis of mean difference?
3. You find that the means of two experimental groups are so divergent that the difference is significant beyond the 0.05 level. Does this mean that if you repeated the study a number of times you would get the same kind of mean difference?

4. An investigator sets the level of significance for rejecting the null hypothesis at 0.05, and the statistical test yields a z value of 6.83. What should the investigator's action be regarding the null hypothesis?

5. If the level of significance for the null hypothesis is set at 0.05, what should the investigator's decision be in each of the following situations?

   (a) if $p < 0.05$ (c) if $p < 0.01$ (e) if $z = 0.19$
   (b) if $p > 0.05$ (d) if $p > 0.01$ (f) if $z = -3.92$

6. Is an investigator who makes a prediction regarding the direction of mean differences between an experimental and control group on the basis of past experimentation permitted to use a one-tailed test?

7. Is a one-tailed test or a two-tailed test more likely to reject the null hypothesis?

8. If a z value of 1.65 is needed to reject a 0.05-level null hypothesis for a one-tailed test, what is the probability level of a z value of 1.65 for a two-tailed test?

9. An educational investigator who rejects the null hypothesis at the 0.01 level is in essence saying, "There is only one chance in 100 that what I have observed in the sample is due to the fluctuations of probability alone." Suppose this rare instance is, in fact, the case and the null hypothesis is rejected erroneously. Would the investigator have committed a Type I or Type II error?

10. A school psychologist discovers that a researcher has demonstrated that one method of counseling yields significantly higher mean achievement with underachievers than another method does. The psychologist consults the research article and learns that a significant mean grade-point difference of 1.32 was produced over a semester by the two different counseling methods. Would the psychologist, who is weighing the merits of introducing the better method, be more interested in questions of hypothesis testing or estimation?

11. A college dean wishes to estimate the average number of hours spent watching television by first-year students. A random sample of 100 freshmen is asked to record the number of hours they watch TV daily for a period of two weeks. The mean number of hours reported is 20.6, and the standard deviation is 6.0.

   (a) Construct the 95 percent and 99 percent confidence intervals the dean could use in estimating mean TV-watching hours for the *population* of first-year students.
   (b) Suppose only 50 students were sampled, and the mean and standard deviation remained unchanged. Repeat (a) with these data and discuss the change in the sizes of the confidence intervals.

SELECTED READINGS

Blalock, Hubert M., Jr. *Social Statistics*. New York: McGraw-Hill, 1979, chaps. 8, 9, and 12.

Dixon, Wilfrid J., and Massey, Frank J. *Introduction to Statistical Analysis*. New York: McGraw-Hill, 1969.

Hoel, Paul G. *Elementary Statistics*. New York: Wiley, 1976, chaps. 5-7.

Kish, Leslie. "Some Statistical Problems in Research Design." *American Sociological Review,* vol. 24, no. 3 (June 1959), pp. 328-38.

Morrison, D. E., and Henkel, R. E. (Eds.). *The Significance Test Controversy.* Chicago: Aldine, 1970.

Shavelson, Richard J. *Statistical Reasoning for the Behavioral Sciences.* Boston: Allyn & Bacon, 1988, chaps. 8-12.

Siegel, Sidney, and Castellan, N. John. *Nonparametric Statistics for the Behavioral Sciences.* New York: McGraw-Hill, 1988, chap. 2.

Walker, Helen M., and Lev, Joseph. *Elementary Statistical Methods.* New York: Holt, Rinehart & Winston, 1969, chap. 9.

5

Correlation

Because one important goal of a science of behavior for education is to isolate and understand more fully the nature of relationships among educational variables, you should not be surprised to learn that techniques for analyzing these relationships are accorded considerable attention in educational statistics texts. Some examples of the types of relationships that interest educators are:

1. The relationship between pupils' aptitude and their achievement in learning situations.
2. The relationship between student reading ability and subsequent performance in schoolwork.
3. The relationship between certain family-school-community conditions and the risk of educational failure.

These are just a few of the many relationships educators must understand if they are to attain their educational goals.

Although correlational techniques were not considered in the chapters on descriptive statistics, indexes of correlation are every bit as descriptive as indexes of central tendency and variability. All such statistics—means, variances, coefficients of correlation—can be tested for statistical significance when it is appropriate to do so.

In this chapter we consider the notion of statistical correlation from an intuitive perspective, that is, from a perspective designed to help you understand what's going on when correlational procedures are used. The following companion chapter will provide you with the computation procedures needed to carry out various correlational analyses.

STATISTICAL CORRELATION

In popular usage the term *correlation* refers to any type of relationship between events or objects. Phrases such as "correlated subject matter" and "the correlation between theory and practice" refer to general kinds of relationships. In statistical analysis, however, **correlation** refers exclusively to a quantifiable relationship between two variables.

In statistical correlations, there must be two measures for each individual (or other entity) in a group. If this condition is satisfied, the data can be inserted into a statistical formulation which will reveal the type and strength of the relationship under study. The most widely employed measure of statistical correlation is the **product-moment correlation coefficient** devised by Karl Pearson. This coefficient estimates both the direction and the strength of a *linear* relationship. Many other techniques used to describe relationships are analogous to the Pearson product-moment correlational approach. This chapter discusses the product-moment statistical correlation coefficient in detail, but several of the more common other types of correlational procedures will also be considered.

The Meaning of Statistical Correlation

Consider what happens when an educator tries to describe the nature of a relationship between two educational variables. For instance, suppose Mrs. Licari wants to study the size of elementary schoolchildren's vocabularies with reference to their performance on achievement tests. She would like to know how vocabulary comprehension is related, if at all, to the way in which pupils score on achievement examinations. It may be that she suspects achievement tests are based largely on vocabulary comprehension.

In order to discover the nature of this relationship, Mrs. Licari decides to administer a suitable vocabulary examination, along with an effective achievement test, to 65 elementary school pupils. She can get a rough idea of the way in which these two measures are related by visually inspecting the scores of the pupils on the two tests. She observes, for example, that many of those who obtained high scores on the achievement test also scored well on the vocabulary quiz, and those who scored low on one test also tended to perform poorly on the other. This visual inspection should tell her that there is probably a degree of relationship between the two variables under study. It is also likely that the relationship is *positive,* rather than *negative,* in nature. In positive relationships, individuals who score high (or low) on one measure tend to score similarly on the other measure as well. In negative relationships, an individual who scores high on one measure tends to score low on the other.

Although it is possible to gain some insights regarding the nature of the relationship under investigation by visually inspecting the scores, this is usually possible only when the relationship is rather clear-cut. If the relationship does not have great strength and is therefore not readily apparent, the visual inspection technique may actually yield erroneous conclusions. This is frequently due to the selective perception of the person scanning the data.

A preferable inspection method Mrs. Licari could use for studying this relationship would be to plot the data in a frequency table such as that depicted in Figure 5–1. The *X* or horizontal scale measures the pupils' scores on the achievement test, and the *Y* or vertical scale measures their scores on the vocabulary quiz. Note that these two measurement scales have been marked off in five-point intervals, to simplify the tabulation. Note also that each tally mark represents the *dual* performance of one individual on measures *X* and *Y*. For example, a student who obtained an achievement test score of 146 and a vocabulary quiz score of 97 would be represented by the single tally mark in the cell at the upper right-hand corner of the table. Similarly, every other tally mark represents *dual* scores of the 65 individuals represented in the frequency table.

Examining a chart such as Figure 5–1, which is called a **scattergram** or correlation chart, provides a more precise notion of the nature of the relationship under investigation. Mrs. Licari can see with more certainty that there is a relationship between vocabulary quiz and achievement test scores that is positive in nature and fairly strong. Yet it still is not possible to attach any precisely quantified label to the strength of the relationship. At this point, the need for an accurate numerical index of the strength and direction of such relationships becomes clear. The product-moment correlation coefficient provides that index.

X = score on achievement test

	90-94	95-99	100-104	105-109	110-114	115-119	120-124	125-129	130-134	135-139	140-144	145-149
95-99									/	/	//	/
90-94		/					/	/		/		
85-89				/		〦〦			//			
80-84						//	/	/			/	/
75-79					//	//	//	/				
70-74			//		/	///	//	//				
65-69			〦〦 /	/		//	/	/				
60-64			/		//	/	/					
55-59		/										
50-54	//	//	/			/						
45-49	/	/										

Y = score on vocabulary quiz

Fig. 5–1. Frequency table for scores of 65 pupils on a vocabulary quiz and an achievement test.

RATIONALE FOR THE PRODUCT-MOMENT COEFFICIENT

One of the first things you need to learn about product-moment correlation is that its coefficient (symbolized r) ranges between $+1.00$ and -1.00. A perfect positive relationship is reflected by an r of $+1.00$; a perfect negative relationship is reflected by an r of -1.00; and a lack of any relationship is reflected by an r of zero. Yet, even though many students have dutifully memorized such notions, it is surprising how few of them really understand what sorts of data relationships yield various types of correlation coefficients.

In establishing the rationale of the product-moment coefficient, we will demonstrate how the following conclusions are reached:

1. That $r = +1.00$ when the data conform to the definition of a perfect, positive linear relationship.
2. That $r = -1.00$ when the data conform to the definition of a perfect, negative linear relationship.
3. That $r = 0$ when there is no relationship in the data.
4. That r can attain all values between -1 and $+1$ for less than perfect (but nonzero) types of relationships in the data.

When $r = +1.00$

Consider a very simple situation involving only five individuals. Each has two scores, one on variable X and one on variable Y. Hypothetical scores for this situation are shown in Table 5.1 for a perfect, positive linear relationship. Looking at the raw scores in columns 1 and 2, you would probably recognize the positive relationship between variables X and Y. But what specific quantitative properties would lead you to this belief? First, note that the *rank order* of each person's score on X is the same as that person's score on Y. For example, individual D obtains the second highest score on X and also has the second highest score on Y. Second, note that the *distance* between the scores of any two subjects on Y is always the same multiple of that between the scores of the same two subjects on X. Thus the distance between the scores of individuals B and E on variable Y is $15 - 9$, or 6, and the distance between the scores of individuals B and E on variable X is $5 - 2$, or 3.

These two criteria for the rank order of and distance between scores are one definition of what is meant by a linear relationship. When the relationships between the five individuals' scores on variables X and Y are graphically plotted in Figure 5–2, the five pairs of points all lie on the same straight line.

Table 5.1   Hypothetical Set of Data for a Perfect, Positive Linear Relationship: $r = +1.0$

Individual	(1) X	(2) Y	(3) z_x	(4) z_y	(5) $z_x z_y$
A	1	7	-1.4	-1.4	2.0
B	2	9	-0.7	-0.7	0.5
C	3	11	0.0	0.0	0.0
D	4	13	0.7	0.7	0.5
E	5	15	1.4	1.4	2.0
				Sum $= +5.0$	
				Mean $= +1.0$	

$$r = \frac{\Sum z_x z_y}{n} \qquad (5.1)$$

where:

z_x = the z score for an individual on variable X
z_y = the z score for that individual on variable Y
n = the number of cases or individuals in the sample

When $r = -1.00$

Now consider what happens when, using the data in Table 5.1, the relative standings of the individuals are completely reversed in terms of their scores on variable Y. This situation is shown in Table 5.2 for a perfect, negative linear relationship. Note that although the same relative distance between any two individuals' raw scores for variables X and Y has been retained, the rank ordering of the individuals' scores for variable X, compared to variable Y, has now been reversed. Thus any individual's z scores on variables X and Y are equal in terms of deviation from the mean, but *opposite in sign*. This is exactly the definition of a perfect, **negative linear relationship** between two variables.

When this relationship between the raw scores on variables X and Y is plotted graphically (see Figure 5–3), the five pairs of points again all lie on the same straight line—but in this case the line slopes downward (from left to right). This property of the slope of the line and the direction of the relationship is consistent. Thus whenever the relationship is positive, the line will slope upward (as in Figure 5–2), and whenever it is negative, the line will slope downward (as in Figure 5–3).

Table 5.2   Hypothetical Set of Data for a Perfect, Negative Linear Relationship: $r = -1.0$

Individual	X	Y	z_x	z_y	$z_x z_y$
A	1	15	−1.4	1.4	−2.0
B	2	13	−0.7	0.7	−0.5
C	3	11	0.0	0.0	0.0
D	4	9	0.7	−0.7	−0.5
E	5	7	1.4	−1.4	−2.0
				Sum =	−5.0
				Mean =	−1.0

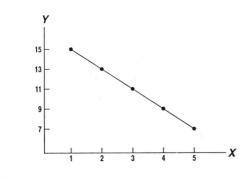

Fig. 5–3. Scattergram for data in Table 5.2.

Because in this case the z scores for an individual are always opposite in sign in the case of perfect negative linear correlation, the product of the z scores will always be *negative*. The sum of the products will also always be negative, and the sum will be equal to *minus* the number of individuals. Thus the mean of these z-score products must be $-5/5$, or -1.00. This is always the case for a perfect negative linear relationship.

When $r=0$

Next, consider another rearrangement of the scores on variable Y for the five individuals in this example. In Table 5.3 for a perfect, **zero linear relationship,** there is no apparent consistency in relative standing on raw scores for the five individuals across variables X and Y. One individual may score relatively high on both X and Y (for example, individual D), whereas another may score relatively high on X but low on Y (for example, individual E). The pattern is reversed for individuals B (low on both X and Y) and A (low on X and high on Y), and individual C retains the same standing on both variables. Thus the patterns of positive and negative relationships within the data should cancel out one another, leaving no relationship whatsoever. This is, in fact, the situation with the z-score products. For every nonzero, positive z-score product, there is a nonzero, negative z-score product having the same magnitude. Thus the sum of these products will be zero, and their mean must be zero.

When this relationship is graphed in Figure 5–4, no one straight line can be drawn through all five pairs of points. In fact, the one straight line that comes closest to all the points (the dotted line) is perfectly horizontal, with no slope whatsoever.

Table 5.3   Hypothetical Set of Data for a Perfect, Zero Linear Relationship: $r=0$

Individual	X	Y	z_x	z_y	$z_x z_y$
A	1	13	-1.4	0.7	-1.0
B	2	7	-0.7	-1.4	1.0
C	3	11	0.0	0.0	0.0
D	4	15	0.7	1.4	1.0
E	5	9	1.4	-0.7	-1.0
				Sum =	0.0
				Mean =	0.0

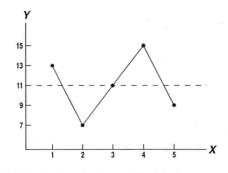

Fig. 5–4. Scattergram for data in Table 5.3.

Other Values of *r* between +1 and −1

Ordinarily, no set of data yields an *r* that is exactly equal to +1, −1, or 0. We have considered these special cases because they provide a certain insight into the nature of Formula 5.1. Typically, the index of relationship given by Formula 5.1 (the Pearson product-moment correlation coefficient) is some decimal value between +1 and −1, indicating a greater or lesser degree of positive or negative linear relationship. For example, if individual A received a score of 9 on variable *Y* in Table 5.1, the relationship, although still positive, would not be as strong; A's new *z* score on *Y* would be −0.71, the new *z* score product would be (−1.42)(−0.71), or 1.01, and Formula 5.1 would yield a new *r* of 4/5 or 0.8.

Perhaps the easiest way of appreciating the possible values that the correlation coefficient can assume is to investigate the scattergram depicting the given relationship. The scattergrams in Figures 5–2 through 5–4 are fairly simplistic in that they are based on only five cases and represent very special values of *r*. Consider, for example, a large number of people obtaining scores on two tests, *X* and *Y*. When the score pairs are graphically plotted, they are usually represented by an elliptical ring as in Figures 5–5 through 5–7. Note that if the direction of the closed oval curve is from lower left to upper right, the *r* is positive (Figures 5–5 and 5–6). If the oval extends from upper left to lower right, a negative *r* is present (Figure 5–7). A careful examination of the points in these scattergrams will give you further insight into the meaning of positive and negative relationships.

The shape of the oval itself should also be inspected. If the oval is fairly narrow, somewhat like a cigar in shape, the relationship is rather strong. The more closely the oval resembles a straight line, the more closely does *r* approach a perfect relationship of ±1.00. At the other extreme, the total absence of relationship would be reflected in a perfect circle shape enclosing the points on the scattergram, as in Figure 5–8.

Even in the case of a perfect correlation, an individual's scores on the two measures are not necessarily *identical*. What must be the same is the *distance* of both of the individual's scores from the means of their respective groups, in terms of standard scores. For example, the very small sample of

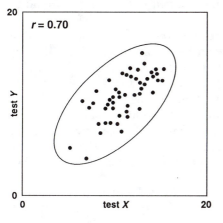

Fig. 5–5. Scattergram with *r* = 0.70.

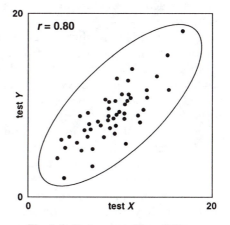

Fig. 5–6. Scattergram with *r* = 0.80.

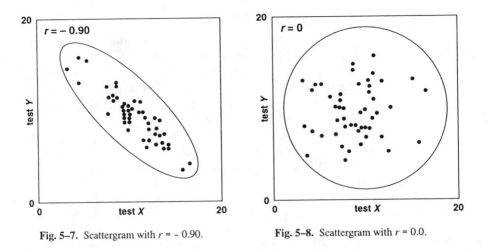

Fig. 5–7. Scattergram with *r* = – 0.90.   **Fig. 5–8.** Scattergram with *r* = 0.0.

scores in Table 5.1 will yield an *r* of + 1.00, even though the scores for any individual on the two tests are not the same. Some students encountering correlation for the first time incorrectly assume that an individual must score precisely the same on both measures in order for a perfect correlation to be produced.

THE STRENGTH AND SIGNIFICANCE OF THE CORRELATION COEFFICIENT

How large must *r* be in order for the relationship between two variables to be considered a strong one? Or, conversely, how small can a correlation coefficient be before it is discounted because it represents a trivial relationship? In general, there are no precise answers to such questions. One valuable guide depends on the notions of probability and statistical significance discussed in Chapter 4. But, leaving aside the question of statistical significance for the moment, it should be noted that for certain purposes an *r* of 0.50 might be considered satisfactory, whereas in other situations an *r* of 0.90 or higher would be required.

For example, in educational measurement, test constructors often must demonstrate the equivalence of two different forms of the same test. A group of students may be required to complete both forms of the test, and then their scores on the two measures are correlated. If the two test forms are to be considered equivalent, a high positive correlation between scores on the two forms, somewhere in the neighborhood of 0.90, would be expected. Yet in other educational situations, for example, relating academic achievement to a predictor test of achievement such as an aptitude test, an *r* of between 0.40 and 0.50 often is considered satisfactory. An *r* of 0.70 in such a situation would be exceptional indeed.

When statisticians refer to "high" and "low" correlation coefficients, they are usually using the absolute scale of 1.00 to 0.00 as their guide. "High" or "strong" correlation coefficients, therefore, should not necessarily be

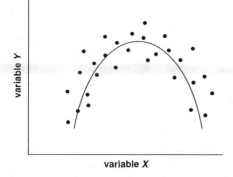

Fig. 5–9. Scattergram of a nonlinear (curvilinear) relationship between variables X and Y.

thought of as "important," nor should "low" or "weak" correlation coefficients necessarily be considered "unimportant."

It should be added that notions of causality, or cause and effect, are not inherent in product-moment correlation. Because two variables are strongly correlated does not imply that one "caused" the other. Though it *may* indeed be true that variable X is causally related to variable Y, causal relationships cannot be imputed to such variables on the basis of the correlation coefficient alone. In fact, variables X and Y may both be "caused" by variable W, which is thus indirectly responsible for the relationship between X and Y. Correlation is a necessary but not sufficient condition for the popular meaning of the word *cause.*

It must be emphasized that the correlation coefficient is a measure of *linear* correlation only. Meaningful relationships between two variables do not necessarily have to be linear. When the correlation coefficient r is low, little *linear* relationship exists between the two variables. That is not to say, however, that no relationship whatsoever exists—in fact, a strong, *curvilinear* relationship may exist in the data. The scattergram in Figure 5–9, for example, would yield a very low value of r but a very high value for any index sensitive to a curvilinear (in this case, quadratic) relationship.

Determining the Statistical Significance of r

As we noted in Chapter 4, in generalizing findings regarding a sample relationship to the population represented by that sample, it is important to ascertain the probability that the observed relationship could be attributed to chance alone. In other words, in order to generalize to a population regarding relationships between variables, you must determine the statistical significance of the sample relationship.

The symbol r, which represents the Pearson product-moment correlation coefficient, is a sample statistic. When working with correlation, we use the phrase "statistical significance of the sample relationship" to mean the statistical significance of this sample statistic. But statistical significance is only meaningful in terms of a specifically stated null hypothesis about the *population* correlation coefficient, denoted by the Greek letter *rho* (ϱ). In general, any hypothesis regarding the value of the parameter ϱ can be tested. Most often, however, the hypothesis concerns whether or not the linear relationship in the population is something other than zero. The null hypothesis most often tested is H_0: $\varrho = 0$. Following the rationale of hypothesis testing discussed in Chapter 4, if the sample value r represents a sufficiently rare event for sampling from a population, with $\varrho = 0$, then the assumption that $\varrho = 0$ is rejected. The conclusion is that there is, in fact, a significant relationship in the population and that r is an estimate of the magnitude and direction of this relationship.

Determining the statistical significance of r is relatively simple because tables of values that must equal or exceed r at given levels of significance have been prepared. These tables are usually designed for two-tailed hypothesis tests, that is, those in which r may be either positive or negative. Table C in the Appendix contains these values.

In using Table C, the table is entered with the number of pairs of scores minus 2. For example, suppose Mr. Rivera, a program evaluator, wants to test a hypothesis regarding a relationship between intellectual aptitude and academic performance. His data consist of the scores of 30 students on an aptitude test and their subsequent scores on a performance test. The significance level he has set before gathering the data is 0.05. Having satisfied all requisite assumptions for the product-moment r, he calculates a coefficient of 0.41. He determines the significance of this coefficient with an n of 30 by entering Table C where the number 28 ($n - 2$) appears under the column headed "degrees of freedom" (*df*). Reading across the four columns to the right, he sees that an r of 0.41 is large enough to be significant at the 0.05 level, but not at the 0.02 level. Because his previously established significance level has been achieved, Mr. Rivera can now reject the null hypothesis and accept the alternative hypothesis that the two variables under study are indeed probably related.

The notion of statistical significance for r is, sensibly enough, tied to the size of the sample. Because a larger sample will provide a more representative index of the nature of a relationship, smaller values of r become statistically significant as the size of n increases.

Some writers on statistics place correlation under the heading of descriptive statistics, for its function is to describe the existing state of relationship between two sets of scores. Most investigators, however, want to generalize to a population their findings about a relationship present in a sample. In our opinion, it is not so important to classify a statistical technique (such as measuring a relationship) as it is to understand the purpose for which the technique is being used.

A Confidence Interval for r

Techniques are also available for computing a confidence interval for a given r. For example, by determining a confidence interval of 95 percent for a particular r based on sample data, an interval can be established so that in 95 percent of similar computations the interval will contain the population correlation coefficient. This is of value to an investigator who must have a relatively precise notion of the limits of the actual population relationship between two variables.

In order to compute confidence limits for a given sample r, it is necessary to transform the r to a special z_r value (**Fisher's z_r coefficient**), by using a logarithmic transformation. Tables are available which give the value of z_r for different values of r. In this text, Table D in the Appendix is used for this purpose. The z_r value is then inserted in a formula that yields the confidence limits for r. The use of Table D and the subsequent computation procedures for determining the confidence interval will be discussed in the next chapter.

ASSUMPTIONS UNDERLYING PRODUCT-MOMENT CORRELATION

As is the case with many of the more complex statistical procedures, there are certain assumptions underlying the proper interpretation of the product-moment r. In the next chapter, several simple formulas are presented which may be applied to data in order to obtain the correlation coefficient. These formulas will yield an r regardless of the kind of data used, as long as there are two numerical scores for each subject. This correctly suggests that a correlation coefficient can be *calculated* with little consideration of the nature of the data. In order to use inferential procedures, however, certain assumptions about the data must be satisfied.

The distinction between the *calculation* of a test of significance and the *defensible interpretation* of a test of significance is an important one in all phases of statistics. In the case of correlation, in order to draw proper statistical inferences regarding the calculated r, the data must fulfill two important assumptions. For all values of one measure (all X scores, for example), the distribution of the other measure's values (Y scores) must be both approximately normal and equal in variability.

The assumption of equality in variance is known technically as **homoscedasticity** (*homo* means equal, *scedasticity* means scattering). The concept can be more readily understood by examining Figure 5–10. For each value of X, a curve has been drawn which depicts the associated Y values. If the variances or standard deviations of these curves are fairly similar, the assumption of homoscedasticity has been satisfied. The other assumption is that each of the distributions is approximately normal in shape. These notions must apply not only to values of Y for X, but also X values for Y.

Ordinarily, the data in a correlation analysis are distributed in normal and homoscedastic fashion when the relationship is linear in nature and sufficient data have been sampled.

MULTIPLE CORRELATION

Sometimes an investigator is interested in the relationship between one variable and a combination of two or more other variables considered simultaneously. It is possible to determine the extent of such a relationship through a procedure known as **multiple correlation,** in which a coefficient (R) is computed which is interpreted in approximately the same way as a simple r. The **multiple correlation coefficient,** however, is not merely a sum of the relationships between one variable and several others. Rather, R is based on *intercorrelations* between variables, so that the highest possible relationship, as in the

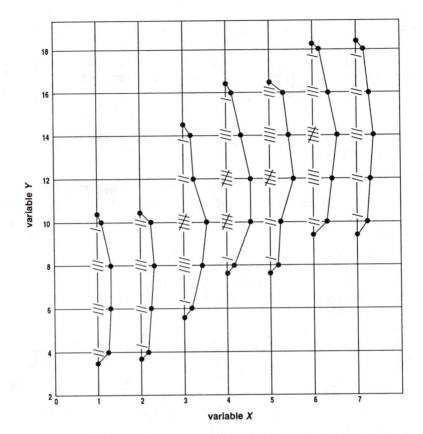

Fig. 5–10. Scattergram with *Y* distributions represented for values of *X* where the assumption of homoscedasticity has been satisfied.

case of *r,* is 1.00. Really, multiple correlation provides an index of the relationship between *two* variables, one variable and a weighted *combination* of more than one other variable.

An example of the type of situation in which an educator might want to compute a multiple *R* would be to find the relationship between a **dependent variable** about which a prediction is to be made, such as student performance on a high school mathematics test, and two **independent variables** to be considered together in making the prediction, such as (1) student verbal aptitude and (2) student performance on a mathematical achievement test taken in junior high school. In educational investigations, the dependent variable often is referred to as the **criterion variable,** and the independent variable is referred to as the **predictor variable.** Predictor (or independent) variables are used in order to make predictions about the criterion (or dependent) variables of interest in the investigation.

The relationship between combined independent variables and a dependent variable might be illuminating because it would indicate whether the resulting *R* is much stronger than the simple *r* between the dependent variable and either of the independent variables alone. Often the strength of the relationship between a criterion and several predictor variables can be increased by computing a multiple *R*.

Table 5.4   **Intercorrelations among One-Semester Grade-Point Ratio, ACE Scores, and SSHA Scores; Multiple Correlation Coefficient between (1) Grade-Point Ratio and (2) ACE and SSHA Scores Considered Simultaneously; for 275 College Students**

Relationship	Coefficient
Grades versus ACE	$r = 0.45$
Grades versus SSHA	$r = 0.48$
SSHA versus ACE	$r = 0.22$
Grades versus ACE and SSHA	$R = 0.60$

Source: W. J. Popham and M. R. Moore, "A Validity Check on the Brown Holtzman Survey of Study Habits and Attitudes and the Borow College Inventory of Academic Adjustment," *Personnel Guidance Journal,* vol. 38, no. 7 (March 1960), pp. 552–54.

This phenomenon is illustrated in Table 5.4. Simple r coefficients have been computed between 275 college students' one-semester grade-point ratios (the criterion variable) and their scores on two predictor measures: (1) the American Council on Education Psychological Examination (ACE), which provides an index of intellectual aptitude, and (2) the Survey of Study Habits and Attitudes (SSHA), which is designed to measure factors associated with student academic success other than intellectual aptitude. Note that, when ACE scores are related to grades, an r of only 0.45 is produced. Similarly, when SSHA scores are related to grades, an r of 0.48 is yielded. But when grades are related by multiple correlation to ACE and SSHA scores *considered simultaneously,* an R of 0.60 is produced.

The reason the separate r coefficients for grades versus ACE and grades versus SSHA have not been simply added to obtain R is that the correlation between the two predictors (0.22) must be taken into consideration. Once the product-moment correlations between the several variables involved in a multiple correlation problem have been computed, the calculation of R is relatively simple. Computation procedures for multiple correlation will be discussed in Chapter 6.

PARTIAL CORRELATION

A different type of investigation involving more than two variables makes use of a technique called **partial correlation.** This technique is used to assess the relationship between two variables when the relationship of another variable with these two has been held constant or *partialed out.*

The relationship between two variables is often unclear because of their mutual relationship with a third variable. For example, if an r were to be computed between verbal fluency and weight for a group of children ranging in age from 1 to 10, a substantially high and positive coefficient would result. Does this mean that verbal fluency is related to a person's weight? Obviously, there is a third variable, chronological age, to which both verbal fluency and weight are related, which must be considered in this analysis. The *mutual* relationship of verbal fluency and weight to chronological age superficially makes it appear that people who weigh more are more verbally fluent.

Another commonly cited example is that the relationship between school grade-point average and students' hours of study has sometimes been found to be negative. If this relationship were to be accepted as it stands, it would appear that students who want to make high grades should be urged to study less. Yet, when the effect of intellectual aptitude is held constant through partial correlation, the relationship between grades and study hours becomes positive and usually significant. The fact that the two variables originally under investigation were mutually related to a third variable confused the picture. The "missing" variable, of course, is intellectual aptitude, which often allows bright students to attain high marks even though they study less than others.

Ideally, investigators could avoid this problem by selecting for their samples only individuals who are alike with respect to the third variable. In the preceding example, only students of the same intellectual aptitude would have been selected. The effect of the third variable on the relationship between the two variables being studied would thereby be controlled through the research design. Unfortunately, such approaches often reduce the sample size to trivial proportions. In addition, educational investigators often want to conduct investigations within an actual school environment, which means intact, heterogeneous groups must be included.

For these reasons, partial correlation offers a convenient method for dealing with such problems, particularly in preliminary phases of an investigation when the investigator is reluctant to spend too much time on rigorously controlling the relevant variables through experimental design. The symbolic representation of a **partial correlation coefficient** is $r_{12 \cdot 3}$. This signifies the relationship between variables 1 and 2 *after* their mutual relationship to variable 3 has been removed, or partialed out. It is also possible to hold constant additional variables, in which case the partial correlation coefficient becomes $r_{12 \cdot 34}$, $r_{12 \cdot 345}$, and so forth. In this notation system the subscript numbers to the right of the dot indicate the controlled variables, while the subscript numbers to the left of the dot indicate the two correlated variables. For example, if $r_{12 \cdot 3} = 0.62$, this signifies that the correlation between variables 1 and 2, when the influence of variable 3 has been controlled, is 0.62. Similarly, if $r_{23 \cdot 14} = 0.34$, then you know that when the influence of variables 1 and 4 has been controlled, the relationship between variables 2 and 3 is 0.34. In other words, *if* all subjects in the study had been alike with respect to variables 1 and 4, the relationship between variables 2 and 3 would have been 0.34. A partial r with only one variable held constant is frequently referred to as a *first-order partial,* while a partial r with two variables held constant is called a *second-order partial,* and so on.

The computation procedures described in the next chapter will provide additional insight into the meaning of partial correlation.

SPECIAL MEASURES OF RELATIONSHIP

There are occasions when the investigator wants to assess the degree of relationship between two variables, but certain features of the data make it impossible to employ the normal product-moment correlation procedure. For some of these situations, special correlation procedures have been developed. For instance, suppose the investigator wishes to assess the degree of relation-

Table 5.5   Four Special Correlation Methods and Relationships between Variables Assessed

Method	Variable Relationship to Be Assessed
Point biserial coefficient (r_{pb})	Continuous versus dichotomous
Biserial coefficient (r_b)	Continuous versus dichotomized
Phi coefficient (∅)	Dichotomous versus dichotomous
Tetrachoric coefficient (r_t)	Dichotomized versus dichotomized

ship between one variable which is distributed over a range of score values, such as college-entrance examination scores, and a second variable which has just two categories, such as (1) living on campus or (2) living off campus. Here is a situation that does not lend itself to standard product-moment correlation procedures, yet a special statistical relationship technique has been designated for precisely this type of problem.

In considering such special correlation methods, it is necessary to draw a distinction between variables that are *dichotomous* and those that have been *dichotomized*. Generally speaking, variables are represented by two or more points on a scale of measurement. Most variables in educational investigations are represented by *many* points on a measurement scale. Almost all test scores fall into this category. Such variables are usually called **continuous variables.** There are some variables, however, that are represented by *only* two points on a scale. These are called **dichotomous variables,** or two-category variables. Examples of dichotomous variables are sex (male or female), marital status (married or unmarried), and residence (living on campus or off campus).[1]

Sometimes investigators encounter continuous variables that, for purposes of analysis, must be artificially dichotomized. A continuous variable such as student scores on a final exam, therefore, might be considered as being either scores below the median or scores at the median and above. This would not be an actual dichotomous variable but would be an artificially **dichotomized variable.**

There are four statistical techniques that are suitable for describing the degree of relationship between various combinations of dichotomous, dichotomized, or continuous variables. These correlation methods are the *point biserial coefficient* (r_{pb}), the *biserial coefficient* (r_b), the *phi coefficient* (∅), and the *tetrachoric coefficient* (r_t). These specialized techniques are not widely used, but some knowledge of them may be helpful. Table 5.5 identifies the particular type of variable relationship assessed by each of these methods.

In the case of the product-moment correlation coefficient, it has been stressed that the relationship between the variables must be capable of being expressed by a straight line. If the relationships depart from linearity in a marked fashion, an alternative technique must be used. For the product-moment coefficient, when a nonlinear relationship is present, the **correlation ratio,** η (*eta*), can be employed.

---

1. There are also variables that are discontinuous but have more than two categories. Marital status, for example, could be considered as a trichotomous variable, that is: (1) married, (2) never married, and (3) formerly married but now single.

A typical example of a nonlinear relationship is found when performance scores are correlated with chronological age. By plotting the values for such a relationship, the investigator will usually discover a noticeable curvature in the array of the paired values. Incidentally, the algebraic sign of η is always positive; hence most statisticians urge that it be considered only as an index of the closeness of the relationship between two variables, not the direction of the relationship.

An extensive examination of these procedures is beyond the scope of this text. See the selected readings cited at the close of this chapter for further treatment of these measures.

■   ■   ■

REVIEW

Correlation techniques provide educational investigators with a procedure for quantifying the nature of relationships between two or more variables. In the case of the most common correlational procedure, the product-moment correlation coefficient of linear relationship, the strength and direction of a relationship between two variables is described by the value of r which ranges from a perfect relationship of ± 1.00 to a nonexistent relationship of zero.

The strength of the correlation coefficient is usually interpreted according to the nearness of r to the perfect correlations of ± 1.00. As with many other statistics, the probabilistic significance of r can be readily determined, so that an observed relationship can be attributed either to chance or nonchance factors.

Multiple correlation and partial correlation are relationship techniques designed to deal with more than two variables. Multiple correlation describes the degree of relationship between a variable and two or more variables considered simultaneously. A multiple R is interpreted in essentially the same way as a product-moment r. Partial correlation allows the statistician to describe the relationship between two variables after controlling or "partialing out" the confounding relationship of another variable or variables.

Special measures of relationship are available for dichotomous, dichotomized, and continuous variables and for the product-moment coefficient when a linear relationship is not present (the correlation ratio).

TERMS TO KNOW

Listed in order of presentation in chapter:

correlation
product-moment correlation coefficient (Pearson's *r*)
scattergram
linear relationship
positive linear relationship
negative linear relationship
zero linear relationship
Fisher's z_r coefficient
homoscedasticity
multiple correlation
multiple correlation coefficient
dependent variable
independent variable
criterion variable
predictor variable
partial correlation
partial correlation coefficient
continuous variables
dichotomous variables
dichotomized variables
correlation ratio

EXERCISES

1. Which of the following correlation coefficients represents the *strongest* relationship between two variables?

   (a) $r = 0.59$ (b) $r = 0.05$ (c) $r = -0.71$

2. Presented below are three simple correlation charts indicating the nature of the relationship between two variables. In each instance, decide whether or not the product-moment correlation coefficient should be used to assess the degree of relationship.

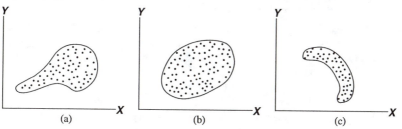

3. If a null hypothesis of relationship between two measures is to be tested by the calculation of *r* and its subsequent interpretation at the 0.01 level of significance, what action regarding the null hypothesis should be taken in each of the following situations?

   (a) $r = 0.65$, $n = 24$ (c) $r = -0.40$, $n = 45$ (e) $r = -0.75$, $n = 9$
   (b) $r = 0.85$, $n = 7$ (d) $r = 0.14$, $n = 590$

4. To assess the strength and direction of a possible relationship between two continuously distributed variables, where it can be demonstrated that the assumptions of homoscedasticity and linearity are satisfied, which statistical relationship technique should be employed?

5. Suppose an educator wishes to test for a relationship between scores on an achievement test and whether or not a group of individuals are foreign-born. Which relationship technique should be employed?

6. In running a standard product-moment correlation computation between achievement scores and scores on a newly devised personality test, a classroom teacher plots the data to determine if the assumption of homoscedasticity and normality can be satisfied. To the teacher's surprise, the data are curvilinearly rather than linearly arranged. Which relationship technique is called for in this instance?

7. If a researcher wishes to assess the degree of relationship between (1) achievement and (2) intelligence and interest considered simultaneously, which relationship technique should be employed?

8. If a school counselor wishes to assess the degree of relationship between achievement and intelligence, while holding constant the variable of reading ability which is related to both achievement and intelligence, which correlational procedure should the counselor select?

9. A county district school psychologist has just completed a correlational analysis in which sixth-graders' scores on the Verbal Skills Aptitude Test (VSAT) were correlated with seventh-grade language arts achievement, *r* equating 0.53. The psychologist, realizing that the *r* of 0.53 is based only on a single sample, wants to supply school personnel in the district with some guidelines for the possible relationship between VSAT scores and language arts achievement that they can expect in the future. To find the high and low boundaries of the correlation coefficient between these measures that will cover this relationship 95 percent of the time, what statistical technique should be used?

SELECTED READINGS

Blalock, Hubert M., Jr. *Social Statistics.* New York: McGraw-Hill, 1979, chaps. 17 and 18.

Edwards, Allen L. *Statistical Analysis.* New York: Holt, Rinehart & Winston, 1969, chaps. 6 and 14.

Guilford, J. P., and Fruchter, Benjamin. *Fundamental Statistics in Psychology and Education.* New York: McGraw-Hill, 1978, chaps. 6, 14, and 16.

Kirk, Roger E. *Elementary Statistics.* Monterey, CA: Brooks/Cole, 1984, chap. 5.

McNemar, Quinn. *Psychological Statistics.* New York: Wiley, 1969, chaps. 8-12.

Pagano, Robert R. *Understanding Statistics in the Behavioral Sciences.* St. Paul, MN: West Publishing, 1986, chap. 7.

Thorndike, Robert M. *Correlational Procedures for Research.* New York: Gardner Press, 1978, chaps. 1 and 2.

Walker, Helen M., and Lev, Joseph. *Statistical Inference.* New York: Holt, Rinehart & Winston, 1953, chap. 11.

6

Correlation
- *computation procedures*

There are many methods by which the product-moment correlation coefficient can be computed, most of them simply variations of the basic formula for *r*. Statistics texts used to give considerable attention to the computation of *r* through the use of a correlation table, similar to Figure 5–1 in the preceding chapter. We believe that such computation methods, which involve great quantities of hand calculation, will rarely be used by educators because the computations are too time-consuming. Educators who have many correlation coefficients to compute usually will either use a personal computer or send their data to a computer specialist for analysis. Few people today have the time to compute many correlation coefficients by the laborious hand-calculation techniques required in the correlation-table method.

There is, however, one advantage to the correlation-table method of computing *r* that should not be overlooked. This is the possibility of visually inspecting the plotted data to see whether the selection of a linear index of correlation is reasonable. The same result can be achieved, however, by plotting a portion of the data on a graph prior to the final calculation of *r*. Fortunately, many computer programs provide graphic plots of correlated data. You will usually find that visually inspecting such graphic displays helps you understand the true nature of the relationship represented.

FORMULAS FOR THE PRODUCT-MOMENT COEFFICIENT

A basic formula which is algebraically equivalent to Formula 5.1 in Chapter 5 is Formula 6.1 for the calculation of the product-moment correlation coefficient:

$$r_{xy} = \frac{\Sigma xy}{ns_x s_y} \tag{6.1}$$

where:

r_{xy} = the correlation coefficient between X and Y
Σxy = the sum of cross products of deviation scores for X and Y
s_x and s_y = the standard deviations of X and Y scores
n = the number of pairs

When this basic formula is manipulated algebraically, the result is Formula 6.2, a **raw-score correlation formula** in which raw scores are used as measurements:

$$r = \frac{\Sigma XY - \dfrac{(\Sigma X)(\Sigma Y)}{n}}{\sqrt{\left(\Sigma X^2 - \dfrac{(\Sigma X)^2}{n}\right)\left(\Sigma Y^2 - \dfrac{(\Sigma Y)^2}{n}\right)}} \tag{6.2}$$

It is important that you understand how this formula works. You will recognize a number of familiar quantities which can be obtained relatively simply with most electronic calculators.[1] In addition to n (the number of *pairs*), the five quantities needed in order to calculate r by this method are ΣX, ΣX^2, ΣY, ΣY^2, and ΣXY.

Table 6.1 Hypothetical Scores for Ten Individuals on Two Tests; Totals Needed for Calculation of r by the Raw-Score Formula

Individual	Test 1 X	Test 2 Y	X^2	Y^2	XY
a	8	3	64	9	24
b	2	1	4	1	2
c	8	6	64	36	48
d	5	3	25	9	15
e	15	14	225	196	210
f	11	12	121	144	132
g	13	9	169	81	117
h	6	4	36	16	24
i	4	4	16	16	16
j	6	5	36	25	30
Σ	78	61	760	533	618

---

1. Relatively inexpensive electronic calculators are available which automatically compute all the usual statistics for bivariate correlation and regression (see Chapters 7 and 8). All you have to do is enter in the n pairs of data points. These are handy devices for small problems, and they provide a way to check your work. For teaching purposes, however, we still recommend that you work through the actual computations.

With small samples, it is instructive to compute Formula 6.2 by hand. Table 6.1 gives the hypothetical scores for ten individuals on two tests and the totals necessary for the calculation of *r* by this method. To calculate *r* for the relationship between the two hypothetical sets of test data in this table, the appropriate values are substituted and the raw-score correlation formula (6.2) is used as follows:

$$r_{xy} = \frac{618 - \dfrac{(78)(61)}{10}}{\sqrt{\left(760 - \dfrac{(78)^2}{10}\right)\left(533 - \dfrac{(61)^2}{10}\right)}}$$

$$= \frac{618 - 475.8}{\sqrt{(760 - 608.4)(533 - 372.1)}}$$

$$= \frac{142.2}{\sqrt{(151.6)(160.9)}}$$

$$= \frac{142.2}{\sqrt{24,392.44}}$$

$$= \frac{142.2}{156.2}$$

$$= 0.91$$

A correlation of 0.91 is, of course, an index of a strong relationship between the two variables under study. Then Table C in the Appendix is entered with 8 degrees of freedom (the number of pairs minus 2), and an *r* of 0.91 is found to be significant beyond the 0.01 level.

The raw-score correlation formula can be used effectively with small samples, even if it is hand calculated. With larger samples, however, use of a calculator or computer is recommended. Anyone who will have to compute many statistics should develop a reasonable degree of competence with such electronic devices, because they can tremendously expedite the computation of statistical tests. High-speed computers have become increasingly available to those who make such computations (see Chapter 21).

If larger samples must be calculated by hand, some of the quantities necessary for the computation may already be available as a result of prior calculation of descriptive statistics. In terms of deviation scores, for example, Formula 6.2 is equivalent to Formula 6.3:

$$r_{xy} = \frac{\Sigma xy}{\sqrt{(\Sigma x^2)(\Sigma y^2)}} \tag{6.3}$$

The sums of squares for the *x* and *y* variables are typically at hand from the computation of standard deviations. (See Chapter 8 for an example illustrating the use of Formula 6.3 as a step in regression computation.)

A second computation example using the raw-score formula is one that

Table 6.2   **Hypothetical Scores for Five Individuals on Two Measures; Totals Needed for Calculation of *r* by the Raw-Score Formula**

Individual	Measure 1 X	Measure 2 Y	X^2	Y^2	XY
1	6	2	36	4	12
2	10	1	100	1	10
3	3	8	9	64	24
4	14	1	196	1	14
5	2	9	4	81	18
Σ	35	21	345	151	78

results in a negative *r*. This example uses the hypothetical data in Table 6.2, the scores for five individuals on two measures, plus the totals needed for the calculation. The appropriate quantities are substituted in Formula 6.2, and *r* is obtained as follows:

$$r_{xy} = \frac{78 - \dfrac{(35)(21)}{5}}{\sqrt{\left(345 - \dfrac{(35)^2}{5}\right)\left(151 - \dfrac{(21)^2}{5}\right)}}$$

$$= \frac{78 - 147}{\sqrt{(345 - 245)(151 - 88.2)}}$$

$$= \frac{-69}{\sqrt{(100)(62.8)}}$$

$$= \frac{-69}{\sqrt{6,280}}$$

$$= \frac{-69}{\sqrt{79.25}}$$

$$= -0.87$$

Table C indicates that an *r* of -0.87 ($df = 3$) is not significant beyond the 0.05 level. The lack of significance, of course, is due to the extremely small sample. If a relationship of such magnitude persisted with larger samples, the result would certainly be significant at a much lower probability level.

Computing the Confidence Interval

As we noted briefly in Chapter 5, in order to compute a confidence interval of a given probability level for *r*, the coefficient must be transformed into a special z_r value through the use of Table D in the Appendix. For example, if the correlation between 52 pupils' scores on two tests is 0.60, the procedure would be as follows:

First, consult Table D to find the z_r value for an *r* of 0.60. The z_r value to be used is 0.69.

Second, determine the *standard error* of the particular z_r, which is $1/\sqrt{n-3}$. In this example, the standard error is $1/\sqrt{52-3}=0.14$.

Third, decide on the probability level you want for the confidence interval and select the normal-curve $\pm z$ values that enclose that proportion (for example, 95 percent of the normal curve). With a 95 percent confidence interval, the z values would be ± 1.96.

Fourth, multiply the ± 1.96 by the standard error of 0.14 and combine the result with the z_r value of 0.69. For this example, $0.69 \pm (1.96)(0.14)$ yields z_r values of 0.96 and 0.42.

Fifth, transform these values, using Table D, back into correlation coefficients to form the boundaries of the 95 percent confidence interval. In this example, the confidence limits for r would be 0.40 and 0.75.

If confidence intervals at a different probability level are to be determined, the same procedure is followed, except different normal-curve z values are employed. For example, a 99 percent confidence interval for these data would be generated as follows: $0.69 \pm (2.58)(0.14) = z_r$ values of 1.05 and 0.33, which yield 99 percent confidence limits for an r of 0.32 and 0.78.

You should be aware that this procedure for constructing a confidence interval for estimating a *population* correlation coefficient is based on exactly the same logic used in Chapter 4 for the construction of a confidence interval in the estimation of a population mean.

MULTIPLE CORRELATION

There are several methods of computing a multiple correlation coefficient (R), which indicates the relationship between one variable (Y) and two or more other variables (e.g., X_1 and X_2) considered simultaneously. One straightforward computation procedure makes use of the individually computed product-moment correlation coefficients between the variables involved in the problem. These r's are then substituted in Formula 6.4 for the multiple correlation coefficient, which is designed for three variables:

$$R_{y \cdot x_1 x_2} = \sqrt{\frac{r^2_{yx_1} + r^2_{yx_2} - 2r_{yx_1}r_{yx_2}r_{x_1x_2}}{1 - r^2_{x_1x_2}}} \qquad (6.4)$$

where:

$R_{y \cdot x_1 x_2}$ = the coefficient of multiple correlation between Y and a combination of X_1 and X_2
r_{yx_1} = the product-moment correlation coefficient between Y and X_1
r_{yx_2} = the product-moment correlation coefficient between Y and X_2
$r_{x_1x_2}$ = the product-moment correlation coefficient between X_1 and X_2

To illustrate the use of Formula 6.4, the correlation coefficients reported in Table 5.4 in Chapter 5 will be used. These values are substituted in the formula as follows:

$$R_{y \cdot x_1 x_2} = \sqrt{\frac{(0.45)^2 + (0.48)^2 - 2(0.45)(0.48)(0.22)}{1 - (0.22)^2}}$$

$$= \sqrt{\frac{0.2025 + 0.2304 - 0.0950}{1 - 0.048}}$$

$$= \sqrt{\frac{0.3379}{0.952}}$$

$$= \sqrt{0.3549}$$

$$= 0.5957$$

The R of 0.60 (by rounding) is, of course, considerably greater than the individual correlations between the criterion variable and either predictor variable.

It is also possible to compute a multiple correlation coefficient between a criterion variable and more than two predictor variables. The interpretation of the resulting R is precisely the same as in the case of two predictors. The formula for such problems is a logical extension of Formula 6.4, but it can be simplified by using previously computed multiple correlation coefficients. Most advanced statistical texts discuss such extensions.

PARTIAL CORRELATION

The technique known as partial correlation is used when an investigator wants to study a relationship between two variables that may be wholly or partly due to the effect of a third variable. This technique makes it possible to control the effects of the third variable. When only one variable is to be held constant, the formula for a **first-order partial correlation coefficient** is Formula 6.5:

$$r_{xy \cdot z} = \frac{r_{xy} - r_{xz}\, r_{yz}}{\sqrt{1 - r_{xz}^2}\,\sqrt{1 - r_{yz}^2}} \tag{6.5}$$

In the above formula, $r_{xy \cdot z}$ represents the amount of relationship between variable X and variable Y after the influence of variable Z has been controlled.

If it is necessary to control the influence of two or more variables, that is, to compute second- or higher-order partials, the formulas are logical extensions of Formula 6.5. A **second-order partial correlation coefficient**, for example, requires the use of Formula 6.6:

$$r_{vx \cdot yz} = \frac{r_{vx \cdot y} - (r_{vz \cdot y})(r_{xz \cdot y})}{\sqrt{1 - r_{vz \cdot y}^2}\,\sqrt{1 - r_{xz \cdot y}^2}} \tag{6.6}$$

In calculating second- or higher-order partials, the lower-order partials required for the formula must first be computed. In Formula 6.6, several first-order partials would have to be computed through Formula 6.5 before they could be substituted in the formula for the second-order r.

The use of Formula 6.5 can be illustrated with correlations between (1) scores on an aptitude test, (2) high school grade-point averages, and (3) hours of study per week. The following correlations indicate the strength of the three relationships for 100 high school seniors:

Relationship	*Coefficient*
(1) Aptitude versus (2) grades	$r_{12} = 0.58$
(2) Grades versus (3) study time	$r_{23} = 0.10$
(1) Aptitude versus (3) study time	$r_{13} = -0.40$

To study each of the possible relationships among these three variables, considered two at a time while holding the third constant through partial correlation, the appropriate coefficients are inserted into Formula 6.5. For example, to obtain $r_{12 \cdot 3}$, that is, the relationship between (1) aptitude and (2) grades while partialing out the influence of (3) study time, then Formula 6.5 is set up and solved as follows:

$$r_{12 \cdot 3} = \frac{0.58 - (-0.40)(0.10)}{\sqrt{1 - (-0.40)^2}\sqrt{1 - (0.10)^2}}$$

$$= \frac{0.62}{(0.917)(0.995)}$$

$$= 0.68$$

Note, from the table, that $r_{12} = 0.58$, whereas $r_{12 \cdot 3} = 0.68$. This indicates that, if study time is held constant (that is, if every student in the sample studied the same number of hours per week), the relationship between grades and aptitude is even stronger than when students are heterogeneous with respect to study hours.

The other partial correlations in this sample would be computed as follows:

$$r_{13 \cdot 2} = \frac{-0.40 - (0.58)(0.10)}{\sqrt{1 - (0.58)^2}\sqrt{1 - (0.10)^2}}$$

$$= \frac{-0.458}{(0.815)(0.995)}$$

$$= 0.56$$

$$r_{23 \cdot 1} = \frac{0.10 - (0.58)(-0.40)}{\sqrt{1 - (0.58)^2}\sqrt{1 - (-0.40)^2}}$$

$$= \frac{0.332}{(0.815)(0.917)}$$

$$= 0.44$$

The partial coefficient $r_{13 \cdot 2} = -0.56$, in contrast to the original r_{13} of -0.40, indicates that if grades are held constant, the negative relationship between aptitude and study hours is even stronger. This indicates that the high-aptitude students in this sample spend fewer hours in study than their less-able classmates.

The relationship between grades and study time, when aptitude is held constant, rises from the original r_{23} of 0.10 to a more reasonable relationship where $r_{23 \cdot 1} = 0.44$. This indicates, as you might expect, that if aptitude is comparable, more time devoted to study is positively related to higher grades.

Second- and third-order partials are computed using Formula 6.6 in a similar fashion, once the first-order partial r's have been calculated.

■   ■   ■

REVIEW

The procedures for computing product-moment correlation coefficients were described. The computation of multiple correlation coefficients and first and second order partial correlation coefficients were also described. These computations can be done by hand, but the use of electronic computation instruments—a calculator or computer—is strongly recommended in practice.

Step-by-step instructions for determining a confidence interval for the product-moment coefficient, using Table D in the Appendix, are similar to those for determining a confidence interval to estimate a population mean.

TERMS TO KNOW

Listed in order of presentation in chapter:

      raw-score correlation formula
      first-order partial correlation coefficient
      second-order partial correlation coefficient

EXERCISES

1. Compute the product-moment correlation coefficient for the 20 pairs of scores given below.

Individual	Measure 1	Measure 2	Individual	Measure 1	Measure 2
a	40	20	k	33	13
b	40	16	l	33	15
c	39	17	m	32	14
d	37	18	n	32	11
e	37	18	o	30	12
f	36	20	p	30	11
g	35	14	q	30	10
h	35	14	r	29	12
i	34	15	s	28	9
j	34	12	t	26	10

2. Is the coefficient obtained in exercise 1 statistically significant? If so, at what level?

3. Compute the product-moment correlation coefficient between the X and Y measures given below:

X	Y	X	Y
49	42	40	38
46	42	38	39
44	44	38	40
44	40	36	29
42	43	34	37

4. Is the r obtained in exercise 3 statistically significant at the 0.01 level?

5. An educational investigator carefully matched 50 pairs of students on the basis of age, sex, and previous achievement. Then one student in a matched pair was randomly assigned to an experimental condition (E), and the other student in that pair was assigned to a control condition (C). The criterion measure used in the investigation was performance on an achievement test. The investigator was interested in the relationship of the achievement-test scores for the two groups. Calculate the product-moment r for the following set of data:

Achievement Test Scores

E	C	E	C	E	C	E	C	E	C
25	18	22	25	20	16	17	14	12	12
25	19	22	20	20	12	17	18	12	9
25	20	22	20	20	24	17	12	12	9
25	21	22	19	19	24	16	11	11	14
24	20	21	19	19	16	16	9	11	18
24	16	21	18	19	16	14	20	11	21
24	15	21	21	18	19	14	21	10	11
24	15	21	21	18	19	13	18	10	9
23	21	20	14	17	21	13	16	9	13
23	25	20	12	17	23	13	13	9	12

6. Is the correlation coefficient in the foregoing problem significant beyond the 0.01 level?

7. A class in educational research was given a 25-question quiz on educational statistics early in the term. At the conclusion of the course, a 100-question final exam was administered. Compute the *r* between students' scores on these two measures. Is the coefficient significant beyond the 0.05 level?

Statistics Quiz Scores	Final Exam Scores	Statistics Quiz Scores	Final Exam Scores
23	82	15	54
20	90	20	95
15	78	21	81
20	74	20	69
21	84	19	84
22	78	17	69
20	82	21	77
12	80	19	78
15	84	18	85
		23	90

8. In the table on the next page are 52 prospective secondary teachers' scores on three tests, *X*, *Y*, and *Z*. Compute multiple correlation coefficients for:
   (a) The relationship between (1) *X* and (2) *Y* and *Z* considered simultaneously, that is, $R_{x \cdot yz}$.
   (b) The relationship between (1) *Y* and (2) *X* and *Z* considered simultaneously, that is, $R_{y \cdot xz}$.
   (c) The relationship between (1) *Z* and (2) *X* and *Y* considered simultaneously, that is, $R_{z \cdot xy}$.

(Continued next page)

	Test				Test		
Individual	X	Y	Z	Individual	X	Y	Z
1	7	23	83	27	4	21	40
2	5	30	87	28	9	20	82
3	10	27	62	29	2	24	160
4	6	18	105	30	6	25	63
5	9	22	55	31	12	29	66
6	10	27	73	32	11	24	92
7	12	26	105	33	10	26	106
8	11	18	71	34	12	31	61
9	10	23	107	35	11	37	96
10	14	22	136	36	12	32	109
11	10	27	110	37	12	29	84
12	14	22	94	38	13	33	38
13	7	29	131	39	5	27	84
14	12	23	108	40	11	35	84
15	4	16	72	41	12	35	76
16	9	22	86	42	11	35	103
17	9	22	106	43	4	33	160
18	2	27	97	44	13	30	80
19	12	24	83	45	13	37	52
20	6	27	109	46	6	34	98
21	7	23	69	47	9	36	77
22	8	24	69	48	8	37	93
23	14	24	67	49	10	36	148
24	11	23	138	50	8	19	48
25	14	27	69	51	2	31	70
26	8	30	136	52	9	30	89

9. For the data in the preceding example, compute:
   (a) The partial correlation coefficient for variables X and Y when Z is held constant, $r_{xy \cdot z}$.
   (b) The partial correlation coefficient for variables Y and Z when X is held constant, $r_{yz \cdot x}$.
   (c) The partial correlation coefficient for variables X and Z when Y is held constant, $r_{xz \cdot y}$.
10. Compute a 95 percent confidence interval for a correlation coefficient of 0.80 when $n = 403$.
11. Compute a 99 percent confidence interval for a correlation coefficient of 0.65 when $n = 28$.

7

Regression

Correlational methods such as those described in Chapters 5 and 6 are used to determine the strength and direction of the relationship between two variables. Sometimes, perhaps to the investigator's surprise, correlation techniques reveal no appreciable relationship between variables that would at first have seemed to be strongly related. Frequently, however, the investigator discovers that a nonzero relationship does exist. For example, a series of research investigations may indicate that student anxiety is related to student achievement, because the correlation coefficient between achievement scores and scores on an anxiety test equals -0.43. Or an investigator may discover a correlation coefficient of 0.52 between the scores of master's degree candidates on a verbal analogies test and their subsequent performance on an objective examination taken at the end of the master's program. In educational settings, such relationships are of value to the extent that classroom teachers and school administrators can profitably employ them once they have been established.

It should be apparent that *any* increase in the fund of knowledge regarding the variables with which educators work will be of some value. Even an awareness of the *general* nature of relationships between variables should help educators reach wiser decisions. For instance, because research indicates that a student's secondary school grade-point average is related to subsequent college achievement, college counselors can identify the first-year students who may need academic assistance. Similarly, teachers who know that prior academic achievement is positively related to classroom performance, and who have access to achievement-test scores for their students, will have a better understanding of why certain students are having difficulty with their lessons.

In addition to understanding such general relationships, educators often want to be able to make accurate predictions for individual students, one at a time. For instance, high school counselors are frequently concerned with the likelihood that a particular student will achieve academic success in college. They know that a general relationship exists between scholastic aptitude and academic performance, but they also have to be able to particularize this relationship in order to make a prediction of success or failure for a certain student. Fortunately, there is a statistical technique designed to do precisely this. The technique of **regression** enables investigators to make predictions regarding a person's performance on one variable (e.g., academic success), given that person's performance on another variable (e.g., scholastic aptitude). This statistical technique is closely related to the product-moment correlation coefficient discussed in Chapters 5 and 6.

As we did with correlation, we will restrict the discussion of regression in this and the following chapter to *linear* relationships. In fact, the statistical prediction technique described in this chapter can be more explicitly referred to as **linear regression.** Moreover, in the same way that important relationships between variables may not be linear in form, so that indexes of relationship other than *r* are needed, the methods of linear regression can be generalized to include *nonlinear* regression. However, the procedures of nonlinear regression are too complicated to be included here, and information on them can be found in more-advanced statistical texts.

In making predictions regarding an individual's theoretical score on some measure from that person's score on an initial measure, *the variable from which the prediction is being made* may be referred to as the independent, variable or the predictor variable. The *variable that is predicted* may be called the dependent, variable or the criterion variable. (These terms were introduced in Chapter 5.) Thus, in predicting a student's score on a history exam from the student's earlier performance on a scholastic aptitude test, the aptitude-test score is the predictor, or independent, variable, and the history exam score is the criterion, or dependent, variable.

RATIONALE OF LINEAR REGRESSION

Briefly, by way of introduction, the following steps are involved in making a **regression prediction** of an individual's performance on a criterion variable, referred to as *Y*, from the individual's performance on a predictor variable, referred to as *X*.

First, a sample is selected in which the individuals are similar to those for whom the predictions ultimately will be made. This is called the **regression sample.** To illustrate, for predictions regarding the success eighth-graders will have in a ninth-grade algebra course, a sample of students in the eighth grade must be secured.

Second, if the predictor variable (*X*) is to be student performance on a group aptitude test, the test must be administered to the sample. (If aptitude scores are already available, ninth-grade pupils could be used for the sample.)

Third, after the students complete the ninth-grade algebra class, their scores on a comprehensive final examination (*Y*) must be secured.

Fourth, if variables *X* and *Y* are correlated, as revealed by a product-moment *r,* it is possible to develop a **regression equation** which can then be used to predict *future* eighth-graders' scores on the ninth-grade algebra examination from previously administered aptitude-test scores. Predictions need not be made for the regression sample, of course, because the criterion test scores are known.

The regression equations, which can also be plotted on a graph, take the form of Formula 7.1[1]:

$$\tilde{Y} = a + bX \tag{7.1}$$

Where $\tilde{Y}$ (~ = *tilde*) is the *predicted* criterion variable score for a student who obtains score *X* on the predictor variable. The lowercase *a* and *b* represent quantities yielded by an analysis of the *X* and *Y* data from the regression sample (more specific definitions of *a* and *b* are given in the next subsection). The size and algebraic sign of *b* depend on the strength and direction of the relationship between *X* and *Y* that is observed in the regression sample originally studied. For instance, in the example of predicted success in the ninth-grade algebra class, the value of *a* might be 5.5 and the value of *b* might be 0.92. In this case, the regression equation would be $\tilde{Y} = 5.5 + 0.92X$. To predict a particular student's expected score ($\tilde{Y}$) on the ninth-grade algebra exam, you would insert the student's actual score (*X*) on the aptitude test and solve the equation. To illustrate, if Marty had obtained a score of 110 on the aptitude test, you would solve as follows: $\tilde{Y} = 5.5 + 0.92(110)$, which reduces to $\tilde{Y} = 106.7$. A score of 106.7 would be the prediction ($\tilde{Y}$) for Marty's performance on the *Y* variable, the algebra examination.

In essence, statisticians make regression predictions for individuals based on data tendencies revealed in a prior study of a sample of similar individuals. In the regression sample, a certain relationship exists between the predictor variable and the criterion variable. Based on that relationship, an individual with a given score on the predictor is likely to achieve a certain score on the criterion. The regression equation of $\tilde{Y} = a + bX$ simply reflects the nature of the linear relationship that was discovered to exist in the regression sample.

In order to make reasonably meaningful predictions for individuals from relationships demonstrated to exist in a regression sample, the individual for whom the prediction is to be made must be, on the whole, similar to the individuals in the regression sample. For example, a regression equation based on the performance of eighth-graders on a general mathematics achievement test could not be used appropriately to predict the success of a fifth-grade pupil in ninth-grade algebra.

Moreover, factors affecting performance on the predictor and criterion variables must remain relatively constant. Consequently, in the example, if a new summer algebra enrichment class is formed for all students between the

---

1. You may recall from elementary algebra that this is the general equation for a straight line.

eighth and ninth grades, a regression scheme based on students who had not taken the summer class would probably prove ineffective. A new sample composed of students who had taken the summer course will have to be studied in order to build a revised regression equation. Similarly, any factors that may significantly alter performance on either the predictor or the criterion variable will usually necessitate the development of a new regression equation.

The Meaning of *a* and *b*

The values of *a* and *b*, the basic components of the regression equation, are determined from a set of sample data in which scores for both X and Y are available. Both *a* and *b* are best understood by referring to the **regression line** formed when the regression equation is plotted on a graph. In Figure 7–1, a regression line for $\tilde{Y}$ is plotted for the regression equation $\tilde{Y} = 2.0 + 0.5X$. This regression line is formed by a technique called the **method of least squares.** In brief, the regression line is placed in a representative position where the *sum* of the squared distances between that line and the points formed by the X and Y scores of the regression sample is at a minimum.

In the regression equation, *a* is known as **the intercept** of the regression line, that is, the value of Y when X is 0. Thus *a* is the value of Y where the regression line *intercepts* or crosses the ordinate (the vertical scale) of the Y variable. The value of *a* in the regression equation example in Figure 7–1 is 2.0; this is the point on the graph at which the regression line *intercepts* the Y axis.

The value of *b* is determined by the angle between the X axis and the regression line, and *b* is called **the slope** of the regression line. (Technically, *b* is the tangent of the angle formed by the regression line and the X axis.) Another way to view *b* is to think of it as the rate of change or increased value of Y with each unit of increase in X. In the example we are using, *b* is 0.5. Note in Figure 7–1 that as X becomes one unit larger, Y becomes 0.5 units larger. For example, if X is 2.0, then Y is 3.0; as X increases to 3.0, Y becomes 3.5. The increase of 0.5 in the value of Y is, of course, the value of *b*, the slope of the regression line. Frequently *b* is called the **regression coefficient.**

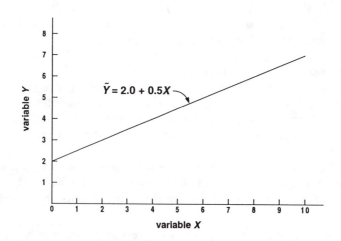

Fig. 7–1. Plot of regression line for $\tilde{Y} = 2.0 + 0.5X$.

The computation of a and b will be considered in much greater detail in the companion chapter to follow. For the present, you can gain insight into the meaning of these terms by considering the computational forms presented in Formulas 7.2 and 7.3. For the computation of b, Formula 7.2 is:

$$b = r\frac{s_y}{s_x} \qquad (7.2)$$

where:

> b = the regression coefficient
> r = the product-moment coefficient of correlation between variables X and Y
> s_x = the standard deviation of variable X
> s_y = the standard deviation of variable Y

Once the value of b has been determined, a is computed with Formula 7.3:

$$a = \overline{Y} - b\overline{X} \qquad (7.3)$$

where:

> a = the intercept of the regression line
> $\overline{Y}$ = the mean of the Y values in the regression sample
> $\overline{X}$ = the mean of the X values in the regression sample

Note that b is a function of the correlation coefficient. Given the variances for X and Y, when the magnitude of the relationship between X and Y, or the size of r, increases (or decreases), the regression coefficient b increases (or decreases) accordingly. Similarly, when the direction of the relationship—the sign of r—is positive (or negative), b is accordingly positive (or negative), and the slope of the prediction line reflects this sign in an upward (or downward) direction, when reading the graph from left to right.

When the X and Y scores are first converted to standard z-score form, the regression line plotted in terms of z scores passes exactly through the origin, or the zero intercept. This line also has a regression coefficient exactly equal to the correlation coefficient; that is, $b = r$. You can ascertain these properties from Formulas 7.2 and 7.3 if you recall that with any distribution of z scores, the mean is always 0, and the standard deviation is always 1.

THE ACCURACY OF REGRESSION PREDICTIONS

Just how accurate will the predicted $\tilde{Y}$ value be for any given value of X? This question must be answered before educators can properly use their predictions of success for particular students. In general, if the assumptions underlying the use of regression have been satisfied, the greater the absolute value of r, the more accurate the predictions will be. In other words, as the observed relationship between the X and Y variables in the regression sample approach $+1.00$ or -1.00, educators can have more certainty of making predictions that are as accurate as possible. Only if the relationship were absolutely perfect (as it never is in educational investigations) would it be possible to predict with complete accuracy.

As in the case of product-moment correlation, there are two assumptions that must be satisfied in order to make legitimate inferences using regression. Both of these assumptions refer to the regression sample and target population on which the regression equation is based. First, the requirement of homoscedasticity must be satisfied. That is, when plotted on a scattergram or a table similar to a correlation chart, the variances in Y values for any given value of X must be comparable (see Figure 5–10 in Chapter 5). To put it another way, the spread of Y scores for individually considered values of X must be about the same. Second, it must be assumed that the values of Y for given values of X are distributed in an approximately normal fashion.

Use of the Regression Line in Making Predictions

To illustrate in more detail what we mean by using the line of regression to make predictions and what we mean by an error in prediction, we will use Table 7.1 and Figure 7–2. In Table 7.1, the scores obtained by five individuals on a predictor variable X and a criterion variable Y are presented. The means, standard deviations, correlation coefficient, regression equation, and predicted $\tilde{Y}$ scores derived from these data are also listed.

In Figure 7–2, the scattergram for the data in Table 7.1 and the line of regression used to predict values of $\tilde{Y}$, given values of X, is shown. The solid lines represent the correspondence between the *observed* (raw) scores on the X and Y variables. The dotted lines represent the paths for the *predicted* Y (the $\tilde{Y}$ scores), given the observed X values. Solid points are used to represent observed values; crossed points are used to represent predicted values. For example, individual D obtained an X score of 8 and a Y score of 13; the predicted $\tilde{Y}$ score for D was 17.8. This prediction could have been obtained by either substituting $X = 8$ into the regression equation and solving algebraically or by using the dotted lines in Figure 7–2 and reading off the Y value corresponding to the X value of 8. Thus, in predicting the $\tilde{Y}$ score for D, an error of -4.8 points was made. These **errors of prediction** $(\tilde{Y} - Y)$ for all five individuals are given in Table 7.1 and are represented in Figure 7–2 by the wavy-line segments.

The regression line is often referred to as the line of "best fit" for the points in the scattergram. The mathematical criterion for finding this line, as we have noted, is to minimize the sum of the squared errors of prediction. The

Table 7.1   **Hypothetical Data for Five Individuals and Variables X and Y, Illustrating Use of Linear Regression**

	Individual				
	A	B	C	D	E
X	2	4	6	8	10
Y	7	1	19	13	25
$\tilde{Y}$	3.4	8.2	13.0	17.8	22.6
Errors $(Y - \tilde{Y})$	3.6	-7.2	7.0	-4.8	2.4

$$\overline{X} = 6 \qquad \overline{Y} = 13$$
$$s_x = 2.8 \qquad s_y = 8.4$$
$$r = 0.80$$
$$\tilde{Y} = 2.4X - 1.4$$

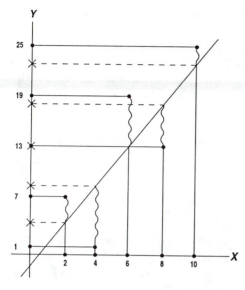

Fig. 7–2. Scattergram and regression line for the data in Table 7.1.

regression line therefore is the line in Figure 7–2 where the sum of the squared lengths represented by the wavy-line segments is at a minimum. This line has the equation given in Formula 7.1. Furthermore, it is always the case that one point on the line of best fit is the point that corresponds to the means of the two variables. Intuitively, it should make sense that the best prediction for the mean of variable X is the mean of variable Y. Thus it is relatively easy to construct the regression line. You locate the points corresponding to the intercept (a) and the pair of means and then draw the line through these two points.

The Standard Error of Estimate

The **standard error of estimate** ($s_{y \cdot x}$) reflects the accuracy of the relationship between predictor and criterion variables. It is used to estimate the agreement of a predicted $\tilde{Y}$ score with the "real" Y score. The standard error of estimate is used in the same way a standard deviation is used as a unit of measurement along the baseline of a normal distribution. In fact, the standard error of estimate is also known as the standard deviation of the errors of prediction.

For example, if the standard error of estimate is 5.0 and the predicted $\tilde{Y}$ score is 100, then, as in a normal curve with a mean of 100 and a standard deviation of 5.0, the actual criterion (Y) score will fall within an area plus or minus 5.0 of the predicted $\tilde{Y}$ score 68 times out of 100. Moving plus or minus two standard errors of estimate from the predicted score, it can be asserted that the actual criterion score will fall within ±10 points of the predicted $\tilde{Y}$ score 95 percent of the time. Moving three standard errors of estimate (that is, ±15) in either direction from the predicted $\tilde{Y}$ score, the prediction, within these margins of error, will be accurate almost 100 percent of the time. This example suggests that a prediction can be more accurately described as follows: For a given X score, 68.3 percent of the time, the actual Y score ($Y = 100$) will be between 95 and 105, and 99.7 percent of the time, the actual Y score will be between 85 and 115.

A similar explanation of the use of the standard error of estimate can be given in graphic form. In Figure 7–3, for any value of X, the predicted $\tilde{Y}$ score would fall on the regression line, but the actual Y score would range within the superimposed normal curves according to the size of the standard error of estimate ($s_{y \cdot x}$).

The Proportion of Predictable Variance.   Additional insight into the nature of the standard error of estimate can be obtained by considering one way to compute this measure, Formula 7.4:

$$s_{y \cdot x} = s_y \sqrt{1 - r^2} \qquad (7.4)$$

In this formula, r^2 represents the **proportion of predictable variance**, which is equivalent to the square of the correlation coefficient.

To show you how Formula 7.4 works, we will use the data for five individuals and two variables that were presented in Table 7.1 and illustrated in Figure 7–2. First, note in Figure 7–2 that the spread (variance) of the predicted $\tilde{Y}$ scores is less than that of the original, observed Y scores. This is always the case when any degree of linear relationship exists between the two variables. Thus the variance of the predicted $\tilde{Y}$ scores is a certain *proportion* of the variance of the observed Y scores. *It can be shown that this proportion is always equal to* r^2, *the square of the correlation coefficient.* For the data in Table 7.1, the variance of the $\tilde{Y}$'s is $(0.80)^2$, or 0.64 of the variance of the Y's. The remaining proportion of the observed Y-score variance $(1 - r^2)$ is due to the errors of prediction. So in the example, $1 - 0.64$, or 36 percent of the observed

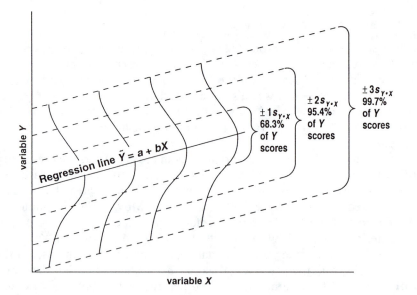

Fig. 7–3. Plotted regression line, with disparity between predicted $\tilde{Y}$ and actual Y scores depicted as a function of the size of the standard error of estimate ($s_{y \cdot x}$).

Y-score variance, is *not* predictable. The *amount* of unpredictable Y-score variance is then $(1 - r^2)s_y{}^2$. For the data in Table 7.1, the amount of unpredictable variance is $(0.36)(8.4)^2$, or 25.9. Taking the square root of this quantity yields a measure in standard deviation units.

You should recognize that the square root of the quantity $(1 - r^2)s_y{}^2$ is exactly the quantity given by Formula 7.4. Thus the standard deviation of the errors in Table 7.1 (otherwise known as the standard error of estimate) is equal to $\sqrt{25.9}$, or 5.1. This value can be obtained directly by using Formula 7.4: $s_{y \cdot x} = 8.4 \sqrt{0.36}$, or 5.1 with rounding error.

The proportion (or percentage) of predictable variance often serves as an index of the *strength* of the correlation between two variables. When using this index, many investigators refer to it as the "percentage of variance shared in common" by the two variables. You should not be confused by this terminology once you realize that the "percentage of shared common variance" refers to the percentage (or proportion) of predictable variance, and this percentage remains the same whether you are predicting Y from X or X from Y. (We will discuss this further in the next subsection.)

At this point, you should be acutely aware of the distinction between statistical significance and statistical meaningfulness. It is possible that an r of 0.20 can be statistically significant ($p < 0.05$), as long as data are available on 100 individuals or more. This indicates that the sample of data is from a population that, in all probability, has a nonzero linear relationship between variables X and Y, and the best guess as to the magnitude of the relationship is 0.20. But how *meaningful* is this relationship? It could be said that, by squaring the r of 0.20, 4 percent of the predictable variance is accounted for; that is, it is *not* possible to predict 96 percent of the observed Y-score variance, given the X-score data. In order to account for at least half of the predictable variance, a correlation of 0.71 is necessary ($0.71 \times 0.71 = 0.50$).

This notion of predictable variance is a troublesome one for most beginning students of statistics. It should help you to consider the regression lines and data for Figure 7-2 versus those for Figure 5-2 in Chapter 5. You have already seen that, in Figure 7-2, the predicting is not done with perfect accuracy. That is, some of the original Y-score variance is "given up" to variability in error due to prediction, as evidenced by the smaller spread of predicted $\tilde{Y}$ scores (crossed points) relative to the larger spread of original Y scores (solid points). Now look at Figure 5-2; imagine constructing the dotted lines to be used for predicting the Y scores for each of the five X scores. These dotted lines would, in fact, be the solid lines as well, because in Figure 5-2 there is a perfect relationship. In other words, the observed and predicted Y scores are one and the same. Thus, the variability of the predicted $\tilde{Y}$ scores is equal to that of the observed Y scores, and *all* Y-score variance is perfectly predictable. Usually, however, the relationship is not perfect, and only r^2 of the Y-score variance can be predicted.

Predicting X from Y

The examples in this section have dealt only with predictions of Y values from given values of X. If you consider the logic underlying regression prediction, however, you will see that with two variables involved, one the predictor and the other the predicted, it should be possible to reverse the roles of the variables. The predictor then becomes the predicted, and vice versa. In this case, the percentage of predictable variance remains the same, because r remains unchanged. Furthermore, the regression line still passes through the point corresponding to the means of the two variables, because $\overline{X}$ and $\overline{Y}$ remain unchanged. But the slope b will always change, unless both variables have the same variances, and the intercept a will always change, unless both variables have the same means *and* variances. To verify these observations, look at Formulas 7.2 and 7.3 again.

Of course, which variable is the predictor and which is the criterion depends on the study design, not an arbritrary designation of X and Y labels.

Reliabilty of the Criterion

In order to make any kind of accurate prediction, it is always necessary to have a reliable criterion variable, that is, one that can be measured with some degree of consistency. The most elaborate prediction scheme, employing several different and highly sensitive predictor variables, is destined for failure if the criterion variable to be predicted is measured in such a way as to yield erratic, unreliable data. The question of reliability is discussed in detail in most measurement texts.

The Value of Prediction to Educators

This section should have made it clear to you that, even with a statistical prediction scheme such as linear regression, statisticians are not able to make errorless predictions. They are, however, able to define and quantify the amount of error involved in the predictions they make. This could not be done on the basis of the correlation coefficient alone between a predictor variable and a criterion variable.

Predictions regarding a student's performance on one variable based on knowledge of the student's performance on another variable can be invaluable in various educational situations, particularly those that deal with vocational and academic counseling. There are also other uses of linear regression in education, such as efforts to predict various types of school-district and class enrollments in planning for staffing or school buildings.

MULTIPLE REGRESSION PREDICTION

One way to increase the accuracy of predictions is by using more than one predictor variable in a regression scheme. In **multiple regression prediction,** two or more predictor variables, both related to the criterion variable, are incorporated into a more complex prediction scheme. Although this technique is more involved than simple regression with a single-predictor variable, multiple regression employs the same rationale in making predictions.

The formula for a multiple regression equation is not too different from the simple, single-predictor variable equation. For two predictors, Formula 7.5 takes the following form:

$$\tilde{Y} = a + b_1 X_1 + b_2 X_2 \qquad (7.5)$$

where:

$\tilde{Y}$ = the predicted criterion score
a = a constant
b_1 = the regression coefficient for the first predictor variable
X_1 = the first predictor variable
b_2 = the regression coefficient for the second predictor variable
X_2 = the second predictor variable

Multiple regression equations involving more than two predictor variables are simply logical extensions of Formula 7.5.

The same assumptions associated with single-predictor regression models must be satisfied in the case of multiple-regression problems. Since a *linear* regression model is used, the assumptions of homoscedasticity and normality of criterion scores must be met. Statistical tests of these assumptions are available and can be found in more advanced statistical texts.

Step-by-step directions for the computation of a multiple regression equation, including the simultaneous solution of several linear equations and determination of the standard error of multiple estimate, are given in Chapter 8. The principal advantage of the extra computations necessary in multiple regression is that, by adding a second predictor variable related to the criterion variable, it is possible to reduce the standard error of estimate that would be present in a single-predictor scheme. The better additional predictor usually is one that is at the same time related to the criterion variable and not too strongly related to the predictor variable already being used. To illustrate, think of a situation in which academic achievement is the criterion variable and performance on an aptitude test is the predictor variable. If you add another aptitude test as a second predictor variable, thus forming a multiple regression scheme, you will have added relatively little to the power and accuracy of the prediction formula, because both predictor variables are doing essentially the same thing. You could augment the accuracy of the prediction scheme more effectively by selecting a second predictor that is strongly related to the criterion but *not* strongly related to the first predictor. A student's performance on a study-habits inventory, for example, would be a suitable second predictor, for it would measure *nonintellectual* factors associated with academic achievement.

Benjamin Bloom and Frank Peters found that school grades, achievement scores, or aptitude-test scores ordinarily correlate with college grades from 0.40 to 0.60, but multiple correlations using two or more of these measures in combination usually range from 0.55 to 0.65.[2] In the same way, the accuracy of regression predictions can be increased by combining different predictors. It is possible to have three, four, or even more predictors in a mul-

---

2. Benjamin S. Bloom and Frank A. Peters, *The Use of Academic Prediction Scales for Counseling and Selecting College Entrants* (New York: Free Press, 1961), p. 25.

tiple regression scheme, but a point is soon reached at which the slightly increased prediction precision provided by each new predictor variable does not justify the additional effort and expense of including more predictors. In most educational situations, little is gained by using more than four or five predictor variables, due to the intercorrelation among such predictors.

With the current widespread availability of personal computers, most multiple regression equations are calculated electronically rather than by hand. Using a computer, an investigator can solve in a few seconds multiple regression problems that would otherwise take many hours to compute.

■   ■   ■

REVIEW

Whereas correlation methods provide a picture of the general relationship between two variables, regression methods provide a way to make a prediction regarding a particular individual's score on a criterion variable, given that individual's score on a predictor variable. A typical example of the use of regression is in predicting a student's academic success in subsequent school programs, based on that student's score on an aptitude test.

The data necessary to set up a prediction equation are gathered from a group of individuals similar to those for whom predictions are to be made. From this regression sample, scores are collected on both the predictor and criterion variables. If the relationship between predictor and criterion is strong, relatively precise predictions can be made for the performance of other individuals in the same category. The use of the standard error of estimate makes it possible to compute margins of error for prediction accuracy.

It is possible to increase the accuracy of predictions through the use of a multiple regression procedure which incorporates more than one predictor variable and accordingly yields smaller or more precise standard errors of estimate.

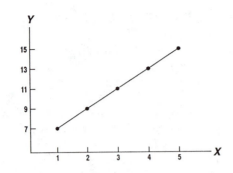

Fig. 5–2. Scattergram for data in Table 5.1.

Another, more precise way of defining a linear relationship is to say that every individual's standard or z score is exactly the same *relative distance* above or below the mean for variable X as it is for variable Y. "Relative distance" means distance in terms of *standard deviation units*. Because z scores indicate how many standard deviations above or below the mean a given raw score is, the above definition can be revised as follows: A perfect **linear relationship** between two variables, X and Y, exists whenever every individual's z score for variable X is the same as that individual's z score for variable Y.

Consider again the data in Table 5.1. The means for variables X and Y are 3 and 11, respectively; the standard deviations are 1.41 and 2.82, respectively. The z scores for each individual can be computed; these are shown in columns 3 and 4. Note that in this table the value and the sign of the z scores are the same for each individual on both variables. The value (or magnitude) of the z score indicates the relative distance of a score from the mean, and the sign (or direction) of the z score indicates whether it is above (+) or below (−) the mean.

The next procedure is to establish a single index of the relationship which will satisfy the following two conditions:

1. The index will increase to the extent that the relationship becomes more linear, that is, comes closer and closer to the above definition.
2. The index will indicate the direction of the relationship, that is, whether the relationship is positive or negative.

Looking again at Table 5.1, note that in a perfect *positive* linear relationship, the *product* of the z scores (column 5) for an individual must always be positive, because these z scores will always have the same sign. For example, the product of the z scores for individual A is $(-1.42)(-1.42)$, or 2.02. Furthermore, the *sum* of these z-score products is exactly equal to the number of individuals. Thus the mean of these z-score products must be 5/5, or + 1.00.

The definition for a perfect, **positive linear relationship**, then, is one in which the z scores on both variables are equal and have the same sign, so the z-score products are always positive. It is always the case that when the data conform to these criteria, the mean z-score product will equal + 1.00. This produces a possible candidate for an index of relationship, the Pearson product-moment correlation coefficient. Formula 5.1 is the formula for this coefficient (r):

TERMS TO KNOW

Listed in order of presentation in chapter:

regression
linear regression
regression prediction
regression sample
regression equation
regression line
method of least squares
the intercept
the slope
regression coefficient
errors of prediction
standard error of estimate
proportion of predictable variance
multiple regression prediction

EXERCISES

1. Will a school counselor who wants to devise a scheme for predicting subsequent achievement performance of sophomore students ultimately be more interested in product-moment correlation or in regression?

2. Is it possible to designate certain variables as criterion variables and others as predictor variables by the very nature of the variables? For instance, would it be safe to say that academic achievement is always a criterion variable?

3. Why is it important for the individuals constituting the regression sample to be like the individuals for whom predictions are to be made?

4. Two regression equations have been developed for different predictions, based on different regression samples of equal size. In situation A the r between predictor and criterion variable was 0.69; in situation B the r between predictor and criterion was 0.58. In which situation will the most accurate predictions be made?

5. What will be the predicted score on a criterion test for a sixth-grader who achieves a score of 30 on a predictor test, when the following regression equation has been set up for the sixth-grade class?

$$\tilde{Y} = 28.5 + 0.50X$$

6. Which of the following standard errors of estimates would allow the most accurate predictions?

   (a) $s_{y \cdot x} = 12.0$ (b) $s_{y \cdot x} = 8.4$

7. Is a single-predictor regression scheme or a multiple-predictor regression scheme apt to result in more precise predictions with reduced error estimates?

SELECTED READINGS

Dixon, Wilfrid J., and Massey, Frank J. *Introduction to Statistical Analysis.* New York: McGraw-Hill, 1969, chap. 11.

Edwards, Allen L. *Statistical Analysis.* New York: Holt, Rinehart & Winston, 1957, chap. 6.

Ferguson, George A., and Takane, Yoshio. *Statistical Analysis in Psychology and Education.* New York: McGraw-Hill, 1989, chap. 8.

Kerlinger, Fred N., and Pedhazur, Elazar J. *Multiple Regression in Behavioral Research.* New York: Holt, Rinehart & Winston, 1973.

McNemar, Quinn. *Psychological Statistics.* New York: Wiley, 1969, chap. 11.

Pagano, Robert R. *Understanding Statistics in the Behavioral Sciences.* St. Paul, MN: West Publishing, 1986, chap. 6.

Thorndike, Robert M. *Correlational Procedures for Research.* New York: Gardner Press, 1978, chaps. 1 and 2.

Walker, Helen M., and Lev, Joseph. *Elementary Statistical Methods.* New York: Holt, Rinehart & Winston, 1969, chaps 12 and 14.

Regression

• *computation procedures*

Most of the formulas needed in the computation of linear regression problems were supplied in Chapter 7, to demonstrate the relative simplicity of the calculations involved in regression prediction. In this chapter the use of these and other algebraically equivalent formulas will be explained, and a number of computational examples will be given. In most of these operations, the use of some type of calculator or computer is strongly recommended.

The purpose in computing a regression problem is to develop the regression equation (Formula 7.1):

$$\tilde{Y} = a + bX$$

With this formula, values of Y can be predicted from known values of X. The standard error of estimate for $Y(s_{y \cdot x})$ should also be computed, to give an idea of how accurate the prediction will be.

As you know from Chapter 7, the first step in developing the regression equation is to select an appropriate regression sample, that is, a sample of individuals who are similar to those for whom the predictions are to be made. Data must then be gathered from this sample regarding both the predictor variable (X) and the criterion variable (Y).

A HYPOTHETICAL COMPUTATIONAL EXAMPLE

We will use a hypothetical example to illustrate the regression operation. Suppose Mr. Major, a counselor in the education department of a college, wants to predict the success that individual M.Ed. degree candidates will have on a comprehensive final examination which must be passed before the degree is granted. If he could make such predictions with a reasonable degree of accuracy, his advice to potential master's degree candidates would be much more effective. He must determine if any measures are available to assist him in making these predictions. To simplify matters, suppose that at this college, all potential M.Ed. candidates must take a nationally standardized entrance examination designed to assess their verbal skills. This measure can probably serve as a predictor. Mr. Major now has a criterion variable (Y)—performance on the comprehensive final examination. He also has a potential predictor (X)—the preliminary verbal skills test administered at the beginning of the M.Ed. program.

Data for past student performance are usually available in such situations. Assume that the counselor can obtain the scores of all M.Ed. candidates for the past three years on both measures, that is, the final comprehensive examination and the preliminary verbal examination. Mr. Major's regression sample is 200 students, and he is willing to defend the proposition that these 200 are similar to the students for whom he will want to make predictions.

To determine the regression equation, the values of a and b must be computed. Formulas for both these quantities were given in Chapter 7. Formula 7.2, the formula for b, is:

$$b = r \frac{s_y}{s_x}$$

This is a "definitional" formula in the sense that it permits a certain amount of insight into the nature of b. If the standard deviations and the correlation coefficient have already been computed, this formula is the easiest one to use. As was the case with the standard deviation and correlation formulas, algebraically equivalent computational formulas exist in terms of the raw scores X and Y (or deviation scores x and y), so b can be calculated directly from the data. Based on deviation scores, b can be computed using Formula 8.1:

$$b = \frac{\Sigma xy}{\Sigma x^2} \tag{8.1}$$

For this equation, the **deviation sum of crossproducts** (the deviation scores for X and Y times one another) and the **deviation sum of squares** (the deviation scores for X and Y times themselves) can be obtained from the following formulas:

$$\Sigma x^2 = \Sigma X^2 - \frac{(\Sigma X^2)}{n}$$

$$\Sigma y^2 = \Sigma Y^2 - \frac{(\Sigma Y^2)}{n}$$

$$\Sigma xy = \Sigma XY - \frac{(\Sigma X)(\Sigma Y)}{n}$$

Now, suppose Mr. Major has the following data for the 200 students in his regression sample:

$$\Sigma xy = 3,200 \quad \Sigma x^2 = 8,000 \quad \Sigma y^2 = 7,000$$

Substituting the appropriate values into Formula 8.1 and solving:

$$b = \frac{3,200}{8,000} = 0.400$$

Thus b, the regression coefficient for Y on X, is 0.400.

In order to compute a for the prediction equation, Formula 7.3 from Chapter 7 is used:

$$a = \overline{Y} - b\overline{X}$$

Assume the means for Y and X are $\overline{Y} = 85.0$, $\overline{X} = 100.0$. Solving for a yields:

$$a = 85.0 - (0.40)(100.0)$$
$$= 45.0$$

The regression equation can now be set up as follows:

$$\tilde{Y} = 45.0 + 0.40X$$

To predict the performance of an M.Ed. candidate on the final comprehensive exam, Mr. Major would simply insert the candidate's score on the preliminary verbal skills exams (X) into the prediction formula. For example, an individual with an X score of 92.0 would have a predicted $\tilde{Y}$ score of 81.8:

$$\tilde{Y} = 45.0 + 0.40(92.0)$$
$$= 81.8$$

The standard error of estimate can then be computed from Formula 8.2 (which is algebraically equivalent to Formula 7.4), as follows:

$$s_{y \cdot x} = \sqrt{\frac{\Sigma y^2 - \frac{(\Sigma xy)^2}{\Sigma x^2}}{n - 2}} \tag{8.2}$$

$$= \sqrt{\frac{7,000 - \frac{(3,200)^2}{8,000}}{200 - 2}}$$

$$= 5.37$$

When applied to the predicted $\tilde{Y}$ score of 81.8, the $s_{y \cdot x}$ can be interpreted as follows: If this study were repeated a great many times, candidates with an X score of 92.0 would have a 68.3% chance of falling within a range of ± 5.37 points from the predicted 81.8, that is, within the interval 76.43–87.17.

A COMPUTATIONAL EXAMPLE WITH REAL DATA

The second computational example of linear regression uses data from an actual set of scores obtained by 18 students on a brief aptitude test administered at the beginning of a course in professional education taught by one of the authors of this text, and a 100-question final examination administered at the end of the course (see Table 8.1). A regression equation can be developed using the aptitude-test scores as the predictor variable (X) and the final-examination scores as the criterion variable (Y). A regression scheme derived from these variables could be of value to instructors in grouping students for teaching purposes or in working with individual students.

The necessary quantities for the various formulas to be used must first be computed. These are Σx^2, Σy^2, Σxy, $\overline{X}$, and $\overline{Y}$:

$$\Sigma x^2 = \Sigma X^2 - \frac{(\Sigma X)^2}{n} \qquad = 16{,}222 - \frac{(532)^2}{18} \qquad = 498.45$$

$$\Sigma y^2 = \Sigma Y^2 - \frac{(\Sigma Y)^2}{n} \qquad = 101{,}533 - \frac{(1{,}345)^2}{18} \qquad = 1{,}031.61$$

$$\Sigma xy = \Sigma XY - \frac{(\Sigma X)(\Sigma Y)}{n} = 40{,}207 - \frac{(532)(1{,}345)}{18} = 454.78$$

$$\overline{X} = \frac{\Sigma X}{n} = \frac{532}{18} \qquad = 29.55$$

$$\overline{Y} = \frac{\Sigma Y}{n} = \frac{1{,}345}{18} \qquad = 74.72$$

Table 8.1   Performance of 18 Students on Aptitude Test at Beginning of Course in Professional Education and Final Examination at End of Course

Student	Aptitude Test X	Final Exam Y	X^2	Y^2	XY
1	21	71	441	5,041	1,491
2	21	57	441	3,249	1,197
3	23	78	529	6,084	1,794
4	23	72	529	5,184	1,656
5	26	72	676	5,184	1,872
6	26	67	676	4,489	1,742
7	26	75	676	5,625	1,950
8	30	67	900	4,489	2,010
9	31	80	961	6,400	2,480
10	31	78	961	6,084	2,418
11	32	71	1,024	5,041	2,272
12	32	77	1,024	5,929	2,464
13	32	74	1,024	5,476	2,368
14	33	84	1,089	7,056	2,772
15	34	75	1,156	5,625	2,550
16	35	70	1,225	4,900	2,450
17	37	91	1,369	8,281	3,367
18	39	86	1,521	7,396	3,354
Σ	532	1,345	16,222	101,533	40,207

The correlation coefficient representing the relationship between these two variables can then be computed according to Formula 6.3 in Chapter 6:

$$r = \frac{\Sigma xy}{\sqrt{(\Sigma x^2)(\Sigma y^2)}}$$

$$= 0.63$$

This computation is not really necessary in setting up the prediction equation, but it is so simply done that many investigators compute r somewhere along the line in a regression operation.

Now b may be computed from Formula 8.1:

$$b = \frac{\Sigma xy}{\Sigma x^2}$$

$$= \frac{454.78}{498.45}$$

$$= 0.912$$

Having found b, a is then computed from Formula 7.3:

$$a = \overline{Y} - b\overline{X}$$

$$= 74.72 - 0.912 \, (29.55)$$

$$= 47.77$$

The regression equation for predicting final-exam scores in the professional education course from scores on the aptitude test therefore is:

$$\tilde{Y} = 47.77 + 0.912X$$

The standard error of estimate is then found, using Formula 8.2:

$$s_{y \cdot x} = \sqrt{\frac{\Sigma y^2 - \frac{(\Sigma xy)^2}{\Sigma x^2}}{n - 2}}$$

$$= \sqrt{\frac{1{,}031.61 - \frac{(454.78)^2}{498.45}}{16}}$$

$$= 6.21$$

With the regression equation of $\tilde{Y} = 47.77 + 0.912X$ and the standard error of estimate of 6.21, fairly accurate predictions can now be made for the success of future students in the professional education class. For example, the final-exam score for a student who gets a score of 30 on the aptitude test could be predicted as follows:

$$\tilde{Y} = 47.77 + 0.912(30)$$

$$= 75.13$$

Using the standard error of estimate, the probability of accuracy in predicting the final examination score within given ranges could then be estimated. For example, given an X score of 30 and the standard error of estimate of 6.21, the actual Y score will fall:

Between $\pm 1 s_{y \cdot x}$ of $\tilde{Y}$ (68.92 through 81.34), 68.3% of the time.
Between $\pm 2 s_{y \cdot x}$ of $\tilde{Y}$ (62.71 through 87.55), 95.4% of the time.
Between $\pm 3 s_{y \cdot x}$ of $\tilde{Y}$ (56.50 through 93.76), 99.7% of the time.

MULTIPLE REGRESSION PREDICTION

When more than one predictor variable is used in a regression scheme, the prediction equation is a logical extension of the one-variable prediction formula. As you learned from Chapter 7, adding one or more predictor variables is a way to increase the accuracy of the predictions to be made through the regression technique. The simplest form of multiple regression employs one additional predictor variable that is related to the criterion variable but also not too strongly related to the predictor variable already being used.

Regression with Two Predictor Variables

For multiple regression with two predictors, Formula 7.5 from Chapter 7 is employed:

$$\tilde{Y} = a + b_1 X_1 + b_2 X_2$$

From Chapter 7, you should know that X_1 and X_2 represent the two predictor variables, and b_1 and b_2 represent the respective regression coefficients of these variables.

Because the computation necessary to set up a multiple regression equation involves the simultaneous solution of linear equations, it is more complicated than that needed for a single predictor. We will take you step by step through a computational example of this process in this section: if you want to learn more about linear equation solutions you should consult any standard college algebra text.

In regression with two predictors, the prediction equation requires the values of a_1, b_1, and b_2. As in the case of single-predictor regression, these values are based on the performance of individuals in the regression sample that has been chosen. The computation of a multiple regression equation can be illustrated with the hypothetical scores of ten students given in Table 8.2. (Although this small sample can be used to illustrate the computation procedure for multiple regression prediction, a much larger regression sample would actually be required for any sort of reliable prediction.) The criterion variable (Y) is performance on a comprehensive high school physical science examination administered at the close of the senior year. One predictor variable (X_1) is the student's final-exam score in freshman science, and the second predictor variable (X_2) is the student's scholastic aptitude as measured by the score received on a standard group aptitude test.

Table 8.2   **Scores on Comprehensive Physical Science Examination, Freshman Science Final Examination, and Scholastic Aptitude Test for Ten High School Students**

	Scores		
Student	Physical Science Examination (Y)	Freshman Science Final Examination (X_1)	Scholastic Aptitude Test (X_2)
1	91	62	118
2	89	63	109
3	79	58	110
4	78	57	112
5	78	59	120
6	72	52	110
7	70	51	104
8	69	47	122
9	67	49	102
10	64	50	98

In order to set up the appropriate linear equations, the following values must be calculated from the data in Table 8.2:

$$n = 10 \qquad \Sigma X_1^{\,2} = 30{,}322$$
$$\Sigma Y = 757 \qquad \Sigma X_2^{\,2} = 122{,}657$$
$$\Sigma X_1 = 548 \qquad \Sigma X_1 Y = 41{,}919$$
$$\Sigma X_2 = 1{,}105 \qquad \Sigma X_2 Y = 83{,}949$$
$$\Sigma Y_2 = 58{,}041 \qquad \Sigma X_1 X_2 = 60{,}683$$

For a two-predictor regression equation, these values are then substituted in the following three equations:

$$\Sigma X_1 Y = b_1 \Sigma X_1^{\,2} + b_2 \Sigma X_1 X_2 + a \Sigma X_1$$
$$\Sigma X_2 Y = b_1 \Sigma X_1 X_2 + b_2 \Sigma X_2^{\,2} + a \Sigma X_2$$
$$\Sigma Y = b_1 \Sigma X_1 + b_2 \Sigma X_2 + a n$$

Substituting, this yields equations 1, 2, and 3:

(1) $41{,}919 = b_1 30{,}322 + b_2 60{,}683 + a548$

(2) $83{,}949 = b_1 60{,}683 + b_2 122{,}657 + a1{,}105$

(3) $757 = b_1 548 + b_2 1{,}105 + a10$

In solving linear equations simultaneously, there are several slightly different approaches. You can use the step-by-step process outlined here with all such problems.

First, divide equations 1, 2, and 3 by their respective coefficients of a, carrying as many digits beyond the decimal as the calculator or computer you are using will allow. This results in equations 4, 5, and 6:

(4) $76.4945255 = b_1 55.3321167 + b_2 110.7354014 + a$

(5) $75.9719457 = b_1 54.9167421 + b_2 111.0018099 + a$

(6) $75.7 \qquad = b_1 54.8 + b_2 110.5 + a$

Second, to remove the a, subtract (or add if the signs of a are unlike) equation 6 from equations 4 and 5, successively. This results in equations 7 and 8:

(7) $\qquad 0.7945255 = b_1 0.5321167 + b_2 0.2354014$
(8) $\qquad 0.27194957 = b_1 0.1167421 + b_2 0.5018099$

Third, divide equations 7 and 8 by their respective coefficients of b_2. This results in equations 9 and 10:

(9) $\qquad 3.3751945 = b_1 2.2604653 + b_2$
(10) $\qquad 0.5419297 = b_1 0.2326421 + b_2$

Fourth, to remove the b_2, subtract (or add if the signs of b_2 are unlike) equation 10 from equation 9. This results in equation 11:

(11) $\qquad 2.8332648 = b_1 2.0278232$

Fifth, solve for b_1 by dividing the quantity at the left of the equals sign by the coefficient of b_1:

$$b_1 = 1.3971952$$

Sixth, substitute the value of b_1 in equation 9 or 10 and solve for b_2:

$$3.3751945 = (1.3971952)(2.2604653) + b_2$$
$$b_2 = 3.3751945 - 3.1583113$$
$$b_2 = 0.2168832$$

Seventh, substitute the values of b_1 and b_2 in equation 4 (or either equation 5 or 6) and solve for a:

$$76.4945255 = (1.3971952)(55.3321167) + (0.2168832)(110.7354014) + a$$
$$a = 76.4945255 - (77.3097679 - 24.0166482)$$
$$a = 76.4945255 - 101.3264161$$
$$a = -24.8318906$$

You have now solved the values necessary for substitution in the multiple regression equation. Before setting up the equation, however, you should check the accuracy of a, b_1, *and* b_2 by substituting your computed values for these quantities in one of the original linear equations (1, 2, or 3). Substituting in 3, you can check as follows:

$$757 = (1.3971952)(548) + (0.2168832)(1,105) + (-24.8318906)(10)$$
$$757 = 765.662969 + 239.655936 - 248.318906$$
$$757 = 756.999999 \text{ (checks)}$$

It is now possible to set up the multiple regression equation to predict student scores on the comprehensive physical science examination as follows:

$$\tilde{Y} = -24.8318906 + 1.3971952X_1 + 0.2168832X_2$$

To illustrate the use of this prediction scheme, suppose Mazie, a student, has achieved a score of 61 on the final examination (X_1) of her freshman science course and has a scholastic aptitude score of 111 on the test (X_2) used in developing the regression formula. Her predicted score ($\tilde{Y}$) on the criterion examination would be computed as follows:

$$\tilde{Y} = -24.8318906 + (1.3971952)(61) + (0.2168832)(111)$$
$$\tilde{Y} = -24.8318906 + 85.2289072 + 24.0740352$$
$$\tilde{Y} = 84.471$$

The Standard Error of Multiple Estimate

In order to gauge the accuracy of the predicted Y in multiple regression, the standard error of estimate must be employed in the same way it is used with a single-predictor regression scheme. The **standard error of multiple estimate** is yielded by Formula 8.3, which employs the coefficient of multiple correlation between the variables involved in the regression problem:

$$s_{y \cdot x_1 x_2} = s_y \sqrt{1 - R^2_{y \cdot x_1 x_2}} \tag{8.3}$$

The analogy between this formula and Formula 7.4 for the standard error of estimate should be clear.

To use Formula 8.3, a multiple R for the variables involved in the problem must first be computed, using the data derived from Table 8.2. To do this, the separate product-moment correlation coefficients are computed according to Formula 6.2 in Chapter 6, and then they are substituted in Formula 6.4 for the multiple R, as follows:

$$r_{yx_1} = \frac{41,919 - \dfrac{(757)(548)}{10}}{\sqrt{\left(58,041 - \dfrac{(757)^2}{10}\right)\left(30,322 - \dfrac{(548)^2}{10}\right)}}$$

$$= 0.940$$

$$r_{yx_2} = \frac{83,949 - \dfrac{(757)(1,105)}{10}}{\sqrt{\left(58,041 - \dfrac{(757)^2}{10}\right)\left(122,657 - \dfrac{(1,105)^2}{10}\right)}}$$

$$= 0.470$$

$$r_{x_1 x_2} = \frac{60,683 - \dfrac{(548)(1,105)}{10}}{\sqrt{\left(30,322 - \dfrac{(548)^2}{10}\right)\left(122,657 - \dfrac{(1,105)^2}{10}\right)}}$$

$$= 0.321$$

$$R_{y \cdot x_1 x_2} = \sqrt{\frac{(0.940)^2 + (0.470)^2 - 2(0.940)(0.470)(0.321)}{1 - (0.321)^2}}$$

$$= 0.957$$

The standard deviation of the criterion variable for the regression sample must also be inserted in Formula 8.3. The value of s_y in this example is 9.043. Now it is possible to compute the standard error of multiple estimate from Formula 8.3.

$$\begin{aligned} s_{y \cdot x_1 x_2} &= 9.043 \ \sqrt{1 - (0.957)^2} \\ &= 9.043(0.290) \\ &= 2.62 \end{aligned}$$

With this standard error of multiple estimate, it is possible to be confident that roughly two-thirds of the time, the predicted $\bar{Y}$ score from the multiple regression equation will be no more than ± 2.62 from the actual Y score a particular student will attain.

More Than Two Predictor Variables

If more than two predictor variables are used in the multiple-regression problem, the necessary formulas are always logical extensions of the two-predictor formulas. For example, with three predictors the regression equation would take the following form:

$$\bar{Y} = a + b_1 X_1 + b_2 X_2 + b_3 X_3 \tag{8.4}$$

The linear equations needed for the determination of a, b_1, b_2, and b_3 would be set up as follows:

$$\begin{aligned} \Sigma X_1 Y &= b_1 \ \Sigma X_1{}^2 + b_2 \Sigma X_1 X_2 + b_3 \Sigma X_1 X_3 + a \Sigma X_1 \\ \Sigma X_2 Y &= b_1 \Sigma X_1 X_2 + b_2 \Sigma X_2{}^2 + b_3 \Sigma X_2 X_3 + a \Sigma X_2 \\ \Sigma X_3 Y &= b_1 \Sigma X_1 X_3 + b_2 \Sigma X_2 X_3 + b_3 \Sigma X_3{}^2 + a \Sigma X_3 \\ \Sigma Y &= b_1 \Sigma X_1 + b_2 \Sigma X_2 + b_3 \Sigma X_3 + an \end{aligned}$$

These linear equations are solved simultaneously in the same fashion described for the two-predictor regression problems.

■   ■   ■

REVIEW

The computational operations necessary for single-predictor and multiple-predictor linear regression described in this chapter may appear formidable at first glance, but, as the step-by-step analysis shows, most of the mathematical operations are quite simple. In solving regression problems, however, the use of some type of calculator or computer is almost a necessity.

The only added complexity in the computations for multiple regression as compared to single-predictor regression is the simultaneous solution of linear equations. If the detailed example of how this is done was not enough for you to understand the process, you are urged to consult a standard algebra text.

Determination of the standard error of estimate is important in the use of both single-predictor and multiple regression prediction techniques.

TERMS TO KNOW

Listed in order of presentation in chapter:

deviation sum of crossproducts
deviation sum of squares
standard error of multiple estimate

EXERCISES

1. Determine the value of a and b in the prediction equation $\tilde{Y} = a + bX$ on the basis of the data on variables X and Y given below for ten individuals:

X	Y	X	Y
50	20	37	11
40	10	36	10
39	15	36	13
38	16	35	11
37	12	34	10

2. Using the values of a and b from the preceding problem, determine the predicted $\tilde{Y}$ score for each of the following values of X:

(a) 48   (c) 40   (e) 31
(b) 42   (d) 38   (f) 28

3. A regression sample of 50 students has been selected in order to develop a prediction scheme to forecast probable achievement in an advanced trigonometry course, based on a specially devised predictor test (X). The predictor test was given to the 50 students before they took a trigonometry course. One academic year later, a comprehensive examination (Y) was given to measure their performance in the course. Develop the prediction equation $\tilde{Y} = a + bX$ on the basis of the scores of these 50 students on these tests:

X	Y	X	Y	X	Y	X	Y	X	Y
62	150	57	111	54	110	51	119	47	125
61	151	57	110	53	119	51	119	46	109
61	143	56	121	53	118	51	114	45	111
61	146	56	120	53	116	51	110	45	107
59	145	56	119	53	110	50	111	44	106
59	140	56	104	52	138	50	111	43	106
58	139	55	143	52	132	49	109	42	104
58	141	55	142	52	130	49	107	42	103
57	142	54	146	52	111	48	124	41	101
57	138	54	111	52	110	47	126	40	101

4. Using the prediction scheme developed in exercise 3, determine the value of $\tilde{Y}$ for each of the following X scores:

(a) 60	(c) 55	(e) 42
(b) 59	(d) 48	(f) 40

5. Compute the value of the standard error of estimate for the prediction equation in exercise 3.

6. On the basis of the standard error of estimate you found in exercise 5, approximately how many times in 100 would an individual with a predicted ($\tilde{Y}$) score of 120 on the trigonometry final examination actually score more than 10.78 above or below the predicted score?

7. Set up the prediction equation $\tilde{Y} = a + bX$ for the following regression sample:

X	Y	X	Y	X	Y	X	Y
20	43	17	38	15	32	12	30
20	43	17	38	14	30	12	29
19	40	16	40	14	30	11	28
19	41	16	36	13	41	11	28
18	40	15	35	13	39	10	27

8. Determine the $\tilde{Y}$ values for the five individuals whose predictor scores are cited below, using this regression scheme:

$$\tilde{Y} = 12.30 + 0.684X_1 + 0.230X_2$$

Individual	$\tilde{Y}$	Predictor I X_1	Predictor II X_2
a	_____	61	37
b	_____	62	39
c	_____	64	42
d	_____	59	31
e	_____	28	29

9. For this practice exercise the data represent a sample far too small to satisfy the requisite assumptions of the technique. However, to illustrate the procedure, set up a multiple regression prediction equation so that the values of X may be predicted from values of Y and Z for the following regression sample:

Individual	X	Y	Z
a	6	3	2
b	7	3	2
c	8	5	4
d	6	4	3
e	5	2	4

9

The *t* Test

Educational situations present numerous problems that require an investigator to determine whether the mean performances of two groups are significantly different. For example, a new method of instruction may be evaluated by using it with an experimental group of students, while a conventional method is used with a comparable control group. If the mean performance of the experimental group on a criterion test is considerably better than that of the control group, it might be concluded that the new method of teaching is so effective that it should be used in classes with enrollments that are similar to the students in the experimental group. The question is, just how great does the difference between the two group means, in favor of the experimental method, have to be to support this conclusion?

Suppose, for example, that on a 100-item spelling test an experimental group, taught by a new spelling technique, attained a mean of 95 correctly spelled words, while the mean of correctly spelled words for the control group was only 30. The decision would easily be in favor of the experimental method. But in educational investigations, mean differences rarely are so clear-cut. If there was only a small mean difference in favor of the experimental group— perhaps a mean of 89, versus a mean of 82 for the control group—the decision would not be so certain. There would be a question whether a seven-point differential is merely the result of chance instead of a genuine difference produced by the experimental method. If the posttest were administered to two randomly selected groups which had *not* been exposed to the new spelling method, would a seven-point difference between such groups be found *by mere chance*?

RATIONALE OF THE *t* TEST

The *t* **test** is used to determine just how great the difference between two means must be in order for it to be judged significant, that is, a significant departure from differences that might be expected by chance alone. Another way of stating the function of the *t* test is to assert that it is used to test the null hypothesis that two group means are not significantly different. In other words, the means are so similar that the sample groups can be considered to have been drawn from the same population (see Chapter 4). Putting this idea in symbols, the null hypothesis H_0: $\mu_1 = \mu_2$ where μ_1 and μ_2 are the two hypothetical population means, states that the two population means are really one and the same. The goal of hypothesis testing is to reject this hypothesis—that is, to accept the alternative hypothesis H_1: $\mu_1 \neq \mu_2$—at some level of statistical significance. In other words, the investigator wants to state with some degree of confidence that the obtained **sample difference**, $\overline{X}_1 - \overline{X}_2$, is too great to be a chance event under the assumption of the null hypothesis.

Remember that just because a mean difference is significant, it is not necessarily an *important* mean difference. Other factors, such as how educationally, socially, or politically meaningful the mean difference is, must be used to judge how important any statistically significant outcome is.

A standard formula for the *t* test is Formula 9.1:

$$t = \frac{\overline{X}_1 - \overline{X}_2}{\sqrt{\dfrac{s_1^2}{n_1} + \dfrac{s_2^2}{n_2}}} \tag{9.1}$$

where:

t = the value by which the statistical significance of the mean difference will be judged
$\overline{X}_1$ = the mean of group 1
$\overline{X}_2$ = the mean of group 2
s_1^2 = the variance of group 1
s_2^2 = the variance of group 2
n_1 = the number of subjects in group 1
n_2 = the number of subjects in group 2

This formula is one of two that are used with different *t* models which will be described in the companion chapter, Chapter 10. In that chapter, Formula 9.1 is identified as the **separate-variance *t* model** and a more complicated formula, Formula 10.1, is identified as the **pooled-variance *t* model**.

From a statistical standpoint, any procedure for testing statistical significance must be based on at least three components:

   1. A sample statistic which reflects (or is sensitive to) the difference or relationship of interest in the population.

2. A well-defined sampling distribution for this statistic.

3. The standard deviation (standard error) of this sampling distribution.

If you are not sure of the meaning of these terms, review the material on sampling distribution and standard error of the mean introduced in Chapter 4. With the *t* test, the sample statistic is a *difference* between means $(\overline{X}_1 - \overline{X}_2)$, the well-defined sampling distribution is the *t* distribution, and the standard deviation of the sampling distribution is the **standard error of mean differences**, $\sqrt{s_1{}^2/n_1 + s_2{}^2/n_2}$.

The *t* value given by Formula 9.1 can be viewed as a kind of standard or *z* score, not for a single $\overline{X}$, but for a *difference* between two $\overline{X}$'s. That is, under the null hypothesis of zero difference between population means, the *t* in Formula 9.1 is simply the ratio of (1) the difference between a sample statistic and its corresponding population parameter to (2) the standard error of the sample statistic. Thus the *t* value is an index of where an observed sample-mean difference is in the distribution of all possible sample-mean differences that might have occurred. Because the form the *t* distribution takes is symmetrical and bell-shaped, much like the normal curve, the larger the *t* value, the smaller the probability of obtaining a sample difference equal to (or greater than) the difference actually observed. When this probability reaches the desired critical level (e.g., 0.05), a significant mean difference can be said to exist.

These statistical notions are admittedly abstract. If we approach the same ideas more intuitively, however, we can set statistical notions aside and reason from a commonsense point of view. There are three separate factors to be considered before a mean difference between two groups can be described as significant:

1. The magnitude of the difference between the two means.

2. The degree of overlap between the two groups, as revealed by the variability of each group.

3. The number of subjects in the two samples.

These three factors will be examined in the following subsections and then summarized with the help of a figure.

Mean Difference

Other things being equal, the larger the value of *t*, the greater the probability that a statistically significant mean difference exists between the two groups under consideration. If you examine the *t*-test model in Formula 9.1, you should see that if the two group means were absolutely identical, there would be no difference between them. Therefore a zero in the numerator of the equation would yield a zero *t* value. Generally speaking, the larger the difference between the two means, the greater the value of *t* (greater in the absolute sense, that is, regardless of algebraic sign), and the less the probability that the difference between the two means is a function of mere chance.

However, the size of *t* that is necessary for statistical significance varies with the sizes of the samples involved. For example, in Table 9.1 you can see how large *t* must be in order to be significant at the 0.05 level with samples of varying size, as reflected in degrees of freedom. Observe that as *df* becomes

Table 9.1   Selected t Values for the 0.05 Level of Significance with Varying-Size Samples, as Reflected in Degrees of Freedom (Two-Tailed Test)

Degrees of Freedom	t at 0.05 Level
1	12.706
2	4.303
3	3.182
5	2.571
10	2.228
30	2.042
60	2.000
120	1.980

larger, a smaller t value is sufficient to reject the null hypothesis. Table 9.1 is based on Table E in the Appendix for the distribution of t values, and degrees of freedom were discussed in Chapter 4 in relation to estimation of the variance. In the t-test situation, two variances must be estimated: $n_1 - 1$ and $n_2 - 1$ degrees of freedom for groups 1 and 2, respectively, or $n_1 + n_2 - 2$ degrees of freedom in all.

Moreover, this notion of "the larger the mean difference, the greater the significance" is complicated by the denominator of the t formula. This is as it should be, because the mere fact that two means differ tells very little, unless something is known about the variability of the two groups under consideration. Obviously, there must be *some* mean difference present, or it would be immediately concluded that there is no significant difference between the identical means of the two groups.

Group Variability

The variability of the groups involved is of considerable importance in determining whether to accept or reject the null hypothesis. If the variances of the two groups are particularly great (that is, there is much spread in the distributions), relatively small mean differences between two groups will result in considerable overlap between the two distributions (see Figure 9–1). With so much overlap between the groups, there would be little basis for concluding that the means of the two distributions are *really* different.

With smaller standard deviations in the samples, the identical mean difference might be judged as reflecting a real-population mean difference. For example, consider the situation depicted in Figure 9–2. Here small standard deviations exist for the two groups under consideration, compared to the very large standard deviations in Figure 9–1. In both cases an equivalent mean difference (ten units) occurs, but in the second instance much more confidence could be placed in the assertion that the two samples were *not* drawn from the same population, since the area of overlap is small, and the groups are clearly distinct.

This notion generalizes to the principle that, other factors being equal, the smaller the variances of the two groups under consideration, the greater the likelihood that a statistically significant mean difference exists.

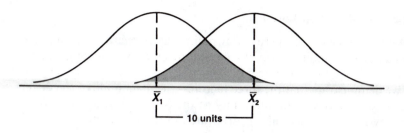

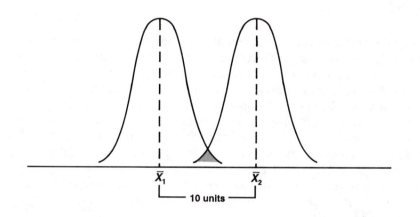

Fig. 9–1. Mean difference of ten units between two groups with relatively large standard deviations, showing area of overlap.

Fig. 9–2. Mean difference of ten units between two groups with relatively small standard deviations, showing area of overlap.

Sample Size

The third factor to be considered in testing for a significant mean difference is the size of the samples involved. To illustrate the necessity of taking sample size into account, suppose that the efficiency of a novel teaching method is being tested by using the new method with only two individuals. A conventional method might also be employed with only two control students. Even if the means of the two student "groups" differed by as much as 100 points, you would probably be unwilling to state with much confidence that the new method was greatly superior to the conventional method.

The size of the sample is extremely important in determining the significance of the difference between means, because with increased sample size, means tend to become more stable representations of group performance. The larger the sample, the greater the confidence that a relatively minor difference between the means exists. However, with an extremely small sample, there is little reason to place much confidence in even a large difference between two means. The larger the sample sizes, the greater the degrees of freedom, and therefore the smaller the critical *t* needed for significance, as we showed in Table 9.1.

Summary of the *t*-Test Formula

To summarize the commonsense viewpoint that there are three factors to be considered in determining the significance of differences between the means of two groups, we will use the model of the *t* test presented in Figure 9–3. In this figure we demonstrate that the three factors—the magnitude of the difference between the two means,the variability of the two groups, and the size of the samples involved—are actually incorporated in the *t* formula.

Difference in Means. The difference between the two means, represented in the numerator of the formula, must be larger than zero, or *t* will be very small. Mean difference therefore is a crucial element in determining the size of *t*.

Size of Group Variances. The sizes of the group variances influence the size of the *t* value because they are incorporated in the denominator of the *t* ratio. Assuming that the sample size is ten for each group, a variance of 5.0 for group 1 would result in a denominator contribution of $5/10$ (or $1/2$), to be divided along with the denominator contribution from group 2 into the mean difference. If the variance of group 1 were doubled, or 10.0, the mean difference would be divided by $10/10$ (or 1), plus the denominator contribution from group 2. Clearly, a smaller quantity divided into the same mean difference yields a larger *t* value. Hence, the *t* model takes into consideration previously discussed notions about variance size and amount of overlap between groups. Smaller variances are more likely to result in significant mean differences, other factors being equal.

Size of Samples. Also incorporated in the denominator is the sample size. The larger the sample size involved in the study, the smaller the value of the fractions under the square root sign. For example, assume that the variance for group 1 is only 2.0. If the number of subjects in group 1 is only four, then the left fraction in the denominator would be only $2/4$, or $1/2$. However, if there are 20 subjects in group 1 and the variance is still 2.0, then the fraction is merely $1/10$. When $1/10$ is divided into *whatever* mean difference exists in the numerator of the *t*-formula fraction, the *t* value will be considerably greater than if $1/2$ is divided into that mean difference.

In essence, then, increased sample size yields a larger *t* value as long as other factors (mean difference and group variances) remain constant. As we showed in Table 9.1, the *t* table (Appendix Table E), by which the significance

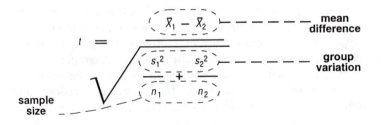

Fig. 9–3. Three factors incorporated in the *t*-test for mean differences.

of the obtained *t* value is judged, also takes into account sample size as reflected in degrees of freedom. Thus a given *t* value is more likely to be significant if the number of individuals in the sample is larger.

The two parts of the denominator of the *t* ratio, group variances and sample sizes, together constitute the **standard error of mean differences**. The computation of this statistic will be described in the companion chapter that follows.

THE TABLE OF *t* VALUES

Once the value of *t* has been determined, it is possible to ascertain whether or not it is statistically significant by comparing it with a table of *t* values such as Table E. An obtained *t* value must equal or exceed the *t* values listed in this table in order for the probability of the mean difference under consideration to be as rare as (or more rare than) the probability proportions given in the top row of the table.

You must know how many degrees of freedom are involved before you can enter Table E (in the column at the left headed *df*). Suppose you were testing a null hypothesis of no difference between means of two samples with 16 individuals in each group. If you were using the 0.05 level to test the null hypothesis, you would enter Table E with 30 degrees of freedom (16 – 1 for each group) and a probability level, or level of significance, of 0.05 for a two-tailed test. The point of intersection of the two columns yields a *t* value of 2.042. This indicates that the obtained *t* value, derived from the actual data for the two samples, must equal or exceed (positively or negatively) 2.042, in order for you to reject the null hypothesis at the 0.05 level.

If the obtained *t* were 2.75, for example, you should reject the null hypothesis and conclude that the two samples were not drawn from the same population. If the obtained *t* were only 1.56, you should consider the null hypothesis tenable and conclude that, based on these samples, there is insufficient evidence to consider the mean difference as being attributable to any factor other than chance.

CONFIDENCE INTERVALS FOR MEAN DIFFERENCES

Confidence intervals can be computed for the difference between means in much the same manner that they are computed for the mean (see Chapter 4) and the correlation coefficient (see Chapter 6). This type of estimation is of considerable value to the educator who must decide whether a new instructional approach should be adopted in preference to conventional procedures. In such a case, it is helpful to know just how large or how small the true population-mean difference is apt to be. For example, the decision to purchase a set of computerized instructional software would be supported by finding a 95 percent mean-difference confidence interval that included an instructionally meaningful difference in favor of the software. This would indicate that if a similar statistical procedure were carried out, similar confidence intervals would be yielded which would contain the true population-mean difference 95 percent of the time. The computation procedures to be followed in setting up confidence intervals for mean differences will be described in the companion chapter that follows.

SITUATIONS CALLING FOR USE OF THE *t* TEST

Investigational situations in which the *t* test can be used to determine the magnitude of mean differences have certain characteristics related to the populations and samples used. A situation that would permit use of the *t* test is conceptualized in Figure 9–4: a comparison of the difference between the means of two populations, each with its own mean and variance, on the basis of statistics computed for samples of a certain size randomly drawn from these populations.

When the two groups are based on a preexisting variable (e.g., sex, political affiliation, brain damage), this conceptualization is quite straightforward. For example, suppose Mrs. Stern, a graduate student in education, wants to compare males and females on a measure of "caring," hoping to find support for her idea that females are more "caring" than males. She can conceptualize a population of males and a population of females, each with the population parameters of mean and variance on the measure of caring. She then would take a sample of males and a sample of females from their respective populations and compute sample estimates (statistics) for the population parameters. For the sake of statistical argument, and to support her contention, she assumes that the population means (μ_1 and μ_2) are equal; that is, there is no difference between males and females on the measure of caring. Then, if the observed difference between her sample estimates ($\overline{X}_1$ and $\overline{X}_2$) is expected to occur by chance only a small percentage of the time (e.g., 5 percent), Mrs. Stern would conclude that what she had assumed for the sake of statistical argument was, in fact, an error. Within a certain level of probability (e.g., 0.05), she was wrong to assume $\mu_1 = \mu_2$, and she is right in accepting that, based on these samples of males and females, at least, $\mu_1 \neq \mu_2$, or there exists a difference in caring between the populations of males and females.

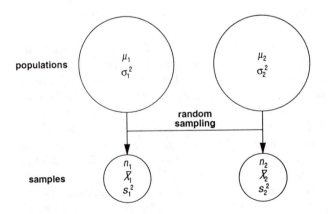

Fig. 9–4. Conceptualization of the *t*-test situation.

When the two groups are based on an experimental variable, as when a treatment group is compared to a control group, this conceptualization is a bit more abstract. For example, in the treatment–no treatment design, the treated and untreated individuals are conceptualized as having been sampled from a population that is hypothetically split into two subpopulations, one treated and one untreated. There then is an analogous situation between the populations and samples. (See Chapter 17 for a more complete discussion of these distinctions.)

Assumptions Underlying the *t* Test

The conceptualization depicted in Figure 9–4 demonstrates the three assumptions that are considered necessary for valid use of the *t* test:

1. The samples must be *randomly drawn* from their respective populations.
2. The scores must be *normally distributed* in the populations.
3. The scores must have the *same variances* in the populations $(\sigma_1^2 = \sigma_2^2)$.

The assumption of random sampling allows use of the notion of a sampling distribution and comparison of the obtained sample difference to all those sample differences that might have occurred. The assumptions of normality and homogeneity of variance allow use of the *t* distribution in making probability decisions.

Despite the necessity of these assumptions, the *t* test can be shown to be a **robust statistical test**. For example, even if the assumptions of normality and homogeneity of variances are departed from quite markedly, a *t* value that can be correctly interpreted will be obtained. This property of statistics being based on assumptions that can be violated without prohibiting a valid statistical test is known as robustness. Certain statistical adjustments are possible when the assumption of equal variances is violated. (This assumption is discussed further in the following section.)

The assumption of random sampling is a *logical* assumption; that is, the logic of the inference procedure rests on the notion of randomness. Therefore, you are urged to employ random selection techniques in selecting samples for an investigation. However, because it is often difficult to draw pure random samples in educational situations, you can make reasonable use of inferential procedures such as the *t* test as long as you are able to demonstrate that the samples are not a biased representation of the population under study. To do this, you have to be able to show that the samples are not unlike those that would have been obtained had the sampling been carried out in a strictly random fashion.

USE OF THE APPROPRIATE *t* MODEL

Although we have dealt with the *t* test as though there were only one *t* formula, there are actually several slightly different models. Use of the appropriate formula is dependent on:

1. The number of individuals in the group.
2. The presence of correlation between group data.
3. The similarity, or homogeneity, of population variances.

For example, when $n_1 = n_2$ and $\sigma_1^2 = \sigma_2^2$, the t formula used is slightly different from the one that is used when $n_1 \neq n_2$ and $\sigma_1^2 \neq \sigma_2^2$. Different degrees of freedom are also involved, depending on the research design and the t formula used. A simple scheme for selecting the appropriate t formula and the accompanying degrees of freedom for different investigational situations is given in the companion chapter Chapter 10.

The Presence of Correlation

Because problems in testing for mean differences arise when a positive correlation is present between data in the two groups, this factor must be taken into consideration in analyzing the data. Suppose, for example, that an investigator wants to test the significance of differences between mean performances on a criterion variable by two groups of matched pairs. If the matching has been done carefully, the investigator would suspect that scores of the two members of a pair would tend to be more similar than if no matching had taken place and the groups had been selected at random. Because the scores would tend to be more similar, there is *less* likelihood that the means of the two groups will be different.

In taking into consideration the presence of correlation, the investigator determines the correlation between the scores of pairs in the groups and adjusts the t value upward to some extent. A special t model designed for correlated data should be used whenever a relationship between data in the two groups of scores has been found. The situations in which correlation between the data in the two groups is usually present are those involving matched pairs (e.g., mothers and daughters) or those in which two measurements have been taken for the same individual, as in pretest and posttest comparisons. The special t formula to be used in computations involving correlated data is presented in the companion chapter.

Homogeneity of Variances

Before a particular t model is chosen, the assumption of **homogeneity of variances** in the two populations should be checked. Whether or not these variances can be considered equal can be determined quickly by using a simple statistical technique known as the **F ratio**, in which the larger sample variance is divided by the smaller one. The resulting quantity, known as F, is interpreted for statistical significance from a table much like the t table. Table F in the Appendix, which contains the values for the F distribution, uses the degrees of freedom for each sample variance, or, as variances are sometimes called, each **mean square**.

As in the interpretation of t, the larger the value of F, the greater is the likelihood of a statistically significant difference between the two variances. If the difference is statistically significant, the null hypotheses of no difference

Table 9.2 Comparison of Scores of "Superior" and "Inferior" Teachers on Minnesota
Teacher Attitude Inventory

Group	Number	Standard Deviation	Mean MTAI Score	t
Superior	72	40.66	23.60	2.81[a]
Inferior	72	38.83	5.30	

[a] Significant beyond the 0.01 level.

Source: W. J. Popham and R. R. Trimble, "The Minnesota Teacher Attitude Inventory as an Index of General Teaching Competence." *Educational and Psychological Measurement*, vol. 20, no. 3 (Autumn 1960), pp. 509-12.

between the population variances is rejected, and the conclusion is that the variances in the two populations are not homogeneous. All of these factors, including the use of Table F, will be explained further in the discussion of the computation procedures for the t test in Chapter 10.

This simple F test may be conducted as an aid in selecting one of several different t formulas. In actual practice, however, few investigators check the assumption of homogeneity of variances. With large enough sample sizes, it is not necessary to worry about the influence of even markedly divergent variances.

REPORTING THE t TEST

Your understanding of the rationale of the t test and procedures for using it now should enable you to interpret an example of the manner in which t tests typically are reported in professional journals. The results of a t-test analysis comparing the performance of two groups of teachers on the Minnesota Teacher Attitude Inventory (MTAI) are presented in Table 9.2. The two samples of teachers were designated as "superior" or "inferior" according to the judgments of teacher raters, and the samples were assumed to be representative of the populations of superior and inferior teachers.

For each group of teachers, the data in Table 9.2 include the number in the sample, the standard deviation, and the mean score on the MTAI. The t value yielded by the analysis of the difference between the two groups also is given. The level of significance of the obtained t is stated below the table.

You can see from Table 9.2 that the t-test result was statistically significant, and the researchers were warranted in rejecting the null hypothesis at the 0.01 level. In other words, the data support the hypothesis that there is a difference in teacher attitude between "superior" and "inferior" teachers, with the superior teachers having a higher score on the attitude scale.

■　　■　　■

REVIEW

The t test is a statistical model designed to determine whether two groups, as represented by their means, are significantly different. In yielding an index of the significance of differences in means, *t* formulas take into account the following factors: (1) mean difference, (2) population variability, and (3) sample size. Where applicable, the presence of correlated data also is a factor in testing for mean differences. Different *t* formulas are used, depending on the design of the study.

The *t* test, like most other significance tests, is computed by analyzing sample data in such a way that a sample statistic (in this case, *t*) is generated. The statistic is subsequently interpreted for statistical significance from a table which indicates the probability that an observed mean difference, or a more extreme difference, could be attributed to chance alone. If the *t* value is sufficiently large, the null hypothesis is rejected, and the investigator concludes that the two samples were not drawn from the same population—that is, they are different. Confidence intervals may be developed for differences between sample means.

Underlying use of the *t* test are the assumptions that (1) the sample data have been drawn randomly from the populations, (2) the population from which each sample has been drawn has a normal distribution, and (3) the populations have the same variance.

TERMS TO KNOW

Listed in order of presentation in chapter:

t test
sample difference
separate-variance t model
pooled-variance t model
standard error of mean differences
robust statistical test
homogeneity of variances
F ratio
mean square

EXERCISES

1. Assume that two investigators are individually testing a null hypothesis which involves a t-test comparison of the means of two groups. Investigator A uses 50 individuals in each group, and investigator B uses 100 individuals in each group. Other factors being equal, which one is more likely to reject the null hypothesis?

2. Assuming that both of the investigators in exercise 1 used identical numbers of subjects in their two samples, suppose A's samples have much smaller standard deviations than those involved in B's t test. If all other factors are equal, which investigator is more likely to reject the null hypothesis?

3. Suppose that, in exercise 1, A has carefully matched pairs of individuals in two groups, and B has drawn two groups at random. Which investigator is more apt to find the greatest mean difference between the two samples?

4. If you *wished* to reject a null hypothesis of mean difference between two samples, would you be happier with a t value of 6.8 with 1 degree of freedom, or a t value of 2.25 with 30 degrees of freedom?

5. Assume that two t tests from different experiments are about to be calculated. In one instance the mean difference is 13.05, and in the other the mean difference is only 6.20. Is it true that the t test with the larger mean difference will always yield the largest t value?

6. If one t test yields a t value of -2.42 and a second yields a t value of 1.99, which t value is least probable and, therefore, more apt to be statistically significant?

7. From Table E in the Appendix, determine whether: (1) a one-tailed t test with $t = 1.90$ and $df = 9$ or (2) a two-tailed t test with $t = 2.10$ and $df = 9$ would entitle a school psychologist to reject a null hypothesis of mean difference between two experimental groups at the 0.05 level.

SELECTED READINGS

Boneau, C. A. "The Effects of Violations of Assumptions Underlying the *t* Test." *Psychological Bulletin*, vol. 57 (1960), pp. 49–64.

Edwards, Allen L. *Statistical Analysis*. New York: Holt, Rinehart & Winston, 1969, chap. 11.

Guilford, J. P., and Fruchter, Benjamin. *Fundamental Statistics in Psychology and Education*. New York: McGraw-Hill, 1978, chap. 9.

Hays, William L. *Statistics for Psychologists*. New York: Holt, Rinehart & Winston, 1981, chap. 8.

McCall, Robert B. *Fundamental Statistics for Behavioral Sciences*. San Diego, CA: Harcourt Brace Jovanovich, 1986, chap. 10.

Spence, Janet T., et al. *Elementary Statistics*. Englewood Cliffs, NJ: Prentice-Hall, 1983, chap. 10.

The *t* Test

- *computation procedures*

An educational investigator who has determined that a *t* test should be used to analyze data is, figuratively speaking, only halfway home. It is clear that a *t* test is appropriate when testing the null hypothesis that two group means are not significantly different, but several decisions must be made before the value of *t* (by which the null hypothesis will be tested) can be calculated and interpreted. For one thing, as you learned in Chapter 9, there are several slightly different models of the *t* test. One decision to be made has to do with which model should be chosen. Another has to do with how many degrees of freedom should be used to interpret an obtained value of *t*. And a third decision concerns what adjustments should be made if there is some relationship (correlation) between the scores of the two groups.

These issues must be resolved before testing the hypothesis under consideration. In this chapter we demonstrate how, in various investigative situations, the appropriate *t* model is selected and the significance of *t* is interpreted after it has been calculated.

In order to select and interpret the appropriate statistical model for the *t* test, an investigator must be able to answer three questions regarding the data in the populations and samples under consideration:

1. Is there a positive correlation of any meaningful magnitude between data in the two populations?
2. Are the variances of the two populations significantly different, or can the two population variances be considered homogeneous?
3. Is there an equal number of individuals in each sample?

The first question to be considered relates to the existence of any appreciable positive correlation between data for the two populations. Such correlation may exist in one of two situations:

1. When the *t* test involves a comparison between two groups composed of matched pairs.
2. When the *t* test compares two measures taken on the same subjects, as in testing the significance of pretest-to-posttest gains for the same pupils.

If there is correlation between data for the two populations, a special *t* model using the correlation coefficient (*r*) must be used.[1]

In any investigation that does not deal with matched pairs or with two measures for the same individuals, a correlation coefficient cannot be computed. The investigator therefore assumes no relationship between data in the two groups. Then the next question is to determine whether the assumption of homogeneity of variances for the two populations can be met. The two population variances are estimated, using the sample variances, and an *F*-ratio test is used to determine whether or not the null hypothesis of no difference in variances should be rejected. To answer the third question, the investigator must note the number of individuals in each sample group to see whether or not they are equal, as well as to find the number of degrees of feedom.

MODELS FOR UNCORRELATED DATA

Before considering the special case of correlated data, we will examine the computational procedures to be used with uncorrelated data. If no positive relationship between the group data has been found, one of two *t* models can be used. The selection depends on whether the variances are homogeneous and whether the *n*'s are equal. One of these two models is the separate-variance *t* model, Formula 9.1, which was introduced in Chapter 9:

$$t = \frac{\overline{X}_1 - \overline{X}_2}{\sqrt{\dfrac{s_1^2}{n_1} + \dfrac{s_2^2}{n_2}}}$$

---

1. In some educational investigative situations, there is no way of discovering whether any correlation exists between the data for the two groups. In such a case, *t* models that do not need to take the presence of relationship into account can be used. This matter should be resolved before the *t* model is selected.

The other is the pooled-variance t model, Formula 10.1:

$$t = \frac{\overline{X}_1 - \overline{X}_2}{\sqrt{\left(\dfrac{(n_1 - 1)s_1^2 + (n_2 - 1)s_2^2}{n_1 + n_2 - 2}\right)\left(\dfrac{1}{n_1} + \dfrac{1}{n_2}\right)}} \tag{10.1}$$

In some instances there is no difference in the t values that are yielded when Formulas 9.1 and 10.1 are applied to the same data, and in other situations there is a considerable difference. Use of the pooled-variance model, however, will result in a t value that usually can be interpreted with more degrees of freedom than could be used with the separate-variance model. When a greater number of degrees of freedom is present, a smaller t value is needed to reject a given null hypothesis. This indicates that a certain t value is more likely to be significant when it has been computed by the pooled-variance formula than when it has been obtained from the separate-variance formula. It follows that the pooled-variance formula is the more-powerful statistical test, that is, more likely to call for rejection of the null hypothesis.

After determining whether the two groups include an identical number of individuals, which is easily done, the remaining concern in choosing the appropriate t test is whether or not the variances of the two populations are homogeneous.

Homogeneity of Variances

To test the homogeneity of the two population variances, that is, the likelihood that $\sigma_1^2 = \sigma_2^2$, the sample variances, s_1^2 and s_2^2, are used to estimate these population parameters. The assumption is that if the null hypothesis of population variability (that is, the hypothesis that the populations are homogeneous) cannot be rejected with the sample statistics, the population parameters can be considered equal for the purpose of conducting the t test.

To test the hypothesis that $\sigma_1^2 = \sigma_2^2$, a simple statistical test, the F ratio, is employed. Formula 10.2, the formula for F, is:

$$F = \frac{s_g^2}{s_l^2} \tag{10.2}$$

where:

    F = the value by which variance homogeneity will be tested

    s_g^2 = the greater (larger) sample variance

    s_l^2 = the lesser (smaller) sample variance

The computation of F is easily accomplished by dividing the smaller variance into the larger variance. Then the resulting quotient, F, is interpreted for statistical significance from a table of the F distribution (Table F in the Appendix). The rows and columns in this table designate the degrees of freedom for each variance, or mean square. Degrees of freedom for the F test are equal to the number of individuals in the group minus 1.

An example will show you how to use the F table. Suppose you are testing the null hypothesis of variance homogeneity for two populations. For sample 1, $s_1^2 = 10.5$, $n_1 = 25$; and for sample 2, $s_2^2 = 3.5$, $n_1 = 29$. You would set up the equation for the *F* ratio by giving the degrees of freedom $(n - 1)$ for both variances as a subscript to *F*, with the *df* for the larger variance on the left in the subscript. Then, with the larger variance in the numerator of the *F* ratio and the smaller variance in the denominator, the *F* value would be determined as follows:

$$F_{24,28} = \frac{10.5}{3.5}$$

$$= 3.0$$

When interpreting the *F* for statistical significance, the degrees of freedom (indicated in the subscript) are used to locate the tabled values that the obtained *F* must equal or exceed if it is to be judged significant.

Then turn to Table F, and you will see that the degrees of freedom for the greater mean square are given in the row across the top of the table, and the degrees of freedom for the lesser mean square are listed in the column at the left margin. Two different values of *F* are given in the table, one printed in regular roman type and the other printed in boldface type (this distinction will be explained in the next paragraph). You would enter the top of the table with the degrees of freedom for the group with the larger variance (24), and enter the left side of the table with the degrees of freedom for the group with the smaller variance (28). These two entries intersect at a point where the value in roman type is 1.91 and the value in boldface type is 2.52. If the computed value of *F* equals or exceeds the tabled values, then the null hypothesis should be rejected, and the hypothesis of variance homogeneity should be considered untenable. If the values exceed the computed *F* value, the variances should be considered homogeneous. In this example, the computed *F* value of 3.0 exceeds both of the tabled values, so you should reject the null hypothesis of variance homogeneity.

The *F* values given in Table F represent the 5 percent probability level (in regular roman type) and the 1 percent level (in boldface type). This table for the distribution of *F* is designed for use with one-tailed tests of significance, and it is usually employed with the statistical technique called analysis of variance (see Chapters 11–14). In the *F*-ratio test of variance homogeneity being considered here for the selection of a *t*-test model, you do not know before the data are collected which of the group variances will be greater, so you are not certain which of the two variances will eventually be placed in the numerator of the ratio. Accordingly, a two-tailed test is used to interpret the *F* ratio. When interpreting the computed *F* value from a test for homogeneity of variance, the roman-type values must be used to represent the 10 percent level and the boldface values to represent the 2 percent level. Computing the 1 and 5 percent levels of significance for two-tailed *F*-ratio tests is an intricate and laborious process, so for these levels a one-tailed *F* table such as Table F is usually used, and the probability levels are doubled.

Selecting the *t* Model and Degrees of Freedom

Once the equivalence of n_1 and n_2 and the homogeneity of σ_1^2 and σ_2^2 have been determined, a four-point scheme can be applied to determine which *t* formula and what degrees of freedom to employ when the data are uncorrelated. This scheme is as follows:

1. When $n_1 = n_2$ and $\sigma_1{}^2 = \sigma_2{}^2$ (that is, the null hypothesis of variance homogeneity cannot be rejected with the *F*-ratio test):
   Use separate-variance or pooled-variance formula, with degrees of freedom equal to $n_1 + n_2 - 2$. (Both formulas are algebraically equivalent when $n_1 = n_2$.)
2. When $n_1 \neq n_2$ and $\sigma_1{}^2 = \sigma_2{}^2$:
   Use pooled-variance formula, with degrees of freedom equal to $n_1 + n_2 - 2$.
3. When $n_1 = n_2$ and $\sigma_1{}^2 \neq \sigma_2{}^2$:
   Use pooled-variance formula or separate-variance formula, with degrees of freedom in each instance equal to $n_1 - 1$ or $n_2 - 1$. (Do not use $df = n_1 + n_2 - 2$.)
4. When $n_1 \neq n_2$ and $\sigma_1{}^2 \neq \sigma_2{}^2$:
   Use separate-variance formula, with tabled *t* value for a given level of significance determined by averaging *t* values for (a) degrees of freedom equal to $n_1 - 1$ and (b) degrees of freedom equal to $n_2 - 1$.

We should clarify the calculation of the *t* value for different levels of significance in the fourth case. To illustrate, suppose you want to use the 0.01 level in such a situation, with $n_1 = 25$ and $n_2 = 13$. You will find in Table E for the distribution of *t* that with a two-tailed test and at the 0.01 level, the *t* value for $df = 24$ is 2.797, and for $df = 12$ it is 3.055. You would calculate the *average* of these two *t* values by dividing the difference between them by 2 and adding this quantity to the smaller value, as follows:

$$3.055 - 2.797 = 0.258; \ 0.258 \div 2 = 0.129; \ 2.797 + 0.129 = 2.926.$$

This value, 2.926, is the value that the computed *t* must equal or exceed in order to be significant at the 0.01 level.

If the calculated *t* had been 2.80, it would not be sufficiently large to reject the null hypothesis at the 0.01 level. Such a *t* would, however, be large enough to reject the null hypothesis at the 0.05 level.[2]

Computational Examples Using Uncorrelated Data

To improve your understanding of how *t* is determined with uncorrelated data, we will take you step by step through an example as you make the necessary decisions and reach a conclusion regarding the tenability of the null hypothesis. Assume that you have developed an experimental design in which you must test the null hypothesis that the means for examination scores of two groups of students do not differ significantly.

First, determine whether the data in the two groups are related, as might be the case in a study involving matched pairs. Assume you are working with

---

2. Another method frequently used for determining the *t* value to be used as the desired probability level in this situation has been supplied by W. G. Cochran and Gertrude M. Cox, *Experimental Designs* (New York: Wiley, 1957).

two unrelated groups, so you do not need correlated t models and can choose either the separate-variance or pooled-variance model.

Second, turn to the sample data before you reach any further decisions on the selection of a t model. Suppose preliminary calculations give you the following set of values for group A and group B, the two samples under investigation:

Group A	Group B
$n = 11$	$n = 25$
$s^2 = 9$	$s^2 = 12$
$\overline{X} = 13.85$	$\overline{X} = 11.20$

Third, check on the data to see whether the variances of the two population groups are homogeneous. You do this by computing an F ratio and dividing the larger variance (in this case, that of group B) by the smaller variance, as follows:

$$F_{24,10} = \frac{12}{9}$$

$$= 1.33$$

From Table F you find that with 24 degrees of freedom for the greater mean square (variance) and 10 degrees of freedom for the lesser mean square, an F value equal to or exceeding 2.74 is required to reject the null hypothesis of variance homogeneity at the 0.10 level (the 0.05 level in Table F). Similarly, the 0.02 level (0.01 in the table) would demand an F of at least 4.33. With an F of 1.33, the hypothesis of variance homogeneity cannot be rejected, so you can conclude that the population variances represented by the two samples are, for statistical purposes, homogeneous.

Fourth, note that the number of individuals in the two groups are not the same; that is, there are 25 individuals in group B and only 11 in group A.

Fifth, now that you are in a position to select a t model as well as the degrees of freedom with which to interpret the t, refer back to the four-point selection scheme outlined above. You can see that when $n_1 \neq n_2$ and $\sigma_1^2 = \sigma_2^2$, you should use the pooled-variance formula (10.1), in which the degrees of freedom for interpreting the significance of t are $n_1 + n_2 - 2$.

Sixth, substituting the necessary data in Formula 10.1, you find that:

$$t = \frac{13.85 - 11.20}{\sqrt{\left(\frac{(10)(9) + (24)(12)}{11 + 25 - 2}\right)\left(\frac{1}{11} + \frac{1}{25}\right)}}$$

$$= \frac{2.65}{\sqrt{\frac{378}{34}(0.091 + 0.040)}}$$

$$= \frac{2.65}{\sqrt{(11.118)(0.131)}}$$

$$= \frac{2.65}{\sqrt{1.456}}$$

$$= \frac{2.65}{1.207}$$

$$= 2.196$$

Seventh, with a t of 2.196, you can now enter Table E (the t table) to determine whether the null hypothesis can be rejected. Since you are using $n_1 + n_2 - 2$ degrees of freedom, $11 + 25 - 2 = 34$ df. Because this is an abridged t table, no value is given for 34 df. You will need to *interpolate* between the t values given for 30 df and 40 df. To be significant at the 0.05 level, t must be 2.042 with 30 df and 2.021 with 40 df. To be significant at the 0.01 level, t must be 2.750 with 30 df and 2.704 with 40 df. In this example, you will find that the t value of 2.196 exceeds the 0.05-level t value but not the 0.01-level t value, so the null hypothesis can be rejected at the 0.05 level but not at the 0.01 level of significance. This is true, of course, for a two-tailed test such as you are using.

Eighth, you can now conclude that the observed mean difference would occur *by chance alone* less than 5 times in 100. Therefore, you can conclude, with odds considerably in your favor, that the observed difference can be attributed to the independent variable under study. To rephrase this statement, a relationship exists between the *dependent* variable represented by the test performance and the *independent* variable represented by the two treatment groups.

You should find that by applying the eight steps described in this computational example in similar situations, you can select t tests easily and interpret them properly. Of course, with different data, the t model selected, as well as the degrees of freedom, could vary.

Suppose, for example, you needed to compute a t test using the following data:

Group 1	Group 2
$n_1 = 100$	$n_2 = 100$
$\overline{X}_1 = 82.6$	$\overline{X}_2 = 68.4$
$s_1^2 = 200.74$	$s_2^2 = 85.63$

You would find that the population variances are not homogeneous, because $F_{99.99} = 200.74/85.63 = 2.42$, $p < 0.02$. You therefore would use the separate-variance formula (9.1) with $n - 1$ degrees of freedom. The pooled-variance formula could also be used with the same degrees of freedom.

Substituting these data in Formula 9.1 would yield the value of t:

$$t = \frac{82.6 - 68.4}{\sqrt{\dfrac{200.74}{100} + \dfrac{85.63}{100}}}$$

$$= \frac{14.2}{\sqrt{2.01 + 0.86}}$$

$$= \frac{14.2}{\sqrt{2.87}}$$

$$= \frac{14.2}{1.69}$$

$$= 8.4$$

With a *t* value of 8.4 and 99 degrees of freedom, you would find from Table E that the mean difference is significant beyond the 0.01 level.

THE *t* MODEL FOR CORRELATED DATA

In testing the mean differences of two groups in which the individuals have been matched or in which two measures for the same individuals comprise the data (as in pretest-posttest comparisons), it is likely that the measurements composing the two groups are positively correlated. The presence of correlation, of course, can be checked by computing the product-moment correlation coefficient, *r*.

If an *r* indicates a relationship between the scores for the two groups, a special *t* model designed specifically for this situation must be used. As we noted in Chapter 9, the reason for using a special model when correlation exists is that the two group means tend to be more similar. If a positive correlation is present, scores in one group will be related to or somewhat like scores in the other group. This tendency of correlated scores to be somewhat more similar than data drawn from uncorrelated groups results in means that are *less* likely to be significantly different than means drawn from independent or unrelated groups. The correlated *t* model embodies a statistical adjustment which is subtracted from the denominator of the separate-variance *t* model, thereby increasing the magnitude of *t*. In other words, the value of *t* is adjusted upward to compensate for the tendency of the means to be similar.

The extent of the adjustment in the correlated *t* model is a function of the magnitude of *r,* as indicated in Formula 10.3:

$$t = \frac{\overline{X}_1 - \overline{X}_2}{\sqrt{\dfrac{s_1^{\,2}}{n_1} + \dfrac{s_2^{\,2}}{n_2} - 2r\left(\dfrac{s_1}{\sqrt{n_1}}\right)\left(\dfrac{s_2}{\sqrt{n_2}}\right)}} \tag{10.3}$$

The value of *t* derived from this correlated model is interpreted for significance according to degrees of freedom equaling the number of *pairs* minus 1.

A COMPUTATIONAL EXAMPLE WITH CORRELATED DATA

As an example using the correlated *t* formula, suppose Miss O'Malley, a high school biology teacher, wants to determine whether a special summer outdoor program has produced any significant gain in knowledge of biology for high school students. To do this, she could administer a pretest and a posttest on the subject matter before and after the program to a representative sample of students. Because the same individuals take both tests, she should anticipate that a positive correlation exists between the students' scores on these two measures. In order to test for significant mean differences between posttest and pretest by use of a *t* model, she must first ascertain whether such a correlation actually exists.

Suppose Miss O'Malley finds that an *r* of 0.41 is present for a sample of 100 pupils' scores on the two tests. She must therefore use the special *t* model in Formula 10.3 to test the null hypothesis. According to her data, the following values are to be used for the computation:

Posttest	Pretest
$n = 100$	$n = 100$
$s^2 = 64.0$	$s^2 = 49.0$
$\overline{X} = 46.4$	$\overline{X} = 42.5$

These values then are substituted in the formula, as follows:

$$t = \frac{46.4 - 42.5}{\sqrt{\dfrac{64.0}{100} + \dfrac{49.0}{100} - 2(0.41)\left(\dfrac{8}{10}\right)\left(\dfrac{7}{10}\right)}}$$
$$= 4.76$$

By consulting the *t* table (Table E) with 99 degrees of freedom, Miss O'Malley can see that a *t* of 4.76 is significant beyond the 0.01 level. Thus she may reject the null hypothesis of pretest and posttest mean equivalence and infer a significant gain in biology knowledge based on the performance of the 100 students. To be more confident that this gain was produced by the special summer program, she would have to contrast the growth in knowledge for these students with that of a comparable group who did not take part in the summer program.

COMPUTING CONFIDENCE INTERVALS FOR *t* MODELS

In computing confidence intervals for differences between means, essentially the procedure used in determining any confidence interval is followed. First, the standard error of mean difference (the denominator of the *t* ratio) is computed. The particular denominator to be used depends on the *t* model used in the analysis. For example, if the separate-variance *t* model is used, the standard error of mean difference would be the denominator of Formula 9.1:

$$\sqrt{\frac{s_1^2}{n_1} + \frac{s_2^2}{n_2}}$$

This standard error is then multiplied by plus and minus the *t* value associated with the desired confidence interval (for example, the 95 percent level) and the degrees of freedom involved. The resulting value is then added to and subtracted from the mean difference observed in the sample, thus yielding the appropriate confidence limits.

The calculation of a confidence interval can be illustrated by using the data from group 1 and group 2 in the second computational example for uncorrelated data given in this chapter. In that example, the mean difference is 14.2, the standard error of mean difference (that is, the denominator or lower part of the *t* model) is 1.69, and the degrees of freedom are 99.

The 99 percent confidence interval for this mean difference would be computed by multiplying 1.69 by the appropriate 99 percent *t* values of ± 2.64 and adding the results to the mean difference of 14.2 points. The result yields 99 percent mean-difference confidence limits of 9.7 and 18.7 points. The 95 percent confidence points would be computed as follows:

$$14.2 \pm (1.99)(1.69) = 10.8 \text{ and } 17.6.$$

■   ■   ■

REVIEW

The preparation for computing a *t* test involves selection of the appropriate *t* model and the correct number of degrees of freedom.

Selection of the correct *t* test hinges on the presence or absence of correlated data and whether or not the variances of the two populations are homogeneous and the number of individuals in the two groups are equal. With uncorrelated data, the choice of *t* model is between the separate-variance model and the pooled-variance model, and there is a special *t* model for use with correlated data.

The size of the samples and the degrees of freedom available in particular situations must be considered because the number of degrees of freedom varies with the different *t* models. A four-point scheme can be used to determine which *t* formula and degrees of freedom to use with uncorrelated data. With the correlated *t* model, the degrees of freedom equal the number of pairs minus 1.

Other statistical procedures used with the *t* test provide for testing homogeneity of variances through the *F* ratio and for setting up mean-difference confidence intervals.

EXERCISES

1. Decide whether to use the separate-variance t model or the pooled-variance t model for each of the following situations. Determine the degrees of freedom that should be used in each instance.

   (a) Group 1   Group 2
        $n = 25$ $n = 14$
        $s^2 = 100.0$ $s^2 = 92.3$
        $\overline{X} = 62.80$ $\overline{X} = 73.42$

   (b) Group 1   Group 2
        $n = 14$ $n = 14$
        $s^2 = 102.0$ $s^2 = 20.0$
        $\overline{X} = 43.71$ $\overline{X} = 36.28$

   (c) Group 1   Group 2
        $n = 18$ $n = 18$
        $s^2 = 161.8$ $s^2 = 154.9$
        $\overline{X} = 72.41$ $\overline{X} = 67.82$

   (d) Group 1   Group 2
        $n = 24$ $n = 16$
        $s^2 = 26.9$ $s^2 = 107.1$
        $\overline{X} = 106.12$ $\overline{X} = 100.22$

2. Compute the value of t for each of the four sets of data (a, b, c, and d) in exercise 1. Using the 0.05 level of significance (two-tailed test), determine whether the null hypothesis of mean difference should be accepted or rejected.

3. To check for homogeneity of population variances before selecting the appropriate t model for the uncorrelated data below, compute F for the five pairs of variances. For each pair, indicate whether the parameters estimated should be considered homogeneous or heterogeneous, using the 0.10 level of significance for rejecting the null hypothesis of variance homogeneity.

   (a) $s_1^2 = 480.42$, $n_1 = 14$ (d) $s_1^2 = 142.81$, $n_1 = 100$
        $s_2^2 = 682.49$, $n_2 = 15$ $s_2^2 = 42.64$, $n_2 = 51$
   (b) $s_1^2 = 286.31$, $n_1 = 62$ (e) $s_1^2 = 1{,}000.67$, $n_1 = 41$
        $s_2^2 = 494.37$, $n_2 = 51$ $s_2^2 = 2{,}527.00$, $n_2 = 61$
   (c) $s_1^2 = 127.42$, $n_1 = 10$
        $s_2^2 = 197.43$, $n_2 = 10$

4. Select the appropriate t model and degrees of freedom for the two unrelated samples (groups A and B) given below. Compute the value of t and, using the 0.01 level, make a decision regarding the rejection of the null hypothesis.

Group A	Group B
42	41
69	38
48	46
37	49
42	37
18	36
64	42
71	18

5. Treat the data for groups X and Y in the manner described for exercise 4.

Group X	Group Y
104	100
102	100
100	97
100	94
98	93
97	92
94	92
90	90
87	86
80	74

6. Using the *t* model for correlated observations, compute the value of *t* and reach a decision regarding the null hypothesis ($p < 0.01$) with the following data for matched pairs:

Group 1, $\overline{X} = 62.70$, $s^2 = 64.00$, $n = 16$
Group 2, $\overline{X} = 42.70$, $s^2 = 49.00$, $n = 25$

Correlation between scores of the two sets of matched pairs is 0.49.

7. A random sample of 20 high-school seniors has been exposed to two experimental treatments designed to produce anxiety. After each treatment the students completed a test designed to measure degree of anxiety. Compute the correlation coefficient between the two anxiety scores of the 20 students, determine the value of *t,* and reach a decision regarding the null hypothesis of mean difference between anxiety level after treatments A and B. Use the 0.01 level of significance.

Student	Score After Treatment A	Score After Treatment B	Student	Score After Treatment A	Score After Treatment B
1	94	62	11	86	60
2	92	60	12	80	55
3	91	63	13	80	56
4	90	68	14	80	52
5	90	71	15	78	48
6	89	60	16	77	45
7	89	54	17	76	45
8	87	54	18	75	43
9	87	52	19	74	49
10	86	59	20	74	42

8. On the basis of a prediction that an experimental group will achieve a higher mean than the comparable control group, an educational investigator uses a one-tailed test to do a *t* analysis which yields a *t* of 1.80 in the predicted direction. At the 0.05 level of significance with 15 degrees of freedom, should the null hypothesis be accepted or rejected?

9. An educational investigator, after considering relevant theory and the results of empirical studies, predicts that boys will outperform girls on a test of mechanical aptitude. To test the null hypothesis, the investigator adopts a one-tailed t test and the 0.05 level of significance. What should the action be on the null hypothesis if, contrary to expectations, the girls perform so much better than the boys that a t value significant at the 0.001 level is yielded?

Single-Classification
Analysis of Variance

A statistical technique known as analysis of variance is routinely employed in the treatment of data collected for an investigation. This technique has several properties that make it particularly suitable for a variety of data analysis procedures. Still, to educators who lack much statistical training, analysis of variance may seem to be particularly baffling and a prime example of statistical symbol-juggling. In this chapter we begin the task of trying to remove the confusion surrounding this useful technique. At the outset, you should be aware that **analysis of variance (anova),** in its most basic form, is simply a statistical method of testing for significant differences between the means of two or more groups. Typically, these group means represent performance on a dependent variable as the result of treatment by one or more independent variables. The objective of the study is to determine the possible relationships among the dependent and independent variables.

Analysis of variance can be used to test the significance of mean differences between more than two groups simultaneously. Although, as you learned in Chapters 9 and 10, a *t* test is usually employed in testing mean differences between only two groups, it actually is a special case of the more general analysis-of-variance test for two groups or more. The same logic underlying Figure 9–4 in Chapter 9 is used here, but it is applied to more than one group. In analysis of variance, any number of populations is conceptualized, samples are drawn from each population, and inferences about the populations are made by analyzing the sample data.

Suppose an educational investigator who is working with three samples wants to determine whether the mean performance of any two of three populations from which the samples were drawn, A, B, and C, is significantly different. To do this, of course, three separate *t* tests could be computed. For example, a *t* test could be employed to assess the significance of mean differences first between groups A and B, then between groups B and C, and finally, between groups A and C. The number of *t*-test calculations in this case is not prohibitive. However, with a large number of groups, the task of computing individual *t* tests becomes more onerous. With ten groups, for instance, the number of separate *t* tests necessary in order to determine if there were significant mean differences between any two of the groups would rise to 45! Obviously, a statistical procedure that uses a single operation to determine whether any significant differences exist between the means of many groups has more merit.

Not only is it more convenient to use analysis of variance instead of a series of *t* tests, but there are some dangers associated with computing many individual *t* tests. For example, when many *t* tests have been computed, a few of the results may appear to be statistically significant by chance alone. Indeed, when many statistical tests have been computed, some results will appear to be significant even when they are not. For instance, if you were to draw 20 different pairs of samples from the *same* population and then compute *t* tests to see if the means of any pair are significantly different, by chance alone one of these pairs of means should be statistically different at the 0.05 level. You should be wary of giving too much importance to such results.

Another point you should be aware of is that investigators who use the analysis-of-variance statistical technique are primarily interested in *mean* differences rather than *variance* differences. Analysis of variance is in fact an ingenious method by which the statistician is able to draw conclusions about mean differences through the process of analyzing variances. This is where the name of the procedure, analysis of variance, comes from.

This very powerful statistical test can be modified for a number of more complex models. But in order to understand how more complex models function, you first need to examine the most basic form of the technique—**single-classification analysis of variance.** By single classification, we mean that the investigator has organized the data in such a fashion as to test for differences in a dependent (or criterion) variable among groups as they relate to a single independent variable.

For example, a college administrator might want to discover if there were any significant differences in general knowledge among students majoring in English, history, philosophy, or mathematics. In this instance, the independent variable would be the college major and the dependent variable would be students' general knowledge. The independent variable is often referred to as a **factor** in the analysis-of-variance design. In this example, the factor is college major, and there are four **factor levels** corresponding to the four majors under study. In single-classification designs, which are often referred to as single-factor or **one-way analysis-of-variance** designs, the investigator is concerned with only one independent variable at a time. If the administrator wants to study general knowledge in terms of other independent variables such as year in college, age, or gender, the students could be regrouped according to these factors. When additional factors are added to the design, a multiple-classification or factorial analysis-of-variance design is created. These models are examined in Chapters 13 and 14.

RATIONALE OF ANALYSIS OF VARIANCE

At first glance, it might appear unlikely that variances could be analyzed in such a way that anything of consequence could be learned about means. Because, as you learned in Chapter 2, variances are measures of variability and means are measures of central tendency, learning about central tendency by examining variability would seem to be a highly suspect process. But remember that in the discussion of a variance as the square of the standard deviation, we pointed out that these variability measures are comparable to an average of the distance of the raw scores in a distribution *from the mean* of that distribution. There is, then, a definite relationship between variances and means. It is this functional relationship that is used in determining the significance of mean differences by analyzing variances in a particular fashion.

In essence, the method employed in the analysis of variance is to compute the variances of the separate groups being tested for mean differences. The scores of all subjects in the subgroups are then artificially combined into one total group. This is done by regrouping, for analysis purposes, all of the scores in the several groups as though they were one, and then computing the variance of the total group. If the variance of the combined total group is approximately the same as the *average* variance of the separate subgroups, then there exists no significant difference between the means of the separate groups. If, on the other hand, the variance of the combined total group is considerably larger than the average variance of the separate subgroups, then a significant mean difference exists between two or more of the subgroups.

Graphic Illustration of the Method

If the explanation of the basic rationale of analysis of variance seems rather obscure, the graphic illustrations of hypothetical analysis-of-variance situations presented in Figures 11–1 and 11–2 should be helpful. The situations represented in these figures vary as to whether or not there exists any significant difference between two or more of the subgroup means, and the effect this has on the decision regarding the null hypothesis.

Four distributions are presented in Figure 11–1. Distributions A, B, and C represent sample groups that are to be tested for significance of mean differences. The distribution depicted at the bottom of the figure represents a regrouped pooling of the other three samples. This is accomplished by combining the scores of groups A, B, and C as though they formed one total group. Note the similarities and differences in the four distributions. The means of all four groups ($\overline{X} = 50$) are identical, as are the variances ($s^2 = 100$). The number of individuals in groups A, B, and C is 25 in each; in the pooled group, of course, there are 75 individuals. The pooled group can be thought of as being composed of three equivalently shaped groups, each with 25 individuals, placed one

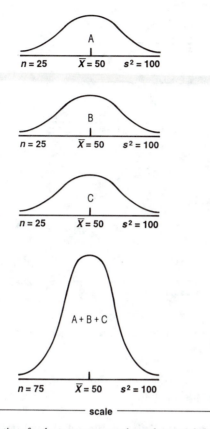

Fig. 11–1. Distributions for three separate samples and one pooled sample composed of the three subgroups considered as a total group.

on top of the other to form a new group of 75 individuals that is more dense but has exactly the same range as the three subgroups. This situation represents data in which absolutely no mean differences exist between any of the three separate groups and in which, therefore, the null hypothesis is tenable and should not be rejected.

Now contrast the situation presented in Figure 11–1 with the four distributions depicted in Figure 11–2. The latter figure represents a situation in which sizable mean differences exist between the separate groups, so the null hypothesis is quite untenable. As in Figure 11–1, distributions A, B, and C are to be tested for mean differences, and the lower distribution represents a pooled group composed of all 75 scores of the other three groups. As before, the variances of groups A, B, and C are equal ($s^2 = 100$). In Figure 11–2, however, the mean differences for these three groups are rather large, and the variation of the scores for the pooled group is radically different from that observed in Figure 11–1, where the pooled-group variance is equal to the average of the separate group variances. Although the average of the variances for groups A, B, and C is still 100 in Figure 11–2, the variance of the pooled group is 517. This situation exists because when scores from the three subgroups are incorporated in the total group, many of them are farther away from the total group's mean.

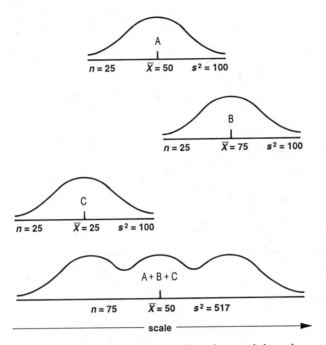

Fig. 11–2. Distributions for three separate samples and one pooled sample composed of the three subgroups considered as a total group.

The pooled distribution is more spread out, and therefore the variance of the pooled group is considerably larger than the average variance of the three subgroups.

In cases where the null hypothesis is tenable, relatively little difference between means will exist, so the average variance of the separate subgroups involved will be about the same size as the variance of the pooled group. In cases where the null hypothesis is untenable, differences between the means of the separate groups will be of a greater magnitude, so the variance of the pooled group will be considerably larger than the average variance of the subgroups. Statisticians have devised analysis of variance as a precise way of determining how great the difference between the variance of the pooled group and the average variance of the separate subgroups needs to be in order to reject the null hypothesis.

Comprehension of the relationship between separate-group mean differences and pooled-group variance is the key to understanding how analysis of variance can reveal important facts about mean differences by treating a measure of variability. If the relationship is not clear to you, we suggest that you reexamine the situations illustrated in Figures 11–1 and 11–2, as well as the accompanying discussion, before proceeding.[1]

---

1. An astute student may find our use of Figures 11–1 and 11–2 and the phrase "significant differences between group means" to be rather nonrigorous. These distributions depict *samples,* randomly drawn from populations with characteristics similar to those depicted for the samples. But when the statistician speaks of significant mean differences, the reference is to *population means.* Differences between sample means are, of course, evident merely upon inspection. Statistically speaking, then, we are testing the null hypothesis H_0: $\mu_1 = \mu_2 = \mu_3$. If this hypothesis is rejected, then we are accepting the alternative hypothesis H_1: $\mu_1 \neq \mu_2$ and/or $\mu_1 \neq \mu_3$ and/or $\mu_2 \neq \mu_3$.

Step-by Step Description of the Method

Analysis of variance is concerned with three different types of variance:

1. Between groups, the amount of variation resulting from mean differences between the separate groups.
2. Within groups, the amount of variation among individuals within the separate groups.
3. Total, the amount of variation present when the separate groups are considered as a single pooled group.

The method underlying analysis of variance involves computation of all three of these variances. A step-by-step description of the general technique used by statisticians is given in this section, and a more detailed explanation, with a computational example, will be given in companion Chapter 12.

First, the sums of squared deviations, or sums of squares (Σx^2), are computed individually for each of the separate groups (see Formula 2.5 and the discussion of the standard deviation in Chapter 2). These sums of squares are then added together to form a quantity referred to as the **within-groups sum of squares,** or the within sum of squares.

Second, the sum of the squares for the pooled group is calculated in the usual manner. This quantity is referred to as the **total-group sum of squares,** or the total sum of squares.

Third, the within-groups sum of squares is subtracted from the total sum of squares. The resulting difference is called the **between-groups sum of squares,** or the between sum of squares.[2] Because the between-groups sum of squares represents the amount of variability in the pooled group that was not present already in the separate groups, it is attributable to the differences in means of the subgroups. The larger the between-groups sum of squares, therefore, the greater the difference between the subgroup means. Conversely, the smaller the between-groups sum of squares, the less divergent are the subgroup means.

Fourth, the within-groups and between-groups sums of squares are divided by the degrees of freedom associated with them. You may recall from the discussion of point estimation of variance in Chapter 4 that, when a sum of squares is divided by the degrees of freedom associated with it, the result is referred to as a variance estimate (or, as it is sometimes called, a mean square). In analysis of variance, the term *mean square* is used to describe the quantities yielded when the within-groups and between-groups sums of squares are divided by their respective degrees of freedom. For the within-groups sum of squares, the degrees of freedom (df) are the number of individuals (n) less the number of groups (k); for the between-groups sum of squares, the degrees of freedom are the number of groups less 1. The **within-groups mean square,** or within mean square, is obtained by dividing the within sum of squares by $n - k$, and the **between-groups mean square,** or between mean square, is obtained by dividing the between sum of squares by $k - 1$.

---

2. It is often easier to calculate the between-groups sum of squares directly and then subtract it from the total sum of squares to obtain the within-groups sum of squares. This is one of the computational sequences described in Chapter 12.

Fifth, the between-groups mean square is divided by the within-groups mean square, which is often called the **error term.** The result of this division yields a value referred to as *F.* (The use of the *F* ratio in testing homogeneity of variance was discussed in Chapters 9 and 10.) The size of the *F* value hinges on the relative magnitude of the two mean squares involved. As we have noted, the between-groups sum of squares becomes larger as the differences between group means increase. This is also true of the between-groups mean square. That is, the greater the magnitude of the differences between subgroup means, the greater the magnitude of the between-groups mean square. Accordingly, *the magnitude of* F *tends to increase as the differences among the group means increase.* This assumes that the within-groups mean square remains relatively constant. Reexamining the graphic illustrations presented in Figures 11–1 and 11–2 should help you see that the within-groups mean squares in the two situations represented would remain the same in both cases.

Sixth, the significance of *F* is interpreted from a table for the sampling distribution of *F* (Table F in the Appendix). If the obtained *F* value is sufficiently large to be statistically significant, the null hypothesis is considered untenable. The conclusion is that there are significant differences between the means of two or more of the populations under investigation.

The steps in the general method of analysis of variance can be summarized as follows:

1. Compute the within-groups sum of squares by totaling the sum of squares of each subgroup.
2. Compute the total sum of squares for the pooled group.
3. Determine the between-groups sum of squares by subtracting the within-groups sum of squares from the total sum of squares.
4. Divide the within-groups sum of squares and between-groups sum of squares by the appropriate degrees of freedom to obtain the within-groups and between-groups mean squares.
5. Obtain the *F* value by dividing the within-groups mean square into the between-groups mean square.
6. Interpret the significance of *F* from a table of the *F* distribution.

ADDING A PRIORI AND POST HOC COMPARISONS

If an analysis of variance has shown the null hypothesis to be untenable, that is, the existence of significant mean differences between two or more groups has been demonstrated, the investigator is not yet able to determine *which* means are significantly different from which other means. Fortunately, methods for carrying out further analysis to determine the exact location of mean differences have been developed.

For example, consider a simple single-classification analysis-of-variance design with five levels—three treatment groups and two control groups. The procedures outlined in this and the following chapter are designed to yield an *F* ratio which answers the question: Are there significant differences among all five groups? If the ratio is found to be significant, the next question usually is: Specifically, *where* are these significant differences? A descriptive analysis of the mean differences can be misleading. The significant F ratio may be due merely to the discrepancy between the highest and lowest treatment means, or it may be due to the discrepancy between the combined effects of the three treatment groups as compared with the two control groups.

An investigator who hypothesizes further mean comparisons at the outset (**a priori comparisons**) can extend the analysis-of-variance computations to include specific **mean contrasts,** each of which can be tested for significance. If the investigator wants to examine mean differences after the fact (**post hoc comparisons**), less powerful computational routines can be used that will systematically test all possible pairs of treatment differences. Additional information on these two types of comparisons and examples of computational procedures for them will be given in Chapter 12, which also introduces a number of new terms related to these procedures.

INTERPRETING *F* AS A RATIO OF SYSTEMATIC VARIANCE TO ERROR VARIANCE

Some statisticians refer to the between-groups mean square as reflecting systematic variability, whereas the within-groups mean square reflects error variability. There is no "mistake" about the presence of variance within groups, however. The term *error* relates to the fact that the investigator has made no attempt to control for individual differences (variance) within each group, such as by adding other independent variables to the design.

For example, suppose the three subgroups in Figure 11-2 represent students instructed under three different computer-assisted instructional sequences for the same course content. An investigator who expected that the only reason for variability in achievement-test scores (the dependent variable) was the differing computer-based programs would also expect all the individuals in group A to receive a score of 50; those in group B, a score of 75; and those in group C, a score of 25. In other words, no variation whatsoever would be expected within treatment groups. The fact that there is such variability may be due to any number of reasons—prior achievement level, scholastic aptitude, gender, socioeconomic status, attitude toward computers, unreliability in measuring achievement, attention level, health, and so forth. All these different sources of variance are *confounded* in the within-groups source of variance. Because these extraneous (but not necessarily irrelevant) sources of variance are not controlled, they are labeled as the within-groups error variance, or unsystematic variance.

Thus the between-groups or **systematic variance** reflects the variability due to the independent variable—in this example, the differences among the three methods of computer-assisted instruction. The unsystematic, within-groups, or **error variance** reflects the variability due to all the remaining uncontrolled factors. To the extent that the systematic variance is less than or equal to the unsystematic or error variance, the investigator would be hard put to claim any real differences due to treatment conditions. The ratio of the between-groups mean square to the within-groups mean square is exactly a reflection of this comparison. When this F ratio is 1.0, there is no more controlled variability than uncontrolled variability; F ratios of 1.0 (or less) can never, in practice, be significant. When the F ratio is sufficiently greater than 1.0 for a given amount of data (or degrees of freedom), the investigator can begin to make a meaningful claim that the results of the experimental treatments made a real difference.

ASSUMPTIONS UNDERLYING ANALYSIS OF VARIANCE

As with other statistical techniques, there are certain assumptions underlying analysis of variance that ought to be satisfied if the method is to be used. From a theoretical viewpoint, these assumptions must be rigorously observed so the technique yields information that is accurately interpretable. There is increasing evidence, however, that despite fairly significant departures from strict theoretical assumptions, analysis of variance is sufficiently robust that the results it yields can be interpreted meaningfully.

The three major assumptions of analysis of variance are random sampling, homogeneity of variances, and normal distribution. In the field of education, it is often difficult to satisfy the condition that the measures within each level or classification must represent random samples. Nevertheless, it is usually possible to approximate random sampling, or at least to rule out the possibility that an obviously biased subgroup is representing a population. For example, there would be less probability of bias in a school where students were assigned to experimental classes on an alphabetical basis than in one where students chose their own teachers or were assigned to classes on the basis of their previous grades.

The assumption that the variances within the populations from which the subgroups are sampled are homogeneous (that is, equal) is usually true when the experimental data were gathered from individuals who had been randomly assigned to subgroups. In any case, the assumption of subgroup homogeneity of variance can be tested by several techniques described in Chapter 12.

The third assumption applies to many statistical techniques: The populations from which the subgroup samples were drawn should be normally distributed.

Investigators must consider these assumptions before choosing to use the technique of analysis of variance. But if the data do not depart from the theoretical assumptions too drastically, it is likely that the investigator can use the technique without fear that the results will be open to spurious interpretations.

USE OF ANALYSIS OF VARIANCE
IN EDUCATIONAL INVESTIGATIONS

Educators who understand the rationale and method of analysis of variance find it useful as a statistical technique in various types of investigations. One common use is to test for mean differences among two or more groups of individuals exposed to different experimental treatments. For example, suppose Mr. Miles, a program developer, wants to contrast the achievement of three groups of college students who were instructed in three essentially different ways. In the first group, conventional lecture-discussion techniques were used; in the second, a problem-based method of teaching; and in the third, a nondirective approach. If Mr. Miles can demonstrate that the composition of the three groups was more or less comparable with respect to variables such as aptitude that are considered relevant to achievement, he could use the results of a final achievement examination administered to all three groups to determine whether their performances were significantly different. He would apply analysis of variance to the examination scores of the three groups to test the null hypothesis of no mean differences among the groups.

Another common use of analysis of variance in education is in test development. Suppose Miss Chen, a measurement specialist, has designed a new test instrument and administered it to a large, normative sample of high school students. She categorizes the students into four subgroups on the basis of year in high school, a variable that she thinks will be related to performance on the test. Then she uses analysis of variance to test for mean differences in the performance of the subgroups on the new test. If, through the magnitude of the F value, the analysis reveals that there are no significant mean differences in performance on the instrument by the four groups, Miss Chen would probably conclude that although she considered year in high school as being potentially relevant to test performance, it appears to have no such relationship. If, however, the subgroups perform at significantly different levels on the test, she would conclude that the variable is indeed related to test performance. She would therefore prepare separate norms taking year in high school into consideration. With separate norms for the four groups, for example, a raw score of 78 might fall at the 35th percentile for juniors and at the 51st percentile for freshmen.

School administrators rely on analysis of variance in making numerous decisions. For example, suppose Mrs. Newcomer, an elementary school principal, needs to determine whether pupils from the several rather distinct socioeconomic areas in the school district differ to any degree with respect to reading readiness. To use analysis of variance in determining this information, she would establish the socioeconomic status of the pupils by a recognized sociological technique and set up the necessary number of socioeconomic groups. Then she could have a reading readiness test administered to all the pupils and categorize their scores into the appropriate socioeconomic groups. By applying analysis of variance to the performance of the groups on the test, Mrs. Newcomer could discern if the pupils in the various socioeconomic categories actually exhibited any significant differences in reading readiness.

EXAMPLE OF AN ANALYSIS-OF-VARIANCE REPORT

To summarize this introduction to single-classification analysis of variance, we will examine a typical report of an analysis of variance as it might be described in the educational literature. A simple, hypothetical analysis-of-variance summary is presented in Table 11.1, similar to what you might find in any educational journal reporting research results. While the form of the table would vary slightly in the various journals, most elements would be comparable to those in this table.

In considering an analysis-of-variance table such as Table 11.1, you

Table 11.1   Analysis of Variance of Final Achievement Performance of Five Groups of Ten Students Taught by Different Instructional Methods

Source of Variation	Degrees of Freedom	Sum of Squares	Mean Square	F
Between groups	4	19.72	4.93	0.873
Within groups	45	254.30	5.65	
Total	49	274.02		

would probably first refer to the *F* value. This quantity, the end result of the entire analysis, indicates whether the null hypothesis should or should not be rejected. In this table the *F* value is only 0.873, which is not statistically significant. When *F is* significant, an asterisk is usually placed on the value and the level of significance (or probability) is indicated below the table. Because *F* values of less than 1 are never significant, in this example you would not even find it necessary to consult the *F* table in order to conclude that the null hypothesis cannot be rejected.

In analysis-of-variance tables the heading "source of variation" identifies the three ways of viewing variation that we have discussed: *between groups,* or the amount of variation resulting from mean differences between the separate groups; *within groups,* or the amount of variation between individuals within the separate groups; and *total,* or the amount of variation present when the separate groups are considered as one pooled group. Remember that the within-groups variation is essentially the variance that is left over when the between-groups variation is subtracted from the total variation.

The mean squares are obtained by dividing the sums of squares for the three sources of variation by their respective degrees of freedom. It is possible to divide the total sum of squares by the total degrees of freedom in order to obtain a total mean square, but this is rarely done because the total mean square is not used to derive the value of *F*. The *F* value is the quotient yielded by dividing the within-groups mean square into the between-groups mean square. This value is subsequently interpreted for statistical significance from the *F* table. Remember, however, that statistical significance might not mean practical significance in terms of actual educational situations.

You should find additional insights into the nature of single-classification analysis of variance in the next chapter, which includes the actual computation of an analysis of variance. For more extensive discussions of this important technique, see the selected readings listed at the end of this chapter.

■   ■   ■

REVIEW

Single-classification analysis of variance provides educational investigators with a technique for simultaneously testing whether the means of two or more population groups are significantly different. This statistical technique capitalizes on the integral relationship between the mean and the variance so that, by analyzing variances of several groups, conclusions can be drawn regarding the similarity of the means of those groups.

You are urged to study the graphic illustration of the logic underlying this important technique that is presented in Figures 11–1 and 11–2. Note that when the null hypothesis is tenable, the average variance in the subgroups will be about the same as the variance in a pooled group representing all scores. When the null hypothesis is untenable, the variance in the pooled groups will markedly exceed the average variance of the subgroups.

Analysis of variance has the advantage of comparing means of many groups in a single statistical test. The F value yielded by this test is interpreted for its level of probability in a table of the F distribution. Typically, however, further tests using a priori or post hoc comparisons are required to locate the exact nature of the statistical differences among means.

TERMS TO KNOW

Listed in order of presentation in chapter:

analysis of variance (anova)
single-classification analysis of variance
factor
factor levels
one-way analysis of variance
within-groups sum of squares
total-group sum of squares
between-groups sum of squares
within-groups mean square
between-groups mean square
error term
a priori comparisons
mean contrasts
post hoc comparisons
systematic variance
error variance

EXERCISES

1. If a statistician makes a few preliminary calculations in a single-classification analysis of variance problem and discovers that the average variances of the five subgroups involved are almost identical to the pooled group variance formed by artificially combining all five sets of data, will the null hypothesis be rejected?

2. Would an investigator who wants to test for mean differences among four groups probably find it more economical to use a series of *t* tests or an analysis of variance? What would the investigator need to do to pinpoint the location of significant differences among groups?

3. Two single-classification analyses of variance have just been computed by an educational research worker. In analysis A the between-groups mean square is relatively large; in analysis B the between-groups mean square is close to zero. In which analysis is the null hypothesis more likely to be rejected, that is, in which analysis are there apt to be significant mean differences?

4. Once a significant *F* value has been yielded from a single-classification analysis of variance involving eight subgroups, can the investigator then identify by inspection the particular group means that are significantly different?

5. If the within-groups mean square is markedly larger than the between-groups mean square, are there significant differences between the group means in an analysis of variance?

SELECTED READINGS

Edwards, Allen L. *Experimental Design in Psychological Research.* New York: Harper & Row, 1985, chap. 6.

Guilford, J. P., and Fruchter, Benjamin. *Fundamental Statistics in Psychology and Education.* New York: McGraw-Hill, 1978, chap. 13.

Kirk, Roger E. *Elementary Statistics.* Monterey, CA: Brooks/Cole, 1984, chap. 16.

Pagano, Robert R. *Understanding Statistics in the Behavioral Sciences.* St. Paul, MN: West Publishing, 1986, chaps. 16 and 17.

Shavelson, Richard J. *Statistical Reasoning for the Behavioral Sciences.* Boston: Allyn & Bacon, 1988, chaps. 14 and 16.

Walker, Helen M., and Lev, Joseph. *Statistical Inference.* New York: Holt, Rinehart & Winston, 1953, chap. 9.

Single-Classification Analysis of Variance

▪ *computation procedures*

The computation of analysis of variance is a rather time-consuming process, but it is also quite simple and straightforward. In order to obtain the *F* value by which the null hypothesis can be assessed, the following quantities are needed:

1. The sums of squares for the total group, between groups, and within groups.
2. The degrees of freedom for the within groups and between groups.
3. The mean squares for the between groups and within groups.

In showing how each of these quantities is calculated, we will refer to the hypothetical sample data presented in Table 12.1. These data represent the achievement-test scores of three groups of students taught by different instructional methods. Though there are five students in each group in this example, equal numbers are not necessary.

A CHECK FOR HOMOGENEITY OF VARIANCE

As you learned in Chapter 11, one of the three assumptions underlying analysis of variance (in addition to random sampling and normal distribution

Table 12.1 Raw Scores (X) and Squared Raw Scores (X^2) on a Final Achievement Test for Students Taught by Three Instructional Methods

	Method 1		Method 2		Method 3
X	X^2	X	X^2	X	X^2
7	49	4	16	2	4
10	100	6	36	2	4
10	100	7	49	3	9
11	121	9	81	7	49
12	144	9	81	6	36
ΣX 50		35		20	
ΣX^2	514		263		102
	$\overline{X} = 10$		$\overline{X} = 7$		$\overline{X} = 4$

for the data) is that the variances within the populations in the analysis are not significantly different (i.e., are homogeneous). It is good practice to check homogeneity of variance at the outset of the analysis.

As we showed in Chapter 10, a simple first test of homogeneity of variance involves calculating the individual variances of the subgroups and using these as estimates of the corresponding population variances. To obtain F, the smallest sample variance is divided into the largest sample variance (see Formula 10.2). The F value then is interpreted for statistical significance using an F table (Table F in the Appendix). If the F yielded by this operation is not statistically significant, the population variances can be considered homogeneous. If the F is significant, a test of homogeneity of variance such as Bartlett's test[1] should be applied to the data, because in some instances the extreme variances will appear heterogeneous but the total set of variances, when tested, will prove to be sufficiently homogeneous.

In the computational example based on the data in Table 12.1 which is used in this chapter, the variances of the three methods groups are $s_1^2 = 3.5$, $s_2^2 = 4.5$, and $s_3^2 = 5.5$. Dividing the smallest into the largest variance yields $F = 5.5/3.5 = 1.57$, which is not statistically significant. Accordingly, the assumption of homogeneity of variance is considered to be satisfied.

COMPUTATION OF SUMS OF SQUARES

Total Sum of Squares

In order to calculate the total sum of squares, the scores in all of the subgroups must be viewed as representing a single set of measurements. The total sum of squares can be computed by using the standard raw-score formula for sums of squares (Formula 2.5 in Chapter 2), as follows:

$$\text{Total SS} = \Sigma X^2 - \frac{(\Sigma X)^2}{n}$$

1. This test was described in M. S. Bartlett, "Some Examples of Statistical Methods of Research in Agriculture and Applied Biology," *Journal of Royal Statistical Society Supplement,* no. 4 (1937), pp. 137–70. Other, less complex tests can be found in Roger E. Kirk, *Experimental Design: Procedures for the Behavioral Sciences* (Belmont, CA: Brooks/Cole, 1982), pp. 77–79.

Substituting the data from Table 12.1, the total sum of squares would be computed as follows:

$$\text{Total SS} = 879 - \frac{(105)^2}{15}$$

$$= 144$$

Between Sum of Squares

To find the between-groups sum of squares, Formula 12.1 can be used:

$$\text{Between SS} = \sum \frac{(\Sigma X_g)^2}{n_g} - \frac{(\Sigma X)^2}{n} \tag{12.1}$$

where:

n_g = the number of individuals in the group
n = the total number of groups
$\Sigma(\Sigma X_g)^2/n_g$ = the sum of each group's raw scores squared and divided by n_g
$(\Sigma X)^2/n$ = the sum of all raw scores squared and divided by n

Substituting the data in Table 12.1, the between-groups sum of squares is computed as follows:

$$\text{Between SS} = \frac{(50)^2}{5} + \frac{(35)^2}{5} + \frac{(20)^2}{5} - \frac{(105)^2}{15}$$

$$= 90$$

Within Sum of Squares

Having obtained the total sum of squares and the between-groups sum of squares, the within-groups sum of squares can be readily found by subtracting the between SS from the total SS. Because of the possibility of making a computational error in calculating the total and between SS, however, it is often desirable to actually compute the within SS by Formula 12.2:

$$\text{Within SS} = \sum \left[\Sigma X_g{}^2 - \frac{(\Sigma X_g)^2}{n_g} \right] \tag{12.2}$$

Here, the raw-score sum of squares formula is applied individually to the several subgroups, and the resulting quantities are then summed. In this computation, each group in the example is identified by a differentiating subscript (1, 2, or 3), and the individual sums of squares are computed as follows:

$$\Sigma x_1{}^2 = 514 - \frac{(50)^2}{5} = 14$$

$$\Sigma x_2{}^2 = 263 - \frac{(35)^2}{5} = 18$$

$$\Sigma x_3{}^2 = 102 - \frac{(20)^2}{5} = 22$$

Adding these three sums of squares together, $14 + 18 + 22 = 54$, yields the within sum of squares.

This same value would have been obtained by subtracting the between SS from the total SS, $144 - 90 = 54$, because of the following property of the total SS:

$$\text{Total SS} = \text{Between SS} + \text{Within SS}$$

COMPUTATION OF DEGREES OF FREEDOM

The degrees of freedom for between groups and within groups are needed in order to obtain the between-groups and within-groups mean squares. The total degrees of freedom is useful as a computational check, since it should equal the sum of the degrees of freedom for the between- and within-groups.

As you learned in Chapter 4, the total degrees of freedom is equal to the number of individuals less 1 $(n - 1)$. Similarly, as you learned in Chapter 11, the between-groups degrees of freedom is equal to the number of groups less 1 $(k - 1)$, and a simple method of obtaining the within-groups degrees of freedom is to subtract the number of groups from the number of individuals $(n - k)$. In the example used in this chapter, the total degrees of freedom would be $15 - 1 = 14$; the between degrees of freedom would be $3 - 1 = 2$; and the within degrees of freedom would be $15 - 3 = 12$.

COMPUTATION OF MEAN SQUARES

To compute the between-groups mean square, the between sum of squares is divided by the between degrees of freedom, as follows:

$$\text{Between mean square} = \frac{90}{2} = 45.0$$

Similarly, the within-groups mean square is computed by dividing the within sum of squares by the within degrees of freedom:

$$\text{Within mean square} = \frac{54}{12} = 4.5$$

COMPUTATION AND INTERPRETATION OF F

The value of F is obtained by dividing the between-groups mean square by the within-groups mean square, as in Formula 12.3:

$$F = \frac{\text{Between groups mean square}}{\text{Within groups mean square}} \qquad (12.3)$$

Substituting in this formula:

$$F = \frac{45.0}{4.5} = 10.0$$

Once the F value has been obtained, it can be interpreted for statistical significance in order to determine whether or not the null hypothesis should be rejected. The F table (Table F in the Appendix) indicates whether the obtained F value is sufficiently large to be significant at the 0.05 or 0.01 levels. These values of F are located in the table by employing the between and within degrees of freedom that were used to obtain the F value. If the obtained F is equal to or larger than the tabled values of F, then the obtained F is considered to be statistically significant. Accordingly, the null hypothesis is rejected.

Table F is used by (1) locating the within degrees of freedom in the column labeled n_1 at the left edge of the table, (2) locating the degrees of freedom corresponding to the between degrees of freedom in the horizontal row labeled n_2, and (3) determining where the row and column intersect. The figure in lightface type at the point of intersection is the value of F that is significant at the 0.05 level, and the figure in boldface type is the value of F significant at the 0.01 level.

In the example of the data given in Table 12.1 for scores of students taught by three different instructional methods, the within degrees of freedom (12) is found in the left-hand column of Table F, and the between degrees of freedom (2) is located in the row at the top of the table. At the point of intersection of this row and column, the figure in lightface type is 3.88, and the figure in boldface type is 6.93. Because the obtained F value of 10.0 exceeds the value of 6.93, it can be concluded that the value of F is significant beyond the 0.01 level. The null hypothesis that there exists no significant difference in the achievement performance of the three groups therefore should be rejected.

If the obtained F value had been as large as or larger than the value in lightface type but not as large as the value in boldface type, then the F would have been significant at the 0.05 level but not at the 0.01 level. If the obtained F were smaller than both of the tabled values, then the null hypothesis cannot be rejected. An F value that is close to but does not reach the magnitude of the tabled values suggests the advisability of further investigation of the problem.

When more groups than the three in the example we are using are involved, the sums of squares for more subgroups must be calculated in order to obtain the within sum of squares. For a further discussion of the computation of single-classification analysis of variance, see the selected readings section at the end of Chapter 11.

A PRIORI AND POST HOC COMPARISONS

The preceding computations for the example being used in this chapter, based on the data for three groups of students taught by different instructional methods (Table 12.1), have shown that the obtained F is significant at the 0.01 level. It can be concluded, therefore, that the achievement performance of students taught by these different instructional methods does vary.

From a purely descriptive standpoint, method 1 ($\overline{X} = 10$) appears to be superior to method 2 ($\overline{X} = 7$), which in turn appears superior to method 3 ($\overline{X} = 4$). From an inferential standpoint, however, it is not possible to be sure of exactly which differences are statistically significant. All that is known to this point is that, overall, there are statistically significant differences between two or more methods or combinations of methods. For more exact information, further statistical tests are needed.

A Priori Comparisons

An investigator who has a conceptual or theoretical basis for hypothesizing specific comparisons in advance of a study can use the method of a priori comparisons to determine whether or not a statistically significant F pertains to these initial hypotheses.

Suppose in our example that method 3 was the conventional instructional method, and it was being used as a *control* against which *experimental* methods 1 and 2 were to be judged. Two important questions of comparison or *contrast* are immediately suggested:

1. Are methods 1 and 2 significantly different from each other?
2. Are methods 1 and 2, together, significantly different from control method 3?

Statistical answers to these questions can be provided by performing what are essentially *t*-test-like comparisons.

These comparisons involve the concept of **contrast coefficients.** In general, the number of useful a priori comparisons or contrasts that can be made is equal to the degrees of freedom for the between-groups source of variance $(k-1)$. In our example, because $k=3$, the investigator can construct as many as two contrasts of potential importance. The construction of contrasts is done through the use of cleverly selected multiplicative coefficients that create the contrast of interest. For example, the three contrast coefficients 1, –1, and 0 are multiplied by the means for methods 1, 2, and 3, respectively. To create the contrast necessary to answer the first question above, add the resultant products:

$$(1)(10) + (-1)(7) + (0)(4) = 10 - 7 = 3$$

This is the mean difference between methods 1 and 2. The second question can be answered by contrasting the average of the means for methods 1 and 2 with the mean of method 3. This is accomplished using the contrast coefficients 1/2, 1/2, and –1, as follows:

$$(1/2)(10) + (1/2)(7) + (-1)(4) = 8.5 - 4 = 4.5$$

This is the mean difference between method 3 and the average of methods 1 and 2. To avoid fractions, use of the coefficients 1, 1, and –2 and the contrast $(1)(10) + (1)(7) + (-2)(4) = 9$ would result in the identical significance test.

To illustrate the general principles at work here, some rather cumbersome notation must be introduced. We will let c_g stand for the contrast coefficient for any group, g. In our example, therefore, $c_1 = 1$, $c_2 = -1$, and $c_3 = 0$ for the first contrast of interest, and $c_1 = 1$, $c_2 = 1$, and $c_3 = -2$ for the second contrast of interest. We will also let C stand for the *value* of any given contrast or comparison of interest. Then, Formula 12.4 can be used to yield the value of C:

$$C = \Sigma c_g X_g \qquad (12.4)$$

According to the computations above, $C = 3$ for the first contrast and $C = 9$ for the second contrast of interest.

Whatever contrast coefficients are selected, they should obviously pinpoint the comparison of interest, and they must meet the following mathematical criterion:

$$\Sigma c_g = 0$$

that is, the sum of the contrast coefficients must equal zero for any particular contrast of interest. This is indeed the case for the above two contrasts: $(1) + (-1) + (0) = 0$ and $(1) + (1) + (-2) = 0$.

One other complication: To get the most out of these a priori comparisons, contrasts should be statistically *independent*—that is, each contrast (and each degree of freedom) should represent a unique portion of the between-groups variance. This would appear to be the case in the above two contrasts, because the first has nothing to do with method 3 and the second has nothing to do with contrasting methods 1 and 2. If we let the notation d_g represent the contrast coefficients for a second comparison of interest, then two comparisons or contrasts will be statistically independent when the following condition is present:

$$\Sigma c_g \, d_g = 0$$

Applying this formula to the two contrasts in the example above:

$$(1)(1) + (-1)(1) + (0)(2) = (1) + (-1) = 0$$

This verifies the independence of the two contrasts.[2]

To test the statistical significance of any given contrast, first the **contrast sum of squares** is computed, using Formula 12.5:

$$\text{Contrast SS} = \frac{C^2}{\Sigma c_g^2 / n_g} \tag{12.5}$$

In our example, the contrast SS for the first question (Are methods 1 and 2 different from each other?) is computed as follows, using the contrast for the mean difference between methods 1 and 2 in the numerator:

$$\text{Contrast SS} = \frac{3^2}{1^2/5 + -1^2/5 + 0^2/5}$$

$$= \frac{9}{2/5}$$

$$= 22.5$$

For the second question (Are methods 1 and 2 combined different from method 3?), the contrast SS is computed using the contrast for the mean difference between method 3 and the average of methods 1 and 2:

$$\text{Contrast SS} = \frac{9^2}{1^2/5 + 1^2/5 + -2^2/5}$$

---

2. If group sizes are unequal, this formula is: $\Sigma c_g d_g / n_g = 0$

$$= \frac{81}{6/5}$$

$$= 67.5$$

Notice that the sum of the squares for both of these contrasts (22.5 + 67.5) equals the between sum of squares (90) for this study. This is not a coincidence. The construction of contrasts is, in fact, based on partitioning the between-groups variance into portions reflecting the specific comparisons of interest. Because these two contrasts are independent and only 2 degrees of freedom are available, all the between SS is accounted for and utilized in these comparisons. You should be able to see from inspection that much more of the between SS is accounted for by the second contrast, suggesting that most of the significant difference between groups is due to the difference between the experimental methods on the one hand and the conventional or control method on the other.

To verify this observation, an *F* test can be computed in a form analogous to Formula 12.3. Because only 1 degree of freedom is involved in any contrast, the mean square for the contrast equals the contrast SS. An *F* ratio based on 1 and $n - k$ degrees of freedom is therefore formed, using Formula 12.6:

$$F = \frac{\text{Contrast SS}}{\text{Within groups mean square}} \qquad (12.6)$$

For the first contrast of interest, $F = 22.5/4.5 = 5.0$ on 1 and 12 degrees of freedom. This is barely significant at the 0.05 level (see Table F, column 1 and row 12). The second contrast yields $F = 65.7/4.5 = 14.6$ on 1 and 12 degrees of freedom, which is significant beyond the 0.01 level. Although the difference between experimental methods 1 and 2 reaches an acceptable level of statistical significance, a *highly* significant result is obtained for the experimental vs. control comparison.

Post Hoc Comparisons

While a priori comparisons are useful when the investigator has a basis for hypothesizing specific comparisons prior to an investigation, this condition is not always met. In such cases, investigations are undertaken from a more *exploratory* viewpoint. When an exploratory study yields a significant *F* for the between-groups variation, the investigator may want to explore the differences among all possible pairs of group means, rather than testing only a few specific comparisons.

There are important reasons for supporting this decision, statistically as well as conceptually. In a priori comparisons, each significance test is performed independently at a chosen level of significance (0.05, 0.01, 0.001, etc.). The more such tests are done, however, the greater are the chances of a Type I error (see Chapter 4). This risk is justified as long as there are good conceptual or theoretical reasons behind each test. Exploratory studies, by their very nature, proceed by testing all possible differences among groups. Therefore, in order to minimize the chances of Type I errors, the statistical methods used must be more *conservative,* that is, they must make it more difficult to reject the null hypothesis with respect to any mean-difference comparison.

There are many post hoc comparison methods from which to choose. Basically, they range from highly conservative statistical tests (e.g., the Scheffé method), to more moderately conservative tests (e.g., the Newman-Keuls method), to even less conservative tests (e.g., the Duncan method).[3] Among the simpler, more moderately conservative procedures is the Tukey **honestly signifi-cant differences (HSD) method.** Performing this test requires nothing more than looking up a *t*-like value called the **studentized range statistic** in a distribution table. This statistic is then used in a formula that provides a critical value that must be exceeded by any mean difference in order for it to be statistically significant, at least at the selected level of significance.

Table G in the Appendix contains values of *q,* the studentized range statistic, for tests at either the 0.05 or 0.01 levels of significance. The *q* value for a given test is located at the intersection of the appropriate row and column of Table G. The row corresponds to the number of degrees of freedom for the within mean square $(n - k)$, and the column corresponds to the number of groups (k). Once *q* is obtained, the **critical value** (CV) that any mean difference must exceed for significance is computed using Formula 12.7:

$$CV = q \sqrt{\frac{\text{Within mean square}}{\text{Number of scores in a group}}} \qquad (12.7)$$

If the numbers of scores in the groups differ, the denominator in this formula must be replaced by an "average" number of scores.[4]

To illustrate with the example in this chapter, recall that the within mean square is 4.5, the number of scores in a group is 5, the degrees of freedom for the within mean square is 12, and the number of groups is 3. In Table G, these data indicate a *q* value of 3.77 at the 0.05 significance level. Substituting the appropriate information into Formula 12.7, the following critical value is obtained:

$$CV = 3.77 \sqrt{\frac{4.5}{5}}$$

$$= (3.77)(0.95)$$

$$= 3.58$$

---

3. For a good discussion of the comparative advantages and disadvantages of the various post hoc comparison methods, see B. J. Winer, *Statistical Principles in Experimental Design* (New York: McGraw-Hill, 1971), pp. 196–201. A comprehensive inventory of multiple comparison methods generally, and post hoc procedures in particular, can be found in A. J. Klockars and G. Sax, *Multiple Comparisons* (Beverly Hills, CA: Sage, 1986).

4. The "average" for groups with different numbers of scores in Formula 12.7 is derived from the following equation:

$$\text{"average"} = k / \Sigma 1/n_g$$

Suppose, in the example, that the groups represented by methods 1, 2, and 3 had 5, 6, and 7 scores, respectively. This "average" number of scores per group would be calculated as follows:

$$\text{"average"} = 3/[(1/5) + (1/6) + (1/7)] = 3/0.51 = 5.88$$

Thus, in the example we are using, any mean difference that exceeds 3.58 is statistically significant, at least at the 0.05 level. More specifically, there are three possible mean differences in this investigation: method 1 vs. method 2 for a difference of $10 - 7 = 3$; method 1 vs. method 3 for a difference of $10 - 4 = 6$; and method 2 vs. method 3 for a difference of $7 - 4 = 3$. Comparing each of these differences with the critical value (3.58), it is clear that only the difference between the first experimental method (1) and the control method (3) is significant.

■   ■   ■

REVIEW

Before computations can be undertaken in single-classification analysis of variance, it is good practice to check the assumption of homogeneity of variance. This can be done by the simple test of dividing the smallest subgroup variance into the largest subgroup variance and interpreting the quotient F value for statistical significance from the F table.

To compute the F value by which the null hypothesis of subgroup mean differences is tested, the following quantities must be calculated: (1) the total, between, and within sums of squares, (2) the between and within degrees of freedom, and (3) the between and within mean squares. F is yielded by dividing the within mean square into the between mean square, and the value is checked for statistical significance with the use of the F table.

Because an overall F test of the differences between group means does not pinpoint where the specific differences are, further comparisons are necessary. If specific comparisons are hypothesized prior to the study, then a priori comparison procedures can be used in further significance testing. However, if the investigator wishes to explore all possible group comparisons, post hoc methods for testing statistical significance are more appropriate.

Computations for a priori comparisons involve the calculation of contrast coefficients, the contrast sum of squares, and an F ratio that is interpreted for significance from the F table. Post hoc comparisons, which are exploratory in nature, use more conservative statistical methods to test all possible differences among groups. The Tukey HSD method uses a value called the studentized range statistic which is interpreted for significance using a special distribution table.

TERMS TO KNOW

Listed in order of presentation in chapter:

contrast coefficients
contrast sum of squares
honestly significant differences (HSD) method
studentized range statistic (q)
critical value

EXERCISES

1. With a between-groups SS of 1,000 ($df = 100$) and a total SS of 2,500 ($df = 105$), determine the F value for a test of mean difference among six groups and decide whether the null hypothesis should be rejected at the 0.01 level.

2. Decide by using Table F whether the following F values would be significant beyond the 0.05 level:

   (a) $F_{7,24} = 3.46$ (b) $F_{6,200} = 2.49$ (c) $F_{7,514} = 1.12$

3. Decide by using Table F whether the following F values would be significant beyond the 0.01 level:

   (a) $F_{14,100} = 2.34$ (b) $F_{2,40} = 84.37$ (c) $F_{9,30} = 5.42$

4. For the following three groups of scores, find the total sum of squares, the within-groups sum of squares, and the between-groups sum of squares:

Group X	Group Y	Group Z
62	60	59
60	60	49
50	58	49
48	53	47
47	49	42

5. Can the variances of the populations from which the three groups in exercise 4 were sampled be considered homogeneous? Use the simple homogeneity-of-variance test described in the chapter.

6. Compute a single-classification analysis of variance on the following data, determining the within-groups mean square, the between-groups mean square, and the value of F.

Group A	Group B	Group C	Group D
14	17	14	8
12	15	12	6
10	12	12	5
10	9	11	4
9	9	11	2
6	7	10	2
6	7	10	2

7. Suppose in exercise 6 that (1) groups A and B represent two alternative methods for teaching a unit in geometry with deductive methods, (2) groups C and D represent alternative inductive methods for accomplishing the same task, and (3) the data represent student scores on the final unit examination. Using the method of a priori comparisons, set up contrast coefficients and apply them in a statistical test for each of the following comparisons:

   (a) A contrast of the two deductive methods.
   (b) A contrast of the two inductive methods.
   (c) A contrast of the deductive with the inductive methods.

8. Are the contrasts in exercise 7 independent? Explain your answer.

9. Thirty high school sophomores have been randomly assigned to three groups, each of which has participated in a series of meetings designed to modify their attitudes toward professional prizefighting. In each of the three groups a different attitude-modification approach was employed. Below are the scores of the 30 students on an attitude scale administered at the close of the series of meetings. Applying single-classification analysis of variance, compute the value of F.

Approach 1	Approach 2	Approach 3
38	35	32
37	34	32
37	33	30
36	33	29
36	31	28
34	30	24
34	29	24
30	26	23
30	25	21
27	25	21

10. In exercise 9, suppose the investigator has no conceptual or theoretical basis upon which to hypothesize specific contrasts between attitude-modification approaches. Compute additional statistical information to help the investigator pinpoint significant differences among the methods.

11. Find the value of the mean square between groups, the mean square within groups, and F for the following data.

Group A			Group B			Group C		
29	24	17	22	18	10	32	24	19
28	24	16	20	17	10	30	21	16
28	20	15	20	16	9	28	20	16
26	18	10	20	14	9	27	20	15
25	18	10	19	11	6	26	19	15

Multiple-Classification
Analysis of Variance

The simplest form of the analysis-of-variance statistical technique—the single-classification model discussed in Chapters 11 and 12—permits an investigator to determine whether there are significant differences among the means of two or more populations. In such analyses, the investigator is basically attempting to discover whether there is a relationship between a dependent variable (such as test performance) and an independent variable (such as method of instruction) represented by several levels of classification. In a more complex form of this model, known as **multiple-classification analysis of variance,** the relationship between one dependent variable and two or more independent variables or factors can be tested. This technique also makes it possible to test for relationships between the dependent variable and various interactions of the factors in the design.

We will use a fairly common educational research example to illustrate the increased utility of multiple-classification analysis of variance compared to the single-classification model. Suppose an investigation is designed to test a research hypothesis regarding the relationship between student achievement and several instructional methods which provide for varying degrees of directiveness in the role for the teacher. The dependent variable in this instance would be student achievement as measured by an achievement test that is relevant to the instructional unit. The independent variable, or factor, would be instructional method. This variable would have three levels represented by three classes of 30 students each, all taught by the same instructor. The instructor deliberately modifies the degree of "directiveness" in the teaching approach, employing a strict instructor-controlled lecture method in the "directive" group, allowing students to completely control structure, content, and procedures in the "nondirective" group, and attempting to use both methods in a "combination" group.

In this example, a one-way or single-classification analysis-of-variance (anova) design could be used to test the null hypothesis and determine whether there were any significant mean differences among the mean performances of the three groups. If no significant mean differences were found, the null hypothesis would be considered tenable, that is, the existence of a relationship between the dependent variable and independent variable would not have been demonstrated by this particular investigation.

It is possible, however, that the investigation was not designed with sufficient sensitivity to yield significant results. There may be other independent variables which, because of their relationship to the criterion variable under consideration, are confounding the results. For instance, there may be reason to expect that students' aptitudes in some way relate to the apparent success of nondirective teaching methods. It is possible to redesign a similar study so that there are *two* independent variables: (1) instructional method and (2) ability level. The student sample can be divided so that each of the three instructional methods groups is partitioned, for example, into two ability groups: those judged "high ability" and those judged "average or below" by their teachers. This would make it possible to test the relationship between the dependent variable (achievement-test scores) and both of the independent variables. This kind of research design is often referred to as **factorial analysis of variance.** In this example the design has two factors, instructional method with three levels and aptitude with two levels. In other terminology that is commonly used, this might be designated as a 3×2 (three-by-two) factorial design, to indicate the number of factors, the number of levels in each factor, and, indirectly, the total number of **treatment combinations** ($3 \times 2 = 6$).

The presence of a relationship in this design is indicated by significant achievement test mean differences among groups or levels representing an independent variable or factor. Also important, the design makes it possible to test for a relationship between the dependent variable and an *interaction* of the two independent variables. The concept of interaction effects will be discussed more extensively later in this chapter.

As in the case of single-classification analysis of variance, the hypotheses would be tested for significance by the size of individual *F* values yielded by the statistical analysis. These values are interpreted for significance from a table of the *F* distribution (Table F in the Appendix), as described in Chapter 12. There would be an *F* value for instructional method, indicating whether the achievement-test means of the methods groups were significantly different. There would also be an *F* value for ability level, indicating whether the achievement-test means of the two ability-level groups differed significantly from each other. Finally, there would be an *F* value for interaction, indicating whether the performance of the students on the achievement test was related to particular combinations of instructional methods and ability levels.

Now suppose this multiple-classification anova design is actually implemented. The independent variables are: (1) instructional method, represented by the "directive," "combination," and "nondirective" student groups; and (2) ability level, represented by the same students who have now been classified for analysis purposes according to whether they have been judged to be "high ability" or "average and below." The dependent variable is student performance on the achievement test. Statistical tests will be made for the significance of the relationship between these variables, as well as for the significance of a relationship of the dependent variable and an interaction of the two independent variables.

After an appropriate instructional period, the criterion achievement test would be administered, and the results obtained might be similar to the hypothetical data presented in Table 13.1. Notice that there is relatively little difference among the performances of the three instructional-method groups overall, but there is a marked disparity between the overall mean performances of the ability-level groups. Observe also that the performance of the higher-ability students is superior when the instructional method is nondirective, while the performance of the less-able students is better in the more-directive teaching situation.

Data such as those in Table 13.1 would probably yield a set of F statistics similar to the hypothetical values presented in Table 13.2. Note that the F for method is nonsignificant, as could be expected from the close similarity of the methods group means indicated in Table 13.1. Also observe that a significant F for ability level reflects the considerable difference between the means of the ability-level groups. The F for interaction is also significant. We have already noted the source of this significant interaction: the fact that the high-ability students tended to achieve better in less-directive teaching situations, with the opposite being the case for students evaluated as average or below.

In studying this example of multiple-classification analysis of variance, you should bear in mind that the data and conclusions are hypothetical, and the investigations were used purely for purposes of exposition. The fictitious

Table 13.1   **Mean Achievement-Test Performance of 90 Students, Classified According to Instructional Method and Ability Level**

	Instructional Method			Total: Ability Level
	Directive	Combination	Nondirective	
Ability level				
"High ability"	$\overline{X}=55.4$	$\overline{X}=59.6$	$\overline{X}=63.0$	$\overline{X}=59.3$
"Average or below"	$\overline{X}=45.2$	$\overline{X}=41.3$	$\overline{X}=38.3$	$\overline{X}=41.6$
Total: Instructional method	$\overline{X}=50.3$	$\overline{X}=50.5$	$\overline{X}=50.7$	

Table 13.2   **Analysis of Variance F Values for Student Performance under Three Different Teaching Methods; Students Classified by Ability Levels**

Source of Variation	F Value	Significance Level
Instructional method	0.13	Not significant
Ability level	10.78	0.01
Interaction	9.42	0.01

data presented in Tables 13.1 and 13.2, of course, should not be used as fuel to stoke the sometimes heated controversies of nondirective and directive teaching-method enthusiasts.

BASIC RATIONALE OF MULTIPLE-CLASSIFICATION ANALYSIS OF VARIANCE

In order to understand how multiple-classification analysis of variance can perform a number of functions, you may find it helpful to review the discussion in Chapter 11 of the rationale of single-classification analysis of variance. The basic technique employed by statisticans in all analysis-of-variance approaches is to use variance, that is, the amount of variation in the scores of a sample from their group mean, in order to learn something about means. Referring back to Figures 11–1 and 11–2, which depict data situations in which the null hypothesis is considered tenable and untenable, respectively, should help you recall the essentials of simple analysis of variance. Briefly, when the variation in the pooled group (formed by considering the scores in separate groups as though they were only one group) is approximately the same as the average variation of the separate groups, then there is no significant difference between the separate group means and the null hypothesis cannot be rejected. On the other hand, if the pooled group variation is much larger than the average variation of the separate groups, then a significant difference between at least two of the group means exists, and the null hypothesis is considered untenable.

It should not be too difficult to apply the more-extensive discussion in Chapter 11 to any independent variable in a multiple-classification anova problem. The same basic logic of the simple analysis-of-variance case is maintained, with only slight modifications.

Two-Way Classification

The sources of variance associated with the independent variables or factors of an anova design are often designated as **main effects,** to distinguish them from the interaction sources of variance. In multiple-classification analysis of variance, the amount of variation that is attributed to each main-effect variable is determined by calculating a **main-effect sum of squares,** or what is essentially a between sum of squares, for the subgroups representing each independent variable. If there are two independent variables, the scores in the groups representing one variable are viewed first, and a between sum of squares is computed for the first main-effect variable. Then the scores in the groups that correspond to the second independent variable are viewed, and a between sum of squares is computed for the second main-effect variable. This process is continued until a between sum of squares has been computed for all independent variables.

Each of these main-effect sums of squares can be thought of as representing the amount of variation caused by the differences between the means of the subgroups representing that variable. For example, if instructional method is one of the independent variables, a sum of squares for method must be computed. The larger this sum of squares, the greater the difference among the means of the methods subgroups.

After a sum of squares has been computed for each independent variable, it is necessary to determine how much variation can be attributed to the interaction between the independent variables. To do this, a sum of squares for interaction must be calculated. To find the interaction sum of squares when there are two independent variables, a special sum of squares must be computed. From this quantity, often called the **subgroup sum of squares,** the total sums of squares for the two main-effect variables are subtracted. The remainder is the **interaction sum of squares,** which reflects the amount of variation attributable to the interaction of the main-effect variables when they are related to the dependent variable. In other words, if all the treatment combinations or subgroups of the two-way design are conceptualized as being laid out as a single-factor or one-way design, the between sum of squares for this "expanded" factor would reflect all three sources of variation—the main effects of the two independent variables and the effect due to their interaction. It is the sum of squares for all these subgroups taken as one factor that is designated as the subgroup sum of squares.

As in single-classification analysis of variance, it is necessary to compute the within sum of squares in order to form the error term to be used in the denominator of the F tests. The within sum of squares is computed exactly as in the one-way design, with the two-way design being conceptualized in its expanded, single-factor form. From a computational standpoint, however, the error sum of squares can be easily found by subtracting all of the main-effect and interaction sums of squares from the total.

The main-effect, interaction, and within sums of squares are then divided by their appropriate degrees of freedom to obtain mean squares. (This operation is discussed in Chapter 14.) These mean squares are then used to form F ratios, with the within mean square always placed in the denominator of the ratio. For example, in a two-way classification with two independent variables, the following F ratios would be formed:

$$\frac{\text{Mean square for main-effect variable No. 1}}{\text{Within mean square}} = F \text{ for main-effect variable No. 1}$$

$$\frac{\text{Mean square for main-effect variable No. 2}}{\text{Within mean square}} = F \text{ for main-effect variable No. 2}$$

$$\frac{\text{Interaction mean square}}{\text{Within mean square}} = F \text{ for interaction}$$

These F ratios are then interpreted for statistical significance from a table of F (Table F in the Appendix), entering the table with the degrees of freedom for the mean squares involved. If the F is sufficiently large to be statistically significant, the particular null hypothesis associated with the ratio that yielded the F is rejected.

Interaction Effects

Multiple-classification analysis-of-variance designs are particularly useful for testing hypotheses about **interaction effects** in educational investigations. An example involving interaction effects should help you gain an intuitive understanding of what is going on when you encounter such effects.

The general principle involved in interaction effects is the same in all anova models—testing for the existence of a relationship between the dependent variable and another variable. Ordinarily, subgroups representing an independent variable are established so that differences between the groups will indicate the existence of such a relationship. In the case of an interaction effect, the potential relationship under analysis is between the dependent variable and the *combined* interaction of the two (or more) independent variables. In the case of a two-way classification model, it is possible to obtain nonsignificant *F* values representing both independent or main-effect variables but a highly significant *F* for interaction.

An example of this situation can be drawn from a practical elementary school situation. A colleague of ours once reported results of an investigation in which the dependent variable was children's reading improvement and two independent variables were gender of teacher and of pupil. Nonsignificant *F* values were obtained in the analysis of variance for both independent variables, that is, there was no relationship in this study between reading improvement and whether the teacher was male or female or whether the pupil was boy or girl. However, a significant *F* for interaction was produced. An inspection of the means revealed that girls made much greater reading gains with female teachers than did boys with female teachers. Conversely, the boys performed somewhat better with male teachers than did girls with male teachers. The differences were of a sufficient magnitude to result in a significant interaction effect.

To illustrate how interaction effects would or would not be produced, Figure 13–1 presents a graph of the mean reading improvement scores for each of the four possible subgroups. The situation in Figure 13–1(a) existed in the actual example. Note the marked crossing of the lines representing boys and girls.

Suppose there had been no significant interaction effects or main-effect differences associated with sex of pupil (main-effect *X*), but there was a signif-

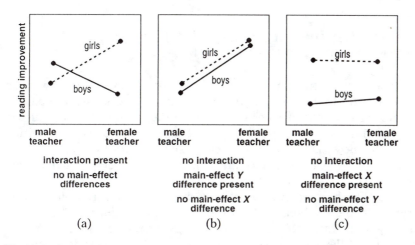

Fig. 13–1. Three graphic representations of data reflecting the presence and absence of interaction and main effects when boys/girls = main-effect *X*, and male teachers/female teachers = main-effect *Y*.

icant difference associated with gender of teacher (main-effect Y). In other words, what if there were a difference in reading-improvement scores of pupils taught by male or female teachers, but no differences associated with the other independent variable. Then the situation would appear something like Figure 13–1(b).

If there were no significant interaction effects and no differences associated with gender of teacher (main-effect Y), but a significant difference associated only with sex of pupils (main-effect X), then the situation would be represented in a fashion similar to that in Figure 13–1(c).

Three-Way and Higher Classifications

The same approach to multiple-classification analysis-of-variance problems is used when two, three, or more independent variables are used to classify the dependent-variable data. The underlying logic of the approach is unchanged; the purpose still is to discover the relationship between a dependent variable and certain independent variables which are represented by two or more subgroups.

With three independent variables (A, B, and C), however, the interaction situation becomes much more complex. Not only is there an interaction between independent variables A and B, B and C, and A and C but there is also a combined interaction of all three independent variables, that is, $A \times B \times C$. In the language of multiple-classification analysis of variance, "factor $A \times$ factor B" may be expressed as "factor A *by* factor B" to indicate the interaction between A and B.

With two main-effect variables, the notion of interaction is not difficult to understand. With three or more independent variables, it becomes increasingly more difficult. What is learned from such complex interactions is that no simple interpretations can be made of single effects. If you recall the simple example of two-way interaction depicted in Table 13.1, and mentally a third factor (e.g., grade level: first graders vs. sixth graders), the interpretation of results becomes more complex. (See the example in Chapter 14.)

ADVANTAGES OF MULTIPLE CLASSIFICATION IN EDUCATIONAL INVESTIGATION

Multiple-classification analysis of variance adds an extremely important tool to the statistical repertoire of educational investigators. Because education is one of the most complex behavioral fields, the investigations conducted in it must employ data analysis techniques that take into consideration not only more than one variable but also extremely subtle interactions among variables. Multiple-classification anova procedures provide such analytic techniques.

Furthermore, because these procedures make it possible to isolate variation attributable to several main effects and to their interactions, they heighten the sensitivity of the various F tests of significance. Increased sensitivity occurs because the size of the within mean square, the error term in the denominator of the F ratio, is reduced with the identification of each new source of variation. A smaller error term results in larger, hence more significant, F values. More will be said about these issues, as well as other design aspects, in the final chapter on analysis of variance, Chapter 17.

A word of caution is warranted: Because analysis of variance is such a powerful and sensitive statistical tool, you must be doubly careful that the data subjected to this type of statistical analysis truly represent the variables under study. There is an old research adage that warns investigators not to "gather data with a rake and study them with a microscope." Figuratively speaking, multiple-classification analysis of variance provides the microscope, and you must guard against indiscriminately raking in the data.

ASSUMPTIONS OF MULTIPLE-CLASSIFICATION ANALYSIS OF VARIANCE

The same assumptions that apply to single-classification analysis of variance also pertain to the multiple-classification models. These assumptions are:

1. The individuals in each subgroup should be random samples from their corresponding populations.
2. The measures must be normally distributed in the subgroup populations.
3. The variances within the subgroup populations must be homogeneous.

As we indicated in Chapter 11, there is increasing evidence of the robustness of analysis-of-variance models. They are able to withstand fairly serious departures from the normality and homogeneity-of-variance assumptions without disturbing the validity of conclusions based on the F tests.

REPORTING A TWO-WAY ANALYSIS OF VARIANCE

To make sure you understand multiple-classification analysis of variance, consider the following example of the way in which multiple-classification anova procedures are reported in the educational research literature. This investigation, conducted by Paul Pimsleur, was reported in the *Journal of Educational Research.*[1]

In this investigation the researcher sought to establish whether incidental learning takes place in a foreign-language learning situation, and if it does, whether the incidental learning is related to a student's overall performance in learning the foreign language. He set up an experiment in which two comparable classes in French, each with 18 students and taught by the same teacher, were exposed to two different types of drills. The experimental group was given a drill task focusing on the position of pronouns in sentences that included a

---

1. Paul Pimsleur, "Incidental Learning in Foreign Language Learning," *Journal of Educational Research,* vol. 54, no. 3 (November 1960), pp. 111–14.

number of new past-participle forms. The control group was given an unrelated task, a pronunciation exercise. Pimsleur was actually interested in the experimental group's mastery of the past participles used in the pronoun-positioning drill. If the experimental group learned the past participles significantly better than the control group did, he would ascribe the result to the influence of the pronoun drill and would describe it as incidental learning.

At the conclusion of the drill, both groups were given several examinations, including an oral recognition test on the past participles. Students received grades in the French class based on their total performance, irrespective of the experiment. Grades of A, B, C, and D were assigned to students in the experimental and control groups.

The researcher was now able to answer the following questions by employing a multiple-classification analysis-of-variance treatment:

1. Did the students in the experimental group, who were incidentally exposed to new past participles, perform significantly better on the oral recognition test than those in the control group who were not exposed to the past participles?
2. Did A, B, C, and D students (irrespective of membership in the experimental or control group) differ in their performance on the oral recognition test?
3. Does the combination of membership in the experimental or control group interacting with level of grade earned make a difference; specifically, did the higher-level A and B students in the experimental group evidence more incidental learning than their lower-level (C and D) classmates?

The data were subjected to a multiple-classification analysis-of-variance treatment in which the first independent variable (exposure to the incidental learning task) was represented by the experimental and control groups, and the second independent variable (grade level) was represented by the four grade groups, those who earned A, B, C, or D in the French course. The interaction between these two variables was also tested.

The report of the analysis is presented in Table 13.3. The F value of 5.23 resulting from the performance difference of the experimental and control groups was found to be significant ($p < 0.05$). Inspection of the means for the experimental and control groups revealed that the former group outperformed the latter, and this was taken as evidence of incidental learning of the past participles by the experimental group. The F value of 6.81 resulting from the differential in performance of the A, B, C, and D students on the oral recognition test was also found to be significant ($p < 0.01$). As expected, those earning higher grades in the course scored better on the test. The F for interaction was not significant, indicating no appreciable relationship between performance on the test and the combination of the two independent variables.

Pimsleur therefore concluded that students do learn incidentally in a foreign-language learning situation and that A, B, C, and D students differ, but that better students (as indexed by their grades) do not appear to learn incidentally any more effectively than poorer students do.

Other investigators would adopt a similar format to report anova results, although the labels they use in tables and text may vary from those used here.

Table 13.3　　Analysis of Variance on Oral Recognition Test Scores

Source of Variation	Sum of Squares	Degrees of Freedom	Mean Square	F
Exposure to material (experimental versus control group)	22	1	22.00	5.23^a
Grade in course (A, B, C, D groups)	86	3	28.67	6.81^b
Interaction	10	3	3.33	0.79
Within	118	28	4.21	
Total	236	35		

[a] Significant at 0.05 level.
[b] Significant at 0.01 level.

Source: Paul Pimsleur, "Incidental Learning in Foreign Language Learning," *Journal of Educational Research,* vol. 54, no. 3 (November 1960), pp. 111–14.

For example, independent variables may be referred to as rows or columns, rather than by the name that describes the variable. This is, in fact, the terminology we use in Chapter 14 in describing the computation of sums of squares. If you keep in mind that rows and columns merely describe subgroups representing specific independent variables, this terminology will not prove confusing.

Greater insight into the nature of multiple-classification analysis of variance is provided in the companion chapter on computation procedures for this statistical technique (Chapter 14). You may also want to consult the selected readings listed at the end of this chapter.

■　　■　　■

REVIEW

Multiple-classification analysis of variance presents educational investigators with a powerful analytic tool that is well adapted to dealing with the complexities of inquiry in the behavioral sciences. This statistical technique is designed to test relationships between a dependent variable and several independent variables or factors in the design. Relationships between the dependent variable and interactions of the independent variables can also be tested. In each case the independent variables are represented by two or more classifications of the data, such as data divided into groups according to different methods of instruction. The dependent variable is some type of numerical data such as student scores on a test.

The rationale underlying multiple-classification analysis of variance is essentially the same as that in single-classification analysis. Variances of groups are analyzed so as to reveal any significant mean differences between the groups.

As with all analysis-of-variance models, multiple-classification anovas yield *F* values which are interpreted for levels of probability from the table of *F*. In multiple-classification designs, *F* values would be yielded for both main effects and interaction effects.

TERMS TO KNOW

Listed in order of presentation in chapter:

> multiple-classification analysis of variance
> factorial analysis of variance
> treatment combinations
> main effects
> main-effect sum of squares
> subgroup sum of squares
> interaction sum of squares
> interaction effect

EXERCISES

1. A secondary-school principal wants to test for differences in reading achievement among five groups of high-school freshmen who are graduates of five different elementary schools. Should the principal use single- or multiple-classification analysis of variance?

2. A school psychologist wants to discover whether there are significant mean differences in personality-test scores among three groups of seventh-grade students representing different religious affiliations. At the same time, the psychologist wants to classify the students according to scholastic ability to see if there are differences between the ability groups on the personality measure. Should the psychologist use single- or multiple-classification analysis of variance?

3. In a two-way multiple-classification analysis-of-variance problem, three F values will be yielded, two for differences in main effects on independent variable groups and one for interaction. Is it possible for the interaction F to be statistically significant if the two main-effect F values are not significant?

4. A single-classification analysis of variance has been computed on a set of data divided into three independent variable subgroups. The F yielded by this analysis is almost, but not quite, significant at the 0.05 level. If a second independent variable had been identified and a multiple-classification analysis of variance been computed on the same data, is it possible that the F value associated with the initial three-groups independent variable would be significant? Why?

5. If the mean squares for every source of variation, that is, independent variables and interactions, are less than the within mean square, will all the null hypotheses be considered tenable or untenable?

SELECTED READINGS

Edwards, Allen L. *Experimental Design in Psychological Research.* New York: Harper & Row, 1985, chap. 12.

Ferguson, George A., and Takane, Yoshio. *Statistical Analysis in Psychology and Education.* New York: McGraw-Hill, 1989, chap. 16.

Guilford, J. P., and Fruchter, Benjamin. *Fundamental Statistics in Psychology and Education.* New York: McGraw-Hill, 1978, chap. 13.

Kirk, Roger E. *Elementary Statistics.* Monterey, CA: Brooks/Cole, 1984, chap. 16.

McNemar, Quinn. *Psychological Statistics.* New York: Wiley, 1969, chap. 16.

Shavelson, Richard J. *Statistical Reasoning for the Behavioral Sciences.* Boston: Allyn & Bacon, 1988, chap. 15.

Spence, Janet T., et al. *Elementary Statistics.* Englewood Cliffs, NJ: Prentice-Hall, 1983, chap. 13.

Multiple-Classification Analysis of Variance

- *computation procedures*

The computation of multiple-classification analysis of variance becomes increasingly tedious as the number of independent variables is increased, for with each additional main-effect variable there are additional interaction analyses to compute. Actually, if it were not for the calculation of the values necessary to compute these interaction F values, the computation of multiple-classification analysis of variance would be almost identical to that for single-classification analysis-of-variance (anova) problems.

TWO-WAY CLASSIFICATION: COMPUTATIONAL EXAMPLE

The first computational example to be described in this chapter involves the most simple multiple-classification design—one with only two independent variables. Suppose a school system curriculum committee has agreed to employ a unique approach to the teaching of mathematics. Members of the curriculum committee believe that the quality of student performance under the new system may be related to students' prior achievement in conventional mathematics and also to their tendency to perseverate in past study patterns. A district research consultant designs a one-semester investigation in which the dependent variable is achievement in mathematics, as measured by a specially designed mathematics problem-solving test.

The first independent variable is designated as level of achievement previously attained by the students in mathematics. According to their performance on an achievement examination administered during the ninth grade, a random sample of the sophomores who will be using the new materials is classified into three groups: (1) "high achievers," those who scored at least one-half standard deviation above the national mean on the ninth-grade mathematics achievement examination; (2) "average achievers," those who scored within the range ±one-half standard deviation from the national mean on that examination; and (3) "low achievers," those who scored at least one-half standard deviation below the national mean.

The second independent variable is designated as students' tendency to perseverate in their prior study routines, as measured by a "rigidity" test administered to all students in the investigation. Those who obtained high scores on the test reflected a greater tendency to persevere in stereotyped behavior on the test; those who scored low revealed a greater tendency to abandon previous behavior patterns. According to their test scores, students were divided into three equal groups designated "high rigidity," "average rigidity," and "low rigidity."

A two-way, multiple-classification anova model allows for the testing of three null hypotheses regarding these variables:

H_{01} There will be no difference among the three achievement populations in their mean performances on the mathematics problem-solving test.

H_{02} There will be no difference among the three rigidity populations in their mean performances on the mathematics problem-solving test.

H_{03} There will be no interaction between student membership in both independent-variable populations and their mean performances on the mathematics problem-solving test.

The 27 scores presented in Table 14.1 will be used in this example, for ease of computation and exposition, though an actual investigation of this type would involve far more individuals. These hypothetical scores represent student performance on the mathematics problem-solving test at the end of a semester during which the new teaching materials were used.

Homogeneity of Variance

The homogeneity-of-variance assumption should be checked with respect to the groups contributing directly to the within mean squares error term. In the one-way design, these groups are simply those that are included in the levels of the factor or independent variable. When the design contains more than one factor, the obtained data can be grouped in different ways. For example, in the design shown in Table 14.1, groups can be formed in three ways:

1. Three nine-member achievement groups, low, average, and high.
2. Three nine-member rigidity groups, high, average, and low.
3. Nine three-member combination rigidity-achievement groups, high-low, high-average, high-high, average-low, average-average, etc.

Table 14.1   **Mathematics Problem-Solving Test Scores of 27 Students Classified According to Prior Mathematics Achievement and Performance on a Test of Rigidity**

Rigidity Tendency	Prior Mathematics Achievement							
	Low Achievers		Average Achievers		High Achievers		Total	
	X	X^2	X	X^2	X	X^2	X	X^2
High rigidity	38	(1,444)	51	(2,601)	59	(3,481)		
	40	(1,600)	43	(1,849)	49	(2,401)		
	35	(1,225)	48	(2,304)	56	(3,136)		
Subtotal	113	(4,269)	142	(6,754)	164	(9,018)	419	(20,041)
Average rigidity	44	(1,936)	50	(2,500)	56	(3,136)		
	43	(1,849)	51	(2,601)	58	(3,364)		
	45	(2,025)	50	(2,500)	55	(3,025)		
Subtotal	132	(5,810)	151	(7,601)	169	(9,525)	452	(22,936)
Low rigidity	50	(2,500)	52	(2,704)	62	(3,844)		
	51	(2,601)	54	(2,916)	62	(3,844)		
	48	(2,304)	57	(3,249)	65	(4,225)		
Subtotal	149	(7,405)	163	(8,869)	189	(11,913)	501	(28,187)
Total	394	(17,484)	456	(23,224)	522	(30,456)	1,372	(71,164)

In our example, the nine combination groups are conceptualized as random samples from nine corresponding populations with normal distributions and equal variances. These nine combination groups or subgroups are referred to as the **cells** in a factorial analysis-of-variance design. They are usually ordered from left to right, starting with the first row. In other words, the multiple-classification design can be conceptualized as a single-classification design with nine groups.

To test the homogeneity-of-variance assumption, the variances for the nine cells, in the order explained, are computed in the usual fashion, using Formula 14.1 (equivalent to Formula 4.2 in Chapter 4):

$$s^2 = \frac{\sum X^2 - \frac{(\sum X)^2}{n_g}}{n_g - 1}$$

(14.1)

The computation of only two of these variances is demonstrated here:

$$\text{High-Low:} \frac{4,269 - \frac{(113)^2}{3}}{2} = 6.34$$

$$\text{High-Average:} \frac{6,754 - \frac{(142)^2}{3}}{2} = 16.34$$

The variances for the other seven cells are 26.34, 0.99, 0.34, 2.34, 2.34, 6.34, and 3.00.

The smallest variance (for the fifth cell, or the average-average combination) is divided into the largest variance (for the third cell, or the high-high combination). The F value obtained is:

$$F_{2,2} = \frac{26.34}{0.34}$$

$$= 77.47$$

According to the values in Table F, with 2 and 2 degrees of freedom, an F value as large as 99.0 would be required to reject the null hypothesis of equal population variances ($p < 0.02$). Because the F value is 77.47, the assumption of variance homogeneity cannot be rejected. The tests of main effects and interactions therefore are in order.

COMPUTATION OF SUMS OF SQUARES

The standard raw-score formulas for computing sums of squares (see Chapter 12) are used to determine the total sum of squares and the sum of squares for all main-effect variables.

Total Sum of Squares

Drawing on the data in Table 14.1, the total sum of squares is computed (using Formula 2.5) as follows:

$$\text{Total SS} = 71,164 - \frac{(1,372)^2}{27}$$

$$= 1,446.1$$

Main-Effect Sums of Squares: Columns and Rows

In computing sums of squares for the main-effect variables, we will use the notions of **columns** and **rows** as descriptions of subgroups representing independent variables. (This usage was introduced in Chapter 13 in the section on reporting a two-way analysis of variance.) By studying Table 14.1, you will see that when the scores are considered from the viewpoint of the independent variable of achievement level, they are grouped in vertical columns. When the scores are viewed in terms of the variable of rigidity tendency, they are grouped in horizontal rows. The descriptive terms *rows* and *columns* are generally applicable to all multiple-classification anova problems, as well as to a number of other statistical operations.

In this example, remember that columns represent the independent variable, achievement-level groups. Thus determining the SS for columns determines the SS for achievement level. Similarly, rows represent the independent variable, rigidity groups, and determining the SS for rows determines the SS for rigidity tendency.

Columns Sum of Squares. The **columns sum of squares** can be found by employing Formula 12.1 for between-groups SS, as given in Chapter 12:

$$\text{Between SS} = \sum \frac{(\Sigma X_g)^2}{n_g} - \frac{(\Sigma X)^2}{n}$$

In this formula, the scores are summed for each achievement group, then squared and divided by the number in the group: $\Sigma X_g^2/n_g$. All of these quantities are then added together. The standard correction term, $\Sigma X^2/n$, which is the square of the sum of all scores divided by the total number in the sample, is then subtracted. In the example we are using, the columns SS would be computed as follows:

$$\text{Columns SS} = \frac{(394)^2}{9} + \frac{(456)^2}{9} + \frac{(522)^2}{9} - \frac{(1,372)^2}{27}$$
$$= 17,248.4 + 23,104.0 + 30,276.0 - 69,717.9$$
$$= 910.5$$

As with the between SS in single-classification analysis of variance, this quantity represents the amount of the total sum of squares that is due to the differences among means of the three achievement groups.

Rows Sum of Squares. The **rows sum of squares** is computed in basically the same way as the columns SS, using Formula 12.1. The raw scores for each rigidity group are summed, then squared, and divided by the number of individuals in the group. The quantities are then totaled. The usual correction term is subtracted from this total, and the result is the rows SS. In our example, the rows sum of squares, for rigidity tendency, is computed as follows:

$$\text{Rows SS} = \frac{(419)^2}{9} + \frac{(452)^2}{9} + \frac{(501)^2}{9} - \frac{(1,372)^2}{27}$$
$$= 19,506.8 + 22,700.4 + 27,889.0 - 69,717.9$$
$$= 378.3$$

This value represents the amount of the total sum of squares that is due to the differences among means of the three rigidity groups.

Interaction Sum of Squares

In order to calculate the interaction sum of squares, a special sum of squares called the subgroup SS is needed. The sums of squares for the rows and columns are subtracted from this value, as follows:

$$\text{Interaction SS} = \text{Subgroup SS} - (\text{Rows SS} + \text{Columns SS}) \qquad (14.2)$$

The sum of squares for subgroups is calculated by considering each of the sets of scores formed by combinations of the rows and columns as distinctive subgroups. As explained earlier, there would be nine such cells or subgroups formed by the three achievement-level and three rigidity-tendency categories. For instance, in the upper left corner of Table 14.1, the three scores made by those who were low achievers and highly rigid ($X = 38$, $X = 40$, $X = 35$) form one subgroup. Again, formula 12.1 is used to calculate the sum of squares, only now all subgroups are considered as one classification factor. That is, each set of subgroup raw scores is totaled, squared, and divided by the number of individuals in the subgroup. All of these values (nine in this example) are then added. From them the usual correction term is subtracted to get the subgroup SS. In this example, the subgroup sum of squares is computed as follows:

$$\text{Subgroup SS} = \frac{(113)^2}{3} + \frac{(142)^2}{3} + \frac{(164)^2}{3} + \frac{(132)^2}{3} + \frac{(151)^2}{3}$$
$$+ \frac{(169)^2}{3} + \frac{(149)^2}{3} + \frac{(163)^2}{3} + \frac{(189)^2}{3} - \frac{(1,372)^2}{27}$$
$$= 4,256.3 + 6,721.3 + 8,965.3 + 5,808.0 + 7,600.3$$
$$+ 9,520.3 + 7,400.3 + 8,856.3 + 11,907.0 - 69,717.9$$
$$= 1,317.2$$

The interaction SS is obtained by subtracting the rows and columns sums of squares from the above value as in Formula 14.2:

$$\text{Interaction SS} = 1,317.2 - (910.5 + 378.3) = 28.4$$

This quantity is the part of the total sum of squares that is due to a relationship between the dependent variable and the interaction of independent variables represented by the rows and columns.

Within Sum of Squares

The within sum of squares is the portion of the total SS that is not already attributed to a given source.

$$\text{Within SS} = \text{Total SS} - (\text{Rows SS} + \text{Columns SS} + \text{Interaction SS}) \quad (14.3)$$

In this example, the within SS is obtained as follows:

$$\text{Within SS} = 1,446.1 - (910.5 + 378.3 + 28.4) = 128.9$$

The within SS, when divided by the appropriate number of degrees of freedom, will serve as the error term in the three F ratios.

COMPUTATION OF DEGREES OF FREEDOM

The degrees of freedom associated with each sum of squares are easily determined in two-way classification analysis-of-variance designs by using the following scheme for sources of variation:

Source	Degrees of Freedom
Rows	number of rows minus $1 = (r-1)$
Columns	number of columns minus $1 = (c-1)$
Interaction	rows minus 1 times columns minus $1 = (r-1)(c-1)$
Within	number in sample minus rows times columns $= (n-rc)$
Total	number in sample minus $1 = (n-1)$

Thus, in the present example, the following degrees of freedom are used:

Rows $r - 1 = 3 - 1 = 2$
Columns $c - 1 = 3 - 1 = 2$
Interaction $(r - 1)(c - 1) = (2)(2) = 4$
Within $n - rc = 27 - (3)(3) = 18$
Total $n - 1 = 27 - 1 = 26$

COMPUTATION OF MEAN SQUARES

The mean squares used in the final statistical operations of this analysis, the F ratios, are obtained by dividing the rows, columns, interaction, and within sums of squares by their respective degrees of freedom. Thus, the computational example yields the following mean squares:

$$\text{Rows MS} = \frac{378.3}{2} = 189.15$$

$$\text{Columns MS} = \frac{910.5}{2} = 455.25$$

$$\text{Interaction MS} = \frac{28.4}{4} = 7.10$$

$$\text{Within MS} = \frac{128.9}{18} = 7.16$$

COMPUTATION AND INTERPRETATION OF *F* VALUES

Once all the necessary mean squares have been obtained, the three null hypotheses posed at the outset of the analysis can be tested by computing and interpreting the F value associated with each hypothesis. In each F ratio, the within mean square value of 7.16 is placed in the denominator. Thus, to test H_{01} that there is no difference among the mean performances of the three achievement groups (represented by columns), the following F ratio is set up with the columns mean square in the numerator:

$$\text{For achievement, } F_{2,18} = \frac{455.25}{7.16} = 63.58$$

When the F table is entered with 2 degrees of freedom for the numerator mean square and 18 degrees of freedom for the denominator mean square, an F of at least 6.01 is shown to be needed for the result to be significant at the 0.01 level. The achievement F value of 63.58 exceeds this figure, so the null hypothesis under consideration is rejected.

To test the second null hypothesis (H_{02}) that there is no difference in the mean performances of the three rigidity groups, the following F ratio is set up with the rows mean square in the numerator:

Table 14.2   **Analysis of Variance of the Performance of 27 Students, Classified by Prior Mathematics Achievement and Rigidity Tendency, on a Mathematical Problem-Solving Test**

Source of Variation	SS	df	MS	F
Achievement level	910.5	2	455.25	63.58[a]
Rigidity tendency	378.3	2	189.15	26.41[a]
Achievement × rigidity	28.4	4	7.10	0.99
Within groups	128.9	18	7.16	
Total	1,446.1	26		

[a] $p < 0.01$.

$$\text{For rigidity tendency, } F_{2,18} = \frac{189.15}{7.16} = 26.41$$

Because the F for rigidity tendency is 26.41, the null hypothesis is again rejected at the 0.01 level.

In testing the final null hypothesis (H_{03}) of a relationship between the dependent variable and an interaction of the two independent variables, an F ratio is set up with the interaction mean square in the numerator:

$$\text{For interaction, } F_{4,18} = \frac{7.10}{7.16} = 0.99$$

This very small F ratio is nonsignificant, because F must be greater than 1.00 to be significant. Therefore, the third null hypothesis cannot be rejected.

If the total analysis of variance described in this example were reported in a research journal, the presentation of the results would resemble Table 14.2. In different journals the terminology or abbreviations used in this table might be slightly altered, but you should have little difficulty interpreting any similar analysis-of-variance presentation.

THREE-WAY CLASSIFICATION: COMPUTATIONAL EXAMPLE

In more complex research designs, the investigator may be concerned with the possible relationship between a dependent variable and three or more independent variables, as well as the presence of significant interactions among the independent variables and the dependent variable. In general, the computation procedure followed for such analyses parallels that described for a two-way classification problem. The total sum of squares and the within sum of squares are computed in the normal fashion.

Each main-effect sum of squares is computed by summing the raw scores for each group representing the main-effect variable. These sums are then squared, divided by the number of measurements in each group, and totaled. From this total the standard correction term is subtracted to yield the particular main-effect SS.

For each interaction sum of squares, a subgroup sum of squares is computed by considering each combination of the main-effect variables involved in the interaction as a separate group. A procedure similar to that for the com-

Table 14.3   **Analysis of Variance of the School-Adjustment Scores of 120 Students Classified by Gender, Grade Level, and Aptitude**

Source of Variation	Degrees of Freedom
Gender	1
Grade level	2
Aptitude	3
Gender × grade level	2
Gender × aptitude	3
Grade level × aptitude	6
Gender × grade level × aptitude	6
Within groups	95
Total	119

putation of a main-effect sum of squares is followed. All SS for main effects included in the interaction are then subtracted from the subgroup SS to yield the interaction SS.

This procedure can be described, without using actual data, in a three-way classification problem in which the dependent variable is a student's score on a school-adjustment scale and the independent variables are gender, grade level, and academic aptitude. The number of students in the study is 120, 40 in each of three grade levels—7th, 8th, and 9th. Aptitude scores are classified into four categories, with 30 students in each group. Gender is represented by two categories of equal size, 60 boys and 60 girls. The sources of variation and their degrees of freedom for this problem are indicated in Table 14.3.

Computing Sums of Squares, Mean Squares, and *F* Values

Total SS.   The total SS is determined in the usual manner, that is, by finding the sum of the squared raw scores for the total sample minus the standard correction term, which is formed by squaring the sum of all raw scores and dividing by the number of scores. The number of degrees of freedom equals 1 less than the number of students: $120 - 1 = 119$.

Gender SS.   The gender SS is computed by disregarding grade level and aptitude, summing the 60 scores in each group, squaring these sums, and dividing each by 60. These two quantities are totaled, and the standard correction term is subtracted from this. The number of degrees of freedom is 1 less than the number of categories: $2 - 1 = 1$.

Grade-Level SS.   The grade-level SS is found by disregarding gender and aptitude, separately summing the 40 scores in each grade level, squaring these sums, and dividing each by 40. These three quantities are totaled, and the standard correction term is subtracted from this. The number of degrees of freedom is 1 less than the number of categories: $3 - 1 = 2$.

Aptitude SS.   The aptitude SS is obtained by disregarding gender and grade level, separately summing the 30 scores in each aptitude group, squaring these sums, and dividing each by 30. These four quantities are then summed, and the standard correction term is subtracted from this. The number of degrees of freedom is the number of categories less 1: $4 - 1 = 3$.

Gender by Grade-Level Interaction SS. Because the SS for gender by grade-level interaction is the interaction between two main-effect variables, it is known as a **first-order interaction**. This SS is found by disregarding aptitude, summing the 20 scores of each gender at each grade level (there will be six such subgroups), squaring these sums, and dividing each by 20. These six quantities are then summed, and the standard correction term is subtracted from this total. The result is the subgroup SS for gender and grade level. The gender SS and the grade-level SS are both subtracted from this subgroup SS to obtain the gender by grade-level interaction SS. The number of degrees of freedom is the product of the number of degrees of freedom for gender and grade level: $(1)(2) = 2$.

Gender by Aptitude Interaction SS. The SS for gender by aptitude interaction, also a first-order interaction, is found by disregarding grade level, summing the 15 scores of each gender in each aptitude group (eight subgroups), squaring these sums, and dividing each by 15. These eight quantities are then summed, and the standard correction term is subtracted from this. The result is the subgroup SS for gender and aptitude. The gender SS and the aptitude SS are subtracted from the subgroup SS to find the gender by aptitude interaction SS. The number of degrees of freedom is the product of the number of degrees of freedom for gender and aptitude $(1)(3) = 3$.

Grade Level by Aptitude Interaction SS. The SS for grade level by aptitude interaction, another first-order interaction, is computed by disregarding gender, summing the ten scores for each grade level in each aptitude group (12 subgroups), squaring these sums, and dividing each by 10. These 12 quantities are then summed, and the standard correction term is subtracted from this. The result is the subgroup SS for grade level and aptitude. The grade-level SS and the aptitude SS are subtracted from this subgroup SS to obtain the grade level by aptitude interaction SS. The number of degrees of freedom is the product of the number of degrees of freedom for grade level and aptitude: $(2)(3) = 6$.

Gender by Grade Level by Aptitude Interaction SS. Because the SS for gender by grade level by aptitude interaction is the interaction among three main effects, it is known as a **second-order interaction.** This SS is found by summing the five scores for each gender at each grade level in each aptitude group (24 subgroups), squaring these sums, and dividing each by 5. These 24 quantities are then summed, and the standard correction term is subtracted from this. The value obtained represents the sums of squares for the gender by grade level by aptitude interaction, together with the sums of squares for the three main effects and the three first-order interactions. The gender by grade level by aptitude interaction SS is obtained by subtracting the main-effect and first-order interaction sums of squares. The number of degrees of freedom is a product of the number of degrees of freedom for gender, grade level, and aptitude: $(1)(2)(3) = 6$.

Within SS.   The within SS can be found by subtracting from the total SS the sums of squares for the three main effects, the three first-order interactions, and the single second-order interaction. The number of degrees of freedom is found by subtracting from the total number of degrees of freedom the product of the number of *categories* in the three main-effect variables: $119 - (2)(3)(4) = 95$.

Mean Squares.   The mean squares for the various sources of variation are found in the usual way, by dividing the sums of squares by their respective degrees of freedom.

F ***Values.***   As in the preceding examples, F values are found by dividing the within mean square into the several main-effect and interaction mean squares. In this example, this procedure would produce seven F values which would then be interpreted from the F table.

UNEQUAL CELL SIZES

The examples for multiple-classification analysis of variance we have used thus far have contained equal numbers of individuals in the various categories and subcategories. It is not always possible to have equal numbers of measurements in each category, nor is it necessary. When inequality exists, either some of the scores can be discarded to equalize the cell sizes, or special methods can be used to allow for the inequality. If the loss of data is not great, it is probably wiser to randomly delete scores in order to achieve equal cell sizes. If the number of deleted scores is large, however, too much information may be lost. Adjustment procedures are available, but such procedures can be quite complex and are best done with the use of statistical programs for computer analysis.[1]

■   ■   ■

REVIEW

Computation procedures for two-way- and three-way-classification analysis-of-variance models differ in degree of complexity and the number of F values involved. Two-way-classification anova designs yield two main-effect F values and an F value for interaction between the two main-effect variables. Three-way-classification anova designs yield three main-effect F values, three first-order interaction F values for interaction between two main effects, and a single second-order interaction F value for interaction among the three main effects.

The degrees of freedom associated with the different F values can be determined from the tables and discussions presented in this chapter. Sums of squares and mean squares are calculated in essentially the same manner as for the single-classification analysis-of-variance model.

---

1. Additional information on these procedures can be found in a more advanced text on experimental design such as B. J. Winer, *Statistical Principles in Experimental Design* (New York: McGraw-Hill, 1971), pp. 402–22.

TERMS TO KNOW

Listed in order of presentation in chapter:

cells
columns
rows
columns sum of squares
rows sum of squares
first-order interaction
second-order interaction

EXERCISES

1. For the following data, compute the main-effect and interaction mean squares and the three F values. In each instance, determine whether the null hypothesis should be rejected at the 0.05 level.

			Methods			
A	B	C	A	B	C
	Males			Females	
8	11	19	16	10	5
9	12	18	10	11	4
9	4	11	11	13	7
5	9	15	9	12	10
4	10	10	7	4	3
8	10	9	14	5	9
3	11	8	10	9	8
10	14	16	8	13	11
9	9	12	17	10	4
7	5	9	18	9	5

2. An educational investigator who has decided to test for significance of mean differences between achievement scores of three groups of students taught by different instructional methods has at the same time classified the students according to scholastic aptitude level. Find the F values for (a) instructional method, (b) aptitude level, and (c) interaction between instructional method and aptitude level. Determine whether any of these F values are significant beyond the 0.05 level. The data are as follows:

Aptitude Level	Instructional Method								
	I			II			III		
High	68	54	49	67	60	54	54	46	39
	60	54	48	63	59	53	50	42	32
	60	50	40	60	56	50	48	40	30
Average	53	49	41	52	50	43	43	40	34
	52	49	40	51	46	40	42	40	30
	50	44	33	50	44	38	42	36	30
Low	57	46	33	49	41	34	38	29	24
	53	40	30	49	40	32	36	29	23
	51	39	28	43	36	27	30	27	22

3. For the following three-way-classification analysis of variance, determine the
   F values (and interpret for statistical significance) for the three main effects
   (A, B, C), the three first-order interactions (A × B, A × C, B × C), and the single second-order interaction (A × B × C).

		A_1		A_2		A_3	
		9	5	10	6	12	7
		9	5	10	6	12	7
	C_1	8	4	9	3	10	7
		7	4	8	3	9	6
		6	4	7	3	8	6
B_1							
		11	7	10	8	11	7
		10	6	10	7	11	7
	C_2	10	5	9	7	10	7
		8	5	9	6	9	6
		7	4	8	5	8	6
		10	6	10	7	12	10
		8	5	9	6	12	9
	C_1	7	4	8	6	12	9
		7	3	8	3	11	9
		6	3	7	3	10	8
B_1							
		9	5	9	6	10	7
		8	4	9	6	9	7
	C_2	7	4	8	6	9	7
		6	3	7	4	7	6
		6	3	7	5	8	6

Analysis of Covariance

Educational investigators often find it necessary to use a student sample from an actual school setting and to derive most of their data from students in preexisting school situations. Often, in fact, the only available source for an appropriate student sample is in the classroom. Moreover, there is a decided advantage in using realistic school situations to investigate relationships among educational variables. Typically, the investigator proposes to generalize research findings to real school situations, and such findings are frequently (but not always) most generalizable when the investigation has been conducted in an authentic school environment.

WORKING WITH PREEXISTING GROUPS

In actual school situations, however, it is often difficult for teachers and administrators to completely accommodate the investigator's need to manipulate students for data-gathering purposes. It may be impractical to move students from one teacher to another or from one curriculum to another in order to help the investigator work out a tight data-gathering design. The investigator therefore often finds it necessary to deal with preexisting student groups. Even if the students can be matched on measures related to the criterion (dependent) variable, the matching operation inevitably reduces the size of the sample because many students cannot be properly matched and must be discarded from the analysis.

The use of preexisting groups, of course, poses certain research design problems. For instance, suppose Mr. Larson, a high school administrator, wants to study the relationship between the dependent variable of students' achievement in physics and the independent variable of their teachers' knowledge of the subject matter. He could ascertain how much the various teachers know about physics by having their subject-matter supervisor rate them according to their knowledge of the science. He could also discover the extent of the students' physics achievement by giving them a postcourse physics test. By dividing the teachers into two or more groups according to knowledge of physics (to represent the variable), he could then see if the students of the most knowledgeable teachers performed better on the postcourse test than students who had studied with teachers who knew less about physics.

But a sophisticated investigator will always try to determine if *other* variables are related, perhaps causally, to the dependent variable under study. In this case, for example, student aptitude is likely to be related to performance on the postcourse test. Suppose Mr. Larson administers an academic aptitude test to the students in his sample and finds that those who were studying with the more knowledgeable teachers also happen to have higher aptitude scores than the other students do. If the results of the study indicate that the students of the better-informed physics teachers score higher than the other students on the examination, how should this be interpreted? Is there indeed a positive relationship between students' physics achievement and teachers' knowledge of the subject matter, or is this merely another case of higher-ability students outperforming their less-able counterparts? Unfortunately, the latter question cannot be answered by this investigation, for an independent variable (academic aptitude) which is relevant to the dependent variable (achievement) has been *confounded* with the relationship between the dependent variable and the independent variable (teachers' knowledge) that is under investigation. Academic aptitude therefore can be described as a **confounding variable**, or, more generally, **covariable**.

If the educational investigator had total freedom in such a situation, the groups composing the samples could be manipulated by stratified random-sampling procedures, so all subgroups representing the independent variable would be equivalent with respect to any variable that potentially could be confounding. In this example, Mr. Larson would have to reassemble the groups in such a way that they were equal in academic aptitude. For that matter, he would try to make the groups comparable with respect to *any* relevant variable that might confound the relationship under investigation. As we have indicated, however, this is usually impossible to do in most school programs. What, then, is the educational investigator to do in such situations?

ANALYSIS OF COVARIANCE AS A STATISTICAL TECHNIQUE

There is a statistical tool of considerable utility, known as analysis of covariance, that can be employed in such instances. This technique, an extension of the analysis-of-variance model combined with certain features of regression analysis, provides a useful statistical device for educational investigators. In brief, **analysis of covariance (ancova)** may be used when a relationship is being studied between a dependent variable and groups formed on the basis of two or more independent variables. This powerful technique allows the investigator to *statistically equate the independent-variable groups with respect to one or more variables that are relevant to the dependent variable.* Thus analysis of covariance allows the investigator to study the performance of several groups that are unequal with regard to a relevant variable *as though* they were equal in this respect. In the example used earlier, it would then be possible for Mr. Larson to equate statistically the academic aptitude levels of the groups taught by teachers with varying degrees of physics knowledge. He could also view any mean differences that resulted as though the groups had been equivalent in academic aptitude.

Sometimes the possible confounding variables will be identified in advance of the data collection. Other times, the investigator discovers such covariables only after the data have been gathered. Both situations can be appropriately handled through the use of the analysis-of-covariance model. It should be emphasized, however, that *individuals (or, in general, cases or experimental units) must be measured on the covariables before any experimental treatment is administered.* If this were not the case, measures on the covariables could, in fact, be affected by (or correlated with) the treatments (independent) variable. Performing the analysis of covariance in these circumstances would tend to equate the treatment groups after the treatments were administered!

Not only can group differences in one relevant variable be compensated for by analysis of covariance but any number of variables relevant to the dependent variable can be taken into account so they do not confound the analysis of the independent-dependent relationship. Obviously, such a tool has important implications for educational investigators because it permits the use of preexisting student groups while controlling variables that might otherwise confound the results of the investigation. Although analysis of covariance should not be indiscriminately applied to educational investigations, it is surprising that it is not used more often in such studies. In many instances the relationships studied would have been more clear if they had been statistically treated with a technique that controls potential confounding variables.

We emphasize, however, that analysis of covariance cannot completely overcome the problems inherent in dealing with preexisting groups. When the independent variable is experimental in nature, as in a treatment group versus control group design, random assignment of individuals to the two groups is, strictly speaking, the only way to ensure the appropriateness of the analysis-of-covariance statistical tests. If the treatment conditions are assigned to preexisting groups, then the ancova results can be meaningfully interpreted *only* to the extent that the investigator can make a case that the preexisting compositions of the groups were not unlike those that would have been obtained with pure random selection. When the independent variable is not experimental (for example, a males versus females design), the pitfalls in interpreting ancova results are even greater. As an extreme example, consider what it would mean to adjust (equate) statistically male and female groups on the variable of height in order to compare the groups on the dependent variable of weight. The potential for erroneous conclusions also exists in many less obvious problem situations.[1] You should be wary of the indiscriminant use of ancova procedures as a cure-all device for equating preexisting groups.

Like analysis of variance, analysis of covariance can be used in both single-classification form, when there is only one independent variable, and multiple-classification form, when there are two or more independent variables. In **single-classification analysis of covariance**, the investigator is interested in the existence of mean differences among two or more groups representing the independent variable, with respect to the measure that represents the dependent variable. It is convenient in ancova problems to refer to the dependent variable as the *criterion variable*, as with other techniques such as regression. The relevant variables for which adjustments are to be made are referred to as the **control variables, covariates,** or **covariables**—synonymous terms used by different authors and investigators.

An example of a single-classification analysis-of-covariance problem would involve a test of the following null hypothesis: There is no difference in the mean performance on an English achievement test of three student groups instructed by different methods that have been statistically equated with respect to verbal aptitude. The independent variable is method of instruction, and the criterion variable is student performance on the English achievement test. The control variable (or covariate or covariable) is verbal aptitude, perhaps measured by a scale on some scholastic aptitude test.

This single-classification design could be turned into a multiple-classification design by adding another factor (independent variable), for example, gender of students. Then additional significance tests would be conducted for the difference between male and female students and the interaction between gender and method of instruction.

RATIONALE OF ANALYSIS OF COVARIANCE

The rationale underlying analysis of covariance involves a combination of analysis of variance and regression concepts. In its most basic form, analysis of covariance can be thought of as nothing more than an analysis of variance of *adjusted* criterion scores. To make the proper adjustment, a regression equation can be computed for each group using the methods described in Chapters 7 and 8 to predict the criterion scores from the scores on the control variable. The groups can be equated on the control variable by selecting any constant score value (usually the overall sample mean) and predicting the criterion mean score for each group (using each group's regression line) for this value. The resulting values are the *adjusted* group means. The **adjusted scores** for group members are simply the *predicted* criterion scores using the group regression line. The analysis of variance is performed with these predicted scores to yield *F* ratios and tests for the amount of variation resulting from differences between the groups.

To help you understand this verbal explanation of the adjustment process, the situation is illustrated graphically in Figure 15–1. These are rather ideal-

1. See F. M. Lord, "A Paradox in the Interpretation of Group Comparisons," *Psychological Bulletin*, vol. 68 (1967), pp. 304–5.

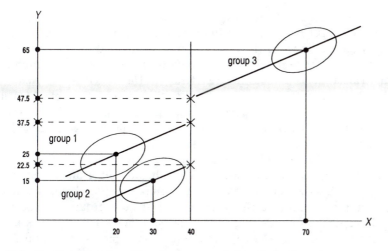

Fig. 15–1. Graphic presentation of the adjustment process in analysis of covariance (solid points = unadjusted values; crossed points = adjusted values).

istic scattergrams for three equal-size, hypothetical groups with control variable X predicting criterion variable Y. Clearly, groups 1, 2, and 3 are initially different on the control variable, having means of 20, 30, and 70, respectively. The overall control-variable mean is 40. The three groups also differ on the criterion variable, with means of 25, 15, and 65, respectively. These values, indicated by solid points, can be read off the graph by following the solid lines between the X axis and the Y axis. The regression lines for each group are also shown, with each one intersecting the vertical ordinate representing the overall control-variable mean. When these points of intersection are transferred to the Y axis, as indicated by dotted lines, the *adjusted* mean scores for each group, indicated by crossed points, can be read off. These scores are 37.5 for group 1, 22.5 for group 2, and 47.5 for group 3. Note that the third group, which was initially much higher on the control variable, is also much higher on the *unadjusted* criterion variable, as would be expected. But when the adjustment is made, this disparity in mean difference between group 3 and groups 1 and 2 is reduced. You should attempt to explain why the unadjusted mean difference between groups 1 and 2 is less than the corresponding adjusted mean difference. (Working out Exercise 6 at the end of the chapter will give you further insight into this adjustment process.)

ANALYSIS OF COVARIANCE: A RESEARCH EXAMPLE

To demonstrate the analysis-of-covariance technique, we will use as an example an actual study of the value of filmed science courses in public schools.[2] A sample of 247 high school physics students was divided into two groups—experimental and control. Students in the control group studied physics under a conventional lecture-discussion instructional method for a full academic year. In the same period, students in the experimental group were using

2. W. J. Popham and J. M. Sadnavitch, *The Effectiveness of Filmed Science Courses in Public Secondary Schools,* Kansas State College of Pittsburg, August 1960, 66 pages.

a series of 30-minute filmed lecture-demonstrations on physics which constituted a full year's course. Although there was some teacher instruction in the experimental group, most of the instruction was provided by the films.

At the end of the school year, a standardized achievement examination was given to all students to measure the efficacy of the filmed and conventional instructional methods. This posttest served as the criterion variable. Measures were also taken of the students' precourse knowledge of physics, their academic aptitude scores, and their previous overall grade-point averages. These latter three measures were used as control variables.

The data were subjected to a single-classification analysis of covariance to test the following null hypothesis: There will be no significant difference int he postcourse physics achievement of the film-taught and conventionally taught students, when initial differences between the two groups have been adjusted with respect to initial knowledge of physics (achievement pretest), academic aptitude (aptitude test), and previous scholastic performance (grade-point average). After the arithmetic computations were completed, the results of the covariance analysis were presented as in Table 15.1. Most of the terms in this table are identical to those used in reporting analysis-of-variance results. The term **residuals** can be thought of as meaning *adjusted*, referring to the fact that the sums of squares and mean squares have been adjusted ~~ont eh~~ on the basis of the control variables. Because a significant F values was yielded, the null hypothesis was rejected.

To be certain which group is significantly superior, it is necessary to inspect the criterion means. Remember that the original criterion means for the groups were adjusted to compensate for initial differences between the groups on the control variables. It is the *adjusted* means that must be inspected now. The research report gives a better ideal of the results of the study if unadjusted and adjusted criterion-variable means, as well as control-variable means, are reported, as in Table 15.2.

Table 15.1   Analysis of Covariance of Achievement Performances of 247 Physics Students in Experimental and Control Groups

Source of Variation	Degrees of Freedom	Residuals Sum of Squares	Residuals Mean Square	F
Between	1	936.465	936.465	14.839[a]
Within	242	15,272.671	63.110	
Total	243	16,209.136		

[a]Significant beyond the 0.01 level.

Table 15.2   Criterion-Variable and Control-Variable Means of 247 Physics Students

		Criterion-Variable Means		Control-Variable Means		
		Postachievement		Pretest	Academic	
	n	Adjusted	Unadjusted	Achievement	Aptitude	GPA
Experimental group	135	55.78	56.78	47.22	116.77	2.92
Control group	112	60.15	59.29	48.77	112.96	2.99

Note in Table 15.2 that the adjustment of the criterion means is rather trivial in this instance, although in other cases the adjustment may be quite great. Observe that the control group's unadjusted original mean has been slightly increased by adjustment, and the experimental group's original mean has been adjusted downward. The reason for these particular adjustments can be inferred from the differences between the experimental and control groups on the control variables. The experimental group's mean was adjusted downward because of that group's initial superiority over the control group in aptitude scores (116.77 to 112.96). This difference outweighed the differences on the other two control variables favoring the control group. The contribution to the mean adjustment made by each control variable is determined primarily by (1) the magnitude of the initial difference between the groups, and (2) the strength of the relationship between the criterion measure and the control measure. In this instance the correlation coefficients between the criterion variable and the control variables were (1) pretest achievement (0.68), (2) academic aptitude (0.51), and (3) GPA (0.30).

By inspecting the adjusted means, you can see that the conventionally taught students performed significantly better than their film-taught counterparts. This research study, then, would not support the use of the particular film series as it was employed during the study.

THE INFLUENCE OF RELEVANT VARIABLES

This example of analysis of covariance illustrates that subtle differences between groups with respect to relevant variables can be extremely influential. An investigator who analyzes only group differences with respect to the dependent variable, without taking into consideration the apparently trivial differences between groups on other measures, often obtains a misleading picture of the true differences between groups. Group criterion means that appear to be highly significant when considered alone may be adjusted to virtual equivalence through analysis of covariance because of the high-scoring group's superiority on relevant variables. Sometimes the reverse occurs, that is, small unadjusted mean differences between groups may become large adjusted differences after each group's performance on relevant variables is taken into account.

The initial differences between groups on the relevant variables do not even have to be statistically significant. Indeed, it is not enough to test for significant differences between groups on variables relevant to the dependent variable and, if no significant differences are found, conclude that the groups are essentially equal. Try to visualize a situation in which one group is superior to a second group on *all* of several relevant variables. None of the differences is significant, but all favor the same group. The composite effect of these minor, but systematic, advantages of the favored group can be most important, and this effect will be detected by analysis of covariance. Computing a number of individual *t* tests on the relevant variables at the outset, for example, would not reveal the important superiority of one of the groups.

One of the advantages of analysis of covariance is that it reduces the size of the error term (the within mean square) which is used as the denominator of the *F* ratio. As a result, the size and significance of the *F* values are increased. However, if an effect is statistically significant *only* after numerous control variables have been employed to reduce the error term, then it may be impossible to see the effect at work in actual school situations. For a teacher employing certain instructional methods to help a particular student, for example, it is no comfort to see the student fall further behind, even if an analysis of covariance showed that academic performance, on average, increases when a number of control variables are taken into account.

MULTIPLE-CLASSIFICATION ANALYSIS OF COVARIANCE

Multiple-classification analysis of covariance is analogous to multiple-classification analysis of variance, coupled with the use of regression analysis. The same general scheme is employed in both models. Thus, in **multiple-classification analysis of covariance**, the investigator is interested in the relationship between a dependent variable and two or more independent variables (represented by subgroups), as well as the possibility of a relationship between the dependent variable and an interaction between the independent variables. Initial differences between the groups representing the independent variables are adjusted as with single-classification analysis of covariance, employing one or more control variables. The resulting *F* values for main effects and interactions are interpreted in the usual way. Adjustments can be made in means representing all independent-variable groups in order to compensate for initial control-variable differences among the groups.

All of the arguments favoring the use of multiple-classification analysis-of-variance models and those favoring analysis-of-covariance approaches can be combined to support the use of multiple-classification analysis of covariance in educational investigations. It is true that the mathematical computations are somewhat lengthy, even if you are using a calculator. But this method is no more complex than any of the techniques you have studied. The companion chapter that follows, which is devoted to computation procedures for single- and multiple-classification analysis of covariance, will demonstrate how the mathematics used in multiple-classification problems can be accomplished.

ASSUMPTIONS FOR ANALYSIS OF COVARIANCE

The assumptions that should be satisfied for valid statistical tests using analysis-of-covariance methods include all those for analysis of variance: random sampling, homogeneity of variances, and normal distributions. There is one additional, important assumption for this technique: The regression coefficients (slopes) for the regression lines in the subgroup populations must be equal. (Note that the regression lines in Figure 15–1 are parallel.) Procedures for testing this assumption can be found in advanced texts on experimental design.

As with the techniques described earlier, stringent satisfaction of these assumptions is probably not required. Nevertheless, in analysis of covariance, departure from them should not be too great. The additional assumption of homogeneity of regression makes analysis of covariance a less robust technique than analysis of variance; that is, it is less able to tolerate marked departures from the requisite assumptions.

■   ■   ■

REVIEW

For the educational investigator, analysis of covariance is a valuable statistical technique because it allows testing for mean differences between two or more groups while compensating for initial differences between groups with respect to relevant variables. This increases the precision of the statistical tests.

Analysis of covariance can be used in the many school situations where, for justifiable practical reasons, the investigator is not able to manipulate groups so that samples can be made equal on such important variables as aptitude and prior achievement. Through analysis of covariance, differences among groups with respect to a criterion variable can be studied more analytically. These adjustment procedures should not be used on preexisting groups without regard to the nature of the *preexisting differences* among groups, however.

This important statistical tool combines analysis of variance and regression models in an intriguing way. Essentially, control measures related to the criterion are used to generate for each individual a predicted criterion score based on that individual's control-measure scores. After the individuals have been equated with respect to the controls, their adjusted scores are then analyzed by analysis of variance.

Adjustments in subgroup means may be made so that a mean difference between groups can be calculated after statistically equalizing the groups on the control measures. As in the case of analysis of variance, the ancova model can be used in single-classification or multiple-classification forms.

TERMS TO KNOW

Listed in order of presentation in chapter:)

confounding variable
covariable
analysis of covariance (ancova)
single-classification analysis of covariance
control variables
covariates
adjusted scores
residuals
multiple-classification analysis of covariance

EXERCISES

1. A school psychologist wishes to study the influence of three new curriculum plans on the history achievement of junior high pupils. Although the groups of pupils involved were selected on a fairly random basis, the psychologist has learned that there is considerable disparity among the groups with respect to verbal aptitude. Should single-classification analysis of variance or single-classification analysis of covariance be used to examine the pupils' postexperiment history achievement? Why?

2. Two samples have *identical* means on a criterion mathematics achievement measure, but group A is markedly inferior to group B with respect to academic aptitude and performance on a pretest of mathematics knowledge. Is it possible that, with the identical means, an analysis of covariance could detect a significant mean difference?

3. If criterion mean adjustments were made in exercise 2, which group's mean would become superior?

4. Is it possible that a series of mean differences among four groups that were found to be significantly different beyond the 0.01 level by analysis of variance could be tested by analysis of covariance (with an added control variable or variables) and found to be statistically insignificant?

5. Discuss the interpretation problems an investigator might encounter in using analysis-of-covariance procedures to test the following null hypothesis: There is no difference in the mean performance on an arithmetic fundamentals achievement test for high, middle, and low socioeconomic student groups that have been statistically equated with respect to academic aptitude.

6. Construct a graph similar to that in Figure 15–1 for the case in which the three groups in the figure do *not* differ in mean scores on the control variable. Does any adjustment take place? Explain.

SELECTED READINGS

Blalock, Hubert M., Jr. *Social Statistics*. New York:McGraw-Hill, 1979, chap. 20.

Dixon, Wilfrid J., and Massey, Frank J. *Introduction to Statistical Analysis*. New York: McGraw-Hill, 1969, chap. 12.

Edwards, Allen L. *Experimental Design in Psychological Research*. New York: Harper and Row, 1985, chap. 24.

McNemar, Quinn. *Psychological Statistics*. New York: Wiley, 1969, chap. 18.

Shavelson, Richard J. *Statistical Reasoning for the Behavioral Sciences*. Boston: Allyn & Bacon, 1988, chap. 21.

Analysis of Covariance

▪ *computation procedures*

As with several of the techniques you have already studied, the mathematics involved in computing analysis of covariance are simple but rather time-consuming. For these procedures, the use of a calculator or computer is almost a must. Routines for analysis of covariance are available in most of the commonly used statistical software packages for computers.

COMPUTATIONAL EXAMPLE FOR SINGLE-CLASSIFICATION ANALYSIS OF COVARIANCE

As you learned in Chapter 15, in single-classification analysis of covariance there is one dependent variable, one independent variable (represented by two or more groups), and at least one control variable. Several control variables may be employed because the investigator considers them to be relevant, or strongly related, to the dependent variable. Such a design requires statistical compensation for differences among the independent-variable groups with respect to the control variables. The criterion or dependent variable is usually represented by the symbol Y and the control variable is represented by X, or, if there is more than one control variable, by X_1, X_2, X_3, and so forth. The inde-

Table 16.1   **Scores of Two Programmed-Instruction Groups of Secondary Mathematics Pupils on Criterion Achievement Test, Prior Mathematics Achievement Examination, and Verbal Aptitude Test**

Pupils	Criterion Achievement Test (Y)	Prior Math Achievement Exam (X_1)	Verbal Aptitude Test (X_2)
Small-step group:			
a	59	68	116
b	58	69	120
c	58	64	114
d	54	63	104
e	53	65	110
f	50	61	101
Group Σ	332	390	665
Large-step group:			
g	56	63	114
h	51	59	102
i	51	56	103
j	49	57	100
k	48	62	111
l	47	61	110
Group Σ	302	358	640
Total Σ	634	748	1,305

pendent variable is represented by the groups whose criterion-variable means are being tested for significance of difference.

The computation procedures for single-classification analysis of covariance can be illustrated by working with the hypothetical data for two groups presented in Table 16.1. The two group samples are extremely small (six individuals in each) and are employed only for purposes of illustration. In actual research situations an investigator working with such small samples would be unable to demonstrate that they have satisfied the assumptions for analysis of covariance, and much larger samples are usually necessary. Though the two groups in the computational example we are using are equal in size, this need not be the case in single-classification analysis of covariance, nor, for that matter, is the technique limited to use with only two groups.

In this example the independent variable or factor is "size of step" in a self-instruction program, that is, the difficulty gap between the items or frames composing the program. Both groups use self-instruction programmed mathematics texts for a period of two months, after which the same criterion achievement test (Y) is administered to all the students. The increase in level of difficulty between successive frames is considerably greater in the large-step programming-method group than in the small-step group. The null hypothesis in this example would be the following: There is no significant difference in achievement between the groups following the experimental self-instruction period (after equating on two control measures).

The variables considered relevant to the criterion are (1) previous mathematics achievement, as measured by a standardized achievement examination, and (2) verbal aptitude, as measured by a verbal analogies test. Data for both control variables are already at hand in the school system's records. Note from

Table 16.1 that the small-step group is superior to the large-step group on both control variables (X_1 and X_2).

Steps in the Analysis

The first step in the analysis is to set up a table similar to Table 16.2, in which sums and means of the criterion and control variables are presented.

The next step in the analysis is to compute the sums of squares for the raw scores and the various crossproducts, which can be easily done with a calculator. These quantities are then summarized in a table such as Table 16.3.

With the data from Tables 16.2 and 16.3, it is possible to compute, *in deviation form,* the various sums of squares and crossproducts associated with the *total* variation in the sample, as well as the amount of variation *within* the two subgroups. As you may recall from the discussion of single-classification analysis of variance in Chapter 11, the part of the total variation present that is not a function of the variation within groups is attributable to the differences *between* groups. (The terms *deviation sum of squares* and *deviation sum of crossproducts* were introduced in Chapter 8.)

In this example, the deviation values must be found first for *total* and then for *within* groups for the following quantities:

$$(1)\ \Sigma y^2,\ (2)\ \Sigma x_1^2,\ (3)\ \Sigma x_2^2,\ (4)\ \Sigma x_1 y,\ (5)\ \Sigma x_2 y,\ (6)\ \Sigma x_1 x_2.$$

Table 16.2   Sums and Means of the Criterion and Control Variables for Two Groups of Programmed-Instruction Secondary Mathematics Pupils

Programming Method		Criterion Variable		Control Variable			
		Achievement		Prior Math Achievement		Verbal Aptitude	
	n	ΣY	$\overline{Y}$	ΣX_1	$\overline{X}_1$	ΣX_2	$\overline{X}_2$
Small step	6	332	55.33	390	65.00	665	110.83
Large step	6	302	50.33	358	59.67	640	106.67
Total sum or mean	12	634	52.83	748	62.33	1,305	108.75

Table 16.3   Summary of Squared Raw Scores and Crossproducts for All 12 Mathematics Pupils

Measure	Symbols	Total for Entire Sample
Squared raw scores		
Criterion achievement test	ΣY^2	33,686
Prior mathematics achievement	ΣX_1^2	46,796
Verbal aptitude	ΣX_2^2	142,399
Crossproducts		
Prior achievement $\times$ criterion	$\Sigma X_1 Y$	39,652
Verbal aptitude $\times$ criterion	$\Sigma X_2 Y$	69,149
Prior achievement $\times$ verbal aptitude	$\Sigma X_1 X_2$	81,587

In the computations for these values, the subscripts *ss* and *ls* denote the small-step and large-step treatment groups, respectively. The computations are as follows:

1. Σy^2 total:

$$\Sigma y^2 = \Sigma Y^2 - \frac{(\Sigma Y)^2}{n}$$

$$= 33{,}686 - \frac{(634)^2}{12}$$

$$= 189.77$$

Σy^2 within:

$$\Sigma y^2 = \Sigma Y^2 - \left[\frac{(\Sigma Y_{ss})^2}{n_{ss}} + \frac{(\Sigma Y_{ls})^2}{n_{ls}}\right]$$

$$= 33{,}686 - \left[\frac{(332)^2}{6} + \frac{(302)^2}{6}\right]$$

$$= 114.66$$

2. Σx_1^2 total:

$$\Sigma x_1^2 = \Sigma X_1^2 - \frac{(\Sigma X_1)^2}{n}$$

$$= 46{,}796 - \frac{(748)^2}{12}$$

$$= 170.67$$

Σx_1^2 within:

$$\Sigma x_1^2 = \Sigma X_1^2 - \left[\frac{(\Sigma X_{1ss})^2}{n_{ss}} + \frac{(\Sigma X_{1ls})^2}{n_{ls}}\right]$$

$$= 46{,}796 - \left[\frac{(390)^2}{6} + \frac{(358)^2}{6}\right]$$

$$= 85.33$$

3. Σx_2^2 total:

$$\Sigma x_2^2 = \Sigma X_2^2 - \frac{(\Sigma X_2)^2}{n}$$

$$= 142{,}399 - \frac{(1{,}305)^2}{12}$$

$$= 480.25$$

Σx_2^2 within:

$$\Sigma x_2^2 = \Sigma X_2^2 - \left[\frac{(\Sigma X_{2ss})^2}{n_{ss}} + \frac{(\Sigma X_{2ls})^2}{n_{ls}}\right]$$

$$= 142{,}399 - \left[\frac{(665)^2}{6} + \frac{(640)^2}{6}\right]$$

$$= 428.16$$

4. $\Sigma x_1 y$ total:

$$\Sigma x_1 y = \Sigma X_1 Y - \frac{(\Sigma X_1)(\Sigma Y)}{n}$$

$$= 39{,}652 - \frac{(748)(634)}{12}$$

$$= 132.67$$

$\Sigma x_1 y$ within:

$$\Sigma x_1 y = \Sigma X_1 Y - \left[\frac{(\Sigma X_{1ss})(\Sigma Y_{ss})}{n_{ss}} + \frac{(\Sigma X_{1ls})(\Sigma Y_{ls})}{n_{ls}}\right]$$

$$= 39{,}652 - \left[\frac{(390)(332)}{6} + \frac{(358)(302)}{6}\right]$$

$$= 52.67$$

5. $\Sigma x_2 y$ total:

$$\Sigma x_2 y = \Sigma X_2 Y - \frac{(\Sigma X_2)(\Sigma Y)}{n}$$

$$= 69{,}149 - \frac{(1{,}305)(634)}{12}$$

$$= 201.50$$

$\Sigma x_2 y$ within:

$$\Sigma x_2 y = \Sigma X_2 Y - \left[\frac{(\Sigma X_{2ss})(\Sigma Y_{ss})}{n_{ss}} + \frac{(\Sigma X_{2ls})(\Sigma Y_{ls})}{n_{ls}}\right]$$

$$= 69{,}149 - \left[\frac{(665)(332)}{6} + \frac{(640)(302)}{6}\right]$$

$$= 139.00$$

6. $\Sigma x_1 x_2$ total:

$$\Sigma x_1 x_2 = \Sigma X_1 X_2 - \frac{(\Sigma X_1)(\Sigma X_2)}{n}$$

$$= 81,587 - \frac{(748)(1,305)}{12}$$

$$= 242.00$$

$\Sigma x_1 x_2$ within:

$$\Sigma x_1 X_2 = \Sigma X_1 X_2 - \left[\frac{(\Sigma X_{1ss})(\Sigma X_{2ss})}{n_{ss}} + \frac{(\Sigma X_{1ls})(\Sigma X_{2ls})}{n_{ls}} \right]$$

$$= 81,587 - \left[\frac{(390)(665)}{6} + \frac{(358)(640)}{6} \right]$$

$$= 175.33$$

You should find it instructive to identify the source of the values used in computing these deviation sums of squares and crossproducts. Note that, although the mathematics involved may appear to be imposing, the various values needed are drawn from Tables 16.2 and 16.3 and inserted into the total and within formulas in a systematic fashion. The actual computation is quite simple.

The next step in the analysis is to compute regression coefficients, first total and then within, for each of the control variables. This is done in a manner similar to that employed in multiple regression analysis as described in Chapter 8. The two linear equations needed to find the values of b_1 and b_2 are:

$$\Sigma x_1 y = b_1 \Sigma x_1^2 + b_2 \Sigma x_1 x_2$$
$$\Sigma x_2 y = b_1 \Sigma x_1 x_2 + b_2 \Sigma x_2^2$$

These equations are solved simultaneously, first with the total sums of squares and crossproducts, then with the within sums of squares and crossproducts. For total, the equations become:

$$132.67 = b_1 170.67 + b_2 242.00$$
$$201.50 = b_1 242.00 + b_2 480.25$$

Dividing both equations by their coefficients of b_2 and then subtracting the second equation from the first (or adding if the algebraic signs of b_2 are unlike) yields the value of b_1:

$$0.54822314 = b_1 0.70524793 + b_2$$
$$0.41957314 = b_1 0.50390422 + b_2$$
$$0.12865000 = b_1 0.20134371$$
$$b_1 = 0.63895713$$

The value of b_2 is found by substituting the value of b_1 in either of the equations yielded by the original division operation. Thus, substituting in the first equation above:

$$0.54822314 = (0.63895713)(0.70524793) + b_2$$
$$b_2 = 0.09759995$$

These values should be checked by substituting them in one of the original equations, as follows:

$$132.67 = (0.63895713)(170.67) + (0.09759995)(242.00)$$
$$132.67 = 109.0508 + 23.6192 = 132.67 \text{ (checks)}$$

By the same process, the values of b_1 and b_2 for within are computed by substituting the necessary within sums of squares and crossproducts into the two linear equations:

$$52.67 = b_1 85.33 + b_2 175.33$$
$$139.00 = b_1 175.33 + b_2 428.16$$

Omitting the mathematical operations identical to those involved in finding the total b_1 and b_2, the values of the within regression coefficients are the following:

$$b_1 = -0.31404788$$
$$b_2 = 0.45324648$$

When the values of b_1 and b_2 for both total and within groups have been determined, the **residual sums of squares** can be computed for total and within. When the within residual sum of squares has been subtracted from the total residual sum of squares, the remainder is called the between residual sum of squares. The between residual sum of squares represents the amount of variation attributable to differences between group means, *after* adjusting for differences between the groups with respect to the control variables. The within and between residual sums of squares are divided by their respective degrees of freedom to obtain the mean squares. As in all forms of analysis of variance, these mean squares are placed in a ratio to yield the F value by which the null hypothesis is tested.

The sum of squares of residuals for both total and within are computed[1] by use of the following equation:

$$\text{Sum of squares of residuals} = \Sigma y^2 - (b_1 \Sigma x_1 y + b_2 \Sigma x_2 y)$$

In computing the *total* residual sum of squares, the values for the equation are the *total* regression coefficients and sums. The *within* residual sum of squares is found by using *within* values in the equation. The equations therefore are:

$$\text{Total SS of residuals} = 189.77 - [(0.63895713)(132.67) +$$
$$(0.09759995)(201.50)]$$
$$= 85.33$$
$$\text{Within SS of residuals} = 114.66 - [(-0.31404788)(52.67) +$$
$$(0.45324648)(139.00)]$$
$$= 68.20$$

Testing for Significance

The final analysis-of-covariance table to test the null hypothesis in the example can now be set up. The table will take a form similar to that in Table

---

1. When only one control variable is involved in the analysis, the residual sums of squares are found by use of the formula:
$$\text{Residual SS} = \Sigma y^2 - [(\Sigma xy)^2 / \Sigma x^2]$$

Table 16.4   **Analysis of Covariance for Achievement Differences between Two Experimental Programmed-Instruction Groups, Controlling for Prior Mathematics Achievement and Verbal Aptitude**

Source of Variation	Degrees of Freedom	Residuals Sum of Squares	Residuals Mean Square	F
Between	1	17.13	17.13	2.01
Within	8	68.20	8.53	
Total	9	85.33		

16.4. Note that the between residual sum of squares is obtained by subtracting the within residual sum of squares from the total residual sum of squares.

The degrees of freedom used in an analysis-of-covariance problem are similar to those used in analysis-of-variance computations, with one important exception. Each control variable used takes 1 degree of freedom from the total degrees of freedom. Thus, for the total df, the number of control variables employed must be subtracted from the usual $n - 1$. Since two control measures are used in the present example, the total degrees of freedom are $12 - 1 = 11$, less the two controls $= 9$. For any single-classification analysis of covariance, the following scheme can be employed for degrees of freedom:

Source of Variation	Degrees of Freedom
Total	$df = n$ minus (1 plus the number of control variables)
Between	$df =$ number of groups minus 1
Within	$df = df$ for total minus df for between

In the example we are using, the degrees of freedom are: for total, $df = 9$; for between, $df = 1$; for within, $df = 8$.

The F value obtained by dividing the between residual mean square by the within residual mean square is 2.01. An inspection of Table F reveals that with 1 and 8 degrees of freedom, an F of 5.32 is needed to reject the null hypothesis at the 0.05 level, so the null hypothesis of no mean difference between the groups cannot be rejected.

The importance of analysis of covariance can be gauged from this example by observing in Table 16.2 that there is a mean difference of five points between the two programmed-instruction groups. Suppose the investigator had not attempted to adjust the data for initial differences by incorporating two control variables in an analysis-of-covariance scheme. *If the criterion data alone* had been analyzed by a pooled-variance t test, the result ($t = 2.56$; $df = 10$) would have been significant beyond the 0.05 level! In other words, if the superiority of the small-step group in verbal aptitude and prior mathematics achievement had not been taken into account, the investigator would have concluded that the small-step programming method is significantly better than the large-step method. You should now be able to see that the two control measures employed in the covariance analysis would have acted to confound the simple t-test design, because one group's superiority in these relevant variables worked to the disadvantage of the other group.

Adjustment of Means

In analysis of covariance, the performance of the groups on the criterion variable is related to their performance on the control variables. Investigators who want to determine how each group would have performed on the criterion measure *if* the groups had been equivalent at the outset with respect to the control measures can use a final step in the procedure. This step permits adjustment of the criterion means to compensate for differences among the groups on the control variables.

For each group's criterion mean, an adjustment term is calculated by using the within regression coefficients and the difference between the group's control-variable mean and the total sample's control-variable mean. This process can be illustrated by adjusting the criterion means in the example, using the data in Table 16.2 and the computations for regression coefficients b_1 and b_2. The adjustment values used for the criterion means of the small-step group ($\overline{Y}_{ss}$) are computed as follows, where the subscript t denotes the total control-variable mean:

$$\begin{aligned}
\text{Values}_{ss} &= b_1(\overline{X}_{1_{ss}} - \overline{X}_{1_t}) \text{ and } b_2(\overline{X}_{2_{ss}} - \overline{X}_{2_t}) \\
&= (-0.31404788)(65.00 - 62.33) \text{ and} \\
&\quad (0.45324648)(110.83 - 108.75) \\
&= -0.84 \text{ and } 0.94
\end{aligned}$$

These adjustment values are then added to or subtracted from the original value of $\overline{Y}_{ss}$ depending on the inferiority or superiority of that group on the control measures. Because the small-step group had an advantage on both control measures, both adjustment values (regardless of the algebraic sign) are subtracted from the original value of $\overline{Y}_{ss}$. Thus the adjusted $\overline{Y}_{ss}$ is $55.33 - (0.84 + 0.94) = 53.55$.

A similar process is followed in the adjustment of $\overline{Y}$ for the large-step group:

$$\begin{aligned}
\text{Values}_{ls} &= b_1(\overline{X}_{1_{ls}} - \overline{X}_{1_t}) \text{ and } b_2(\overline{X}_{2_{ls}} - \overline{X}_{2_t}) \\
&= (-0.31404788)(59.67 - 62.33) \text{ and} \\
&\quad (0.45324648)(106.67 - 108.75) \\
&= 0.84 \text{ and } -0.94
\end{aligned}$$

The adjustment is again made in terms of the original superiority or inferiority of the large-step group on the control measures. Because the large-step group's control variable means were smaller than the total control-variable means in both instances, the 0.84 and 0.94 are added to the original value of $\overline{Y}_{ls}$. The adjusted $\overline{Y}_{ls}$ is $50.33 + (0.84 + 0.94) = 52.11$. Note that the adjusted $\overline{Y}_{ls}$ of 52.11 is only slightly lower than the adjusted $\overline{Y}_{ss}$ of 53.55.

When more than one control variable is employed, there may be situations in which a group is inferior with respect to one or more control measures but superior with respect to other controls. In such cases the adjustment values usually cancel each other to a great extent. However, the adjustment value that usually makes the most difference is the one based on the control variable that is most strongly related to the criterion, particularly when there is a sizable difference between the groups on that measure. The difference between the total control-variable mean and the group control-variable mean should always be noted and the adjustment made accordingly.

COMPUTATIONAL EXAMPLE FOR MULTIPLE-CLASSIFICATION ANALYSIS OF COVARIANCE

As in analysis of variance, in analysis of covariance the basic logic of the single-classification procedure can be extended to a multiple-classification scheme for studying the relationship between a criterion variable and more than one independent variable (as represented by subgroups). With multiple-classification analysis of covariance it is possible to test for group differences on the independent or main-effect variables, as well as for significant interactions between the independent variables. At the same time, adjustments can be made for differences between the independent-variable groups with respect to one or more control variables considered relevant to the criterion. Thus the more sensitive analysis available through multiple-classification analysis of variance can be refined even further.

The computation procedures for multiple-classification analysis of covariance can be illustrated by an example in which the two independent variables are (1) type of instructional film, and (2) previous exposure to educational television. The dependent variable is geography achievement, and the control variables are (1) scholastic aptitude, (2) previous overall academic achievement, and (3) pretest geography achievement.

Suppose a researcher is testing the efficacy of a unique new filmed method of teaching geography principles, in contrast to a more conventional filmed approach to the subject. The new method might include a number of opportunities to respond to instructional questions posed throughout the film and subsequently answered in it. Suppose also there are five films of the new type and five conventional films that treat the same topic in almost an equivalent fashion, except for the questions interspersed throughout the experimental films. And suppose that a classroom educational television (ETV) project is currently underway in which many, but not all, of the students in the school are participating. If the researcher's opinion is that previous exposure to ETV may affect the response of the students to the films in some way, the students may be classified so that participation in the ETV project is considered as a second independent variable.

An experiment can be conducted using the two sets of films with a sample of 40 high school students, 20 of whom use the new films for a week and 20 of whom use the conventional films for the same period.[2] The former students are designated as the experimental group and the latter students as the control group. In addition, the students are selected so that ten in each group are participating in the educational television project.

In this experiment the researcher uses an achievement test based on the content of the films as the dependent variable, with (1) the approach employed in the films and (2) participation in ETV as the two independent variables. The control variables are (1) students' scholastic aptitude test scores, (2) grade-

---

2. Though unequal frequencies in the subgroups can be employed, extensive adjustments must then be made in the analysis. Most computer-based statistical programs with a general linear model or multivariate analysis-of-variance routine can perform the required computations. See B. J. Winer, *Statistical Principles in Experimental Design* (New York: McGraw-Hill, 1971), pp. 792–96.

point averages earned by students during the previous semester, and (3) performance on a pretest administered before the films are used.

Steps in the Analysis

Once the necessary data have been obtained, the first step in the analysis is to set up a table such as Table 16.5 in which the sums and means of the four subgroups are presented. Another table (such as Table 16.6) is also needed to summarize the raw-score sum of squares and crossproducts needed for the computations to follow.

Next, as in the single-classification model, all possible sums of squares and crossproducts for the total sample and for within groups must be computed in deviation form. In multiple-classification analysis of covariance, it is also necessary to compute the deviation sums of squares and crossproducts for each main-effect variable and for all possible interactions between the main-effect variables. In this example, it is necessary to compute these values for (1) total, (2) film type used, (3) ETV participation, (4) interaction, and (5) within for all of the following quantities: Σy^2, $\Sigma x_1{}^2$, $\Sigma x_2{}^2$, $\Sigma x_3{}^2$, $\Sigma x_1 y$, $\Sigma x_2 y$, $\Sigma x_3 y$,

Table 16.5   **Sums and Means of Experimental and Conventional Film-Taught Student Groups, Classified According to Participation in Educational Television Project**

Group	n	Criterion Posttest Scores		Scholastic Aptitude Test Scores		Controls Grade Point Averages		Pretest Scores	
		ΣY	$\overline{Y}$	ΣX_1	$\overline{X}_1$	ΣX_2	$\overline{X}_2$	ΣX_3	$\overline{X}_3$
Experimental films									
ETV participants	10	828	82.80	1,134	113.40	28.32	2.832	209	20.90
ETV nonparticipants	10	776	77.60	1,231	123.10	29.43	2.943	259	25.90
Subtotal	20	1,604	80.20	2,365	118.25	57.75	2.887	468	23.40
Conventional films									
ETV participants	10	814	81.40	1,174	117.40	27.30	2.730	239	23.90
ETV nonparticipants	10	692	69.20	1,074	107.40	27.18	2.718	232	23.20
Subtotal	20	1,506	75.30	2,248	112.40	54.48	2.724	471	23.55
Total sums or means	40	3,110	77.75	4,613	115.33	112.23	2.806	939	23.47

Table 16.6   **Summary of Raw-Score Squares and Crossproducts for Criterion and Control Variables**

Measure	Symbol	Total
Posttest	ΣY^2	247,847
Scholastic aptitude	$\Sigma X_1{}^2$	541,256
Grade-point average	$\Sigma X_2{}^2$	325.76
Pretest	$\Sigma X_3{}^2$	24,172.14
Crossproducts	$\Sigma X_1 Y$	360,483
	$\Sigma X_2 Y$	8,779.99
	$\Sigma X_3 Y$	73,920
	$\Sigma X_1 X_2$	12,999.82
	$\Sigma X_2 X_3$	2,654.34
	$\Sigma X_1 X_3$	108,603

$\Sigma x_1 x_2$, $\Sigma x_1 x_3$, $\Sigma x_2 x_3$. Examples of the computation procedures for computing the sums of squares will be given first, followed by examples of the procedure for computing the crossproducts.

The criterion variable will be used to illustrate the computation of sums of squares. The five Σy^2 values are determined as follows:

1. For total:

$$\Sigma y^2 = \Sigma Y^2 - \frac{(\Sigma Y)^2}{n}$$

$$= 247,847 - \frac{(3,110)^2}{40}$$

$$= 6,044.5$$

2. For film type used, where the subscripts e and c denote the experimental and conventional film groups:

$$\Sigma y^2 = \frac{(\Sigma Y_e)^2}{n_e} + \frac{(\Sigma Y_c)^2}{n_c} - \frac{(\Sigma Y)^2}{n}$$

$$= \frac{(1,604)^2}{20} + \frac{(1,506)^2}{20} - \frac{(3,110)^2}{40}$$

$$= 240.1$$

3. For ETV participation, where the subscripts p and np denote participants and nonparticipants:

$$\Sigma y^2 = \frac{(\Sigma Y_p)^2}{n_p} + \frac{(\Sigma Y_{np})^2}{n_{np}} - \frac{(\Sigma Y)^2}{n}$$

$$= \frac{(828 + 814)^2}{20} + \frac{(776 + 692)^2}{20} - \frac{(3,110)^2}{40}$$

$$= 756.9$$

4. For interaction:

$$\Sigma y^2 = \frac{(\Sigma Y_{ep})^2}{n_{ep}} + \frac{(\Sigma Y_{enp})^2}{n_{enp}} + \frac{(\Sigma Y_{cp})^2}{n_{cp}} + \frac{(\Sigma Y_{cnp})^2}{n_{cnp}} - \frac{(\Sigma Y)^2}{n}$$

$$- (\text{SS for films} + \text{SS for ETV})$$

$$= \frac{(828)^2}{10} + \frac{(776)^2}{10} + \frac{(814)^2}{10} + \frac{(692)^2}{10} - \frac{(3,110)^2}{40} - (240.1 + 756.9)$$

$$= 122.5$$

5. For within:

$$\Sigma y^2 = \Sigma Y^2 - \left[\frac{(\Sigma Y_{ep})^2}{n_{ep}} + \frac{(\Sigma Y_{enp})^2}{n_{enp}} + \frac{(\Sigma Y_{cp})^2}{n_{cp}} + \frac{(\Sigma Y_{cnp})^2}{n_{cnp}}\right]$$

$$= 247{,}847 - \left[\frac{(828)^2}{10} + \frac{(776)^2}{10} + \frac{(814)^2}{10} + \frac{(692)^2}{10}\right]$$

$$= 4{,}925.0$$

The deviation sums of squares for the control variables are computed in a similar fashion.

The computation of deviation crossproducts is illustrated using the cross-product of the posttest criterion and scholastic aptitude test scores, as follows:

1. For total:

$$\Sigma x_1 y = \Sigma X_1 Y - \frac{(\Sigma X_1)(\Sigma Y)}{n}$$

$$= 360{,}483 - \frac{(4{,}613)(3{,}110)}{40}$$

$$= 1{,}822.25$$

2. For film type used:

$$\Sigma x_1 y = \frac{(\Sigma X_{1e})(\Sigma Y_e)}{n_e} + \frac{(\Sigma X_{1c})(\Sigma Y_c)}{n_c} - \frac{(\Sigma X_1)(\Sigma Y)}{n}$$

$$= \frac{(2{,}365)(1{,}604)}{20} + \frac{(2{,}248)(1{,}506)}{20} - \frac{(4{,}613)(3{,}110)}{40}$$

$$= 286.65$$

3. For ETV participation:

$$\Sigma x_1 y = \frac{(\Sigma X_{1p})(\Sigma Y_p)}{n_p} + \frac{(\Sigma X_{1np})(\Sigma Y_{np})}{n_{np}} - \frac{(\Sigma X_1)(\Sigma Y)}{n}$$

$$= \frac{(1{,}134 + 1{,}174)(828 + 814)}{20} + \frac{(1{,}231 + 1{,}074)(776 + 692)}{20}$$

$$\quad - \frac{(4{,}613)(3{,}110)}{40}$$

$$= 13.05$$

4. For interaction:

$$\Sigma x_1 y = \frac{(\Sigma X_{1ep})(\Sigma Y_{ep})}{n_{ep}} + \frac{(\Sigma X_{1enp})(\Sigma Y_{enp})}{n_{enp}} + \frac{(\Sigma X_{1cp})(\Sigma Y_{cp})}{n_{cp}}$$

$$+ \frac{(\Sigma X_{1cnp})(\Sigma Y_{cnp})}{n_{cnp}} - \frac{(\Sigma X_1)(\Sigma Y)}{n}$$

$$- (\text{SS for films} + \text{SS for ETV})$$

$$= \frac{(1,134)(828)}{10} + \frac{(1,231)(776)}{10} + \frac{(1,174)(814)}{10} + \frac{(1,074)(692)}{10}$$

$$- \frac{(4,613)(3,110)}{40} - (286.65 + 13.05)$$

$$= 344.75$$

5. For within:

$$\Sigma x_1 y = \Sigma X_1 Y - \left[\frac{(\Sigma X_{1ep})(\Sigma Y_{ep})}{n_{ep}} + \frac{(\Sigma X_{1enp})(\Sigma X_{enp})}{n_{enp}} + \frac{(\Sigma X_{1cp})(\Sigma Y_{cp})}{n_{cp}} + \frac{(\Sigma X_{1cnp})(\Sigma Y_{cnp})}{n_{cnp}} \right]$$

$$= 360,483 - \left[\frac{(1,134)(828)}{10} + \frac{(1,231)(776)}{10} + \frac{(1,174)(814)}{10} + \frac{(1,074)(692)}{10} \right]$$

$$= 1,177.80$$

You should attempt to trace the origin of the various values in these equations to their sources in Tables 16.5 and 16.6. Although the numbers involved may seem imposing and confusing, careful consideration will reveal that each of the sums of squares and crossproducts reflects the variation in the data that can be attributed to a specific source. To do this, the data are artificially reclassified, or simply looked at in another light. The process is something akin to viewing a phenomenon from different angles in order to note the contribution made by each of several factors.

After the necessary deviation values have been computed, all deviation values are presented in a table similar to Table 16.7. In viewing this table, you might consider the number of mathematical calculations to be enormous. But the calculation of the 50 deviation sums of squares and crossproducts by calculator, although time-consuming, is really quite routine, because the computations for each source of variation, that is, for total, within, main effects, and interaction, are very similar. Of course, the use of a computer for this type of analysis would be the preferred choice for these and subsequent computations to be described.

The next step in the analysis is to add the within value of each sum of squares and sum of crossproducts to each main-effect and interaction value. In the example we are using, the values for Σy^2 would be treated as follows:

Table 16.7   Deviation Values for Sums of Squares and Crossproducts

Source of Variation	Σy^2	Σx_1^2	Σx_2^2	Σx_3^2
Type of films used	240.1	344.20	0.2673	0.22
ETV participation	756.9	2.20	0.0245	46.22
Interaction	122.5	968.25	0.0378	81.23
Within	4,925.0	7,949.10	10.5425	2,001.44
Total	6,044.5	9,263.75	10.8721	2,129.11

Table 16.8   Deviation Values for Sums of Squares and Crossproducts, Combined with Within

Within Plus	Σy^2	Σx_1^2	Σx_2^2	Σx_3^2
Type of films used	5,165.1	8,293.30	10.8098	2,001.66
ETV participation	5,681.9	7,951.30	10.5670	2,047.66
Interaction	5,047.5	8,917.35	10.5803	2,082.67

For within plus type of films used:	$4,925.0 + 240.1 = 5,165.1$
For within plus ETV participation:	$4,925.0 + 756.9 = 5,681.9$
For within plus interaction:	$4,925.0 + 122.5 = 5,047.5$

In the same fashion the within values are added to each film used, ETV participation, and interaction sum of squares and sum of crossproducts. These values are then summarized in a table such as Table 16.8, in which the required deviation values for the sums of squares and crossproducts are presented.

At this point in the analysis, linear equations are set up to determine the regression coefficients associated with each control variable, considered separately for each source of variation. For three control variables the equations take the following form:

$$\Sigma x_1 y = b_1 \Sigma x_1^2 + b_2 \Sigma x_1 x_2 + b_3 \Sigma x_1 x_2$$
$$\Sigma x_2 y = b_1 \Sigma x_1 x_2 + b_2 \Sigma x_2^2 + b_3 \Sigma x_2 x_3$$
$$\Sigma x_3 y = b_1 \Sigma x_1 x_3 + b_2 \Sigma x_2 x_3 + b_3 \Sigma x_3^2$$

By substituting the values for within plus films used in the above equations, the values of b_1, b_2, and b_3 for this particular source of variation can be determined. Using these regression coefficients, the sum of squares (amount of variation) attributable to the difference between the two film groups after the groups have been statistically equalized with respect to the three control variables can then be obtained.

The within plus ETV participation values and the within plus interaction values must also be substituted in the equations in order to obtain adjusted sums of squares for these two sources of variation. Finally, an adjusted sum of squares for within alone must be calculated. This is done by substituting the required within values in the equations and solving simultaneously. In all, then, four sets of simultaneous equations must be solved. If you need to be reacquainted with the solution procedures for such equations, see the step-by-step explanation in Chapter 8.

For the within plus films used values, the equations are as follows:

Table 16.7   *(continued)*

$\Sigma x_1 y$	$\Sigma x_2 y$	$\Sigma x_3 y$	$\Sigma x_1 x_2$	$\Sigma x_2 x_3$	$\Sigma x_1 x_3$
286.55	8.01	−7.35	9.57	0.25	−8.77
13.05	−4.31	−187.05·	0.07	1.07	−3.22
344.75	2.17	99.75	5.91	1.26	280.72
1,177.80	48.24	1,007.40	41.35	17.16	44.10
1,822.15	54.11	912.75	56.90	19.74	312.83

Table 16.8   *(continued)*

$\Sigma x_1 y$	$\Sigma x_2 y$	$\Sigma x_3 y$	$\Sigma x_1 x_2$	$\Sigma x_2 x_3$	$\Sigma x_1 x_3$
1,464.35	56.25	1,000.05	50.92	17.41	35.33
1,190.85	43.93	820.35	41.42	18.23	40.88
1,522.55	50.41	1,107.15	47.26	18.42	324.82

$$1,464.35 = b_1 8,293.30 + b_2 50.92 + b_3 35.33$$
$$56.25 = b_1 50.92 + b_2 10.8098 + b_3 17.41$$
$$1,000.05 = b_1 35.33 + b_2 17.41 + b_3 2,001.66$$

Simultaneous solution of the above equations yields the following regression coefficients for within plus films used:

$$b_1 = 0.15162103$$
$$b_2 = 3.74108924$$
$$b_3 = 0.46461978$$

In a similar fashion, the following regression coefficients are found for within plus ETV participation, within plus interaction, and within alone:

For Within Plus ETV Participation	For Within Plus Interaction	For Within Alone
$b_1 = 0.13223981$	$b_1 = 0.13561500$	$b_1 = 0.12836266$
$b_2 = 2.99838559$	$b_2 = 3.32121139$	$b_2 = 3.30372611$
$b_3 = 0.37129422$	$b_3 = 0.48107613$	$b_3 = 0.47218366$

The "within plus" residual sum of squares can now be computed for each of the four sources of variation needed for the F tests. Sometimes the residual sums of squares are called *adjusted* sums of squares. In each instance, the following equation (using "within plus" values) is solved to obtain the residual sum of squares:

$$\text{Residual SS} = \Sigma y^2 - (b_1 \Sigma x_1 y + b_2 \Sigma x_2 y + b_3 \Sigma x_3 y)$$

The equations for the sources of variation are:

1. For type of films used:

$$\text{Residual SS} = 5,165.1 - [(0.15162103)(1,464.35) + (3.74108924)(56.25)$$
$$+ (0.46461978)(1,000.05)] = 4,267.995$$

2. For ETV participation:

$$\text{Residual SS} = 5,681.9 - [(0.13223981)(1,190.85) + (2.99838559)(43.90) \\ + (0.37129422)(820.35)] = 5,088.202$$

3. For interaction:

$$\text{Residual SS} = 5,047.5 - [(0.13561500)(1,522.55) + (3.32121139)(50.41) \\ + (0.48107613)(1,107.15)] = 4,140.974$$

4. For within:

$$\text{Residual SS} = 4,925.0 - [(0.12836266)(1,177.80) + (3.30372611)(48.24) \\ + (0.47218366)(1,007.40)] = 4,138.764$$

To arrive at the residual sums of squares that represent the amount of variation attributable to the two main effects and interaction, the within residual SS must be subtracted from each of the other three "within plus" sums of squares. The resulting values are then reported in a table similar to Table 16.9.

The degrees of freedom used in multiple-classification ancova are determined in much the same way as in multiple-classification ancova (see Chapter 14). The exception is that the number of within degrees of freedom is found by subtracting from the total *df* (39 in this example) the number of degrees of freedom for main effects and interaction (3 in the example), as well as a degree of freedom for each control variable (3 in the example). Thus the number of degrees of freedom for within is 33.

Mean squares are then obtained by dividing the sums of squares by their respective degrees of freedom. *F* values for each main effect and for interaction are yielded by dividing the other mean squares by the within mean squares.

As you can see in Table 16.9, only the *F* value resulting from students' participation in the educational television project is statistically significant. This indicates that the following null hypothesis should be rejected: Having statistically adjusted for initial differences in scholastic aptitude, grade-point averages, and pretest scores between students who participated in the school ETV project and those who did not, there is no significant difference between the two groups. The null hypotheses concerning the type of film used and concerning interaction could not be rejected.

To carry the analysis one step further, means are adjusted in the same

Table 16.9   Analysis of Covariance Significance Tests

Source of Variation	Degrees of Freedom	Residuals		F
		Sum of Squares	Mean Square	
Films used	1	129.231	129.231	1.03
ETV participation	1	949.438	949.438	7.57[a]
Interaction	1	2.210	2.210	0.02
Within	33	4,138.764	125.417	

[a]Significant beyond the 0.01 level.

fashion as described in this chapter for single-classification analysis of covariance.

■   ■   ■

REVIEW

The computation procedures for single- and multiple-classification ancova models are lengthy, and the extensive calculations associated with the technique may seem awesome. Use of a calculator or computer, however, makes possible relatively rapid solution of most such problems.

In essence, analysis of covariance involves the computation of series of deviation sums of squares and crossproducts. Ultimately, these quantities are substituted in formulas to yield residual or adjusted sums of squares for the sources of variation typically seen in analysis of variance. The adjusted sums of squares incorporate the modifications made because of initial disparities between groups with respect to control measures.

The adjustment of criterion means is a function of the differences between subgroups on the control measure, as well as the strength of relationship between the criterion and the controls.

TERMS TO KNOW

residual sum of squares

EXERCISES

1. Two groups of elementary school pupils have been involved in a semester-long experiment in which different methods of geometry instructions have been used with each group. At the beginning of the experiment all pupils were given a standardized arithmetic test (X_1) and a standardized verbal analogies test (X_2). None of the students had had any formal instruction in geometry prior to the experiment. At the close of the training period, both groups were given a specially designed geometry examination (Y).

   Employ a single-classification analysis-of-covariance model, in which the arithmetic achievement and verbal analogies measures serve as the control variables and the geometry examination scores serve as the criterion variable, to determine the value of F. Then decide whether the null hypothesis that group I is not significantly different from group II should be rejected.

Pupil	Arithmetic Achievement	Verbal Analogies	Geometry Examination
		Group I	
1	7.1	83	82
2	4.9	77	45
3	5.8	75	19
4	6.1	74	55
5	5.6	71	22
6	8.0	67	72
7	5.3	68	33
8	4.0	66	33
9	7.2	65	31
10	4.9	64	47
11	5.9	58	51
12	4.0	55	7
		Group II	
1	7.2	76	33
2	5.2	78	24
3	6.2	75	51
4	6.8	74	60
5	5.4	73	55
6	6.8	70	43
7	4.2	66	16
8	6.4	63	31
9	5.9	62	71
10	3.6	62	14
11	5.2	56	29
12	5.7	62	39

2. Recognizing that the samples in this practice problem are probably too small to demonstrate that the requisite assumptions for multiple-classification analysis of covariance have been satisfied, compute the F values for the two main effects (A and B) as well as the interaction of the two main effects (A $\times$ B). Let Y represent the criterion variable and X_1 and X_2 the control variables. Decide whether any of the null hypotheses associated with the three F values should be rejected.

Main Effect B		Main Effect A						
		A_1				A_2		
	Individual	X_1	X_2	Y	Individual	X_1	X_2	Y
B_1	a	5	9	9	k	5	8	9
	b	5	9	6	l	4	6	9
	c	4	9	6	m	4	6	9
	d	4	8	5	n	3	7	9
	e	4	8	5	o	3	5	8
	f	3	6	4	p	2	4	8
	g	3	7	4	q	1	4	8
	h	2	4	3	r	1	3	7
	i	1	4	2	s	1	3	7
	j	1	7	1	t	1	4	7
B_2	u	7	8	6	ee	8	9	9
	v	6	8	6	ff	6	7	9
	w	6	7	5	gg	6	7	9
	x	5	6	5	hh	5	6	9
	y	5	7	4	ii	4	8	8
	z	4	5	4	jj	4	2	8
	aa	4	4	4	kk	4	2	7
	bb	4	5	3	ll	4	2	7
	cc	2	5	3	mm	4	4	7
	dd	2	2	3	nn	4	3	6

17

Using Analysis of Variance

- *further considations*

Perhaps one of the major sources of confusion leading to the misuse and misinterpretation of analysis of variance is its traditional association with experimental design. Many popular introductory texts on analysis-of-variance (anova) procedures for the behavioral sciences have the phrase "experimental design" (or some variation) in their titles. These may be excellent textbooks on the subject and may include many of the design considerations discussed in this chapter. Nevertheless, the beginning student of statistics tends to lose sight of the fact that anova is a statistical tool, whereas **experimental design** is a set of research considerations: the definition of experimental units, random selection of units, random assignment of units to treatment conditions, identification of important independent and dependent variables, and so forth. Such considerations often have a direct bearing on three major design concepts: the *validity* of the statistical procedures and the *sensitivity* and *generalizability* of the data analysis and results. Before discussing these concepts in more detail, we will briefly consider the distinction between experimental and nonexperimental research designs in educational investigations.

EXPERIMENTAL AND EX POST FACTO DESIGNS

Analysis of variance is often used as the quantitative technique in ex post facto and experimental types of research. From a statistical viewpoint, the analysis in ex post facto studies is indistinguishable from that used in experimental studies. The research design considerations as well as the kinds of inferences that can be made, however, are markedly different in these two categories.

In **ex post facto designs,** the levels of the factors exist after the fact, that is, the research units belong to the levels *by definition.* This means that the investigator cannot assign research units at random to the levels of the factor. Some examples of factors that might be used in ex post facto designs with students as the research units are gender (levels = male, female) and ethnicity (levels = black, white, Asian, Hispanic, Native American). Clearly, the investigator is not able to randomly assign students to the levels of such factors, which are often referred to as organismic or **selection factors.**

By contrast, in experimental designs the levels of the factors do not preclude the assignment of research (or experimental) units to them. These factors are often referred to as **treatment factors,** in that the levels constitute different treatments. The investigator has control over which research units receive (are assigned) which treatments. Some examples of factors that might be found in experimental designs are type of instructional grouping (levels = heterogeneous, homogeneous), drug use (levels = high, medium, low), and teaching strategy (levels = inductive, deductive).

It should be clear that the crucial concept distinguishing experimental and ex post facto types of design is **randomization.** This concept also lies at the heart of the distinction between causal and noncausal inferences. Consider, for example, a one-way anova design with two experimental levels: teaching methods 1 and 2. Suppose students are randomly assigned to either method and are measured on some achievement variable. Consider also the same situation with one exception—instead of teaching method, the factor is gender, and the levels are males and females. In the former case, significant differences in achievement between the two groups can be logically attributed to the differences in teaching method. In the latter case, it is possible to infer whether a significant relationship exists, but not its causality. That is, significant differences in achievement between the groups could be attributed not only to gender differences but to many other unknown (in the sense that they were not included in the study) variables related to gender differences.

Because of these distinctions, investigations other than experiments are often referred to as **correlational studies.** (Remember, from Chapter 5, that *correlation does not imply causation.*) We prefer not to use this terminology, however, because establishing relationships between dependent and independent variables lies at the heart of any research design. The implication of causation depends on the nature of the independent variable or factor and whether it is experimental or ex post facto.[1]

Even the use of the experimental-nonexperimental design terminology is troublesome in view of the fact that most research designs include both experimental and ex post facto variables. An example would be a study investigating

---

1. Although randomization is a logical guarantee for causal interpretations, there are methods for increasing the *plausibility* of causal interpretations when randomization has not occurred. This methodology is generally referred to as *path analysis.* See, for example, David A. Kenny, *Correlation and Causality* (New York: Wiley, 1979).

the effect of multiple-choice versus short-answer items on achievement test performance of high-, middle-, and low-ability students. Ideally, students would be randomly assigned to either of the treatment conditions (multiple-choice or short-answer item tests) *within* the ability groupings. Then, the variance of the resulting test scores could be analyzed using a 3×2 factorial design.

The use of the term *ideally* with respect to randomization in experimental designs is significant. As we have noted, often (if not usually), the educational investigator does not have the flexibility to randomly assign experimental units (students, classrooms, and so forth) to treatment conditions. In this case, the procedures and resulting inferences are not truly experimental in nature, and these designs are often referred to as **quasi-experimental.**[2]

VALIDITY, SENSITIVITY, AND GENERALIZABILITY

In descriptions of research design, the terms *validity, sensitivity,* and *generalizability* have been used to signify a variety of concepts. For example, Donald T. Campbell and Julian Stanley used the expression *internal validity* to describe the extent to which the results of an experiment have actually been caused by the experimental (independent) variable, and the expression *external validity* to describe the degree to which the results of an experiment can be legitimately generalized to other, similar situations.[3] Their distinction between internal and external validity was a valuable one which led to much discussion in the research community about the relative importance of internal versus external validity.

In a subsequent reformulation of these distinctions, Campbell and Thomas Cook added two additional concepts: statistical conclusion validity and construct validity. *Statistical conclusion validity* is an internal issue pertaining specifically to the validity of tests of statistical significance. *Construct validity* is an external issue pertaining specifically to the validity of the variables being measured.[4]

If you are planning to conduct research or evaluation studies, we strongly advise that you study these issues further. (See the Selected Readings section at the end of the chapter.) In the following sections, we will use the terms *validity, sensitivity,* and *generalizability* merely as placeholders for the specific concepts we need to clarify in this chapter.

VALIDITY

The term **validity** is used here in reference to potential violations of the mathematical and logical bases on which rest analysis-of-variance procedures and the resulting statistical conclusions. In other words, asking a question

---

2. Donald T. Campbell and Julian C. Stanley, *Experimental and Quasi-Experimental Designs for Research* (Chicago: Rand McNally, 1966). This work was revised considerably in Thomas D. Cook and Donald T. Campbell, *Quasi-Experimentation: Design and Analysis Issues for Field Settings* (Chicago: Rand McNally, 1979). See, in particular, chapter 2.
3. Campbell and Stanley, *Experimental and Quasi-Experimental Designs.*
4. Cook and Campbell, *Quasi-Experimentation.*

about validity is asking a question such as: Can I be sure that this so-called F value is really a statistic with a sampling distribution given by the F table at the back of my book and with the degrees of freedom I think I have? To the extent that the answer is no, the resulting probabilities (or levels of significance) that you read from the table may be in error. As a result, the statistical decisions you make may be based more on illusion than on fact.

Statistical Assumptions

Investigating the validity of an analysis of variance is a matter of looking for possible violations of the statistical assumptions detailed in Chapters 11 and 13. The assumptions of normality and homogeneity of variance can themselves be statistically tested. As we indicated in these chapters, anova is a fairly robust technique with respect to violations of these assumptions. Ideally, the investigator conducts a pilot test of the dependent variables to investigate the shape and variability of their distributions.

The assumption of random sampling, however, cannot be statistically tested; it is satisfied or not satisfied by the data-gathering design. Whereas the normality and homogeneity-of-variance assumptions guarantee the mathematical basis of the statistical tests, the random-sampling assumption guarantees the *logical* basis of the test. That is, if your set of data was not one of any number of possible random sets of data, then your F statistic is not one of any number of possible F statistics. In such a case, using the F distribution as a sampling distribution to generate probability values would make no sense.

The Principle of Randomization

The concepts of **random sampling** and **randomization,** or **random assignment**, are frequently confused because they are regarded interchangeably as the third anova assumption. The confusion is clearly related to the distinction between ex post facto and experimental factors. For example, if the factor is gender, it is easy to conceptualize two distinct populations (male and female) from which random samples can be obtained. In this case, of course, randomization (i.e., random assignment to gender groups) is not possible. (This process was conceptualized in Figure 9–4 in Chapter 9.)

If, however, the factor is teaching strategy (inductive vs. deductive), the conceptualization of two populations and random sampling is not immediately obvious. It becomes clear when the population of individuals (or, more generally, experimental units) to which the anova results are to be generalized is, first, conceptualized and then randomly split into two "treatment" populations. Finally, the inductive and deductive groups in the experiment are conceptualized as *random samples* from the separate treatment populations. In this case, random sampling has *implicitly* randomized the assignment of individuals between experimental conditions by definition of the original treatment populations. The concepts of randomization by random sampling and random assignment are graphically portrayed in Figure 17–1.

Thus, while random sampling supplies the logical basis for valid inference in ex post facto designs, in experimental designs this basis is ultimately supplied by random assignment of experimental units to treatment conditions. The

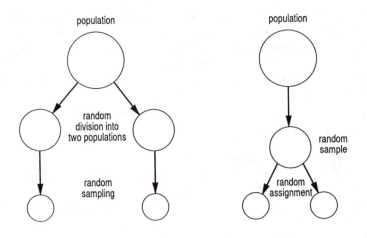

Fig. 17–1. Two equivalent conceptualizations of the process of randomization.

power of randomization can be seen most clearly, however, by eliminating the
need for conceptualizing treatment populations.

Consider for an example a hypothetical experiment in which the factor is
teaching strategies in arithmetic, with inductive and deductive levels. Suppose
the investigator has 20 students *available* (not sampled) for the experiment and
randomly assigns 10 of them to each of the treatment conditions (inductive or
deductive). An achievement test covering the arithmetic content is used to obtain 20 scores for analysis. A simple one-way anova yields an F statistic (on 1
and 18 *df*) which can be used to compare the mean performances of the two experimental groups. (See Tables 17.1 and 17.2.)

Table 17.1   Data for Hypothetical Teaching Strategies Experiment

Treatment Condition	
Inductive (A) Scores	Deductive (B) Scores
18	11
8	4
20	12
17	5
9	13
17	13
7	6
7	12
19	5
9	4
Treatment Means	
13.1	8.5

Table 17.2   One-Way Anova for the Teaching Strategies Experiment Data in Table 17.1

Source of Variation	SS	*df*	MS	*F*
Treatments	105.80	1	105.80	4.61
Within (error)	413.40	18	22.97	

But nowhere has any random sampling been performed. To what population, then, is any inference being made? The answer lies in the fact that the investigator randomized individuals over treatment conditions. The "population" is all possible *randomizations* of the students (and their scores) that could have occurred under the null hypothesis of no treatment differences.

In other words, the randomization process has implicitly created a sampling distribution of F statistics to which the particular F statistic obtained belongs. Ten scores in each of two conditions are available. Given the null hypothesis of no treatment differences, plus the fact that the assignment of students was randomized across treatments, Ted's score of 18, say, could have been in treatment condition B instead of A, and Sarah's score of 6 could have been in condition A instead of B. In fact, any of the possible 184,756 rearrangements of the ten scores in condition A and the ten in condition B could have occurred.[5] In addition, the anova and resulting F statistics could be computed for each of the 184,756 possible arrangements. The set of 184,756 statistics constitutes the sampling distribution and includes the statistic originally computed by the investigator.

The significance test is merely the way of determining the probability of the occurrence of the original statistic in the sampling distribution that was empirically generated. This probability could be computed directly from the sampling distribution.

At this point, you may be wondering if all possible randomizations of data have to be analyzed every time you conduct an experiment. The answer is no, because it can be shown that sampling distributions empirically created, like the one in this example, always have the approximate properties of an F distribution.[6] In other words, the distribution of the 184,756 statistics computed is closely approximated by an F distribution for 1 and 18 degrees of freedom. The test of significance is thus performed as usual by looking up the obtained F statistic in Table F in the Appendix. The teaching strategies experiment would then be reported as in Table 17.2.

You should now see that in the case of experimental factors, randomization is the sine qua non for the validity of the statistical test. You do not need to worry about the normality, homogeneity-of-variance, or random-sampling assumptions.

Selection of Experimental Units

In most of our examples of experimental designs we have used students or individuals as the experimental units. Unfortunately, in much of educational research design, there has been a subtle equation of experimental unit with individual student. Many times anova procedures have been applied to

---

5. The number of possible arrangements is determined by asking the question: In how many ways can 20 scores be combined, taking 10 at a time? Students familiar with combinatorial arithmetic will recognize the computation of the answer to be:

$$20!/10!\,10! = (1 \cdot 2 \cdot 3 \cdots 20)/(1 \cdot 2 \cdot 3 \cdots 10)(1 \cdot 2 \cdot 3 \cdots 10) = 184,756$$

6. See E. J. G. Pitman, "Significance Tests Which May Be Applied to Samples of Any Population. III. Analysis of Variance Test," *Biometrika,* vol. 29 (1937), pp. 322–25.

scores obtained by individuals when they should have been applied to scores obtained by *groups* of individuals. It might be argued that the choice of experiment unit is not a topic for discussion in a section on validity, in view of the fact that anova procedures per se are immune to the meaningfulness of the data. However, the choice of experimental unit has a direct bearing on the number of degrees of freedom in the anova and, consequently, the appropriate *F* distribution for the test of significance.

Consider the following experimental design in which the investigator wants to compare the effects of presenting certain instructional material with a series of slides or with a film. Suppose there are 30 students in each group (those that see the slides and those that see the film), and both groups are given an achievement test at the conclusion of either the slide presentation or the film. If each student were treated as the experimental unit, the anova would yield an *F* value based on 1 and 58 degrees of freedom.

But the **experimental unit** is the smallest *independently treated* unit, which, in this case, is clearly the group. This can be seen by considering what sources of variance will absorb the various uncontrolled effects of treatment malfunctions. For example, suppose the film breaks three minutes into the presentation for the film group, and five minutes are lost due to splicing and reloading. This would affect all 30 students in that group simultaneously, and, in that sense, the variability resulting from the breakdown would be reflected in the difference between treatments. The film treatment would virtually be re-defined as "film plus five-minute breakdown." But if the treatments were administered to each student in a separate cubicle, complete with its own projection system, a breakdown in any system would be reflected in the variability among individuals *within* treatment conditions—that is, error variance. Only in such circumstances could the individual be regarded as the experimental unit.

Because the group is the appropriate unit for analysis in this experiment, the investigator is left with only one observation in each treatment condition, namely, the mean achievement-test score for the 30 students in each condition. At least two such mean scores would be needed in each treatment condition in order for there to be any variance to analyze. An anova would then yield an *F* statistic based on 1 and 2 degrees of freedom—quite a change in *df* from the analysis when the student was used as the experimental unit.

The choice of appropriate experimental units is one of the most difficult research design problems encountered by educational investigators. When, as is often the case, the investigation involves the comparison of two or more instructional methods, the investigator is fortunate to gain the cooperation of two or more *classes,* one for each method of instruction. But if the class is the appropriate unit of analysis, at least two classes are needed for each treatment condition in order to perform the anova. In fact, depending on the expected variability between classes, it may be desirable to use 10 to 15 classes for each instructional method. Given the time, staff, and other economic restrictions prevalent in most educational systems, such an allocation of resources often is extremely difficult—if not impossible—to obtain.

The point to keep in mind is this: You must be aware of the decision-making purpose for which the experiment is intended and, in particular, the unit receiving the direct impact of decisions made. If it is clear that the individual student is the focus of attention, then every effort should be made to experimentally treat individuals. For example, comparing different strategies for individualization of instruction clearly calls for individual students as the unit of analysis. Nevertheless, it may be more feasible to administer the treatments to intact classes. In this case, where the treatments are clearly individually oriented, we suggest that you can still analyze your data meaningfully on an individual-score basis as long as you interpret statistical probabilities with caution. You should also maintain detailed anecdotal records regarding all unintended (nontreatment-related) events occurring in the classes that could potentially contribute to mean differences between the treatment groups.

SENSITIVITY

Recall the simple one-way analysis-of-variance design for the experiment on teaching strategies in arithmetic, with inductive and deductive instruction formats and ten students in each of the treatment conditions. In this design, the total variability of the 20 arithmetic achievement-test scores would be partitioned into two basic sources: the *between* source of variance, reflecting the difference between the treatments, and the *within* source of variance, reflecting the differences between students within the treatments (see Table 17.2 above). This latter source of variance (often called the error variance) reflects all possible independent variables, other than the treatment variable, that could conceivably cause individuals to differ on their scores. Any attempt to identify and control these additional sources of variability, thereby decreasing the error variability, is an attempt to increase the **sensitivity** of the anova design. Sensitivity is increased when the within-group or error variance is decreased relative to the remaining systematic sources of variance. This kind of increase in sensitivity is directly reflected in the F ratio, because F is the ratio of the mean square for a systematic source of variance to the mean square for the error source of variance. When the denominator decreases relative to the numerator, the ratio (or quotient) increases.

Another way to increase the F value is to bring about an increase in the numerator (systematic source) while holding the denominator (error source) relatively constant. The easiest way to increase sensitivity in this manner is to increase the sample size.

Sample Size

Increasing the sample size, that is, the number of experimental units, is one way to increase the sensitivity of an analysis-of-variance design without necessarily identifying and controlling additional sources of variability. From an intuitive point of view, it stands to reason that the more data you sample, the more confidence you can have in believing that the relationships observed in the sample actually exist in the population.

This can be seen more clearly by investigating the effect on the arithmetic of a simple anova table when the sample size is increased while keeping the mean differences and within-group variances the same. Suppose the number of students in the teaching strategies experiment were doubled, so that both the

Table 17.3   One-Way Anova for the Teaching Strategies Experiment When Data in Table 17.1 Are Replicated and Sample Size Is Doubled

Source of Variation	SS	df	MS	F
Treatments	211.60	1	211.60	9.73
Within (error)	826.79	39	21.76	

treatment means and the within-group variance remain the same.[7] Comparing Table 17.3 to Table 17.2 reveals the effect of doubling the sample size, from 20 to 40 students. First, the degrees of freedom for error are more than doubled, resulting in a substantial decrease in the critical F value needed for statistical significance. Second, the mean square for the treatment source of variance is greatly increased, while that for the within source remains almost the same. (Actually, the sum of squares for the within source is doubled, while the degrees of freedom are slightly more than doubled. Thus the mean square for the within source is slightly less than it was originally.) The net effect, of course, is to substantially increase the F value. In this particular case, you can see that whereas the mean difference of 4.6 based on 20 cases (see Table 7.1) was not significant at the 0.01 level, that same difference based on 40 cases reaches significance beyond the 0.01 level.

You might well wonder how useful the whole notion of inference can be if *any* mean difference can be constructed to be significant if you have a large enough sample size. But remember that if sampling resources were unlimited, you might as well measure every experimental unit in the population, thereby eliminating the need for any inferential procedure at all! Moreover, although any mean difference could be found to be statistically significant, given the right conditions, only some mean differences are large enough to be *meaningfully* considered. You have to bear in mind that statistical significance does not necessarily imply substantive meaningfulness.

A good anova design will contain a statement on how large a treatment difference must be in order to be considered meaningful in terms of the topic under investigation. In addition, the maximum Type I error the investigator is willing to risk, that is, the level of statistical significance that is to be reached, can be stated in advance. If an estimate of the within-group variance is available (from pilot testing of the dependent variable, for example), formulas exist for determining the minimum sample size that is necessary to realize the statistical significance of the desired mean differences at the desired probability level. For further discussion, consult any of the texts on experimental design listed at the end of the chapter.

Blocking

Given a reasonably sized sample of experimental units, the best and most useful way of increasing the sensitivity of an experimental design is by **blocking,** or identifying the important additional sources of variability and incorpo-

---

7. Although this would never happen in reality, the mean treatment differences and variability among individuals within treatments would remain relatively constant to the extent that the original sample was random and representative of the population.

rating them as additional factors into the experimental design. For example, suppose in the teaching strategies experiment that the investigator had good reason to suspect that the students' initial level of general, quantitative achievement would substantially contribute to individual differences. Furthermore, suppose the investigator was wise enough to recognize this fact before conducting the experiment. Therefore those students in the sample who were high or low in quantitative achievement were identified (say there were 10 high-achievement students and 10 low-achievement students in the sample of 20), and five students in each achievement grouping were assigned *at random* to each of the treatment groups (inductive or deductive teaching strategy). Table 17.4 portrays how the data might look if the design were revised to reflect high- and low-achievement **blocks.**

Now look again at the anova results in Table 17.2. In this one-way analysis, the potential two-way analysis, namely the achievement by treatment, 2×2 factorial design, is "hidden." The hiding occurs in the error or within source of variance: The SS for the achievement-group main effect and the SS for the interaction of achievement and treatment factors are included in the SS for the within source of variance, while 1 *df* for the achievement-grouping main effect and 1 *df* for the interaction and treatment factors are included in the *df* for the within source. This becomes clear when the data are reorganized in the 2×2 design shown in Table 17.4. When this new design is analyzed, as in Table 17.5, note the decrease in error mean square and the increase in design sensitivity, inasmuch as the mean difference between the two treatment groups is now significant well beyond the 0.01 level.

Table 17.4   Reorganization of Data in Table 17.1 to Include High- and Low-Achievement Blocks

Achievement Levels	Treatments		Means
	Inductive	Deductive	
High	18	11	
	20	12	
	17	13	15.2
	17	13	
	19	12	
Low	8	4	
	9	5	
	7	6	6.4
	7	5	
	9	4	
Means	13.1	8.5	

Table 17.5   Two-Way Anova for Data on Teaching Strategies Experiment in Table 17.4

Source of Variation	SS	*df*	MS	F
Treatments (T)	105.80	1	105.80	103.24
Blocks (B)	387.20	1	387.20	377.83
T × B	9.80	1	9.80	9.56
Within (error)	16.40	16	1.02	

In addition, the investigator has "bought"[8] two extra hypotheses which may or may not be of substantive interest. The mean difference between high- and low-achievement groups is not surprising, in light of their definition. The difference does, however, support the investigator's decision to include the achievement factor for the purpose of increasing sensitivity. Moreover, the interaction could have been of theoretical interest. The investigator could have hypothesized that low-achieving students would profit more from a straight-forward deductive strategy, whereas high-achieving students would perform better using the more-challenging inductive approach. Or the investigator could have hypothesized that prior achievement level is irrelevant in respect to well-devised inductive and deductive strategies. In any case, the interaction source of variance is necessary to explore the issue further.

Blocking as a means for increasing sensitivity is usually discussed under the heading of *randomized block designs* in most textbooks on experimental design. This has often led to some confusion, however, because anova procedures are basically no different from those included under the heading of *factorial designs* (see Chapter 13). When a factor has been introduced in the design for the purpose of increasing its sensitivity, it is usually conceptualized as a blocking factor and, as such, is a nonexperimental factor. When a factor is present for investigative purposes, it is usually not regarded as a blocking factor and can be either experimental or nonexperimental.

Analysis of Covariance

In Chapters 15 and 16, analysis of covariance (ancova) was discussed in detail from the viewpoint of statistically eliminating one or more sources of bias in the interpretation of group differences. In this section, we will discuss the technique of analyzing the variance of statistically adjusted scores with a view toward increasing the sensitivity of the data analysis. To the extent that the investigator makes a judicious selection of control variables or covariables, the error term will generally be reduced relative to the systematic sources of variance. For every covariable used in the analysis, 1 degree of freedom is removed from the error term.

Consider again the teaching strategies experiment. Instead of blocking on achievement level, the investigator could have performed an ancova using the general-achievement measure as a covariable. In other words, the continuous arithmetic-achievement variable, used previously to arrive at the high-low classification, would now be used to adjust statistically the criterion variable, arithmetic achievement-test scores. Even as gross a scoring system as 1 for high-achieving and 0 for low-achieving students can illustrate the effect analysis of covariance can have on sensitivity (see Table 17.6). Because the experiment was originally balanced in terms of prior achievement, the adjusted treatment means are identical to the unadjusted means. Yet the adjusted ratio of the systematic to unsystematic variance (the *F* ratio) is now significant well beyond the 0.01 level.

As to the question of when blocking, rather than analysis of covariance, should be used as a technique for increasing sensitivity, we take the position that the answer is, "Always, except when not possible." We recommend that

---

8. The unit of exchange might be conceptualized as degrees of freedom.

Table 17.6   Analysis of Covariance for the Teaching Strategies Data of Table 17.1

Source of Variation	SS	df	MS	F
Treatments	105.80	1	105.80	68.65
Within (error)	26.20	17	1.54	

blocking in anova designs "always" should be used rather than ancova designs, in view of the following considerations:

1. Anova assumptions are more robust in contrast to those of ancova, especially in regard to the homogeneity of regression assumption needed in ancova. In fact, the violation of this assumption implies the existence of an interaction between the covariable and one or more treatment factors—an interaction that can easily be accounted for when the covariable is included as a blocking factor in the anova design.
2. Nonlinear relationships between covariable and dependent variable cannot be handled by conventional ancova techniques, whereas the validity of blocking is not bound by any functional relationship.
3. The analysis is more straightforward with more easily interpreted results and more potentially interpretable information (additional main effects and interactions).
4. For most anova designs used in education, nearly all the information contained in a given covariable can usually be accounted for in three to five blocks.[9]
5. The analysis of covariance is logically incapable of "equating" nonexperimental or ex post facto groups.

Given randomization across treatment conditions, however, ancova may prove to be the only viable analytical technique for the following reasons:

1. It may not be possible to meaningfully determine discrete blocks from a continuous covariable.
2. Even though blocks may be meaningfully determined, the investigator may not be able to randomize subjects *within* blocks before the actual experimental treatment. As a result, some cells of the blocks-by-treatment design may contain too few subjects for a valid anova.

GENERALIZABILITY

The concept of **generalizability** refers to the "size" and "quality" of the "span" of inference that investigators can make with their data. Interpreted broadly, generalizability pertains to questions of representativeness and replicability on at least three fronts: the independent variables or factors, the dependent variables or criterion measures, and the experimental units (students, classes, schools, and so forth) used in the anova design. We will limit this discussion to issues concerning the experimental units and the population from

---

9. Optimal numbers of blocking levels for various design conditions have been determined by Leonard Feldt and are given in "A Comparison of the Precision of Three Experimental Designs Employing a Concomitant Variable," *Psychometrika,* vol. 23 (1958), pp. 335–54.

which they were sampled. Equally important issues such as the confounding of experimental treatments, maturation and mortality of study participants, pretest contamination, and unreliability and invalidity of measurement are explicated at length in texts dealing with data-gathering designs. Many of these additional sources of variance can be expected to contribute to within-cell variability and are thus important considerations in the *sensitivity* of an anova design as well.

Random Sampling and Randomization

We have discussed the processes of random sampling and randomization as necessary conditions for the logical validity of nonexperimental and experimental designs, respectively. Implicit in that discussion was the concept of generalizability, the intent on the part of the investigator to make statements about some larger set of experimental units using the results obtained from a subset of these units. The logical basis for this process of generalization rests on *randomly sampling* the subset of units. (The quality of generalizability can be improved by allowing chance to operate within a structured, representative framework, as in *stratified* random sampling.)

In nonexperimental designs (males-females, high-middle-low achievers, and so forth), therefore, the guarantee for logical validity serves also as the basis for generalizability. An investigator who has no interest in extrapolating from the data (in other words, the sample *is* the population) has no need for anova or any other inferential technique. Such instances may arise, for example, in some program evaluation studies.

In experimental designs, however, the basis for logical validity (randomization) has no direct bearing on generalizability. To illustrate, we will turn once more to the teaching strategies experiment. Even if the investigator considers the "sample" to be the population, a valid probability statement concerning the observed mean difference can be made. If, however, the investigator intends to generalize beyond the sample, no amount of random assignment to treatment conditions will help. The investigator must also, strictly speaking, have randomly sampled from the target population.

We have used the phrase "strictly speaking" often in this text. We reiterate that the educational investigator is often at the mercy of educational realities, that is, not able to randomize subjects across treatment conditions or to randomly sample subjects from well-defined populations. Nevertheless, the investigator must try to make valid comparisons with general implications. We advocate that investigators ought to be entitled to the power of statistical methodology so long as they are well aware that many of their probability statements must be qualified with phrases such as "assuming the sample at hand is not unlike that which would have been obtained had it been randomly sampled from the population of interest."

SOME ADDITIONAL CONSIDERATIONS

Until this point, we have avoided discussing several concepts and issues related to the use of analysis of variance. In this section, we alert you to the existence of these concepts and issues and direct you to more definitive sources on them.

Fixed, Random, and Mixed Models

All the examples and procedures for analysis that we have illustrated thus far have contained only **fixed factors.** Factors having levels such as males versus females, inductive teaching versus deductive teaching, high versus middle versus low achievement groups, and so forth, are *fixed* insofar as:

1. The levels have not been sampled from a potentially larger set of levels.
2. The investigator does not intend to generalize the result beyond the levels of the included factors.

Often in educational data-gathering designs, a blocking factor such as schools has levels corresponding to only a small number of the available target population of schools. An investigator considering the relative merits of traditional and modern algebra textbooks, for example, may wish to generalize the results to all schools in a large local district. If the resources for conducting the study are available at only, say, four schools, the investigator can choose the schools to be used at random, thus introducing a four-level **random factor** to the design. The anova computations remain unchanged until the point of constructing the appropriate F ratios, because when random factors are present, the within-groups variation is not always the appropriate error term. Anova designs can contain all fixed, all random, or both fixed and random factors **(mixed models)**. The procedures for determining the correct error terms can be found in advanced texts such as those listed in the readings section.

Nonorthogonal Designs

All the analysis-of-variance designs containing two or more factors that we have considered also have contained the same number of research units in each cell or treatment combination. When this is the case, or when proportionality exists between the cell sizes on a row-by-row (or column-by-column) basis, the computational procedures presented here are appropriate. When the cell sizes are unequal (or disproportional), these computations would lead to a source table whose sum of squares lacked **orthogonality** (statistical independence). Because this mathematical property is required to form valid F ratios, other computational procedures (based on least-squares regression) have been developed. The computations are tedious and best left to the computer; but if you are interested in learning about them, consult the texts in the Selected Readings section.

Multivariate Analysis of Variance

A third complication that we have avoided thus far is the use of more than one dependent variable for any given analysis-of-variance design. More often than not, the educational investigator obtains several cognitive and/or affective (and perhaps even psychomotor) measures in a single investigation. In the preceding example, the investigator might have also constructed an attitude questionnaire to assess student sentiment toward teaching strategies, expecting differential results depending on the format of the instruction.

Investigators often perform and interpret separate anovas for each of their dependent variables. Unfortunately, these dependent variables are usually correlated, so the separate anovas are also "correlated," and their independent interpretations are rendered potentially misleading. If student sentiment toward teaching strategies and student achievement were substantially correlated, it would not be surprising to obtain similar results for both analyses—and it would not be particularly insightful to treat the results as two separate phenomena.

Multivariate analysis of variance (manova) is basically a technique whereby the "generalized" variance (a multidimensional analog of the common, unidimensional variance of a single variable) of two or more dependent variables considered simultaneously is analyzed and partitioned into systematic (main effects and interactions) and unsystematic (error) sources. Ratios of systematic variance to error variance are formed (analogous to the univariate F ratio), so that the significance of main effects and interactions can be determined. When a ratio of this type is significant, the computations can be further extended to determine which dependent variable (or set of dependent variables) contributes most to the significance of the main effect or interaction.

The computations involved in manova are extremely laborious and are best left to the computer. Furthermore, manova has more stringent assumptions regarding the statistical properties of the data than ordinary **univariate analysis-of-variance** techniques. Educational investigators often find themselves in the familiar position of having access to statistical methodology that is sophisticated beyond the level of their data. An investigator who does not feel that the data warrant the application of manova procedures should at least be compelled to interpret the univariate anovas in light of the correlations among the dependent variables. For more insight into manova procedures, see the readings section.

Research Designs to Measure Change

The assessment of change is particularly relevant to research in education. Educational principles and practices are investigated not so much in terms of comparing individual measurements at a single point in time as in terms of comparing individuals on their measured growth (cognitive, affective, or psychomotor) over points in time. In the teaching strategies experiment that has been used as an example in this chapter, the investigator should have been asking the question: Which instructional format results in better student achievement (or attitude) *than was evidenced at the start?*

Fortunately, the traditional "posttest minus pretest" difference score analysis has been exposed as a simplistic, misleading, and statistically unsound design for the assessment of change.[10] Unfortunately, a great deal of controversy and difficulty accompanies attempts to determine a useful procedure to

---

10. Lee J. Cronbach and F. Furby, "How Should We Measure 'Change'—Or Should We?" *Psychological Bulletin,* vol. 74 (1970), pp. 68–80.

take its place. Measuring change is closely related to the concept of sensitivity; each individual being measured more than once functionally serves as that individual's own control. This has the net effect of generally reducing appropriate error terms relative to systematic sources.

In fact, perhaps the best way of assessing change in the common pretest-posttest design is to block on the pretest (e.g., high-middle-low pretest-score groups) and incorporate these blocks as a factor in the design. The next best way is to perform an analysis of covariance using the pretest score as the covariable and the posttest score as the dependent variable. The difference between posttest score and *predicted* posttest score is generally a better growth index than the raw post-minus-prescore difference.

Further complications arise when the individual is repeatedly treated over time. There are anova models, commonly referred to as repeated-measure designs, whereby these effects, as well as possible linear and curvilinear trends across treatment means, can be analyzed. For a discussion of the conceptual and analytical difficulties and possible methodologies in the assessment of change, see the text by C. W. Harris referenced in the Selected Readings section.

TERMS TO KNOW

Listed in order of presentation in chapter:

experimental design
ex post facto designs
selection factors
treatment factors
randomization
correlational studies
quasi-experimental
validity
random sampling
randomization
random assignment
experimental unit
sensitivity
blocking
blocks
generalizability
fixed factors
random factors
mixed models
orthogonality
multivariate analysis of variance (manova)
univariate analysis of variance

EXERCISES

Education officials of a certain state are interested in determining whether or not to adopt either of two new 11th-grade U.S. history textbooks in lieu of the text currently in use. There are 50 school districts in the state, ten secondary schools in each district, four 11th-grade classes in each school, one teacher for every two classes, and 30 pupils in each class. The state officials are concerned with pupils' learning outcomes on both achievement and attitude dimensions.

Construct an experimental design to help the state officials make their determination. Where applicable, comment on the following design considerations:

1. Validity
2. Random sampling and/or randomization
3. Sensitivity
4. Generalizability
5. Mixed or fixed models
6. Specific treatment comparisons
7. Nature and number of dependent variables
8. Appropriate experimental units
9. Measurement of change

SELECTED READINGS

Campbell, Donald T., and Stanley, Julian C. *Experimental and Quasi-Experimental Designs for Research*. Chicago: Rand-McNally, 1966.

Cook, Thomas D., and Campbell, D. T. "The Design and Conduct of Quasi-Experiments and True Experiments in Field Settings." In M. D. Dunnette (Ed.), *Handbook of Industrial and Organizational Psychology*. Chicago: Rand McNally, 1976.

Cook, T. D., and Campbell, D. T. *Quasi-Experimentation: Design and Analysis Issues for Field Settings*. Chicago: Rand McNally, 1979.

Cronbach, Lee J., Ambron, S. R., Dornbusch, S. M., Hess, R. D., Hornik, R. C., Phillips, D. C., Walker, D. F., and Weiner, S. S. *Toward Reform of Program Evaluation*. San Francisco: Jossey-Bass, 1980.

Dayton, C. M. *The Design of Educational Experiments*. New York: McGraw-Hill, 1970.

Harris, C. W. *Problems in Measuring Change*. Madison: The University of Wisconsin Press, 1967.

Kempthorne, O. *The Design and Analysis of Experiments*. New York: Wiley, 1952.

Kirk, R. E. *Experimental Design: Procedures for the Behavioral Sciences*. Belmont, CA.: Brooks/Cole, 1968.

Lindquist, E. F. *Design and Analysis of Experiments in Psychology and Education*. Boston: Houghton Mifflin, 1953.

Lunneborg, Clifford E., and Abbott, Robert D. *Elementary Multivariate Analysis for the Behavioral Sciences*. New York: North-Hollad, 1983.

Myers, J. L. *Fundamentals of Experimental Design*. Boston: Allyn and Bacon, 1979.

Tabachnick, Barbara G., and Fidell, Linda S. *Using Multivariate Statistics*. New York: Harper & Row, 1983.

Tatsuoka, M. M. *Multivariate Analysis: Techniques for Educational and Psychological Research*. New York: Macmillan, 1988.

Winer, B. J. *Statistical Principles in Experimental Design,* 2nd ed. New York: McGraw-Hill, 1971.

18

Nonparametric Statistics

A characteristic of statistical techniques that we have not considered to this point involves the distinction between parametric and nonparametric procedures. All of the inferential techniques we have described thus far are of the parametric type, in contrast to the nonparametric procedures we will discuss in this and the following companion chapter.

PARAMETRIC AND NONPARAMETRIC PROCEDURES

The chief distinction between parametric and nonparametric techniques hinges on the assumptions that must be made regarding population parameters. In most **parametric techniques,** such as the t test and analysis of variance, certain assumptions are made regarding the nature of the population data from which the sample data under analysis have been drawn. For example, it is assumed in the case of the t test that the parent populations are distributed normally and with equal variability. **Nonparametric techniques** require far fewer assumptions about population data. For that matter, these techniques have often been referred to as "distribution-free" procedures. Actually, it is somewhat misleading to think of nonparametric tests as though they could be legitimately conducted without considering population data. Though nonparametric tests never require population normality, in some instances they do involve limited assumptions regarding the nature of population distributions. It is certainly true, however, that the assumptions associated with nonparametric statistical tests are much weaker than those that must be satisfied for many parametric tests. Statisticians generally agree that when the investigator is working with data that seriously violate the assumptions required by appropriate parametric tests, nonparametric procedures are suitable alternatives.

Levels of Measurement

In addition to parameter assumptions, another distinction that is made between parametric and nonparametric procedures involves the measurement level of the data to be analyzed. A brief examination of three measurement levels—nominal, ordinal, and interval—that are applicable to nonparametric tests is given in this section.

In the least powerful level of measurement, a **nominal scale,** symbols or numbers are used to identify different categories of a variable. The investigator simply attaches a name (*nomen*) to categories on the scale. Thus the numbers on football players' jerseys represent a nominal scale. For that matter, any classification scheme, such as rural and urban, that labels objects, characteristics, or persons without signifying any ordered relationship between the categories is a nominal scale.

While a nominal scale carries no notion of order, in an **ordinal scale** actual rank order is implied. Not only is there a difference between categories but there is an *ordered* relationship between the categories. Such ordered relationships are frequently designated by the caret symbol ($>$), which is interpreted as "greater than."[1] For example, the rank system employed in the military would constitute an ordinal scale, for sergeant $>$ corporal $>$ private. Note that there is *no notion of equidistance* between points or categories on the scale, only a notion of rank order. In other words, the distance between sergeant and corporal may not be the same as the distance between corporal and private, but all sergeants are ranked higher than either corporals or privates. In educational investigations, a common example of data gathered on an ordinal scale is the ratings of observers who are asked to evaluate teachers or pupils in terms such as "good," "average," or "poor."

An **interval scale** has all the characteristics of an ordinal scale and, in addition, is composed of units that are equal. For example, the distance between points 55 and 65 on a scale must be the same as the distance between points 38 and 48. Moreover, an equal distance *numerically* is assumed to be an equal distance *in fact*. A common example of an interval scale is the measurement of temperature on either a Fahrenheit or centigrade scale.

Use of Measurement Scales in Educational Investigations. Statisticians are divided in their opinions as to whether most of the measurement scales used in education (for example, the scales produced by aptitude tests, achievement tests, and interest tests) should be treated as ordinal or interval. There is,

---

1. Once you have $>$, the symbol for "greater than," you also have $<$, the symbol for "less than."

however, a growing tendency to consider such data as though they were somewhere *between* ordinal and interval scales.

It has been argued by some that, unless data have been measured on a scale with interval properties, parametric techniques such as analysis of variance should not be used in investigations.[2] The contention is that one of the prime considerations in selecting a particular statistical test is whether the data to be treated are nominal, ordinal, or interval in nature. The principal reason for this concern over measurement scales is a belief that only certain types of mathematical operations are permissible with data of a given measurement strength. According to this point of view, ordinal data should not be subjected to the mathematical operations (addition, subtraction, multiplication, division) used in parametric analysis, because such operations require equidistance between the points on the scale. Since most of the data dealt with in educational research are measured on scales that are probably not as strong as an interval scale, proponents of this point of view have generally concluded that in *most* data analyses, the data should be treated by nonparametric rather than parametric procedures.

This view has been rejected by most statisticians on the grounds that it confuses a measurement question with a statistical question. It is not true that parametric analyses such as a *t* test cannot be *computed* on data that are only ordinal in nature. Actually, parametric procedures can be computed as long as the data are represented in numerical form. For example, a *t* test could be computed to determine whether the numbers on the basketball uniforms of one team are significantly greater than the numbers on the uniforms of another team. The question, however, would be whether there would be any sense in carrying out such an analysis.

An investigator always tries to find data that accurately reflect the variables the data represent before subjecting them to some kind of statistical analysis. A number of empirical studies have demonstrated that when parametric procedures have been employed with *ordinal* data, they rarely distort a relationship between variables which may be present in the data. More often than not, such parametric analysis results are nearly identical to those yielded by nonparametric procedures. Because the majority of data encountered in educational investigations probably falls somewhere between ordinal and interval strength, the educational investigator is usually on safe ground in applying parametric tests to numerical (ordinal or interval) data. This rule requires, of course, that other assumptions of the particular parametric test have been satisfied.

PARAMETRICS VERSUS NONPARAMETRICS

Parametric methods have several advantages over nonparametric methods. For one thing, parametric techniques, particularly analysis of variance, offer more analysis flexibility. The ability to categorize variables in such a way as to simultaneously study relationships between a dependent variable and many

---

2. Sidney Siegel and N. John Castellan, *Nonparametric Statistics for the Behavioral Sciences* (New York: McGraw-Hill, 1988).

different independent variables, as well as the interaction relationships between such variables, is tremendously advantageous. In addition, parametric procedures are often markedly more powerful than their nonparametric counterparts. That is, in general, a parametric procedure will reject a false null hypothesis more frequently than will a nonparametric test designed to perform the same function. This can be attributed to the fact that the parametric procedure uses more of the available information, such as the deviations from the mean of the scores in the analysis. Nonparametric procedures frequently rely more on frequency count and ranking procedures, thus discarding some of the information available in the data.

With respect to the power differences of parametric and nonparametric techniques, an important point concerns the generality of findings from the less powerful nonparametric tests. To illustrate, if a difference is highly significant when the sign test, a popular nonparametric technique, is used, then it has a very high probability of being significant when more powerful parametric statistics are used. However, the reverse is not true. Consequently, if an investigator can show a high level of significance with a rather weak statistical test, this makes the findings much more general than other possible ways of analyzing the data.

However, nonparametric tests do have certain advantages. For one thing, nonparametric tests are usually much easier to compute than parametric tests. This may not be important to investigators who have invested considerable time in conducting investigations and who can easily analyze even the most complex designs using available computer-based statistical software. But for classroom teachers and school administrators, whose hours for investigative purposes are at a premium and who are ordinarily concerned only with differences or relationships of considerable magnitude that can be detected by a less powerful test, nonparametric procedures often suffice. In such cases, recourse to nonparametric techniques can be a time-saving way of dealing with educational questions that are amenable to statistical analysis.

Another advantage of certain nonparametric procedures is that they can be used to treat data that have been measured on nominal, or classificatory, scales. Because such data cannot be ordered numerically on any logical basis, there is no possibility of using parametric statistical tests, which require numerical data.

The primary reason for using nonparametric procedures, however, is that while certain parametric methods rest on strong assumptions regarding the nature of the population data, nonparametric procedures generally do not. Numerous articles on theory written over the years have debated the appropriateness of using parametric procedures with ordinal data, but the conclusion has generally been in favor of using these procedures with ordinal as well as interval data.

RELATIONSHIPS AND DIFFERENCES

Though most inferential statistics procedures are ultimately designed to test relationships between variables, it is convenient to consider them in terms of either difference tests or relationship tests. Difference tests are also concerned with relationships, however. Difference techniques are used to test for the existence of a relationship between a dependent variable, such as pupil achievement, and an independent variable *represented by two or more classifications,* such as two groups taught by different methods of instruction. For example, a parametric procedure, the *t* test, might be used to *test* for a significant *difference* between the two groups. If a significant difference were found, the investigator would conclude that the *variables* of achievement and instructional method are *related.*

Relationship techniques such as product-moment correlation gauge relationships in a different fashion. A statistician who obtains an *r* of 0.89 when correlating two variables will conclude that the variables are strongly related. Relationship tests can provide not only an index of the existence of a relationship but also an estimate of its magnitude.

At any rate, as you have seen in the chapters on parametric techniques, the *t* test, analysis of variance, and analysis of covariance are parametric difference-testing procedures, while the correlation measures are parametric relationship-testing procedures. The same distinction can be drawn in regard to nonparametric techniques. As long as you remember that, in the final analysis, inferential statistical techniques are really concerned with relationships between variables, the descriptions of these two types of nonparametric techniques should be helpful.

NONPARAMETRIC PROCEDURES

The general pattern of nonparametric procedures is much like that for parametric tests. To investigate a statistical relationship between two or more variables, data pertaining to the relationship are sampled from the population(s) of interest. These data are treated by a statistical model which yields a numerical value or statistic that reflects the particular relationship. The likelihood of the chance occurrence of this value is then interpreted according to some type of statistical probability distribution. If the value is such that it would occur very infrequently by chance, then the relationship is assumed to be a product of a nonchance factor. In other words, the relationship under investigation is assumed to be real, and the null hypothesis of no relationship is rejected.

As with parametric procedures, it is possible to develop confidence intervals for nonparametric tests. Methods for computing nonparametric confidence intervals are less widely used, but they have been described by several authors.[3]

While the nonparametric tests described in the remainder of this chapter in no way exhaust the nonparametric procedures suitable for particular purposes, they are representative of similar procedures of a nonparametric nature. Some of the tests can be used with nominal data, while other techniques require ordinal or interval data. Deeper insight into any of the procedures de-

---

3. See, for example, Leonard A. Marascuilo and Maryellen McSweeney, *Nonparametric and Distribution-Free Methods for the Social Sciences* (Monterey, CA: Brooks/Cole, 1977).

scribed in this chapter can be secured by consulting the computation procedures in the companion chapter, Chapter 19.

Our discussion of nonparametric procedures will of necessity be brief, touching only on the more prominent procedures. The topic of nonparametric statistics has been ably treated by other authors, and if you want to study it further, see the texts cited in the Selected Readings section at the end of the chapter.

DIFFERENCE TESTS: ONE-SAMPLE

Nonparametric difference tests can be classified according to whether they are concerned with one, two, or more than two samples, as well as whether the samples are independent or related. This section and the four that follow describe difference tests that take into account the number and independence of the samples.

Educational investigators are often concerned with questions of whether sample data are distributed in a particular fashion, such as in the shape of the normal curve. The assumption of normal distribution for a particular population can be checked, for example, by seeing whether a sample drawn from that population departs significantly from the shape of a normal distribution. Investigators also may want to see whether sample data are distributed in other ways, in other kinds of probability distributions, perhaps, or according to previously established empirical distributions.

Chi-Square Test

A nonparametric technique which may be used to test the difference between the distribution of one sample and some other hypothetical or known distribution is the **chi-square (χ^2) test.** The χ^2 test can be used with data measured on nominal or stronger scales. Essentially, this procedure involves a **goodness-of-fit test** wherein the sample frequencies that actually fall within certain categories are contrasted with those that might be expected on the basis of the hypothetical distribution. If a marked difference exists between the *observed* or *actual* frequencies falling in each category and the frequencies *expected* to fall in each category on the basis of chance or a previously established distribution, then the χ^2 test will yield a numerical value large enough to be interpreted as statistically significant.

To provide an example of this process, suppose Mr. Ortiz, an elementary school principal, wants to determine whether a set of his students' achievement scores are distributed in a nonnormal fashion. If he has a range of achievement scores from 40 to 90 and a large enough number of students, he can classify the scores into categories or intervals of five points: 40-44, 45-49, 50-54, and so on. Then he can count the frequencies of the scores *actually* falling within each of these categories. Next, he could construct a table of the normal curve to determine, in terms of the mean and standard deviation of the sample, how many scores would be *expected* to fall within each of the five-point categories *if the distribution were perfectly normal*. By contrasting the observed or actual frequencies with these *expected* or *hypothetical frequencies,* he can determine through the χ^2 test whether the sample departs significantly from normality.

In brief, the χ^2 test yields a value which is produced by the disparity in each of the data categories or cells between expected and observed frequencies. If the sample distribution were *perfectly* normal, there would be no difference in any category between expected and observed frequencies, hence the resulting value of χ^2 would be zero. The greater the disparity between the observed and the expected frequencies, the larger χ^2 becomes. As usual, the final value of this statistical test is interpreted for significance from a probability curve, in this instance from a set of χ^2 curves. Each χ^2 value is interpreted according to the number of degrees of freedom in the analysis in a fashion similar to the way the various *t* distributions are used. A chi-square table is then used to secure the probability level of the χ^2 value yielded by the analysis. In this text, χ^2 values at various levels of significance are given in Table H.

The chi-square one-sample test can also be used to determine whether the data depart significantly from a previously established distribution. For example, Miss O'Brien, a high school administrator, might want to determine whether the proportion of students in last year's senior class who continued their formal education after graduation was essentially the same as the proportions in previous years had been. By checking follow-up data for the past five years, she might determine that 29 percent of the previous seniors had continued their formal education, while 71 percent had not. This previously established ratio, that is, 29:71, determines the *expected* frequencies for the χ^2 test for last year's class. The *actual* frequencies are drawn from the follow-up data for last year's senior class. As in all chi-square analyses, the actual frequencies are contrasted with the expected frequencies in such a way as to yield a χ^2 value, which is subsequently checked for statistical significance according to a chi-square probability curve.

Additional Tests

Another test suitable for the one-sample case involving nominal data is the binomial test. With ordinal data, appropriate one-sample tests are the Kolmogorov-Smirnov test and the one-sample runs test. For information on these techniques and other "additional tests" identified but not described in this chapter, see the text by Sidney Siegel and N. John Castellan as well as others cited in the Selected Readings section.

DIFFERENCE TESTS: TWO RELATED SAMPLES

Investigators who want to contrast the performance of two groups must first consider whether or not the two samples are independent. If the two groups consist of matched pairs or two measures on the same individuals, as in pretest and posttest comparisons, the answer is no; that is, the samples are *related*. In such cases, statistical techniques are used that take this relationship into consideration. In parametric procedures, for example, certain modifications of the *t* test are employed. In nonparametric procedures, special tests have been devised for related samples.

Wilcoxon Matched-Pairs Signed-Ranks Test

A procedure frequently used for testing differences between related samples is the Wilcoxon matched-pairs signed-ranks test. When, for example, two measures for the same individual are taken in an investigation, these measures are considered to represent a *pair*. The **Wilcoxon matched-pairs signed-ranks test** takes into account not only the *direction* of differences between pairs but also the *magnitude* of the differences. Therefore the Wilcoxon test requires numerical data and cannot be employed when the data are only nominal.

In essence, the Wilcoxon matched-pairs signed-ranks test is based on the notion that investigators can determine whether one member of a pair exceeds the other, and by roughly how much. If most of the *major* differences between pairs favor one group, then that group is significantly superior to the other. If the null hypothesis is true, then the number and magnitude of differences favoring the superior group will be about the same as those favoring the other group.

Computing the Wilcoxon test is simple: The investigator notes the difference between each pair; ranks the differences, irrespective of algebraic sign; and then totals the ranks with the *less-frequent* sign. The resulting value is called T and is interpreted for statistical probability from a statistical table. In this text, the critical values of T are given in Table I.

Consideration of the process involved reveals that the smaller the value of T, the greater the preponderance of differences between pairs in favor of one group, and therefore the more significant the value of T is. If the two related samples were perfectly identical, there would be an equal quantity and magnitude of negative ranks and positive ranks, so the value of T would be large. To put it another way, if the members of *each* pair in one group always exceed their matched counterparts in the other group, the value of the less frequent rank sum (that is, T) would be zero and, of course, quite significant.

Sign Test

The **sign test** also is frequently used in testing for differences between two related samples, but it utilizes only the direction and not the magnitude of the differences between pairs. Therefore it is less powerful than the Wilcoxon test. The sign test also requires data that have been measured by at least an ordinal scale. This very useful test has a wide range of applications and is extremely simple to compute. The basic rationale of the sign test is that if two groups of related individuals are contrasted when the null hypothesis holds true, approximately half of one group should be judged better than or greater than the other group. If a markedly greater proportion of one group is favored, the sign test detects the existence of a significant difference. Procedures for testing this significance with the use of Table J or a special formula are described in the following chapter.

A Nominal-Data Test

A model suitable for checking differences between related samples when the data are only at the nominal level is the McNemar test for the significance of changes.

DIFFERENCE TESTS: TWO INDEPENDENT SAMPLES

If the two samples used in an investigation do not consist of *matched* pairs, a variety of nonparametric difference tests is available. The Mann-Whitney U test and the chi-square test are two that are frequently used.

Mann-Whitney U Test

This powerful nonparametric technique can be employed in place of the parametric *t* test, with little loss in power. Briefly, the **Mann-Whitney U test** is based on the notion that if scores of two similar groups are ranked together (as though the two groups were one), there will be a considerable intermingling of rankings for the two groups. If the groups are quite different, however, most of the superior group's rankings will be higher than those of the inferior group.

The value of U is computed by concentrating on the lower-ranked group and counting the number of ranks of the high group that fall *below* the lower-ranked group. Thus if *all* the ranks of the higher-ranked group exceeded all the ranks of the lower-ranked group, none of the superior group's rankings would be below those of the inferior group, and the value of U would be zero. As in the Wilcoxon tests, this is an instance where the lower the value of the statistic yielded by the test, the more significant it is.

The Mann-Whitney test can be used with extremely small samples. Probability tables are available (in this text, Tables K and L in the Appendix) for samples as small as three individuals in one group and only one in the second group.

Chi-Square Test

When the data from two independent samples are not numerical but only at the nominal level, the chi-square test can again be used to detect significant differences. For two samples, the chi-square analysis follows a pattern similar to that described for the one-sample goodness-of-fit test. In the two-sample application, however, the expected frequencies are drawn not from some hypothetical distribution but directly from the actual or observed frequencies themselves.

To illustrate the process, the hypothetical data in Table 18.1 contrast the supposed performance of high school juniors and seniors on their initial automobile driver's license tests. In this example the independent variable is year in high school, as represented by the junior and senior groups. The dependent variable is performance on the driving test, classified into categories of pass or fail. The data represent the *actual* or observed scores of the 100 students taking the driving test.

Studying Table 18.1 will help you understand how the *expected* frequencies are determined in such a two-sample case. You can see that 60 of the 100 students passed the driving test, and 40 failed. Note also that the subtotals for both juniors and seniors are 50, or exactly half of the total of 100 students. Now, according to simple logic, because 50 percent of the students were seniors, you should expect that 50 percent of the 60 persons who passed the test would be seniors. Thus the *expected* frequency for seniors who passed the test is 50

Table 18.1   Hypothetical Data on Performance of 50 High School Seniors and 50 High School Juniors on Initial Automobile Driver's License Tests

Year in School	Passed	Failed	Row Subtotal	
Seniors	40	10	50	
Juniors	20	30	50	
Column subtotal	60	40	100	Total

percent of 60, or 30; the actual frequency is 40. Similarly, for juniors who should have passed the test, the expected frequency is 30; the actual frequency is 20. For seniors who failed the test, the expected frequency is 20 (50 percent of the 40 students who failed), and for juniors who failed, the expected frequency is also 20.

The value of χ^2 depends on the *disparity* between the actual frequencies and the expected frequencies, with χ^2 becoming larger as the disparity increases. In other words, if the value of χ^2 is large enough to be statistically significant, there is a considerable difference between the *category proportions* of two independent-variable groups with respect to the dependent variable. For the hypothetical data in Table 18.1, the value of χ^2 is 15.04, which is significant beyond the 0.01 level. This result indicates that in the hypothetical example, there is indeed a difference of considerable consequence between the seniors and juniors in passing the driver's license test.

Additional Tests

When nominal data are involved, differences may also be assessed by the Fisher exact probability test. If ordinal data are available, differences between two independent groups may be tested by the median test, the Kolmogorov-Smirnov two-sample test, the Wald-Wolfowitz runs test, and the Moses test of extreme reactions.

DIFFERENCE TESTS: MORE THAN TWO RELATED SAMPLES

To determine if three or more *matched* samples differ significantly with respect to data measured at least on an ordinal scale, the Friedman two-way analysis of variance may be employed.

Friedman Two-Way Analysis of Variance

This technique is applicable when the investigator is working with sets of matched pairs, or when the same individuals have been exposed to different treatment conditions. To illustrate the **Friedman two-way analysis of variance,** suppose Mrs. Carson, a physical education teacher, wants to see whether there are any significant performance differences among students who were taught to play a new kind of game by three different methods. She decides to determine their performance in the new game by the combined ratings of five judges, who rate the performance of each student without knowing which method of instruction had been used to teach that student the game. Essentially, the research is designed to discover the existence, or lack, of a relationship between performance as reflected by judges' ratings and method of instruction as represented by the three groups of students.

Because prior physical ability is probably related to the success of the students in mastering the new skill, Mrs. Carson assembles five *sets* of three individuals, with each of the students in a given set *matched* to the other members of the set on the basis of previous performance on a test of physical aptitude. She then assigns the three individuals in each set, on a random basis, to one of the three instructional methods.

After the students receive instruction with one of the three methods, the performance of each one is rated by the judges so that, during the analysis, a student's *rank within the set of three students* can be determined. Now, if one of the three instructional methods is markedly superior to the other two, Mrs. Carson might expect that the students taught by that method would receive rankings of 1 rather than 2 or 3. As a result, the total of ranks for the superior instructional method would be only five, because each student in the five matched sets who had been taught by that method would be ranked higher than the two members of that set who were exposed to the other methods. In other words, the total of ranks for the superior method will be much smaller than the total of ranks for the inferior methods. In contrast, if the three instructional methods are about equally effective, the ranks within each of the five sets will be fairly well scattered, and the sum of the ranks for each instructional method will be similar.

To summarize, the rationale of the Friedman two-way analysis of variance is based on the fact that if matched sets of individuals (or the same individuals exposed to differential treatments) are assigned to different groups representing an independent variable, their *within-sets* rankings, which are based on the dependent variable, will be distributed in a fairly random pattern when the null hypothesis is tenable. When the null hypothesis is untenable, that is, when there are differences between two or more of the groups representing the independent variable, there will be a marked disparity between the sums of ranks for the independent-variable groups.

To test for significant differences between the condition (independent-variable) groups, the sums of ranks are inserted in a formula which yields a value (χ_r^2) to be subsequently interpreted for significance according to a chi-square table. If the value is sufficiently large, the null hypothesis is rejected, and it is concluded that significant differences between the condition groups exist. Special probability tables must be used for this test when the number of subjects and conditions is particularly small. In this text, Table M in the Appendix is the table of probabilities associated with values as large as observed values of χ_r^2 in the Friedman test.

DIFFERENCE TESTS: MORE THAN TWO INDEPENDENT SAMPLES

To test for significant differences among more than two independent (or unrelated) samples, the parametric analysis-of-variance design is the usual choice. However, if the sample data appear to depart markedly from the requisite assumptions of anova, it may be preferable to use nonparametric techniques such as the Kruskal-Wallis one-way analysis of variance or the chi-square test.

Kruskal-Wallis One-Way Analysis of Variance

If the dependent-variable data are numerical in nature, the **Kruskal-Wallis one-way analysis of variance** may be employed. This technique requires that the dependent variable under analysis be continuously distributed; that is, there should be no extended "gaps" in which no scores appear.

The basic rationale for this test is quite simple. If there are no differences among the several groups representing the independent variable, then when all scores are ranked from highest to lowest, irrespective of groups, the average sum of ranks for each group should be roughly comparable. If there are significant differences among the groups, then there will be a marked disparity among the average sums of ranks for the various groups.

For example, a school psychologist who wanted to contrast the scores of students from three grade levels on a personality test would compute ranks for the entire set of students, sum the ranks for each of the three grade-level groups, and then average these sums according to how many students were in each group. If these average sums of ranks are relatively similar, then it is likely that no significant difference exists among students from the three grade levels. If marked differences do exist among the several average sums of ranks, then the null hypothesis should be rejected, and grade level should be taken into consideration when interpreting scores of the personality test.

The sums of ranks are inserted in a formula which yields a value known as *H*. When the number of samples and subjects is small, a special table of probabilities (Table N in the Appendix) is used to interpret the significance of *H*. When the number of samples and subjects is larger, *H* is interpreted for significance from a chi-square table.

Chi-Square Test

For data that are only nominal in nature, a chi-square analysis is used to test for differences between more than two independent samples. The procedure involved is simply an extension of that used in the case of two independent samples where the observed frequencies are contrasted with expected frequencies drawn from row and column totals. If the disparity between expected and observed frequencies is quite large, this reflects a significant difference between the groups. The larger the value of chi square, the greater the difference between the groups.

Chi square can also be applied to ordinal and interval data, but it then represents a markedly less powerful test than those designated for use with numerical data.

RELATIONSHIP TESTS

Thus far in this chapter we have considered statistical models designed to test for differences between a sample and a hypothetical distribution; two samples, either related or independent; and more than two samples, either related or independent. A nonparametric relationship test that is comparable to the parametric product-moment correlational procedure described in Chapters 5 and 6 is the Spearman rank-order procedure.

Spearman Rank-Order Correlation Coefficient

The **Spearman rank-order correlation coefficient** (r_s), or *rho,* as it is sometimes called, can be employed to determine the degree of relationship between two variables measured at the ordinal level. For example, this would be an appropriate technique to assess the degree of relationship between students' academic rank in high school and their rank on a test of attitudes toward study habits. The rank-order correlation coefficient is encountered frequently in the literature on education.

The rationale for this statistic is based on the notion of *differences* between ranks of individuals on two measures. For example, if a perfect positive relationship between the two variables is present, then an individual who ranked first on one measure would also rank first on the second measure, and so on. In each instance, the difference between the two ranks of each individual would be zero. If the relationship between the variables is less than perfect, an individual who ranked first on one measure might rank seventh in the second measure, with a resulting difference of six points between the two ranks. An index of the disagreement in ranks, or the lack of relationship between the two variables, is drawn from the size and number of these differences. To remove the negative sign from certain differences that occur between ranks, all differences are squared, then summed. The sum of squared differences is the crucial value in the formula that yields the Spearman coefficient. If the sum of the squared differences is small, then a strong relationship exists. If the sum of the squared differences is moderately large, a low-order relationship exists. If the sum of the squared differences is extremely large, a negative relationship exists.

When inserted in the formula that yields the Spearman coefficient, a sum of squared differences of zero (from a perfect positive relationship) would yield a coefficient of $+1.00$. A perfect negative relationship would occur if the ranks were perfectly reversed, with the resulting large sum of squared differences yielding a coefficient of -1.00. You should see, then, that the range and meaning of the Spearman coefficient are identical to those of the Pearson product-moment correlation coefficient. Generally speaking, r_s can be interpreted in the say way as *r.* In reality, the Spearman coefficient is nothing more than the Pearson product-moment formula applied to the two sets of ranks.

The significance of r_s for samples of from 4 to 30 can be ascertained readily from a specially prepared probability table (Table O in Appendix). For larger samples, a formula which yields a *t* value is used to check the significance of the Spearman coefficient.

Additional Tests

Other nonparametric relationship techniques, particularly a set of coefficients developed by Kendall, are also available.

REVIEW

Nonparametric statistical tests require far less stringent assumptions than do parametric tests such as analysis of variance. Although the argument is not fashionable these days, some maintain that the use of parametric procedures with much educational data yields spurious results, so nonparametric techniques should be employed. We believe, to the contrary, that because of the greater power and flexibility of parametric procedures, they should ordinarily be used where there is a choice between a nonparametric and a parametric test. However, in cases where parametric assumptions are seriously violated or where the samples are so small that it would be difficult to demonstrate the satisfaction of parametric assumptions, nonparametric techniques have their place.

The numerous parametric tests can be classified as difference-testing or relationship-testing procedures. This chapter has introduced representative nonparametric models to fit the more common requirements for educational investigations.

For testing differences between one sample and a hypothetical distribution, the chi-square test is appropriate. Because it may be applied to nominal or classificatory data, this test is widely used.

With ordinal or stronger data, the difference between two related (matched) samples can be tested by the Wilcoxon matched-pairs signed-ranks model. A less powerful test for the same situation is the sign test.

For two independent samples with ordinal or stronger data, the Mann-Whitney U test is an excellent choice. With data of only nominal strength, the χ^2 test for two independent groups may be used.

For three or more related groups with data of at least ordinal strength, the Friedman two-way analysis of variance is a suitable model. With three or more independent samples and ordinal or stronger data, the Kruskal-Wallis one-way analysis of variance model is recommended. Chi square can be used with three or more independent groups and data of only nominal strength.

The Spearman rank-order correlation coefficient is a relationship technique suitable for dealing with data of ordinal or greater strength. This coefficient is interpreted in much the same way as the Pearson product-moment correlation coefficient.

TERMS TO KNOW

Listed in order of presentation in chapter:

> **parametric techniques**
> **nonparametric techniques**
> **nominal scale**
> **ordinal scale**
> **interval scale**
> **chi-square test**
> **goodness-of-fit test**
> **Wilcoxon matched-pairs signed-ranks test**
> **sign test**
> **Mann-Whitney *U* test**
> **Friedman two-way analysis of variance**
> **Kruskal-Wallis one-way analysis of variance**
> **Spearman rank-order correlation coefficient (r_s)**

EXERCISES

1. In general, will a nonparametric or a parametric test, each of which has been designed to accomplish the same analytic functions, more frequently reject the null hypothesis?

2. If an educator wants to use a *t* test to contrast differences between two independent groups but finds that the assumptions of the *t* test cannot be satisfied, which nonparametric test should be used?

3. An educational investigator wants to test for a relationship between two sets of ranked data. Which nonparametric test should be employed?

4. To test the null hypothesis that the students from three different private schools differ with respect to their religious affiliation (Protestant, Catholic, other), which nonparametric statistical technique should be used?

5. A teacher wants to test for pretest and posttest differences in scores on an attitude scale for a class which has just seen a lengthy movie on the problems of racial intolerance. Which two nonparametric tests might be employed in this situation? Which of the two is the more powerful test?

6. Which nonparametric technique would an investigator use to test whether a large set of data was distributed in a significantly nonnormal fashion?

7. Five sets with three matched students in each have been exposed to three different attitude-modification self-instruction programs. For each student, a "gain" score based on the difference between performances on a preexperiment and postexperiment attitude inventory has been obtained. Which nonparametric test might be used to test for differences in the effectiveness of the three self-instruction programs?

8. An educator wishes to test for differences among four independent groups. With nominal data, which nonparametric test should be used? With ordinal data, which nonparametric test should be used?

SELECTED READINGS

Anderson, Norman H. "Scales and Statistics: Parametric and Nonparametric." *Psychological Bulletin,* vol. 58 (July 1961), pp. 305-16.

Blalock, Hubert M., Jr. *Social Statistics.* New York: McGraw-Hill, 1979, chaps. 14-15.

Edington, Eugene S. *Statistical Inference: The Distribution-Free Approach.* New York: McGraw-Hill, 1969.

Marascuilo, Leonard A., and McSweeney, Maryellen. *Nonparametric and Distribution-Free Methods for the Social Sciences.* Monterey, CA: Brooks/Cole, 1977.

McCall, Robert B. *Fundamental Statistics for Behavioral Sciences.* San Diego, CA: Harcourt Brace Jovanovich, 1986, chap. 13.

McNemar, Quinn. *Psychological Statistics.* New York: Wiley, 1966, chap. 19.

Savage, Richard J. "Nonparametric Statistics." *Journal of the American Statistical Association,* vol 52, no. 332 (1957).

Siegel, Sidney, and Castellan, N. John. *Nonparametric Statistics for the Behavioral Sciences.* New York: McGraw-Hill, 1988.

Nonparametric Statistics

- *computation procedures*

This companion chapter describes computation procedures for the non-parametric tests that were described in some detail in Chapter 18. These tests are the chi-square test, the Wilcoxon matched-pairs signed-ranks test, the sign test, the Mann-Whitney U test, the Friedman two-way analysis of variance, the Kruskal-Wallis one-way analysis of variance, and the Spearman rank-order correlation coefficient. The rationale and purposes of these tests will be only briefly referred to here. For a more extensive discussion, see Chapter 18 and the Selected Readings section at the close of that chapter.

CHI-SQUARE TEST

The chi-square (χ^2) test is undoubtedly the most important member of the nonparametric family of statistics. This test can be used with data that are only nominal in strength, such as categories representing college major or parental occupation. Chi square is employed to test the difference between an actual sample and another hypothetical or previously established distribution, and it can also be used to test differences between two or more actual samples. With only slight differences, the computation procedures for chi square are basically the same in either of these situations.

Chi square can be used to treat data that are classified into nominal, non-ordered categories. It can also be employed with numerical data, though it may be desirable to analyze such data with more-powerful parametric tests. For nominal data, however, few alternatives to chi-square analysis exist.

The basic computational formula for chi square is Formula 19.1:

$$\chi^2 = \sum \frac{(\text{Observed frequency} - \text{Expected frequency})^2}{\text{Expected frequency}} \qquad (19.1)$$

The use of this formula to determine the value of χ^2 and the subsequent interpretation of its significance will be illustrated both in the one-sample case and in the case of two or more samples.

Whenever χ^2 is calculated from a 1×2 or 2×2 table (instances in which there is only 1 degree of freedom), an adjustment known as the Yates correction for continuity must be employed.[1] To use this correction, a value of 0.5 is subtracted from the absolute value (irrespective of algebraic sign) of the numerator contribution of each cell to Formula 19.1, as follows:

$$\frac{(|\text{Observed frequency} - \text{Expected frequency}| - 0.5)^2}{\text{Expected frequency}}$$

One-Sample Case

Educational investigators often want to know whether a sample departs significantly from some known or hypothetical distribution. For example, suppose a superintendent of a large school system wants to know whether the district's recently employed, first-year teachers are being drawn from state-supported or private colleges in a proportion significantly different from the pattern observed in the preceding decade. A chi-square analysis could be used to settle this issue. The basic analytic task is to contrast the proportion of state-college and private-college graduates between (1) the recently employed teachers and (2) an established proportion drawn from district records over the past ten years. The recently employed teachers represent the *observed* frequencies, and the previously established proportions serve as the basis for calculating the *expected* frequencies. In any one-sample application of chi square, the sample to be contrasted with the known or hypothetical distribution constitutes the observed frequencies. The data to be used in this example are summarized in Table 19.1.

The expected frequencies needed for the chi-square formula (19.1) are

Table 19.1   District Teachers Hired Recently and Employed During Preceding Ten Years, Classified According to Graduation from State or Private College

	State-College Graduate	Private-College Graduate
Number of teachers hired recently	30	20
Percentage of teachers employed in preceding 10 years	40%	60%

---

1. F. Yates, "Contingency Tables Involving Small Numbers and the χ^2 Test," *Journal of the Royal Statistical Society Supplement,* vol. 1 (1934), pp. 217–35.

Table 19.2   Observed and Expected Frequencies for the Data in Table 19.1

	State-College Graduates	Private-College Graduates
Observed	30	20
Expected	20	30

calculated as follows. First, based on the data available for the past decade, the proportions of state-college and private-college graduates in the previously established distribution are noted, namely, 40 percent state-college graduates to 60 percent private-college graduates. Then these proportions are applied to the 50 recently employed teachers, because, according to the previously established distribution, it would be "expected" that 40 percent, or 20, of the 50 new teachers would be state-college graduates, and 60 percent, or 30, of the 50 new teachers would be private-college graduates. The observed frequencies (the actual frequencies of the sample in question) as well as the expected frequencies can be displayed in a frequency table such as Table 19.2.

Once the quantities necessary for the solution of the chi-square analysis have been obtained in this manner, they are substituted in Formula 19.1 and chi square is computed. Remember that in calculating χ^2 from 1×2 or 2×2 tables, the Yates correction should be used:

$$\chi^2 = \frac{(|30 - 20| - 0.5)^2}{20} + \frac{(|20 - 30| - 0.5)^2}{30}$$

$$= 4.5 + 3.0$$

$$= 7.5$$

As in the inferential significance tests previously discussed, this χ^2 value of 7.5 is interpreted from a table of probability values. The table for the chi-square distribution in this text is Table H in the Appendix. To determine the appropriate number of degrees of freedom needed to enter the table for a one-sample case, it is not necessary to calculate expected proportions from the sample data. Therefore, *df* is always the number of cells (as seen in Table 10.2), less 1. In this example, there are two cells, so $df = 2 - 1 = 1$. It can be seen in Table H that with 1 degree of freedom, a χ^2 value equal to or greater than 3.84 is needed to reject the null hypothesis at the 0.05 level, while a χ^2 value of 6.64 or greater is needed to reject the null hypothesis at the 0.01 level. Because the obtained χ^2 value of 7.5 exceeds both of these, the null hypothesis that the recently employed teachers are being drawn from state and private colleges in the same proportion as in previous years is rejected. The district administrator may now begin to search for reasons behind this statistically significant departure from previous practices.

Goodness of Fit

Basically, the χ^2 one-sample case is an instance of checking the "goodness of fit" between an actual sample and some known or hypothetical distribution. Frequently, the educational investigator wants to check the assumption of normality by seeing if the sample data depart significantly from the shape of a normal distribution. This can be accomplished through a chi-square analysis by assessing the "goodness of fit" of the sample data with a normally shaped distribution.

The procedure is essentially the same as described in the preceding section. The exception is that the expected frequencies are calculated on the basis of the normal curve rather than on the basis of prior information. Thus two additional degrees of freedom are lost, due to the need to estimate the parameters (the mean and standard deviation) of the hypothetical normal curve. First, the actual sample data (that is, the observed frequencies) are cast in a number of categories. Then, in terms of the mean and standard deviation of the sample, the normal-curve table is checked to see what proportion of the distribution should fall in a particular category if the distribution were perfectly normal.

For example, suppose a sample of data had a standard deviation of 10. Suppose, further, that this sample distribution were divided into *half* standard deviation intervals (5 units each), with an equal number of intervals above and below the mean. If the distribution were perfectly normal, then consulting the normal-curve table (Table A in the Appendix) would indicate that 19 percent of the cases would fall in the first interval, 15 percent in the second interval, and so on. (See Chapter 3.)

When these hypothetical proportions are multiplied by the actual number of cases in the sample, the result represents the expected frequencies. The observed and expected frequencies are then used in Formula 19.1 as in the preceding example, except that the number of *df* now equals the number of categories or cells less 3.

How Many Categories?

While there is some controversy among statisticians as to the question of number of categories, the following guidelines are generally accepted. In some cases the investigator has relatively little control over the number of categories in the analysis, because they consist of some type of unique nominal classes such as "living" or "deceased." In many cases, however, a certain amount of control over categories can be exercised. For instance, five attitude inventory categories such as "strongly agree," "agree," "neutral," "disagree," and "strongly disagree" could be regrouped into three categories: "agree," "neutral," "disagree." Similarly, a range of achievement-test scores could be subdivided into a variety of categories, ranging from two, such as "100 and above" and "below 100," to a host of categories with two- or three-point ranges in each. Even nominal-scale categories can be recategorized under new, more or less inclusive headings.

The general rule in setting up χ^2 categories is to have as many as possible, for the test will then be more sensitive. (Clearly, when testing for "goodness of fit," at least two categories must be used to have at least 1 *df* for the statistical test.) The limitations are that no more than 20 percent of the cells have an *expected* frequency smaller than 5.0, and no cell has an *expected* frequency smaller than 1.0. These limitations are not placed on the size of the observed or actual frequencies; only the expected frequencies should not be any smaller. If too many small expected frequencies exist, the categories should be combined, unless such combinations are meaningless. For example, a category of "agreement" should not be combined with one of "disagreement." This rule means that when only two-, three-, or four-cell χ^2 analyses are set up, *no* cell can have an expected frequency of less than 5.0.

If categories are combined to the point where there are only two categories and still an expected frequency of less than 5.0 exists, χ^2 should not be used. Instead, the *binomial test* may be used to treat the data.[2] The same rules about the required magnitude of expected frequencies apply to the two-or-more sample cases to be described next.

Two-or-More Sample Cases

In contrasting differences between two or more samples by a chi-square test, the same principles apply as in the one-sample application. Only the methods of determining expected frequencies and the number of degrees of freedom vary.

Difference between Two Samples.   The computational example we will use to illustrate the procedure for testing the null hypothesis that two samples are drawn from the same population concerns an investigator who wants to see if boys and girls respond differently to an attitudinal question. The responses of 100 boys and 100 girls to a question regarding the educational value of extracurricular activities are summarized and the row and column subtotals are given in Table 19.3.

The expected frequencies for such a problem are determined in a logical fashion. Because of the equal numbers of girls and boys in this investigation, as indicated by the row subtotals, it is logical to *expect* equal proportions of the column subtotals to be divided between the girls and boys. Thus 50 percent of the 100 frequencies in the "very valuable" column would be expected to go to the girls and 50 percent to the boys. Similarly, the 60 "uncertain" and 40 "of little value" frequencies should be divided equally between the boys and girls. The expected frequencies for this example have been added parenthetically in Table 19.4.

If you are unclear about how the expected frequencies were computed, study Tables 19.3 and 19.4 carefully. Note, for example, that to obtain the ex-

Table 19.3   Responses of 200 Boys and Girls to Question Regarding Value of Extracurricular Activities

	Very Valuable	Uncertain	Of Little Value	Row Subtotal	
Boys	40	40	20	100	
Girls	60	20	20	100	
Column subtotal	100	60	40	200	Total

2. See Sidney Siegel and N. John Castellan, *Nonparametric Statistics for the Behavioral Sciences* (New York: McGraw-Hill, 1988), pp. 49–50.

Table 19.4   Observed and Expected Frequencies^a for the Data in Table 19.3

	Very Valuable	Uncertain	Of Little Value	Row Subtotal	
Boys	(50) 40	(30) 40	(20) 20	100	
Girls	(50) 60	(30) 20	(20) 20	100	
Column subtotal	100	60	40	200	Total

^{a}Expected frequencies in parentheses.

pected frequency for the upper-left corner cell, the proportion of upper *row subtotal* to *total* (100/200) is multiplied by the left *column subtotal* (100) to yield the desired quantity (50). Expected frequencies for other cells are computed in a similar fashion.

The observed and expected frequencies are then inserted into the χ^2 calculation formula (19.1) as follows and solved accordingly:

$$\chi^2 = \frac{(40-50)^2}{50} + \frac{(40-30)^2}{30} + \frac{(20-20)^2}{20} + \frac{(60-50)^2}{50} + \frac{(20-30)^2}{30}$$

$$+ \frac{(20-20)^2}{20}$$

$$= 2.0 + 3.3 + 0 + 2.0 + 3.3 + 0$$

$$= 10.6$$

For two or more samples, the degrees of freedom necessary to interpret χ^2 values such as the above are always determined from the frequency table by the number of rows minus 1 times the number of columns minus 1; $(r-1)(c-1) = df$. In this case, using the data in Table 19.4, the computation is $(2-1)(3-1) = 2\ df$.

Examination of Table H (the chi-square table) reveals that, with 2 degrees of freedom, the χ^2 value of 10.6 in this example is significant beyond the 0.01 level. If this satisfies the previously set rejection level, the result indicates that the null hypothesis should be considered untenable and that there is a relationship between gender and response to the question. *The actual nature of the relationship must be discerned by a visual inspection of the frequency table.*

Differences between More Than Two Samples.   The technique for computing a chi-square analysis in which three or more samples are involved is quite similar to that for the two-sample case. In Table 19.5, the number of yearly truancy reports is cited for student samples in three secondary schools in a metropolitan school district of lower socioeconomic status. Expected frequencies have been added in parentheses.

The expected frequencies are computed as in preceding examples. To illustrate, the expected frequency for the upper-right corner cell is determined by taking the proportion between the upper *row subtotal* and the *total* (600/1200) and multiplying it by the right *column subtotal* (125) to yield the expected

Table 19.5   **Annual Truancy Reports for Three High Schools**[a]

| School | Number of Truancy Reports, by Individual Student | | | | Row Subtotal |
	None	1 – 3	4 – 6	More than 6	
A	(400) 400	(87.5) 100	(50) 50	(62.5) 50	600
B	(266.6) 300	(58.3) 50	(33.3) 25	(41.7) 25	400
C	(133.3) 100	(29.2) 25	(16.7) 25	(20.8) 50	200
Column subtotal	800	175	100	125	1200 Total

[a]Expected frequencies in parentheses.

frequency (62.5). The expected and observed frequencies are then inserted in Formula 19.1, and χ^2 is produced as follows:

$$\chi^2 = \frac{(400-400)^2}{400} + \frac{(100-87.5)^2}{87.5} + \frac{(50-50)^2}{50} + \frac{(50-62.5)^2}{62.5}$$

$$+ \frac{(300-266.6)^2}{266.6} + \frac{(50-58.3)^2}{58.3} + \frac{(25-33.3)^2}{33.3} + \frac{(25-41.7)^2}{41.7}$$

$$+ \frac{(100-133.3)^2}{133.3} + \frac{(25-29.2)^2}{29.2} + \frac{(25-16.7)^2}{16.7} + \frac{(50-20.8)^2}{20.8}$$

$$= 0 + 1.79 + 0 + 2.50 + 4.18 + 1.18 + 2.07 + 6.69 + 8.32 + 0.60 + 4.13 + 40.99$$

$$= 72.45$$

This value of chi square is interpreted for statistical significance from Table H with degrees of freedom equaling $(r-1)(c-1) = (3-1)(4-1) = 6$. The χ^2 value of 72.45 is well beyond that needed for significance at the 0.001 level; thus the null hypothesis should be rejected. It is necessary to consult the frequency table (Table 19.5) to discover the precise manner in which the truancy reports of the three high schools differ. An examination of the frequencies should reveal that school C has a markedly greater proportion of truancy reports than the other two schools.

When interpreting the meaning of a significant χ^2 value, it is often helpful to note the contribution made by each cell in the frequency table to the total χ^2 value. Observe in this example, for instance, that the lower-right cell makes a contribution of 40.99 to the final χ^2 of 72.45. Such observations can prove valuable in explaining the relationship indicated by the significant χ^2. It is also useful for interpretation and presentation purposes to table the observed frequencies as percentages of row or column totals. In Table 19.6, these percentages (by row totals) are shown for the truancy data. It should be clear from this table that the percentage of students with no truancy reports was relatively higher at schools A (67 percent) and B (75 percent), compared to only 50 percent with no reports at school C.

In computing χ^2 values by the method described here, care should be

Table 19.6   Observed Data in Table 19.5 as Percentages by Row

| School | Percentage of Truancy Reports, by Individual Student | | | | |
	None	1 − 3	4 − 6	More than 6	Total
A	66.7	16.7	8.3	8.3	100%
B	75.0	12.5	6.3	6.3	100
C	50.0	12.5	12.5	25.0	100

taken to check that the subtotal of the expected frequencies in any row or column equals the subtotal of the observed frequencies in the same row or column. Trivial differences between the expected and observed frequency subtotals created by rounding should be disregarded, however.

WILCOXON MATCHED-PAIRS SIGNED-RANKS TEST

The Wilcoxon matched-pairs signed-ranks test is used to assess the significance of difference between two samples consisting of matched pairs. Matched pairs would include two measures taken on the same individual, as in a pretest-posttest comparison. This test is the nonparametric counterpart of the *t* test for correlated data. Like most nonparametric techniques, the Wilcoxon test is quite simple to compute.

The computation procedures for this test will be illustrated by a hypothetical example in which an educational investigator has carefully matched eight pairs of students so that both members of each pair have equivalent scores on a verbal aptitude test and a physics achievement test. The eight pairs are separated into two groups, one member of a pair in each group. Over a two-week period, one of the groups is shown a series of filmed lectures covering a rather esoteric topic in the field of physics. These students are given no other instruction on the topic, which, incidentally, is so uncommon that students would have difficulty finding additional study materials on it. After each film, a 20-item, multiple-choice examination is given to the students, but they are not given the correct answers, nor do they receive corrected test papers.

The second group receives the same treatment as the first, with one exception. At the conclusion of each 20-item examination, the second group's papers are quickly corrected and returned to the students. The second group, therefore, receives *knowledge of results* regarding their performance, while the first group does not. At the close of the experimental period, an extensive examination is administered to both groups. The scores on the test are then analyzed by the Wilcoxon matched-pairs signed-ranks test.

The data from this example are summarized in Table 19.7. In the second and third columns, the posttraining test scores of the eight matched pairs are cited. In the remaining three columns at the right of the table, all of the operations that are necessary to compute *T,* the statistic on which the Wilcoxon test is based, are depicted.

The first step in computing *T* is to calculate all of the differences, either positive or negative, between the pairs by subtracting the scores of those who had no knowledge of results from their matched counterparts. These differences are then listed in a separate column.

Table 19.7   **Posttraining Test Scores of Eight Matched Pairs of Students, Classified According to Whether or Not Knowledge of Results Was Given**

Pair	Posttraining Test Scores		Difference	Rank of Difference	Rank with Less Frequent Sign
	Knowledge of Results	No Knowledge of Results			
1	65	61	4	2.5	
2	72	59	13	7	
3	58	63	−5	−4	4
4	48	41	7	5	
5	62	64	−2	−1	1
6	59	55	4	2.5	
7	74	54	20	8	
8	69	60	9	6	
					$T = 5$

Next, the differences are ranked, *regardless of algebraic sign*. A rank of 1 is given to the smallest difference, a rank of 2 to the next smallest, and so forth. Because the ranking is done without considering algebraic signs, a difference of −3 is given a *lower* rank than either −4 or +4. Pairs whose difference is zero are dropped from the analysis. If more than one pair has an identical difference, all of these pairs are given the mean of the totaled rankings. This is the case for pairs 1 and 6 in the example, where each difference has been assigned a ranking of 2.5.

After the differences have been ranked, regardless of algebraic sign, the sign is affixed once more to the rank of the differences. Essentially, this identifies those ranks that arose from negative differences and those that arose from positive differences.

Now T is obtained by summing the *smaller* number of the like-signed ranks. In this example, the negative ranks are fewer, so T equals 5. If the number of pairs is 25 or less, the significance of T can be determined by consulting Table I in the Appendix. In this example, with $n = 8$, a T value of 4 or less is needed to yield significance at the 0.05 level, and a T of zero is needed for significance at the 0.01 level. Both of these values are for two-tailed tests (direction not predicted). Note that, unlike many other statistics, the smaller T is, the more significant it is.

Table I covers only cases involving from 6 to 25 pairs. When n exceeds 25, Formula 19.2 is used to determine the value of z (the standard score for the normal curve), and the significance of T is then determined from a table of the normal curve (Table A in the Appendix). Formula 19.2 is:

$$z = \frac{T - \dfrac{n(n+1)}{4}}{\sqrt{\dfrac{n(n+1)(2n+1)}{24}}} \tag{19.2}$$

To indicate how satisfactory this formula is, even for small samples, the values of T and n from the example in this section can be used to compute the value of z. Substituting $T = 5$ and $n = 8$ in the formula, z is found as follows:

$$z = \frac{5 - \dfrac{8(8+1)}{4}}{\sqrt{\dfrac{8(8+1)(2)(8+1)}{24}}}$$

$$= -1.77$$

Notice that a z of -1.77 nears but does not quite reach statistical significance at the 0.05 level (a z of ± 1.96 would be required for a two-tailed hypothesis test). This is basically the same as the result noted in Table I, where the obtained T of 5 barely missed the required T of 4.

The computation procedure followed for the Wilcoxon matched-pairs signed-ranks test thus is quite simple. If n is 25 or less, Table I can be used to interpret the probability of T. If n exceeds 25, Formula 19.2 is used, and the resulting z value is interpreted from Table A.

SIGN TEST

The sign test is used in situations similar to those for which the Wilcoxon test is employed, but it may be utilized when only the direction, not the size, of difference between matched pairs can be determined. For example, suppose matched pairs are subjected to an experimental condition so that one member of the pair can be identified as superior to the other, but no notion of the degree of superiority can be obtained. This is an ideal situation for the application of the sign test.

The computation of this widely used nonparametric procedure will be illustrated by an example drawn from a high-school wrestling class in which 12 pairs of boys, matched on previously administered tests of physical strength and coordination, were taught a particular wrestling stunt by two different instructional methods. Following training, the boys performed their stunt in pairs before judges who, without knowing which member of each pair had been taught by which method, rated the performance of one member of the pair as superior to that of the other pair member. Data from the study are summarized in Table 19.8. In this table the member of each pair who was rated superior by the judges is identified by teaching method. In the column at the right a sign has been given to each difference, depending on the direction of difference. In the event that no direction of difference can be discerned between members of a pair, the individuals are dropped from the analysis, as in the Wilcoxon test. The symbol x is used to represent the number of the fewer signs. In this case, the value of x is 3.

For samples of 25 or fewer pairs, Table J can be used to interpret the significance or probability of x. According to this table, with n equal to 12, an x of 3 has a one-tailed probability of occurrence of 0.073; accordingly, it has a two-tailed probability of 0.146. The null hypothesis therefore would be considered tenable.

With an n larger than 25, the significance of the sign test is determined in a manner similar to that for the Wilcoxon test. In this case, Formula 19.3 is used to yield a z value:

Table 19.8   Performance Ratings of 12 Pairs of Boys Taught by Method A and Method B

Pair	Teaching Method Used with Boy Judged Superior	Sign
1	A	+
2	A	+
3	B	−
4	B	−
5	A	+
6	A	+
7	A	+
8	B	−
9	A	+
10	A	+
11	A	+
12	A	+
		$x = 3$

$$z = \frac{(x \pm 0.5) - \frac{1}{2}n}{\frac{1}{2}\sqrt{n}} \tag{19.3}$$

In this formula, $x + 0.5$ is used when x is less than $\frac{1}{2}n$, and $x - 0.5$ is used when x is greater than $\frac{1}{2}n$.

The use of Formula 19.3 can be illustrated by data from 36 matched pairs in which the number of fewer difference signs is 8; thus $n = 36$ and $x = 8$. Because x is less than $\frac{1}{2}n$, $x + 0.5$ is used in the formula, as follows:

$$z = \frac{(8 + 0.5) - 18}{\frac{1}{2}\sqrt{36}}$$
$$= -3.17$$

A z value of -3.17, interpreted from Table A, is significant beyond the 0.01 level, and the null hypothesis would be rejected.

MANN-WHITNEY U TEST

When the difference between two independent or nonmatched groups is to be assessed, the Mann-Whitney U test represents a powerful alternative to the parametric t test for uncorrelated samples. The U test needs data that can be ranked. With small samples, U can be calculated in an extremely brief manner. The statistic on which this test is based (that is, U) is interpreted for statistical significance in one of three different ways, depending on the size of the sample involved.

Very Small Samples

Before proceeding, you must understand that n_1 is defined as the number of cases in the smaller of the two groups being compared in the Mann-Whitney U test, and n_2 is defined as the number of cases in the larger of the two groups.

When n_1 and n_2 are very small, U is computed as follows. First, the scores of the two groups are ranked together, but the identity of each score's rank (that is, the group from which it was drawn) is retained. For example, with the eight scores presented below, the ranking is conducted in order of increasing size, as follows:

Group A Scores: 4, 6, 7, 12, 15
Group B Scores: 3, 8, 9

Now in combined ranking:

Rank	3	4	6	7	8	9	12	15
Group	B	A	A	A	B	B	A	A

Next, focusing on the B group, the number of A scores that are ranked below, or precede, each score in the B group is counted. For the B score of 3, no A score is ranked lower. For the B score of 8, three A scores precede, as is the case with the B score of 9. Hence, $U = 0 + 3 + 3 = 6$; that is, six is the number of times an A score preceded a B score.

When neither n_1 nor n_2 is larger than 8, Table K of the Appendix may be used to determine the probability of the occurrence of U. To use this table, the separate subtable that has n_2 equal to the number of cases in the larger sample is consulted. In this example, $n_2 = 5$, so the subtable for $n_2 = 5$ is consulted. Next, the value of n_1 (the number of cases in the smaller sample) is located in the top row of the table. The column of probability values below the appropriate n_1 indicates the significance level for the U values in the column at the extreme left. In the example, a U of 6, when $n_2 = 5$ and $n_1 = 3$, has a 0.393 probability of occurrence. Because *all probability values in Table K are for one-tailed tests,* the two-tailed probability of this U would be 0.786. The investigator would not reject the null hypothesis under the circumstances. The U test is another example of a statistical test in which the smaller the statistic is, the more significant it is.

It sometimes happens that the value of U is so large that it is not cited in the appropriate subtable. This situation occurs when the investigator has focused on the "wrong" group to determine U. A value of U too large for the table is called U' (U prime). In this example, U' would have been obtained had the values of B scores that were ranked below the values of A scores been used, instead of the other way around. To illustrate, U would then have been $1 + 1 + 1 + 3 + 3 = 9$. In the subtable with $n_2 = 5$, there is no probability value for a U of 9 when $n_1 = 3$. Thus this U is actually U', which can be quickly converted or transformed to U by the use of Formula 19.4, as follows:

$$U = n_1 n_2 - U' \qquad (19.4)$$

In the example, Formula 19.4 would be used to obtain the U originally found by counting the number of B scores that preceded A scores. Substituting the values in the example, the equation would be:

$$U = (3)(5) - 9 = 6$$

Moderately Large Samples

When n_2 is between 9 and 20, Table K is not used to determine the significance of U. Instead, Table L in the Appendix is used. This table consists of four subtables which give critical values for U for one- and two-tailed tests at commonly used significance levels. The particular subtable of Table L that is appropriate for the significance level employed by the investigator must be used. For example, if $n_1 = 8$ and $n_2 = 16$ in a two-tailed null hypothesis test where the rejection level has been preset at 0.05, a U value of 31 or less is needed to reject the null hypothesis.

It may occasionally be necessary to compute the value of U'. This can be quickly ascertained by inserting the obtained value in Formula 19.4 and computing a second U value. The smaller of the two U values is U, while the larger is U'.

Large Samples

When n_2 is larger than 20, a special formula has been developed for interpreting the probability of U by a z value and the normal curve. Formula 19.5 is as follows:

$$z = \frac{U - \frac{n_1 n_2}{2}}{\sqrt{\frac{(n_1)(n_2)(n_1 + n_2 + 1)}{12}}} \qquad (19.5)$$

Like some of the nonparametric formulas for treating large samples, Formula 19.5 yields a z value whose probability of occurrence is determined through use of Table A for the normal curve.

With large or even moderately large samples, the computation of U by the counting method described earlier is far too time-consuming. A procedure which yields identical results is carried out by considering the scores in both groups as though they were in one group and then ranking all scores, giving a 1 to the lowest score, a 2 to the next lowest, and so forth. Then the value of U is found by using Formula 19.6:

$$U = n_1 n_2 + \frac{n_1 (n_1 + 1)}{2} - R_1 \qquad (19.6)$$

where:

$R_1 = $ the sum of the ranks assigned to the n_1 group

Use of Formula 19.6 with large or *moderately large* groups readily yields the value of U. This value should be inserted in the transformation formula (Formula 19.4) to see if U' rather than U has been obtained. The smaller value is U.

We will illustrate the use of Formulas 19.5 and 19.6 with the hypothetical data presented in Table 19.9 for behavioral rigidity scores and ranks of an experimental group and a control group of students. The first step is to give overall rankings to the scores, considering them as a combined group. The

Table 19.9   **Behavioral Rigidity Scores of 15 Students: 9 in Experimental Group and 6 in Control Group**

Experimental Group		Control Group	
Score	Rank	Score	Rank
49	13	59	15
47	11	56	14
41	9	48	12
39	9	46	10
35	6	37	7
30	5	26	2
29	4		
28	3		
24	1		
			$R_1 = 60$

rankings of the smaller group are then summed; in this example, this yields an R_1 of 60. This value is then inserted, along with n_1 and n_2, into Formula 19.6:

$$U = (6)(9) + \frac{(6)(6+1)}{2} - 60$$

$$= 15$$

To be certain that this value is U rather than U', Formula 19.4 is used:

$$U = (6)(9) - 15$$

$$= 39$$

The smaller of these two values is U; therefore, $U = 15$ and $U' = 39$.

The next step in the analysis is to insert U, n_1, and n_2 into Formula 19.5 and solve for z, as follows:

$$z = \frac{15 - \frac{(6)(9)}{2}}{\sqrt{\frac{(6)(9)(6+9+1)}{12}}}$$

$$= \frac{-12}{8.49}$$

$$= -1.41$$

Because a z value of -1.41, as interpreted from the table of the normal curve, is not significant at the 0.05 level, the null hypothesis would not be rejected.

In computing U through Formula 19.6, ties in ranks are assigned the average of the tied ranks. If the tied ranks are many and U is close to the previously decided rejection level, a special correction formula which takes ties into account may be used.[3] The effect of this correction is to slightly increase the value of z, thus making it more significant.

---

3. See Siegel and Castellan, *Nonparametric Statistics,* pp. 134–36.

FRIEDMAN TWO-WAY ANALYSIS OF VARIANCE BY RANKS

The Friedman two-way analysis of variance by ranks is designed to test the null hypothesis that several matched samples have been drawn from the same population. The matched samples may be the same group of individuals who have been exposed to several conditions, or they may be sets of individuals who have been matched on relevant variables and are randomly assigned to different conditions. In either situation, the condition represents the independent variable, while the criterion data, which must be amenable to ranking, represent the dependent variable.

The use of the Friedman test will be illustrated with the data presented in Table 19.10. Four elementary school pupils, each of whom has been exposed to three different programmed-instruction methods, have ranked each method according to how "interesting" they believed it to be. The most interesting method was ranked 1, the next most interesting method ranked 2, and the least interesting method ranked 3.

It makes no difference in the Friedman test whether rankings are from lowest to highest or highest to lowest. Tied ranks are assigned the average ranks of the ties. After the ranks in each column are summed (as in Table 19.10), Formula 19.7, which yields χ_r^2, the statistic on which the Friedman test is based, can then be used. Formula 19.7 is:

$$\chi_r^2 = \frac{12}{Nk(k+1)}\Sigma\,(R_j)^2 - 3N(k+1) \tag{19.7}$$

where:

N = the number of rows
k = the number of columns
$(R_j)^2$ directs that all column rank totals are to be first squared and then summed

When the necessary values are inserted in Formula 19.7, the equation is as follows:

$$\chi_r^2 = \frac{12}{(4)(3)(3+1)}[(8)^2 + (5)^2 + (11)^2] - 3(4)(3+1)$$

$$= 4.5$$

Table 19.10   Ranks of Three Programmed-Instruction Methods by Four Elementary School Pupils

	Programming Method		
Pupil	1	2	3
A	2	1	3
B	3	1	2
C	1	2	3
D	2	1	3
	$R_1 = 8$	$R_2 = 5$	$R_3 = 11$

The probability of χ_r^2 is generally determined by using the standard χ^2 table (Table H in the Appendix), with the degrees of freedom equaling the number of columns less 1. However, when the number of columns is three and the number of rows is two through nine, or when the number of columns is four and the number of rows is two through four, Table M in the Appendix should be used. Because in this example there are only three columns and four rows, Table M is consulted. With $k = 3$ and $N = 4$, a χ_r^2 value of 4.5 is shown in the table to be significant at the 0.125 level. Thus the null hypothesis would not be rejected.

KRUSKAL-WALLIS ONE-WAY ANALYSIS OF VARIANCE BY RANKS

The Kruskal-Wallis one-way analysis of variance by ranks is designed to test the null hypothesis that several independent samples are drawn from the same population. This test is basically used to test for differences among three or more groups when the data involved are capable of being ranked. It can be applied to situations involving extremely small samples. In fact, probability values are available for three samples involving as few as one, one, and two individuals.

To illustrate the computation procedures used with the Kruskal-Wallis test, consider an example in which the performances of three small samples of public-school special-services personnel on an attitude inventory are contrasted. The inventory is designed to measure the likelihood that school nurses, counselors, and psychometricians will establish good rapport with colleagues. Scores and ranks of the individuals in the three sample groups of personnel are presented in Table 19.11.

The first step in the computation procedure is to consider all scores as though they were drawn from one group and assign ranks to each score. This has been done in Table 19.11 in the rank columns adjacent to the score columns. These ranks are then summed for each column; in this example, the sums are $R_1 = 28$, $R_2 = 42$, and $R_3 = 21$. Now Formula 19.8 can be used to determine the value of H for the Kruskal-Wallis test, as follows:

$$H = \frac{12}{n(n+1)} \sum \frac{R_j^2}{n_j} - 3(n+1) \tag{19.8}$$

Table 19.11 **Scores of Three Groups of Public-School Special-Services Personnel on Test of Potential Rapport with Colleagues**

School Nurses		Counselors		Psychometricians	
Score	Rank	Score	Rank	Score	Rank
64	9	72	13	66	11
59	8	70	12	49	5
56	6	65	10	48	4
47	3	57	7	42	1
44	2				
$R_1 = 28$		$R_2 = 42$		$R_3 = 21$	

where:

n = the number of cases in all the samples combined

$\sum \dfrac{R_j{}^2}{n_j}$ directs that each sum of column ranks is to be squared, each of these squares is to be divided by the number of ranks in the column, and then the resulting quantities are to be added together

Substituting the data in Table 19.11, the value of H in the example would be computed as follows:

$$H = \frac{12}{13(13+1)}\left[\frac{(28)^2}{5} + \frac{(42)^2}{4} + \frac{(21)^2}{4}\right] - 3(13+1)$$

$$= 4.73$$

When the number of cases in each sample exceeds five, H may be interpreted for level of statistical significance from a chi-square table (Table H in the Appendix) with df = the number of columns, or samples, less 1. However, when there are only three samples and the number of cases per sample is five or less, then Table N of the Appendix should be used to interpret the probability of the occurrence of H. This situation exists in the example, where $n_1 = 5$, $n_2 = 4$, and $n_3 = 4$. From Table N, it can be seen that, with samples of this size, an H of 4.73 has a probability of occurrence significant at the 0.10 level (where H must equal or exceed 4.6187) but not at the 0.05 level (where H must equal or exceed 5.6176). Thus, had the investigator previously set the null hypothesis rejection level at 0.05, the null hypothesis would have to be considered tenable. This result indicates that on the basis of these samples, at least, there was no significant difference among the three groups of special-services personnel with respect to scores on the test of potential rapport with colleagues.

You may note from the data, however, that there are apparently certain score differences among the three samples. With larger n's in the groups, if the trend of these differences persisted, the results would definitely be statistically significant. This situation, therefore, illustrates how the size of samples is so instrumental in yielding probabilistic significance.

SPEARMAN RANK-ORDER CORRELATION COEFFICIENT

The Spearman rank-order correlation coefficient is one of the more widely used nonparametric techniques. We designate this statistic, often referred to as *rho,* as r_s. The function of r_s is essentially the same as that of the Pearson product-moment correlation coefficient, namely, to assess the degree of relationship between two variables. However, while the Pearson r requires that certain assumptions such as homoscedasticity be satisfied, the Spearman coefficient does not. Thus it may be used in certain instances when the investigator finds it impossible to apply the Pearson r. Because it is computed rapidly with small samples, r_s is often used by educators who want to secure a quick estimate of relationship between variables.

The computation of the Spearman rank-order correlation coefficient will be illustrated with the hypothetical attitude-scale data presented in Table

Table 19.12   **Scores and Ranks of Seven Individuals on Two Attitude Inventories**

Individual	Attitude Inventory X Score	Attitude Inventory X Rank	Attitude Inventory Y Score	Attitude Inventory Y Rank	d	d^2
a	124	1	62	2	−1	1
b	123	2	59	3	−1	1
c	119	3	67	1	2	4
d	117	4	57	4.5	0.5	0.25
e	110	5	57	4.5	0.5	0.25
f	104	6	50	7	−1	1
g	94	7	52	6	1	1
						$\Sigma d^2 = 8.5$

19.12. All scores of the individuals on both of the variables are listed and ranks are assigned to each individual, first for the X scores and then for the Y scores. The difference between the two ranks for each individual is then listed in a separate column, and the squares of these differences are listed and summed in the column at the right-hand side of the table. Note that tied scores (the score of 57 in Table 19.12) are assigned the average of the ranks. Though quite a large number of tied ranks can be tolerated without affecting the size of r_s, a correction for an excessive number of ties is available.[4]

Once these values are available, r_s can be readily computed by the use of Formula 19.9:

$$r_s = 1 - \frac{6 \Sigma d^2}{n^3 - n} \tag{19.9}$$

where:

        $n =$ the number of individuals
        $\Sigma d^2 =$ the sum of the squared differences between individuals' ranks

The sum of the squared differences (Σd^2) in this case is 8.5. Inserting this quantity and the number of individuals in Formula 19.9 yields r_s, as follows:

$$r_s = 1 - \frac{6(8.5)}{7^3 - 7}$$

$$= 0.85$$

The Spearman coefficient is interpreted in basically the same way as the standard product-moment r. A coefficient near $+1.00$ reflects a strong positive relationship, a coefficient near -1.00 reflects a strong negative relationship, and a coefficient near zero reflects little or no relationship.

Determining the Significance of r_s

The statistical significance of r_s can be determined quite readily with small samples of 4 to 30 cases by using Table O in the Appendix. This table

---

4. See Siegel and Castellan, *Nonparametric Statistics*.

supplies one-tailed significance levels for critical values of r_s at the 0.05 and 0.01 levels. It can be seen in Table O that with the r_s of 0.85 obtained in the example, where $n = 7$, a one-tailed significance level of 0.05 has been reached. The 0.05 critical value in Table O with this size sample is 0.714, while the 0.01 critical value is 0.893.

When n is ten or greater, the significance of the Spearman coefficient may be tested by the use of Formula 19.10:

$$t = r_s \sqrt{\frac{n-2}{1-r_s^2}} \tag{19.10}$$

This yields a t value that is interpreted from the table for the distribution of t (Table E in the Appendix), with $df = n - 2$.

To illustrate the use of Formula 19.10, a Spearman coefficient value of 0.70 can be inserted, with the number of individuals involved being 32. The formula is then set up and computed as follows:

$$t = 0.70 \sqrt{\frac{32-2}{1-(0.70)^2}}$$

$$= 5.37$$

With 30 df $(n-2)$, it can be seen from Table E that the obtained t value of 5.37 is significant beyond the 0.01 level.

■   ■   ■

REVIEW

Chi square is an important nonparametric test. It is widely used to test for goodness of fit between a sample and some known or hypothetical distribution, as well as to test differences between two or more samples. For data at the nominal level, there are few alternatives. Particular attention should be given to the requirements for expected frequencies, including suggestions for regrouping categories to meet these requirements.

In addition to chi square, this chapter has presented computation procedures and examples for the other nonparametric procedures discussed in Chapter 18. These include the Wilcoxon matched-pairs signed-ranks test, the sign test, the Mann-Whitney U test, the Friedman two-way analysis of variance, the Kruskal-Wallis one-way analysis of variance, and the Spearman rank-order correlation coefficient.

Almost all of these tests can be quickly calculated and readily interpreted, a point of some importance to time-pressed teachers and administrators.

EXERCISES

1. During seven preceding years, the average percentage of students electing particular foreign languages in a metropolitan high school has been the following: French, 35%; Spanish, 40%; German, 15%; Latin, 10%. This year the school counselors note an apparently marked divergence from previous enrollments for these classes. The 500 students electing foreign languages are distributed as follows: French, 200; Spanish, 150; German, 100; Latin, 50. Using a χ^2 analysis, determine whether this year's enrollment in foreign languages is significantly different (at the 0.01 level) from the average distribution pattern during the seven preceding years.

2. Determine by a χ^2 goodness-of-fit test whether the following distribution of scores can be considered to depart significantly from the shape of a normal distribution. Remember that a score such as 17 actually represents an interval from 16.5 through 17.5. Set up a 1×8 χ^2 table and compute the expected frequencies based on the normal-curve table.

Score	Frequency
20	20
19	40
18	60
17	80
16	80
15	60
14	40
13	20

3. Below are responses of two groups of students to a questionnaire item. Using a chi-square two-sample test, determine whether the null hypotheses regarding group differences should be rejected.

	A	B	C	D
Group X	60	50	40	50
Group Y	0	10	30	30

4. Fifty first-year elementary teachers and fifty first-year secondary teachers have completed an attitude inventory regarding professional organizations in education. Their responses have been summarized in the 2×5 table below. If necessary, combine categories of scores, so that χ^2 can be applied without violating generally accepted notions regarding minimum expected frequencies. Compute a chi-square value to see whether the two samples of teachers can be considered to have been drawn from the same population.

	Attitude Inventory Score				
	40 and Below	41–50	51–60	61–70	71 and Above
Elementary teachers	4	10	12	18	6
Secondary teachers	3	11	13	15	8

5. Two samples consisting of matched pairs of elementary pupils have been given different sets of spelling materials. The two students in each pair were matched on language-arts scores from a standardized achievement test and scores on an extensive spelling pretest. Below are their scores in a posttraining spelling examination. Using a Wilcoxon matched-pairs signed-ranks test, determine whether the performance of the groups using spelling materials X is significantly different beyond the 0.05 level from the group using spelling materials Z.

Pair Number	Spelling Examination Score	
	Materials X	Materials Z
1	28	31
2	33	35
3	40	39
4	36	39
5	40	43
6	14	21
7	16	19
8	21	26
9	32	30
10	43	56

6. Twelve matched pairs of primary-grade students have undergone a month-long reading-improvement training session, with one group using conventional reading-improvement materials and the other group using an approach based on a modified form of our alphabet symbols known as the *Augmented Roman Alphabet*. At the conclusion of the training period, 10 of the 12 pupils in the Augmented Roman Alphabet group exceed the performance of their material counterparts on a standardized reading test. Using a sign test, determine whether this difference is significant beyond the 0.05 level.

7. By employing a Mann-Whitney U test, determine the value of U and decide whether Group I significantly outperformed Group II at the 0.05 level. Assume that you have made a prediction in advance of the data gathering that Group I will perform better (that is, secure higher scores) than Group II, so you are entitled to use a one-tailed test.

Group I scores	2	3	5	6	9	9	10
Group II scores	1	1	4	4			

8. Test the null hypothesis that the following scores of 20 boys and 18 girls are not significantly different from one another on an inventory of interest in social welfare work. Use the Mann-Whitney U test and Formulas 19.5 and 19.6 to analyze the data.

Boys	Girls	Boys	Girls
42	54	33	41
40	53	30	41
40	50	30	41
39	48	30	38
38	48	28	34
37	47	28	33
36	47	27	30
35	46	26	30
35	46	25	
34	43	24	

9. Using a Friedman two-way analysis-of-variance model, determine the value of χ_r^2 and decide whether to reject the null hypothesis at the 0.01 level for the following data, in which three matched sets of individuals have been trained by four different instructional techniques and subsequently ranked in terms of performance.

Set of Individuals	Instructional Technique			
	1	2	3	4
A	4	2	1	3
B	4	3	1	2
C	4	3	1	1

10. The following are personality-test scores for three groups of secondary teachers whose college majors were English, psychology, and sociology. Using the Kruskal-Wallis one-way analysis of variance, determine the value of H and decide whether the three samples should be considered part of the same population.

Psychology	English	Sociology
64	65	59
63	42	42
58	39	29
43	30	
40		

11. Compute a Spearman rank-order correlation coefficient on the data given in exercise 7 in Chapter 6. Note how r_s compares with the product-moment r of 0.35.

12. Determine the size of r_s for the following two sets of rankings by two teachers of a set of essay examinations. Assuming that r_s will be positive and, therefore, using a one-tailed test, is r_s significant beyond the 0.05 level?

Test Paper	Ranking by Teacher I	Ranking by Teacher II
1	1	1
2	3	2
3	2	3
4	5	4
5	4	5
6	6	6
7	7	7

Choosing the
Appropriate Technique

- *a programmed-learning exercise*

This chapter is designed to serve several purposes. It will help you select statistical procedures for use in analyzing data from educational investigations. It will help you study reports of educational investigations and program evaluations and improve your conceptual understanding of the purposes for which these techniques are commonly used. And of course, the chapter will also serve as an interesting way for you to review the material presented in Chapters 1–19.

The scheme we have employed is quite simple. A hypothetical situation is presented which represents a general class of data-gathering design that might be encountered by an educator. After you read the description of the situation, we ask you to select from several choices the statistical technique most appropriate for the analysis of the situation and to turn to a page in this chapter associated with that choice. If the correct choice is made, you will be so informed and will be directed to another hypothetical situation. If the incorrect choice is made, additional information will be presented in order to clarify why another technique is more suitable. You will then be directed to choose another statistical technique for the situation, until you find the correct answer.

The pages that follow are numbered in sequence, as in the rest of this text, but *they are not to be read consecutively.* In proceeding from one situation to the next, you will respond to a multiple-choice question by turning to the page indicated to the left of your answer choice. If the right answer appears on that page, you will be directed to proceed to a new hypothetical situation and multiple-choice question. If you have chosen the wrong answer, directions will be given regarding the selection of another answer. In each case, for maximum learning, you should read the entire answer section before proceeding, and refer to the pages cited in italics to review.

Now please begin on the following page.

SITUATION A

A pilot experiment, designed to test the effectiveness of a new approach to spelling proficiency, has been conducted over a semester-long period in a junior high school. Two different classes of 29 seventh-grade pupils participated in the study. Both classes received their formal spelling instructions from Mr. Jordan, an experienced teacher. With group X, he employed conventional methods of spelling instruction such as are commonly used in upper elementary grades. He met with group X five times a week for a period of one hour, but only one of these periods was devoted to spelling instruction. Group Y also met with Mr. Jordan daily and devoted one hour a week to spelling instruction, but in the formal spelling teaching for this group computer-assisted lessons were presented to the students via personal computers. Because all of the students involved in the pilot study had been preselected, Mr. Jordan had matched them in pairs in two groups with respect to academic aptitude and preexperiment performance on an orally administered spelling quiz of 150 words. At the conclusion of the semester's experiment, the spelling quiz was readministered to both groups.

Which of the statistical procedures listed below should Mr. Jordan select to test whether there is a significant difference between his conventional instruction techniques and the computer-assisted method of teaching spelling, as determined by postexperiment performance on the spelling quiz?

Page 290   Product-Moment Correlation
Page 292   The *t* Test
Page 294   Analysis of Covariance

YOUR ANSWER (from page 293): Determination of a Confidence Interval

As you may recall, confidence intervals are used to estimate, from sample statistics, the limits within which population parameters such as means, correlation coefficients, and mean differences probably fall. Estimation of such intervals or ranges is an extremely important operation in educational investigations. However, the task facing the program evaluator in situation B is to determine whether a statistically significant difference exists between any two of the four groups. Having determined that a significant difference exists, the next step might be to determine the confidence interval.

In selecting a technique to use in this situation, Miss Adams must choose a statistical model capable of testing for mean differences between two or more groups.

Now return to page 293 and select the most appropriate technique for situation B.

To review the purposes of estimation procedures, see pp. 54–60.

YOUR ANSWER (from page 288): Product-Moment Correlation

Well, let's see. You have learned that correlation procedures are used in determining the degree of relationship between two variables. In order to calculate such a relationship, there must be two measures for the same individuals. The measures available in situation A are preexperiment spelling scores, postexperiment spelling scores, and aptitude test scores. Mr. Jordan could, then, compute correlation coefficients between any two of these measures. Which correlation coefficient, however, would tell him anything about the effectiveness of the two methods of teaching spelling? Would the correlation between pre- and postexperiment spelling indicate anything about the value of the new approach to spelling, even if he considered the groups one at a time? No, he could gain little insight into the efficacy of the new method by correlating students' scores on any of the available measures.

Mr. Jordan needs a statistical technique that will indicate if those who studied spelling by the new method *exceeded* the performance of those who studied by the conventional method. A *difference-testing* technique is called for in this situation, not product-moment correlation.

In light of this additional information, return to page 288 and select the correct technique for situation A.

To review the function of product-moment correlation, see pp. 64–66.

YOUR ANSWER (from page 326): Spearman Rank-Order Correlation Coefficient

The Spearman rank-order correlation approach yields an index of the relationship between two ranked variables. As such, it is often employed in situations where the assumptions of the product-moment r cannot be satisfied. It is true in the prediction problem presented in situation E that Mrs. Sparks, the counselor, would have a better idea of which students to recommend for university work if she knew more about the general nature of relationships between the variable of college-grade performance and the potential prediction variables she has available, such as students' high school grade averages, ninth-grade verbal aptitude scores, and college entrance examination scores. The Spearman r_s will provide such a general estimate of the strength and direction of relationships between prediction variables and the criterion variable, but it does not provide a method for making appropriate predictions for *individual* students.

Such a technique is needed in this situation. Mrs. Sparks must use a model that makes it possible to set up a prediction equation in which she can insert a student's scores on the predictor variables to yield an estimate of that student's performance on the criterion measure—in this case, university grades.

Return to page 326 and select the appropriate technique for situation E.

To review the purposes of the Spearman rank-order correlation coefficient,
see pp. 280–81.

YOUR ANSWER (from page 288): The *t* Test

CORRECT. The problem at hand is to test the null hypothesis that the postexperiment performances of the two matched groups are equivalent. Because the groups have been matched on measures considered relevant to the criterion, the major remaining factor that is potentially related to the criterion is type of treatment (i.e., mode of instruction). Because the groups consist of matched pairs, the correlated *t* model should be used. If the null hypothesis is tenable, as indicated by a nonsignificant *t* value, then Mr. Jordan would conclude that no difference favoring the new method of teaching spelling exists, at least on the basis of this pilot study. If the null hypothesis is untenable, as manifested by a significant *t* value, and the group favored by the mean differences is the experimental group, the evidence to support the use of the new method has been provided by the pilot study. Further large-scale experimentation to assess the relative efficacy of the new method is probably warranted.

Now proceed to hypothetical situation B on the following page.

To review the different types of t-*test models, see pp. 129–31.*

Now consider another experimental situation. Assume that Miss Adams, a program evaluator, wants to contrast *three* new methods of teaching spelling with a conventional method. As in situation A, only one instructor is involved in the experiment. Miss Adams randomly assigns 15 students to each of four groups. She wants to determine whether there were significant differences in the scores of the four groups (three experimental, one control) on a postexperiment spelling test. Which of the following statistical procedures would be most appropriate for her to use?

YOUR ANSWER (from page 288): Analysis of Covariance

You have probably recalled that analysis of covariance may be used to test for differences among two or more groups, while statistically controlling for group differences on variables that are relevant to the criterion variable under consideration. In situation A, the criterion measure is student performance on the postexperiment spelling examination. Available measures that are relevant are undoubtedly preexperiment spelling scores and aptitude-test scores. However, there is really no need to statistically equate group differences on these relevant variables, because students in the two groups *were already matched in pairs* before the experiment was begun. Hence, while analysis of covariance *could* be employed in this situation to yield the necessary information regarding the efficacy of the experimental method, a technique that did not involve the computation associated with the statistical equalization of groups would be more economical. This would probably be a better choice under these circumstances.

Return to page 288 and select the correct technique for situation A.

To review the function of analysis of covariance, see pp. 199–202.

YOUR ANSWER (from page 293): Single-Classification Analysis of Variance

CORRECT. When testing for mean differences among several randomly drawn samples, single-classification analysis of variance is appropriate if only one independent variable is employed in the design. In the present situation, the single independent variable is method of instruction as represented by the four groups, and the dependent variable is performance on the spelling test.

Now proceed to hypothetical situation C on the following page.

To review the assumptions underlying analysis of variance, see pp. 162–63.

SITUATION C

To continue with the same problem, suppose Miss Adams, the program evaluator, obtained an F value indicating significant differences among the four experimental groups. How would she pinpoint exactly where these differences are? For example, suppose she had hypothesized, among other things, that all three new methods of teaching spelling were superior to the conventional method. How could she statistically analyze the data further to follow up specifically on this hypothesis?

Page 324   Post Hoc Comparisons
Page 329   A Priori Comparisons
Page 327   Nonparametric Tests

YOUR ANSWER (from page 293): Chi Square

There are research situations quite similar to situation B in which chi square might be used to test for differences between several groups. Because it is a nonparametric statistical model and uses only frequency-count data rather than deviations from the mean, however, chi square is a markedly *less powerful* statistical test than its parametric counterparts. Chi square *can* be used to test for differences among two or more groups when the criterion data appear only in classificatory, rather than numerical, form.

In this example, because the postexperiment scores of the pupils are numerical, a parametric approach is probably preferable to chi square. Miss Adams should select a parametric model that will test for mean differences between two or more samples.

Return to page 293 and choose the appropriate statistical technique for situation B.

To review the applications of the chi-square model, see pp. 264–71.

YOUR ANSWER (from page 326): Regression

CORRECT. Through the use of a linear regression model, Mrs. Sparks, the counselor, could set up a prediction equation so that by inserting a student's score on one or more prediction variables, such as high school grade-point average, a predicted college grade-point average for that student could be determined, with certain known error limits for inaccurate predictions. To secure the data necessary for the development of a regression prediction equation, she would have to consider the high school's previous graduates who had entered the university as the regression sample. On the basis of the relationships between these students' performances on the criterion and one or more predictive variables, she could set up the prediction equation for the present high school seniors.

Now proceed to hypothetical situation F on the following page.

To review the assumptions that should be satisfied before using regression procedures, see pp. 99–100.

For the next hypothetical situation, imagine that Mr. Brown, a teacher, wants to demonstrate that two forms of an achievement test he has developed are parallel, or more-or-less equivalent. If so, he can administer one form as a pretest and the second as a posttest in a study of certain new instructional procedures he proposes to introduce to his class. The actual experiment Mr. Brown wants to conduct involves a comparison of the achievement of three matched groups of pupils who have been taught a series of concepts by three relatively distinct instructional procedures. The results of the experiment will help him decide which of the instructional procedures to use with future classes.

SITUATION F

To prepare for this project, Mr. Brown has written a large number of test items and randomly divided them into two sets representing different forms of the test. After instructing his class using a combination of the three new instructional procedures, he administers the two forms of the test to 110 pupils in four sections (classes) of the same course. He notes with pleasure that the means for the two test forms are practically identical. By employing which of the following techniques can he now secure a statistical notion of the degree to which the two forms of the test are equivalent?

Page 301   Multiple-Classification Analysis of Variance
Page 303   The *t* Test
Page 306   Product-Moment Correlation

YOUR ANSWER (from page 326): Standard Deviation

The standard deviation, like the mean, median, and variance, is a descriptive statistic, suitable for describing a certain facet of a set of data. More specifically, the standard deviation is an index of the variability of a set of data. Though it is in some cases desirable to know something about how widely scores diverge from the mean of a distribution, the particular task faced by the counselor is to select a rigorous predictive model. For these purposes, standard deviation would not suffice.

Now return to page 326 and select the appropriate *predictive* statistical model for situation E.

To review the differences between descriptive and inferential statistics, see pp. 6–7.

YOUR ANSWER (from page 299): Multiple-Classification Analysis of Variance

Multiple-classification analysis of variance is a particularly powerful tool at the disposal of the educational investigator, and it can be appropriately used in a variety of situations. Unfortunately, this is not one of them. Multiple-classification analysis of variance allows the investigator to determine whether there are differences among two or more sets of groups (representing independent variables) with respect to a dependent variable. It is also possible to detect a significant interaction effect of two or more independent variables upon a dependent variable.

For example, with achievement-test scores as a dependent or criterion measure, it would be possible to determine if there were (1) any difference between scores of males and females, as well as (2) any differences among high-aptitude, average-aptitude, and low-aptitude pupils. In such a design, the two independent variables would be sex and aptitude. It would also be possible to see if an interaction between sex and aptitude resulted in any achievement-score differences.

What Mr. Brown, the teacher in situation F, needs is an index of the relationship, not difference, between his previous pupils' scores on the two test forms.

Now return to page 299 and select the appropriate technique for situation F.

To review the applications of multiple-classification analysis of variance, see pp. 174–77.

YOUR ANSWER (from page 307): Single-Classification Analysis of Variance

Single-classification analysis of variance allows the investigator to test the null hypothesis that means of several samples have been drawn from the same population. To phrase it another way, single-classification analysis of variance makes it possible to tell whether there are any significant mean differences among two or more groups. The problem for Miss Perez is somewhat the same because she wants to learn if there is a significant difference in the responses of the two groups composed of males and females. But there are no *means* of the two groups to analyze. Instead of numerical criterion data from which means and standard deviations could be computed, she has a set of nominal, or classificatory, data with three classes of responses to the questionnaire item. In this instance, the difference between the two samples will be determined by the *frequency* of the responses to the three categories. Analysis-of-variance models cannot be used with such data. Instead, a nonparametric difference-testing technique is required.

Now return to page 307 and select the appropriate technique for situation G.

To review the measurement-level requirements of nonparametric tests, see pp. 248–50.

YOUR ANSWER (from page 299): The *t* Test

Well, at first glance this might appear to be a situation where a *t* test could be appropriately used, for a *t* test does allow the investigator to tell whether two sample means are significantly different. And there are two scores for each of the 110 pupils, so each set of scores could be considered to represent a different sample. By means of a *t* test, Mr. Brown, the teacher, could determine whether the means of the scores for the two forms were significantly different. But is this what he really wants to know?

Since the means of the scores on the forms are practically identical, it is a foregone conclusion that a *t* test will allow Mr. Brown to consider the null hypothesis tenable. Does this help him, however? Such an occurrence might result from a situation where a number of students obtained high scores on form A and low scores on form B, but a similar number of students had low scores on form A and high scores on form B. In other words, the two forms might not be yielding similar scores for individual pupils; only their means would be similar. Mr. Brown would want to know whether one form is more difficult than the other, but what he really needs to know is whether a student who scores high on one form tends to score high on the other, and, conversely, whether a low scorer on one form is also a low scorer on the other. To discover how an individual's scores on both forms are *related* is what the teacher wants to determine in this situation.

Now return to page 299 and select the appropriate technique for situation F.

To review the purposes of the t *test, see pp. 121–22.*

YOUR ANSWER (from page 307): Chi Square

CORRECT. To conduct a chi-square analysis of these data, Miss Perez would cast the responses into a 2×3 frequency table (with sex and questionnaire items) and determine whether the pattern of boys' responses departed significantly from the pattern of girls' responses. Chi square can be used, of course, in a variety of related situations ranging from one-sample tests (a sample vs. a known or hypothetical distribution) to k-sample tests, where a host of different groups are contrasted with respect to response frequencies in nominal categories.

Now proceed to hypothetical situation H on the following page.

To review the requirements for chi-square tests, see pp. 264–71.

Now consider the situation of Mrs. O'Shea, an educational investigator who wants to test whether there are any significant differences among the achievement scores of three samples of students taught by three rather distinctive varieties of lecture-based instruction. The first lecture approach features a multitude of rhetorical, unanswered questions designed to stimulate the students to think about the content of the lecture. The second lecture approach embodies many rhetorical questions which the lecturer quickly answers. The final lecture technique has few, if any, rhetorical questions.

Mrs. O'Shea also wants to see if the students' level of academic aptitude interacts in any significant fashion with their performances under the three varieties of lecture techniques. She gathers posttest achievement scores for three sets of students, for each of which a different lecture method has been used. Aptitude-test scores are also secured for each student, so that the total sample of 300 students (100 taught by each method) can be classified as having above-average aptitude, average aptitude, or below-average aptitude.

In order to test the null hypotheses that (1) there are no significant differences among students taught by the three lecture methods, and (2) there is no significant interaction of aptitude level and lecture method on achievement, which of the following techniques should Mrs. O'Shea select?

Page 308   The *t* Test
Page 311   Single-Classification Analysis of Variance
Page 314   Multiple-Classification Analysis of Variance

YOUR ANSWER (from page 299): Product-Moment Correlation

CORRECT. Mr. Brown needs to know the type and strength of the relation-ship, if any, between the 110 pupils' scores on the two test forms. The result he would like to see is a strong, positive r, perhaps in the neighborhood of 0.80 or 0.90. Such a coefficient would indicate that an individual who scored high on one form would very likely score high on the other, as would be true conversely with low scorers. A markedly lower r would suggest that Mr. Brown needs to do further work on equating the two forms. An inspection of the means for the two forms has revealed that neither form is more difficult than the other. By studying the difficulty and discrimination efficiency of individual items over a period of time, the teacher should be able to increase the comparability of the two test forms.

Now proceed to hypothetical situation G on the following page.

To review the assumptions required for the product-moment correlation method, see p. 75.

In the next hypothetical situation, Miss Perez, a school administrator, is studying the results of a year's tryout of a team-teaching approach. Though achievement standards have been as high as in previous years, she is puzzled by results from a postcourse questionnaire which was administered to the 95 pupils who took part in the team-teaching project. In particular, she is perplexed by the following responses to one question:

(7) Which type of teaching situation do you prefer?	Number checking
Team-teaching with more students per group	12
Team-teaching with fewer students per group	57
Conventional teaching with one teacher per 25–35 pupils	26

Of the 26 students who chose conventional teaching as their answer in this item, all but five were boys. Miss Perez wonders whether the fact that all three teachers constituting the teaching team were women might have influenced the answers. Specifically, she speculates that there may be a significant difference between the responses to question 7 given by the 55 boys and those given by the 40 girls in the group. Which of the following techniques should she use to determine this?

Page 302   Single-Classification Analysis of Variance
Page 304   Chi Square
Page 309   Spearman Rank-Order Correlation Coefficient

YOUR ANSWER (from page 305): The *t* Test

Well, a *t* test might be used to test one of the null hypotheses under consideration, that is, the hypothesis that there is no significant achievement differential among the three groups. But, because a *t* test can only be used with two groups at a time, Mrs. O'Shea would have to compute three *t* tests to tell whether there were any mean differences among the three lecture groups. Further, *t* tests offer no hope of detecting *interaction* effects of two or more independent variables upon a dependent variable. Thus, a *t* test would not be a suitable choice for this situation.

Return to page 305 and select the appropriate technique for situation H.

To review the functions of the t *test, see pp. 121–22.*

YOUR ANSWER (from page 307): Spearman Rank-Order Correlation Coefficient

To the extent that this situation requires a nonparametric technique, you are correct. However, the Spearman correlation approach requires data of ordinal or interval strength. What we have here are nominal data represented by the three classes of response to the questionnaire item. Further, the Spearman rank-order correlation coefficient is a *relationship-testing* technique rather than a *difference-testing* technique. What Miss Perez needs is a nonparametric technique suitable for use with nominal data that can be used to test for differences between two groups.

Return to page 307 and select such a technique for situation G.

To review the measurement-level requirements of the Spearman correlational method, see pp. 280–81.

YOUR ANSWER (from page 315): Kruskal-Wallis One-Way Analysis of Variance

The Kruskal-Wallis test is an excellent alternative to single classification analysis of variance when the assumptions of the more powerful parametric test cannot be met or when the samples are very small. In situation I, however, a statistical test is needed that can be used to control, or statistically compensate for, differences in relevant variables among two or more groups. Because the Kruskal-Wallis one-way analysis of variance has no such potential, Mr. Simon must turn to another model with built-in provisions for handling initial differences among groups on important variables.

Now return to page 315 and select the appropriate technique for situation I.

To review the function of the Kruskal-Wallis test, see p. 259.

YOUR ANSWER (from page 305): Single-Classification Analysis of Variance

Well, a single-classification analysis of variance model *could* be used to test the null hypothesis that there were no significant mean differences among the three student samples taught by different lecture methods. But what about the second null hypothesis regarding *interaction* between aptitude level and lecture approach? Single-classification analysis of variance cannot cope with this kind of question. Thus, a more sophisticated analysis of variance model is required for this situation.

Return to page 305 and select such a model for situation H.

To review the meaning of interaction, see pp. 178–80.

YOUR ANSWER (from page 321): Mann-Whitney *U* Test

CORRECT. To test for differences between two samples, the Mann-Whitney *U* test is an extremely powerful model. The *U* test compares favorably, in fact, with the parametric *t* test, but it can be applied to situations where the assumptions of the *t* test cannot be satisfied. Situation J, in which nonnormal population data preclude the use of the *t* test, is an instance in which the Mann-Whitney test should be used.

Now proceed to hypothetical situation K on the following page.

To review the function of the U *test, see p. 274.*

The final hypothetical situation in this chapter presents the predicament of the curriculum-instruction committee in a large school system which is faced with the task of recommending for district adoption a set of remedial reading materials for the intermediate grades in elementary schools. After several months of study, the committee has narrowed the choice to two sets of materials. It has conducted several short-term experimental studies to contrast the gain performance of two groups of students using different materials. Results of these projects, in several of which significant performance differences were detected, strongly suggest that one set of the reading materials does produce somewhat better achievement results than the competing materials. Unfortunately, these superior materials are also more expensive.

Because the committee is obliged to consider economic factors, members are undecided as to which of the two sets of materials to endorse. One member proposes that the experimental data that has been gathered by the committee should be subjected to additional analysis in such a way as to make defensible the choice of the more effective but more expensive set of materials. Which of the following statistical procedures should be used to accomplish this purpose?

Page 322   Sign Test
Page 328   Product-Moment Correlation
Page 331   Determination of a Confidence Interval

SITUATION

K

YOUR ANSWER (from page 305): Multiple-Classification Analysis of Variance

CORRECT. By the use of this powerful model, Mrs. O'Shea could test both of her null hypotheses. Incidentally, she could easily test a third interaction hypothesis regarding performance difference between achievement-level groups. The results of such an analysis, however, are a foregone conclusion; that is, the brighter students will outperform their peers. Yet there are many occasions when the investigator tests for criterion mean differences between groups representing one independent variable, then a second independent variable, and finally, the interaction effect of the two independent variables.

Now go on to hypothetical situation I on the following page.

To review the assumptions required for multiple-classification analysis of variance, see p. 181.

In the next hypothetical situation, suppose Mr. Simon, a school psychologist, is studying the influence of nondirective versus directive teaching approaches on the social studies achievement of 200 high school juniors. Three teachers have participated in the experimental project, each teaching one class by a highly directive approach in which the instructor assumes primary responsibility for the students' learning, and a second class by a nondirective approach in which the student is urged to take the chief responsibility for learning. At the beginning and end of a three-month instructional period, during which all three instructors cover identical content, achievement examinations are administered to all the students. In addition, a test of verbal aptitude is administered to all pupils midway through the experiment.

Because Mr. Simon had to use pupils in this experiment who had already been assigned to the three participating teachers, he wants to rule out differences between the pupils who were directively taught and those who were non-directively taught, with respect to their verbal aptitude and pretest achievement levels. He then wants to see if there is a significant achievement difference between the two groups. Which of the following techniques should he select to accomplish these tasks?

Page 310   Kruskal-Wallis One-Way Analysis of Variance
Page 317   Regression
Page 320   Analysis of Covariance

YOUR ANSWER (from page 321): Wilcoxon Matched-Pairs Signed-Rank Test

The Wilcoxon test, an important nonparametric technique, can be used to test for differences between two groups. However, the individuals in the two groups must consist of matched pairs. In situation J, the two groups are composed of randomly drawn, and therefore *independent*, members.

Now return to page 321 and choose the technique that can be used with two smaller independent samples for situation J.

To review the function of the Wilcoxon matched-pairs signed-ranks test, see
p. 255.

YOUR ANSWER (from page 315): Regression

To some extent, regression analysis could be used in situation I. Mr. Simon, the school psychologist, needs to predict what a pupil's criterion (posttest) achievement score would be if that pupil were equal to all others regarding pretest score and verbal aptitude test score. But there is a more complex parametric technique which combines regression analysis with the analysis-of-variance model to perform this operation, while testing for mean differences between *statistically equalized* groups.

Return to page 315 and select such a technique for situation I.

To review the purposes of regression analysis, see pp. 95–96.

YOUR ANSWER (from page 321): Chi Square

It is true that chi square might be considered appropriate in Mrs. Martin's situation, for differences between two groups can be tested by means of chi square. Yet this technique is less powerful than several other nonparametric tests that can perform the same function. If an alternative exists, the more powerful test is usually selected.

Another limitation of situation J which would preclude the use of chi square is the small number of individuals involved. You may recall that chi-square analyses require the expected frequencies in most cells of a chi-square table to be five or larger. Certainly, considering six individuals in each of Mrs. Martin's two groups, even in a 2×2 chi-square table, would lead to insufficient expected frequencies.

Now return to page 321 and select the appropriate technique for situation J.

To review the data requirements of chi-square models, see pp. 264–71.

YOUR ANSWER (from page 330): Multiple *t* Tests between All Possible Pairs of Mean Differences

Miss Adams could certainly perform such tests. However, in general, performing multiple *t* tests greatly increases the chances of making Type I errors. Moreover, *t* tests are more powerful and, like a priori comparisons, are warranted only when the investigator has good conceptual reasons for testing specific comparisons. Such is not the case for Miss Adams in situation D.

Return to page 330 and select the more appropriate statistical procedure.

To review issues concerning Type I errors, see pp. 54–56.

YOUR ANSWER (from page 315): Analysis of Covariance

CORRECT. Through analysis of covariance, the differences between the two groups in pretest achievement and verbal aptitude could be statistically adjusted so that a test between means of the directive and nondirective groups could be computed, *as if* there were no disparity between the groups in aptitude or pretest achievement. Because of its utility in school situations such as this, where intact groups must often be used, analysis of covariance is an invaluable implement in the educational investigator's tool kit.

Now proceed to situation J on the following page.

To review the assumptions required for the use of analysis of covariance, see pp. 206–07.

For the next problem situation, imagine that Mrs. Martin, an educational ex-perimenter, has studied the influence of a number of instructional variables on certain aspects of students' attitudes toward school and study activities. Using a newly developed attitude inventory, she has sampled a large number of pupils, attempting to establish norms for the inventory. From these early studies, she is convinced that the attitude scores yielded by the inventory are not normally dis-tributed in the student population. Rather, samples of the numerical scores ac-quired through use of the inventory are always negatively skewed. She therefore reasons that analyses of such data should not be conducted with parametric techniques that require relatively normal population distributions.

SITUATION

J

Mrs. Martin is currently conducting an experiment in which two groups of six pupils have been exposed to different instructional procedures. All 12 pu-pils were randomly selected and randomly assigned to one of the two groups. At the conclusion of the instructional period, both groups were given the atti-tude inventory. Which of the following techniques should be used to test whether the attitude scores of the two groups are significantly different?

Page 312   Mann-Whitney *U* Test
Page 316   Wilcoxon Matched-Pairs Signed-Rank Test
Page 318   Chi Square

YOUR ANSWER (from page 313): Sign Test

The sign test might seem like an appropriate choice for this type of situation, for it is a difference-testing technique which may be used with matched pairs of subjects. However, the curriculum-instruction committee does not merely need to know *whether* one set of reading materials is superior to the other. This, evidently, has already been established. They need an estimate of *how much* better the superior materials are likely to be in continued usage. This type of information is needed to weigh against the higher cost of the superior materials.

In other words, a hypothesis-testing technique is not needed here, for it only answers the questions "Is there a difference?" and "Is there a relationship?" What the committee needs is a statistical method of estimating from sample data the probable magnitude of mean difference in the population.

Now return to page 313 and select such a procedure for situation K.

To review the function of the sign test, see p. 255.

YOUR ANSWER (from page 330): Three Specific A Priori Comparisons

Only when investigators have good conceptual reasons to hypothesize specific comparisons between groups are they entitled to use the power of a priori comparison procedures. In this case, Miss Adams does not have this warrant, but she does want to explore further the mean differences among spelling methods.

Return to page 330 and select a more appropriate procedure for her to use in situation D.

To review the appropriate application of a priori comparisons, see pp. 167–69.

YOUR ANSWER (from page 296): Post Hoc Comparisons

Post hoc comparisons can certainly be used to statistically test all possible mean differences among the four experimental groups. But they are conservative tests designed particularly for those cases where the investigator is exploring the data ex post facto. An investigator who has a good hypothesis about where the differences between groups might be is entitled to use more powerful statistical tests that follow up an overall significant F ratio.

Return to page 296 and select a more appropriate statistical procedure for situation C.

To review the role of post hoc comparison procedures, see pp. 169–70.

YOUR ANSWER (from page 330): Tukey Test of Honestly Significant Differences

CORRECT. The Tukey HSD test is a post hoc comparison procedure that would be appropriate to apply in this instance. In fact, Miss Adams would probably use it to test all possible differences among the four experimental groups (the three new spelling methods and the conventional method). Of particular interest to the question at hand in situation D would be the three possible comparisons among the new spelling methods.

Now go on to situation E on the following page.

To review the Tukey post hoc comparison procedure, see p. 170.

**SITUATION
E**

In a different situation, Mrs. Sparks, a high school counselor, is faced with the task of setting up a systematic procedure for predicting the likely success her school's seniors will have at a nearby private university. In previous years, students with a grade-point average lower than B+, regardless of verbal aptitude or any other factors, have been advised not to enroll in this university, on the grounds that they would probably fail to maintain its grade standards.

Both the admission officials at the university and the administrators at the high school have asked that the counseling office develop a more precise scheme for predicting potential success at the university. A number of the high school's graduates who had maintained C averages throughout high school and who had entered the university against the advice of Mrs. Sparks' office had achieved excellent scholastic results there.

Mrs. Sparks is given complete access to students' academic records at the university as well as the high school for all students who had graduated and entered the university. Records are quite complete for the past 12 years. Included in the university records are college grades and entrance examination scores. The high school records have grades, scores on a verbal aptitude test administered during the ninth grade, and certain personal data such as sex and ethnicity.

Which of the following statistical techniques should Mrs. Sparks use to develop the prediction scheme that will permit her to be more precise in advising high school students who want to enter the university?

Page 291   Spearman Rank-Order Correlation Coefficient
Page 298   Regression
Page 300   Standard Deviation

YOUR ANSWER (from page 296): Nonparametric Tests

There are, in fact, nonparametric procedures for following up on significant, overall results when comparing more than two groups. However, in situation C, the data are such that the program evaluator has already chosen to use parametric analyses, namely, the analysis of variance and appropriate parametric procedures for further testing differences between groups.

Now return to page 296 and select the most appropriate technique for situation C.

To review the purpose and application of nonparametric tests, see pp. 250–53.

YOUR ANSWER (from page 313): Product-Moment Correlation

Although product-moment correlation methods frequently are employed in varied aspects of educational research, situation K does not call for this approach. Recall that correlation indicates the strength and direction of the relationship between two variables, whereas the present situation is more amenable to treatment by a difference-testing technique. Yet, a difference-testing technique is needed which will reveal whether students exposed to one set of reading materials perform better than students exposed to the other set. Further, an estimate is needed of *how much* better one set of materials is, because the performance differential must be considered against the higher cost of the superior materials. Product-moment correlation is not suitable for supplying answers to such questions; hence a different technique is required for this situation.

Return to page 313 and select the appropriate technique for situation K.

To review the function of product-moment correlation, see pp. 64–66.

YOUR ANSWER (from page 296): A Priori Comparisons

CORRECT. When specific hypotheses regarding the differences between groups are suggested, the investigator is entitled to follow up an overall significant F ratio with a priori or specific comparison procedures. In this case, using the contrast coefficients 1, 1, 1, and -3, Miss Adams can test the specific hypothesis of interest.

Now proceed to hypothetical situation D on the following page.

To review the application of a priori comparison procedures, see pp. 167–69.

SITUATION D

Continuing with the same example, suppose there is no conceptual basis on which to base hypotheses regarding how the three new spelling programs may differ from one another. Yet the significant F value and a descriptive analysis of the group means suggest that these experimental groups are performing differently on the postexperiment spelling test. How might Miss Adams follow up these observations with more specific statistical tests?

Page 325   The Tukey Test of Honestly Significant Differences
Page 323   Three Specific A Priori Comparisons
Page 319   Multiple t Tests between All Possible Pairs of Mean Differences

YOUR ANSWER (from p. 313): Determination of a Confidence Interval

CORRECT. Use of an estimation approach to assist the educational decision maker is a most suitable choice. In this particular situation, a confidence interval should be determined for the difference between performance means of the students using the two different sets of materials. For example, a 95 percent confidence interval for mean difference could be developed so that the committee could tell, with odds of 95 to 5, the probable student mean performance superiority that could be expected by using the better, but more expensive, reading materials. With such estimates, perhaps computed for each experimental study that has been previously conducted by the group, the committee is in a far better position to reach a prudent decision regarding the remedial reading materials.

Estimation procedures are strongly recommended as a statistical operation that can be carried out after hypothesis testing to help the investigator evaluate the importance of results that have been found to be statistically significant.

This is the final hypothetical situation in the chapter.

To review the role of estimation in educational research, see pp. 54–60.

Number Crunching

· *making use of computer technology*

Throughout this text, we have deliberately invited you to become involved not only with the concepts underlying statistical procedures but also with their computational details. We are convinced that conceptual understanding is enhanced with hands-on involvement with the arithmetic underlying such statistical matters as t, F, r, R, chi square, variance, $p < 0.05$, and the like.

But enough is enough! Although educational investigators should (*must*, we think) get their hands "dirty" with their own raw data to some extent, ordinarily their data bases will be sufficiently large, and their analyses sufficiently time-consuming, to mitigate against extensive analyses "by hand" (i.e., using calculators). As the student who has worked through the problems in this book knows, even a small data set (say, 15 or 20 scores) and a fairly straightforward analysis (say, a single-classification analysis of variance) can make for a quite lengthy exercise. Moreover, there are the inevitable mistakes—slips of the hand or mind—that create all that much more work in recomputations or, even worse, trying to make sense out of erroneous results.

Fortunately, we are well into the age of computer technology. In the old days, when the authors were graduate students, we had to make do with mechanical calculators the size of large typewriters and about as noisy as an old-fashioned cash register. When reasonably functional mainframe computer technology became available, we all breathed a sigh of relief. All we had to do then was to punch up a bunch of IBM cards, run them through something called a card sorter a time or two, repunch the cards that were mangled, carry the lot over to the computer center, and hope for the best. The best would be computer output in a day or two. Usually, however, we would discover in that output keypunching or programming errors. These would need to be corrected, the job resubmitted, and the cycle repeated until error-free computer output was obtained.

You might well wonder why we didn't just do the calculations by hand. Well, once the input of data and processing requests to the computer was done correctly, the resultant calculations were error-free. Moreover, the sum total of all the analyses to be conducted in typical research studies would take much more than several days to accomplish by hand. Furthermore, many complicated multivariate analyses would not have even been attempted without the computing power of these early computers.

Today, the personal computers (PCs) most of us have sitting on our desks have upwards of three times or more the computing capacity of those earlier, room-filling mainframe computers. Today's mainframes, of course, have upwards of 100 times the capacity of earlier models. IBM cards and sorting machines are things of the past. Whether using PCs or mainframes, data entry is accomplished with keyboards and display monitors and a command system no more complicated than that for most word-processing programs.

But still, why should you, as a student, bother to become familiar with this stuff? Perhaps only for your own edification, if you are so inclined. However, becoming familiar with computerized data processing may be essential if you are planning to conduct educational research or evaluation studies (or investigations, as we have frequently referred to them in this text) at the master's or doctoral levels and will need to analyze data for your thesis or dissertation. And if you are planning a career in education or any applied field of social science, a working knowledge of computerized data processing may be a required part of the job.

Perhaps you are still not convinced. Perhaps you have decided that you will simply hire a statistical consultant to analyze your data for your thesis or dissertation and postpone (hopefully forever) having to learn computer data processing yourself. We sincerely wish you the best of luck, because luck is what you will need. We have seen many a naive student mislead (or be misled by) statistical consultants who quickly process data with little thought about the research or evaluation design or intent of the investigative questions. For example, we have lost count of the number of times students, relying on someone else for their analyses, end up with independent-group (uncorrelated data) *t* tests all neatly done for them on paired-comparison or correlated data!

No matter how facile you may be with a computer, the adage, "garbage in, garbage out" applies. At minimum, you must be familiar enough with statistics and computerized statistical processing to be able to communicate clearly with a consultant and to read and critically inspect the computer output presented by a consultant. At best, you should be skilled enough to analyze your own data.

This chapter is designed to help you become familiar with, *not* expert in, data processing by computer. However, depending on your instructor's intentions, this chapter can be used with other materials in a more rigorous, hands-on, data-processing instructional unit. We have selected one of the most popular computer data analysis systems to illustrate most of the statistical procedures discussed in this text. The SPSS system—Statistical Package for the Social Sciences—is a user-friendly conglomeration of nearly all of the kinds of statistical procedures likely to be needed by educational investigators. If you and your instructor wish to augment this chapter with a more hands-on approach to SPSS, we recommend the use of *The SPSS Guide to Data Analysis* (see Selected Readings).

In the sections that follow, we will present a brief overview of how data are arranged for computer processing and how to "talk" to SPSS by way of requesting statistical analyses. We will then illustrate computer data processing using SPSS by reanalyzing examples presented in preceding chapters for most of the statistical procedures discussed in this text.

ARRANGING DATA

For illustrative purposes, consider this simple experimental study on creative writing via computer involving ten upper-elementary students. In one group, five randomly assigned students write a one-paragraph essay using traditional paper-and-pencil technology. In the other group, the other five students compose their one-paragraph essays using computers and a simple word-processing program. The essays are scored holistically on a 10-point scale by raters trained in such matters. As part of the study, information on students' age, gender, and verbal ability are also collected.

An easy way to think about all of the information collected in a research study is to imagine a two-dimensional matrix or box of data in which rows correspond to cases and columns correspond to variables. Cases are typically individuals, like students in the above example; however, in other types of studies, cases might represent other entities, like classrooms or schools. For each case, there are a number of variables designating the discrete pieces of information collected. In our example, there are four obvious variables: age, gender, measure of verbal ability, and essay rating. Additionally, there are two less-obvious variables. One is an identification number that should be arbitrarily assigned to each student in order to keep track of who is who in the data base. The other is an indication of which experimental group the student is in, the paper-and-pencil or the computer group.

Using simple acronyms as labels for each of the six variables, a hypothetical matrix of data could be arrayed as follows:

ID	GROUP	AGE	SEX	VERBAL	ESSAY
01	1	08	1	55	06
02	1	11	1	42	09
03	1	09	2	63	08
04	1	10	1	37	03
05	1	10	2	65	10
06	2	12	2	58	07
07	2	09	1	60	05
08	2	11	2	49	06
09	2	10	2	51	07
10	2	12	1	45	04

Where do these numbers come from? The numbers for ID are arbitrarily assigned identification labels for each of the ten students in the study. We chose to assign the ID numbers 1 through 5 to the students in the computer group and the numbers 6 through 10 to those in the paper-and-pencil group. The variable GROUP designates the experimental group to which the student was assigned. GROUP is a *nominal* variable as defined in Chapter 18—that is, it simply identifies categories or labels rather than a measured quantity. Thus, we arbitrarily assigned the number 1 to the computer group and 2 to the paper-and-pencil group.

The rest of the data should now be pretty obvious. The variable AGE is just that, the actual age (in years) of each of the hypothetical students in the study. SEX represents the gender of each student, another nominal variable, coded 1 for males and 2 for females. The numbers indicated for the variable VERBAL are hypothetical scores on a verbal-ability test. Finally, the variable ESSAY contains the hypothetical scores (using the 10-point rating scale) for each student's paragraph.

Note the "width" of the variables in the above example. Some are one digit wide and some are two digits wide. This, of course, has to do with the largest possible value or score that the variable could have. Notice, also, that one-digit values in two-digit variables are padded with a leading 0; for example, case 10 received a rating of 4 on his essay, which is recorded as 04 for the variable ESSAY. This process of recording data, known as right-adjusting, ensures that every piece of information will be in exactly the same position in every case or *record*.

In other words, each student in our example generates one record-worth of information that is always ten digits long. If we arrayed all the data into one unlabeled matrix, it would look like this:

```
0110815506
0211114209
0310926308
0411013703
0511026510
0621225807
0720916005
0821124906
0921025107
1021214504
```

The record for student 03, for example, is 0310926308, and the record for student 06 is 0621225807. However, since the variables and records have been coded systematically, the 09 and the 12 in the fourth and fifth positions of the records for students 03 and 06, for example, both refer to their ages.

Thus, with a simple set of instructions, the above box of numbers can be turned into an orderly set of data. These instructions, and how to communicate them to a statistical computer program, are the topics of the next section.

COMMUNICATING WITH SPSS

Communicating with a computer is simply a matter of learning a new language. The language is invented by programmers who are themselves using a more basic language that instructs computers to perform the arithmetic and algebraic operations necessary for any given statistical procedure. Once you get the hang of this lingo, an SPSS setup (i.e., list of commands, specifications, and the like) can be read as easily as a novel. None of the language or syntax, however, need be memorized; SPSS provides extensive documentation in a number of manuals and guides (see Selected Readings). We will discuss below only a handful of the most elementary SPSS instructions. Most statistical processing programs, like SPSS, have many more instructions and options for labeling, selecting, sorting, and transforming information. If you are interested, you will want to take at least one course specifically directed at data processing.

We should also note that different versions of SPSS have slightly different language and syntax conventions. Likewise, minor differences exist between versions designed to run on mainframe computers and those designed for PCs or microcomputers. The illustrations to follow are based on SPSS-X, Release 2.0, run on a CYBER mainframe computer at the University of Washington in late 1989. We have been advised by the marketing department at SPSS headquarters in Chicago that the newest version of SPSS will contain few (if any) syntax changes; moreover, the microcomputer and mainframe versions will be nearly identical.

When running SPSS jobs using a mainframe computer, the actual SPSS language is often preceded by several lines of instructions. These instructions— job-control language—are specific to the particular type of computer and computer installation. They tell the computer who you are, identify you as a legitimate user of the computer system, and request that the system make available the SPSS program for your use. Since job-control language is idiosyncratic, we will not pursue it further. Your computer installation should have ample documentation and consultant help.

The Basic SPSS Setup

Several lines of instruction plus your actual data are all that are necessary to run most of the statistical procedures we have discussed in this text. In the old days, these lines corresponded to keypunched cards. Now they correspond to 80-column lines on a display terminal as they are input and stored in a PC or mainframe.

The basic SPSS language is a series of *commands*. Each command is one or two words that must begin in the first position or column of the instructional line. Subsequent lines of the command must be indented one or more columns so that they are not confused with a new command. Each command usually requires more information (called *specifications*) separated by one or more spaces from the command words. Commands and specifications involve *key words* that instruct SPSS as to labeling output, defining variables, selecting statistical options, and so forth. Only a few commands and their more basic options are illustrated in this section.

TITLE.   The first instructional line(s) is typically a TITLE command. Often, as in this case, an SPSS command specifies exactly what it suggests. The keyword TITLE suggests a title for the computer output as indicated by the user in the specification part of the instruction. If we assigned the title CREA-

TIVE WRITING EXPERIMENT in our example, that title would appear at the top of every page of computer output using the following SPSS command:

```
TITLE     CREATIVE WRITING EXPERIMENT
```

In the SPSS analyses presented in the figures in this chapter, we will use TITLE commands in the input but eliminate the titles from the output in consideration of space.

DATA LIST.　The second instructional line(s) typically define the data to be analyzed. Since each case of data is merely a stream of numbers, SPSS needs to know which digits go with which variables. Moreover, SPSS needs to know where the data are; for example, on some storage device like a tape or disk or as part of the instructions themselves. In reference to our creative writing example, consider the following lines of instruction:

```
DATA LIST     FILE=INLINE RECORDS=1
              /ID 1-2 GROUP 3 AGE 4-5 SEX 6 VERBAL 7-8 ESSAY 9-10
```

Much information is communicated to SPSS with these two lines of instruction. DATA LIST is simply the command name that alerts SPSS to the specifications to come. FILE = INLINE tells SPSS that the actual data will be part of the instructions rather than coming from some other storage device. RECORDS = 1 informs the system that it only takes one line of information per case to include all the variables in the study. The slash (/) is simply a syntax convention that SPSS uses to separate specifications. In this case, / informs SPSS that variable names and their column locations are to follow. Using the acronyms we invented for our own study, each variable is given a name and is located by the column number(s) of its position in the record. These variable names are very important. The computer user will use them to tell SPSS which variables are involved in subsequent analyses. SPSS will use them as labels in the computer output.

BEGIN DATA and END DATA.　These commands, with the actual data sandwiched in between, obviously identify for SPSS the raw data for statistical analysis. For the above study, the lines of instruction would appear as follows:

```
BEGIN DATA
0110815506
0211114209
0310926308
   .
   .
   .
0821124906
0921025107
1021214504
END DATA
```

The dots between cases 03 and 08 are *not* part of the data. They are simply intended to indicate that the data for cases 04–07 should be inserted. We will use this device in order to save space in the examples to follow.

Task Definition Commands.   There are a number of commands depending on the type of statistical analysis you wish to perform. Suppose, for example, you wanted to see frequency distributions and basic descriptive statistics for each variable in our study. The following command and specifications will do the job:

```
FREQUENCIES    VARIABLES=GROUP,AGE,SEX,VERBAL,ESSAY/
               STATISTICS=MEAN,MEDIAN,MODE,STDDEV/
```

FREQUENCIES refers to a specific SPSS command that invokes a number of analysis and statistical options, all amply documented in the SPSS manual.

Another command, for example, is ANOVA. You guessed it—this command invokes a whole set of procedures for performing single- or multiple-classification analyses of variance. Suppose we wanted to see if composing on the computer enhanced creative writing performance over the traditional paper-and-pencil method. Suppose, also, that we had reason to believe that gender might interact with the experimental conditions. This suggests a 2×2, gender-by-group design, with the essay rating as the dependent variable. One line of instructions is all it takes to do the job:

```
ANOVA     ESSAY BY SEX,GROUP(1,2)/
```

Putting It All Together.   A complete set of instructions is nothing more than putting all of the above commands together in one SPSS setup (the *input*):

```
TITLE          CREATIVE WRITING EXPERIMENT
DATA LIST      FILE=INLINE RECORDS=1
               /ID 1-2 GROUP 3 AGE 4-5 SEX 6 VERBAL 7-8 ESSAY 9-10
BEGIN DATA
0110815506
0211114209
    .
    .
    .
1021214504
END DATA
FREQUENCIES    VARIABLES=GROUP,AGE,SEX,VERBAL,ESSAY/
               STATISTICS=MEAN,MEDIAN,MODE,STDDEV/
ANOVA          ESSAY BY SEX,GROUP(1,2)/
```

We did not bother to actually run the above analyses on our hypothetical data set, since analyses like these will be illustrated in the sections to follow.

COMPUTER DATA PROCESSING IN ACTION

In the preceding chapters we have discussed and illustrated the conceptual and computational details of a number of descriptive and inferential statistical procedures. By way of illustrating how these analyses can be accomplished using a computer and statistical software, selected examples in the preceding chapters will be reanalyzed using SPSS.

In each case, we will refer back to the appropriate chapter, statistical procedure, and tables of raw data and computational results. Only brief discussions of the SPSS setups and results will be provided. For the most part, the input and output should be self-explanatory once you have studied the other chapters of this text. We are not attempting to make you proficient in the use of SPSS. Rather, we are seeking to give you an initial level of familiarity with the use of computers and their power as tools for data processing. Our hope is that instructors who assign this chapter do so in the larger context of actual, hands-on experience with computers. For this purpose, exercises (with answers) are provided at the end of this chapter.

Frequency Distributions and Descriptive Statistics

In Chapter 2, we discussed various ways in which a distribution of measurements, for example, test scores, could be described—in terms of a frequency distribution, or central tendency (mean, median, and mode), or variability (range, standard deviation, and variance). Using the data in Table 2.1 in Chapter 2, we have done a computer analysis using the SPSS setup (the *input*) listed in Figure 21–1. Also shown in Figure 21–1 are the results of the computer analysis (the *output*).

INPUT

```
TITLE          EXAMPLE OF FREQUENCIES PROCEDURE WITH 18 SCORES
DATA LIST      FILE=INLINE RECORDS=1
               /SCORE 1-2
BEGIN DATA
14
13
12
 .
 .
 .
 8
 7
 6
END DATA
FREQUENCIES    VARIABLES=SCORE/
               STATISTICS=MEAN,MEDIAN,MODE,STDDEV,VARIANCE/
```

OUTPUT

SCORE

VALUE LABEL	VALUE	FREQUENCY	PERCENT	VALID PERCENT	CUM PERCENT
	6	1	5.6	5.6	5.6
	7	1	5.6	5.6	11.1
	8	2	11.1	11.1	22.2
	9	3	16.7	16.7	38.9
	10	4	22.2	22.2	61.1
	11	3	16.7	16.7	77.8
	12	2	11.1	11.1	88.9
	13	1	5.6	5.6	94.4
	14	1	5.6	5.6	100.0
		-------	-------	-------	
	TOTAL	18	100.0	100.0	

MEAN 10.000	MEDIAN 10.000	MODE 10.000	
STD DEV 2.058	VARIANCE 4.235		

VALID CASES 18	MISSING CASES O	

Fig. 21–1. Descriptive analysis of the data in Table 2.1.

Looking at the input, you will see that we have not bothered to give ID numbers to each case. (However, in actual studies, ID numbers should always be part of each record.) We selected the variable name SCORE, a two-digit number, for the measurements in Table 2.1. We requested SPSS to compute the frequency distribution for SCORE as well as the statistics on central tendency and variability.

Looking at the output, you will see the name of the variable, SCORE, reproduced in the upper left-hand corner. The first column heading, VALUE LABEL, refers to user-selected names for each possible score value. Since we have not designated such labels (nor will we in any of the analyses to follow), this column is blank. The next columns contain the actual score values, the frequencies of their occurrence, the relative percentages, and the cumulative percentages. With these values, the distribution can be graphed or tabled in any number of forms. (Actually, SPSS can be instructed to produce histograms and frequency tables with different groupings of the same data.) The computed values for the mean, median, mode, standard deviation, and variance are listed below the frequency distribution.

You should compare these SPSS results with the graph in Figure 2–6 and the description of computed statistics in the narrative accompanying Table 2.1. The only discrepancies will be found in the computations for the standard deviation and variance. In Chapter 2, we were discussing descriptive statistics only, and therefore these statistics were computed using N in the denominators. SPSS, however, operates in an inferential mode, so $N-1$ is used in the denominator. (You may wish to review the discussions accompanying Formulas 2.6 and 4.2 in Chapters 2 and 4, respectively.)

Finally, note at the bottom of the output in Figure 21–1 that all 18 cases are VALID CASES. In other words, there are zero MISSING CASES. In actual studies, there will almost always be some missing cases, that is, some score values missing for one or more variables for one or more individuals in the study. Since there are no missing values in our example, the PERCENT and the VALID PERCENT columns are identical. If there had been missing values, the PERCENT column would have included them in the computations, whereas the VALID PERCENT column would have excluded them. (They would have also been excluded from the statistical computations.)

Pearson Product-Moment Correlation

In Chapter 6, an example of the computation and statistical test of a Pearson correlation coefficient is given using the data in Table 6.1. In Figure 21–2, we show the same results using SPSS.

The input should by now look familiar to you or should at least be easy to interpret. TEST1 and TEST2 are the names given to the two tests, and PEARSON CORR is the SPSS command for computing correlations, as in TEST1 WITH TEST2. The output simply presents the computed correlation along with the number of cases on which it is based and the level of its statistical significance. Since SPSS prints probabilities only to the nearest thousandth, we can conclude that the correlation of .91 is significant at $p < .0005$.

INPUT

```
TITLE              EXAMPLE OF PEARSON CORRELATION
DATA LIST          FILE=INLINE RECORDS=1
                   /TEST1 1-2 TEST2 4-5
BEGIN DATA
  8    3
  2    1
  8    6
       .
       .
       .
  6    4
  4    4
  6    5
END DATA
PEARSON CORR       TEST1 WITH TEST2
```

OUTPUT

```
              TEST2

TEST1          .9105
             (   10)
             P=  .000
```

Fig. 21-2.   Pearson correlation for the data in Table 6.1.

Bivariate Regression

A two-variable regression example is given in Chapter 8 based on the data in Table 8.1, using an aptitude test (APTST) to predict scores on a final exam (FINAL). The SPSS instructions and results are shown in Figure 21-3.

Notice in the REGRESSION command that both variables are listed, and then one is designated as the dependent variable. This designation, of course, depends on the design of the particular study. In this case, the final examination score is considered to be dependent on an initial measure of aptitude.

The output is considerably more informative than we had prepared you for in Chapters 7 and 8. Suffice it to say that regression analysis and analysis of variance are complementary statistical methods, and SPSS presents both kinds of results. Of interest to us are a few of the many statistics listed. In a bivariate regression, the multiple R, Pearson correlation, and standardized regression coefficient (BETA) are identical; in this example, they equal the value of .63. If you were to construct the regression or prediction equation (using Formula 7.1 from Chapter 7), the values of a (the intercept or constant) and b (the slope) would be needed. These values can be found in the column headed B under VARIABLES IN THE EQUATION (.91 and 47.76, respectively). The standard error of estimate (6.21) is also computed (see Formula 7.4). Finally, if you want to test the relationship for statistical significance, the F test, indicating that the regression coefficient is significant at $p < .005$, does the job.

INPUT

```
TITLE          REGRESSION EXAMPLE WITH 18 STUDENTS
DATA LIST      FILE=INLINE RECORDS=1
               /APTST 1-2 FINAL 4-5
BEGIN DATA
21 71
21 57
23 78
  .
  .
  .
35 70
37 91
39 86
END DATA
REGRESSION     VARIABLES=APTST,FINAL/DEPENDENT=FINAL/TEST=(APTST)/
```

OUTPUT

VARIABLE(S) ENTERED ON STEP NUMBER   1..   APTST

HYPOTHESIS TESTS

DF	SUM OF SQUARES	RSQ CHG	F	SIG F	SOURCE
1	414.93657	.40222	10.76578	.0047	APTST
1	414.93657		10.76578	.0047	REGRESSION
16	616.67454				RESIDUAL
17	1031.61111				TOTAL

		ANALYSIS OF VARIANCE			
MULTIPLE R	.63421		DF	SUM OF SQUARES	MEAN SQUARE
R SQUARE	.40222	REGRESSION	1	414.93657	414.93657
ADJUSTED R SQUARE	.36486	RESIDUAL	16	616.67454	38.54216
STANDARD ERROR	6.20823				

F =   10.76578   SIGNIF F =   .0047

----------------- VARIABLES IN THE EQUATION ------------------

VARIABLE	B	SE B	BETA	T	SIG T
APTST	.91239	.27807	.63421	3.281	.0047
(CONSTANT)	47.75591	8.34787		5.721	.0000

Fig. 21–3.   Bivariate regression analysis of the data in Table 8.1.

Multiple Regression

Computations become considerably more complicated, as do interpretations, when more than one predictor (or independent) variable is involved. In Chapter 8, Table 8.2, the procedures for a two-predictor, multiple regression analysis are illustrated. In Figure 21–4, we present the same analysis using SPSS.

INPUT

```
TITLE              REGRESSION EXAMPLE WITH TWO PREDICTORS
DATA LIST          FILE=INLINE RECORDS=1
                   /PHZSCI 1-2 SCIFINL 4-5 APTST 7-9
BEGIN DATA
91 62 118
89 63 109
79 58 110
      .
      .
      .
69 47 122
67 49 102
64 50  98
END DATA
REGRESSION         VARIABLES=PHZSCI,SCIFINL,APTST/DEPENDENT=PHZSCI/
                   TEST=(SCIFINL)(APTST)/
```

OUTPUT

```
VARIABLE(S) ENTERED ON STEP NUMBER   1..    APTST
                                     2..    SCIFINL

HYPOTHESIS TESTS

             SUM OF
   DF        SQUARES   RSQ CHG           F    SIG F    SOURCE

    1       510.66227   .69374    57.11388   .0001    SCIFINL
    1        23.39842   .03179     2.61694   .1498    APTST

    2       673.51214             37.66373   .0002    REGRESSION
    7        62.58786                                 RESIDUAL
    9       736.10000                                 TOTAL
```

```
MULTIPLE R              .95654      ANALYSIS OF VARIANCE
R SQUARE                .91497                  DF     SUM OF SQUARES    MEAN SQUARE
ADJUSTED R SQUARE       .89068      REGRESSION   2          673.51214      336.75607
STANDARD ERROR         2.99017      RESIDUAL     7           62.58786        8.94112

                                    F =    37.66373     SIGNIF F =  .0002
```

```
----------------- VARIABLES IN THE EQUATION -----------------

VARIABLE             B          SE B        BETA        T    SIG T

APTST            .21688       .13407      .18824    1.618    .1498
SCIFINL         1.39719       .18488      .87939    7.557    .0001
(CONSTANT)    -24.83190     15.05691               -1.649    .1431
```

Fig. 21–4. Multiple regression analysis of the data in Table 8.2.

In the input, note that the REGRESSION command now includes three variables, with one designated as the dependent variable. In the output, note that there are two regression coefficients and a constant listed in the B column under VARIABLES IN THE EQUATION. These values are used to construct the multiple regression equation, which, you will see, is identical to that computed in Chapter 8. The multiple correlation coefficient and standard error of estimate also were computed in Chapter 8, and the same values appear here in the SPSS output. Additionally, you can get an idea of the relative contribution of each of the predictor variables to the overall relationship by inspecting the standardized regression coefficients listed under the BETA column. The variable SCIFINL has a relatively higher coefficient (.88) than APTST (.19), indicating a stronger contribution of the freshman science exam in predicting scores on the physical science exam than the aptitude measure. (Moreover, you can verify that the Pearson correlation between SCIFINL and PHZSCI is much higher than that between APTST and PHZSCI.)

The *t* Test

In Chapter 10, computational procedures were illustrated for both the independent or uncorrelated groups *t* test and the paired-comparison or correlated groups *t* test. In both cases, raw data were not presented. Instead, computations began with the statistics (means, standard deviations, and correlations) already available. Computer programs generally expect raw data as input. Thus, in order to illustrate how SPSS performs *t* tests, we will develop two new examples.

Uncorrelated Data.   A statistics teacher is curious about the educational benefits of the textbook she is using. In particular, she wonders if reading chapters first and then hearing the instructor's lecture is more or less beneficial than reading the chapters after the lecture. She decides to conduct an experiment over the first eight weeks of her elementary statistics class of 42 students. She instructs a random half of the students to always read the material before class. The remaining group is instructed to always read the material after class. She then compares the two groups on the midterm examination. (There are a number of experimental-design issues to be concerned about in this study. They could be the subject of a good class discussion. There is at least one ethical issue, as well, and the teacher decides to inform all students that their midterm scores will be favorably adjusted if the group to which they were assigned scores relatively lower on the exam.)

The midterm examination scores for group 1 (the "before" group) and group 2 (the "after" group) are as follows:

Group 1: 62,60,60,59,58,57,57,56,55,55,54,53,52,51,50,50,48,47,40,37,32
Group 2: 69,68,68,67,65,64,64,64,63,62,61,60,58,58,56,56,54,54,51,50,48

In Figure 21–5, the SPSS input required to analyze these data and the resultant output are presented. Note that each case contains a numerical code (named GROUP) corresponding to the group it is in. On the T-TEST command card, SPSS is informed that the variable GROUP is to be used as the basis for forming two independent groups for analysis. The dependent variable is SCORE, the scores on the midterm exam.

All the relevant statistics required to interpret the *t* test are indicated in the output as labeled. Note, first, the *F* test value of 1.56. This is a test of the homogeneity of variance as described in Chapter 10, which, in our example here, suggests that the two experimental groups are close enough in variance to proceed with the *t* test using the pooled-variance formula. The significant *t* of

-3.64 ($p < .001$) indicates that group 2 appears to have benefited more by reading after the lecture (mean $= 60.0$) than group 1 did by reading before the lecture (mean $= 52.0$).

Correlated Data. In a study of ego needs, a psychologist wonders if there is a difference between firstborn and second-born siblings. He obtains a sample of ten families with two children each and administers an ego-needs test to each child. (Students may wish to discuss design and ethical issues in relation to this hypothetical study.) The following results are obtained:

Family Number:

	1	2	3	4	5	6	7	8	9	10
Firstborn	8	2	8	5	15	11	13	6	4	6
Second born:	3	1	6	3	14	12	9	4	4	5

The SPSS input and output for this study are presented in Figure 21–6. Note that cases correspond to families, that is, *pairs* of first- and second-born siblings, and the records for each case contain corresponding pairs of scores: 8 and 3, 2 and 1, and so forth. The output shows a mean difference of 1.70 between pairs, with firstborns having higher ego needs than second borns. The *t* value of 3.04 is nearly significant at the .01 level. Note also that the Pearson correlation between the ego-need scores of first- and second-born siblings is .91 (significant at $p < .0005$).

Single-Classification Analysis of Variance with A Priori and Post Hoc Comparisons

Single-classification or one-way analysis of variance is discussed in Chapters 11 and 12. In the latter, a computational example is given using the data in Table 12.1. These same data were input to the SPSS system using the program ONEWAY. Input and output are shown in Figure 21–7.

Notice on each record that a code for method of instruction, the variable GROUP, appears. The code 1, 2, or 3 indicates, respectively, method 1, 2, or 3. The ONEWAY command designates the achievement-test scores (ACHTEST) as the dependent variable. Also indicated in the command are requests for a priori and post hoc comparisons, corresponding with those computed for these data in Chapter 12.

In the output labeled ANALYSIS OF VARIANCE, you can see a typical source table indicating between and within sources of variance, the degrees of freedom, sum of squares, mean squares, and *F* test. All these values are identical to those computed in Chapter 12. The *F* of 10.0 on 2 and 12 *df* is significant at the .0028 level.

Thus there *are* statistically significant differences among the three methods. But where among them are these differences? Follow-up significance tests are required; these can be a priori or post hoc, as discussed and described in Chapters 11 and 12. As you saw in Chapter 12, methods 1 and 2 were barely significantly different at the 0.05 level, whereas, taken together, they were highly significantly different from method 3 (designated as the control method). The

INPUT

```
TITLE          T-TEST EXAMPLE FOR INDEPENDENT GROUPS
DATA LIST      FILE=INLINE RECORDS=1
               /GROUP 1 SCORE 3-4
BEGIN DATA
1 62
1 60
1 60
   .
   .
2 51
2 50
2 48
END DATA
T-TEST         GROUPS=GROUP(1,2)/VARIABLES=SCORE/
```

OUTPUT

- T - T E S T -

GROUP 1 - GROUP   EQ   1.
GROUP 2 - GROUP   EQ   2.

VARIABLE	NUMBER OF CASES	MEAN	STANDARD DEVIATION	STANDARD ERROR	F VALUE	2-TAIL PROB.	POOLED VARIANCE ESTIMATE T VALUE	DEGREES OF FREEDOM	2-TAIL PROB.	SEPARATE VARIANCE ESTIMATE T VALUE	DEGREES OF FREEDOM	2-TAIL PROB.
SCORE												
GROUP 1	21	52.0476	7.813	1.705	1.56	.327	-3.64	40	.001	-3.64	38.17	.001
GROUP 2	21	60.0000	6.253	1.365								

Fig. 21-5. The *t* test for uncorrelated data.

INPUT

```
TITLE        EXAMPLE OF T-TEST FOR PAIRED SCORES
DATA LIST    FILE=INLINE RECORDS=1
             /TEST1 1-2 TEST2 4-5
BEGIN DATA
8 3
2 1
8 6
.  .
6 4
4 4
6 5
END DATA
T-TEST       PAIRS=TEST1 TEST2/
```

OUTPUT

- - - - - - - - - - - - - - T - T E S T - - - - - - - - - - - - - - -

VARIABLE	NUMBER OF CASES	MEAN	STANDARD DEVIATION	STANDARD ERROR	*	(DIFFERENCE) MEAN	STANDARD DEVIATION	STANDARD ERROR	*	2-TAIL CORR. PROB.	*	T VALUE	DEGREES OF FREEDOM	2-TAIL PROB.
TEST1	10	7.8000	4.104	1.298	*				*		*			
					*	1.7000	1.767	.559	*	.910 .000	*	3.04	9	.014
TEST2		6.1000	4.228	1.337	*				*		*			

Fig. 21-6. The *t* test for correlated data.

INPUT

```
TITLE       ONE-WAY ANOVA EXAMPLE
DATA LIST   FILE=INLINE RECORDS=1
            /GROUP 1 ACHTEST 3-4

BEGIN DATA
1 7
1 10
1 10
  .
  .
3 3
3 7
3 6
END DATA
ONEWAY      ACHTEST BY GROUP(1,3)/
            CONTRAST 1 -1 0/
            CONTRAST 1 1 -2/
            RANGES=TUKEY
```

OUTPUT

SOURCE	D.F.	SUM OF SQUARES	MEAN SQUARES	F RATIO	F PROB.
BETWEEN GROUPS	2	90.0000	45.0000	10.0000	.0028
WITHIN GROUPS	12	54.0000	4.5000		
TOTAL	14	144.0000			

CONTRAST COEFFICIENT MATRIX

	GRP 1	GRP 2	GRP 3
CONTRAST 1	1.0	-1.0	.0
CONTRAST 2	1.0	1.0	-2.0

			POOLED VARIANCE ESTIMATE				SEPARATE VARIANCE ESTIMATE		
	VALUE	S. ERROR	T VALUE	D.F.	T PROB.	S. ERROR	T VALUE	D.F.	T PROB.
CONTRAST 1	3.0000	1.3416	2.236	12.0	.045	1.2649	2.372	7.9	.044
CONTRAST 2	9.0000	2.3238	3.873	12.0	.002	2.4495	3.674	7.0	.007

```
TUKEY-HSD PROCEDURE
RANGES FOR THE  .050 LEVEL -

        3.77   3.77

THE RANGES ABOVE ARE TABLE RANGES.
THE VALUE ACTUALLY COMPARED WITH MEAN(J)-MEAN(I) IS..
        1.5000 * RANGE * SQRT(1/N(I) + 1/N(J))

   (*) DENOTES PAIRS OF GROUPS SIGNIFICANTLY DIFFERENT AT THE   .050 LEVEL


                                    G G G
                                    R R R
                                    P P P

                                    3 2 1

    MEAN        GROUP

    4.0000      GRP 3
    7.0000      GRP 2
   10.0000      GRP 1        *


HOMOGENEOUS SUBSETS    (SUBSETS OF GROUPS, WHOSE HIGHEST AND LOWEST MEANS
                        DO NOT DIFFER BY MORE THAN THE SHORTEST
                        SIGNIFICANT RANGE FOR A SUBSET OF THAT SIZE)


SUBSET   1

GROUP       GRP 3       GRP 2
MEAN        4.0000      7.0000
 -  -

SUBSET   2

GROUP       GRP 2       GRP 1
MEAN        7.0000      10.0000
 -  -
```

Fig. 21-7. One-way analysis of variance of the data in Table 12.1 with a priori and post hoc comparisons.

SPSS output for a priori contrasts verifies these results. Note on the input instructions how the contrasts are specified using contrast coefficients. Note also that SPSS uses t tests instead of F tests for each contrast. (It is a mathematical fact that the square root of an F value on 1 and x degrees of freedom is equivalent to a t value on x degrees of freedom. You can verify this by computing the square roots of the F values for the contrasts computed in Chapter 12; the results will be equal to the pooled-variance t values in the SPSS output.)

The Tukey test for honestly significant differences is also quite easily called for in the input instructions. The results are identical to the computations in Chapter 12. Note how the computer output neatly arranges a matrix of all possible pairs of differences and then indicates with an asterisk which pair(s) is(are) significantly different.

Multiple-Classification Analysis of Variance: A Two-Way Example

Extending one-way anovas to anovas where two or more factors are involved in the design is discussed and illustrated in Chapters 13 and 14. We will illustrate how SPSS handles computational matters using the two-way design and data displayed in Table 14.1. The SPSS input and output are shown in Figure 21–8.

INPUT

```
TITLE           TWO-WAY ANOVA EXAMPLE
DATA LIST       FILE=INLINE RECORDS=1
                /ACHV 1 RIGID 3 PSOLV 5-6
BEGIN DATA
1 1 38
1 1 40
1 1 35
   .
   .
   .
3 3 62
3 3 62
3 3 65
END DATA
ANOVA           PSOLV BY ACHV,RIGID(1,3)/
```

OUTPUT

SOURCE OF VARIATION	SUM OF SQUARES	DF	MEAN SQUARE	F	SIGNIF. OF F
MAIN EFFECTS	1288.815	4	322.204	45.075	.000
ACHV	910.519	2	455.259	63.689	.000
RIGID	378.296	2	189.148	26.461	.000
2-WAY INTERACTIONS	28.593	4	7.148	1.000	.433
ACHV RIGID	28.593	4	7.148	1.000	.433
EXPLAINED	1317.407	8	164.676	23.038	.000
RESIDUAL	128.667	18	7.148		
TOTAL	1446.074	26	55.618		

Fig. 21–8. Multiple-classification ANOVA of the data in Table 14.1.

The first thing to notice is how the data are arranged in each record. In a two-way analysis, two group identifiers are needed. For our example, we need to know in which achievement category and which rigidity category the student is classified. The variable ACHV (coded 1, 2, or 3 for low, average, and high, respectively) and the variable RIGID (coded 1, 2, 3 for high, average, and low, respectively) provide the needed information. The third variable, PSOLV, represents the scores on the problem-solving test.

The output contains essentially the same calculated values as are displayed in Table 14.2 in Chapter 14. (The results in Table 14.2 contain slight errors due to rounding off intermediate computations to the nearest thousandth.) The five lines of results in Table 14.2 correspond to the lines in the output labeled ACHV, RIGID, ACHV RIGID, RESIDUAL, and TOTAL. (Other important statistics, not shown in the output, are the number of cases and the means and standard deviations for the rows, columns, and cells of this 3×3 design. These data would be easy to generate using the SPSS program MEANS.)

Analysis of Covariance

You will recall from the discussions in Chapter 15 that analysis of covariance is simply analysis of variance, *except* that the dependent variable is statistically adjusted based on its correlation and regression equation with one or more control variables. Conceptually, the analysis is relatively straightforward. Computationally, it is a nightmare. If you have attempted these computations, you will appreciate the ease with which SPSS does the job.

We will illustrate this for the single-classification analysis of covariance design and data displayed in Table 16.1, Chapter 16. Figure 21–9 presents the corresponding SPSS analysis.

The input data are arranged in exactly the same order as they were in Table 16.1, except that each case contains a 1 or 2 depending on the experimental group to which it was assigned. The ANOVA command is almost readable: "Analyze dependent variable Y BY independent variable GROUP WITH X1 and X2 as covariates."

Because the intermediate calculations in Chapter 16 were not as precise as those done by computer, the results presented in Table 16.4 for the data in Table 16.1 are close to but not quite identical with the SPSS output. In Table 16.4, the Between and Within lines correspond to the GROUP and RESIDUAL lines in the SPSS output. Additional information is contained in the SPSS output, namely tests of each covariate's influence on the dependent variable. These are essentially tests of their regression coefficients. In this example, the results (although not significant) indicate that X1 (prior mathematics achievement) had a relatively larger effect on achievement in the programmed-instruction methods than did the measure of verbal aptitude.

Nonparametric Statistical Analyses

In Chapters 18 and 19, the rationale and computational details for a number of nonparametric procedures are discussed. We will illustrate here how SPSS can be used for most of these analyses.

INPUT

```
TITLE              ANALYSIS OF COVARIANCE EXAMPLE
DATA LIST          FILE=INLINE RECORDS=1
                   /GROUP 1 Y 3-4 X1 6-7 X2 9-11
BEGIN DATA
1 59 68 116
1 58 69 120
1 58 64 114
              .
              .
              .
2 49 57 100
2 48 62 111
2 47 61 110
END DATA
ANOVA              Y BY GROUP(1,2) WITH X1,X2/
```

OUTPUT

SOURCE OF VARIATION	SUM OF SQUARES	DF	MEAN SQUARE	F	SIGNIF. OF F
COVARIATES	104.434	2	52.217	6.125	.024
X1	19.890	1	19.890	2.333	.165
X2	1.306	1	1.306	.153	.706
MAIN EFFECTS	17.028	1	17.028	1.997	.195
GROUP	17.028	1	17.028	1.997	.195
EXPLAINED	121.462	3	40.487	4.749	.035
RESIDUAL	68.205	8	8.526		
TOTAL	189.667	11	17.242		

Fig. 21-9.   Single-classification analysis of covariance in the data in Table 16.1.

Chi Square.   A chi-square test is typically employed when the relationship between two or more qualitative or categorized variables is being studied. Table 19.5 in Chapter 19 is illustrative. Each of the 1,200 students can be categorized in one of three schools and in one of four levels of truancy reports. Figure 21–10 contains the corresponding input and output for an SPSS analysis of these same data.

If this were a real study, we would have data records for all 1,200 cases containing the variables SCHOOL and NUMREP, as indicated. Because this is a hypothetical study and we already know how many cases fall into each cell (see Table 19.5), we can simplify matters by weighting. We create one case for each cell and weight the case by the actual frequency in each cell. This device need not concern you. The important thing is to note the CROSSTABS command, which simply calls for a crosstabulation of the two variables in this study.

The SPSS output nearly duplicates Table 19.5, except for a few variations in format. Cell frequencies and expected cell frequencies are presented, along with row and column totals and percentages. The output also gives the chi-square statistic, degrees of freedom, and level of significance. Actually, much

INPUT

```
TITLE           CROSSTABS EXAMPLE
DATA LIST       FILE=INLINE RECORDS=1
                /SCHOOL 1 NUMREP 3 WGHT 5-7
BEGIN DATA
1 1 400
2 1 300
3 1 100
       .
       .
       .
1 4  50
2 4  25
3 4  50
END DATA
WEIGHT BY WGHT
CROSSTABS       TABLES=SCHOOL BY NUMREP
OPTION          14
STATISTICS      1
```

OUTPUT

```
               NUMREP
        COUNT  I
        EXP VAL I                                           ROW
               I                                            TOTAL
               I     1I       2I       3I       4I
SCHOOL  -------+--------+--------+--------+--------+
            1  I    400  I   100  I   50  I   50  I   600
               I  400.0  I  87.5  I  50.0 I  62.5 I  50.0P
               +--------+--------+--------+--------+
            2  I    300  I    50  I   25  I   25  I   400
               I  266.7  I  58.3  I  33.3 I  41.7 I  33.3P
               +--------+--------+--------+--------+
            3  I    100  I    25  I   25  I   50  I   200
               I  133.3  I  29.2  I  16.7 I  20.8 I  16.7P
               +--------+--------+--------+--------+
        COLUMN      800      175      100     125     1200
        TOTAL      66.7P    14.6P    8.3P    10.4P   100.0P
```

CHI-SQUARE	D.F.	SIGNIFICANCE	MIN E.F.	CELLS WITH E.F.< 5
72.32143	6	.0000	16.667	NONE

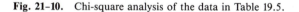

Fig. 21-10.   Chi-square analysis of the data in Table 19.5.

more information can be obtained by selecting additional output options, and many more statistics (besides chi square) can be computed for crosstabulation tables.

Other Nonparametric Procedures

Six other nonparametric tests are described and illustrated in Chapter 19. The corresponding SPSS analyses, in terms of both input and output, are relatively straightforward and easy to read. We present them in the following pages (Figures 21–11 through 21–16) with no further explanation. In each case, the data are from the examples in Chapter 19.

INPUT

```
TITLE           WILCOXON EXAMPLE
DATA LIST       FILE=INLINE RECORDS=1
                /KNO 1-2 NOKNO 4-5
BEGIN DATA
65 61
72 59
58 63
   .
   .
   .
59 55
74 54
69 60
END DATA
NONPAR TESTS    WILCOXON=KNO WITH NOKNO
```

OUTPUT

```
MEAN RANK     CASES

    5.17         6  -  RANKS  (NOKNO LT KNO)
    2.50         2  +  RANKS  (NOKNO GT KNO)
                 O     TIES   (NOKNO EQ KNO)
                 -
                 8     TOTAL

    Z =   -1.8204              2-TAILED P =   .0687
```

Fig. 21–11.   Wilcoxon matched-pairs signed-ranks test on the data in Table 19.7.

INPUT

```
TITLE           SIGN TEST EXAMPLE
DATA LIST       FILE=INLINE RECORDS=1
                /A 1 B 3
BEGIN DATA
1 O
1 O
O 1
  .
  .
  .
1 O
1 O
1 O
END DATA
NONPAR TESTS    SIGN=A WITH B
OPTION          6
```

OUTPUT

```
CASES

    9   -  DIFFS (B LT A)
    3   +  DIFFS (B GT A)        (BINOMIAL)
    O      TIES                  2-TAILED P =       .1460
   --
   12      TOTAL
```

Fig. 21–12.   Sign test on the data in Table 19.8.

INPUT

```
TITLE           MANN-WHITNEY EXAMPLE
DATA LIST       FILE=INLINE RECORDS=1
                /GROUP 1 SCORE 3-4
BEGIN DATA
1 49
1 47
1 41
  .
  .
  .
2 46
2 37
2 26
END DATA
NONPAR TESTS    M-W=SCORE BY GROUP(1,2)
```

OUTPUT

```
MEAN RANK     CASES

    6.67          9   GROUP = 1
   10.00          6   GROUP = 2
                 --
                 15   TOTAL

                              EXACT           CORRECTED FOR TIES
     U          W          2-TAILED P        Z          2-TAILED P
   15.0       60.0          .1810         -1.4142         .1573
```

Fig. 21–13. Mann-Whitney *U* test on the data in Table 19.9.

INPUT

```
TITLE           FRIEDMAN EXAMPLE
DATA LIST       FILE=INLINE RECORDS=1
                /PM1 1 PM2 3 PM3 5
BEGIN DATA
2  1  3
3  1  2
1  2  3
2  1  3
END DATA
NONPAR TESTS    FRIEDMAN=PM1 PM2 PM3
```

OUTPUT

```
MEAN RANK     VARIABLE

    2.00       PM1
    1.25       PM2
    2.75       PM3

   CASES        CHI-SQUARE        D.F.     SIGNIFICANCE
     4           4.5000            2           .1054
```

Fig. 21–14. Friedman two-way ANOVA by ranks on the data in Table 19.10.

INPUT

```
TITLE           KRUSKAL-WALLIS EXAMPLE
DATA LIST       FILE=INLINE RECORDS=1
                /GROUP 1 SCORE 3-4
BEGIN DATA
1 64
1 59
1 56
     .
     .
     .
3 49
3 48
3 42
END DATA
NONPAR TESTS    K-W=SCORE BY GROUP(1,3)
```

OUTPUT

```
MEAN RANK      CASES

    5.60         5      GROUP  =  1
   10.50         4      GROUP  =  2
    5.25         4      GROUP  =  3
                --
                13      TOTAL
```

			CORRECTED FOR TIES	
CASES	CHI-SQUARE	SIGNIFICANCE	CHI-SQUARE	SIGNIFICANCE
13	4.6846	.0961	4.6846	.0961

Fig. 21–15.   Kruskal-Wallis one-way ANOVA by ranks on the data in Table 19.11.

INPUT

```
TITLE           SPEARMAN RANK-ORDER CORRELATION EXAMPLE
DATA LIST       FILE=INLINE RECORDS=1
                /ATTX 1-3 ATTY 5-6
BEGIN DATA
124 62
123 59
119 67
    .
    .
    .
110 57
104 50
 94 52
END DATA
NONPAR CORR     ATTX WITH ATTY
OPTION          6
```

OUTPUT

```
            ATTY


ATTX          .8469
          N(    7)
          SIG .008
```

Fig. 21–16.   Spearman rank-order correlation on data in Table 19.12.

REVIEW

For even a rather small-sized study, say, several variables and 15 to 20 cases, you will find that much can be saved in the way of time, energy, error correction, and overall grief by using a computer and statistical software to analyze the data. If nothing else, this chapter should have demonstrated how easy and straightforward such analyses can be.

But remember that computer analysis is not a substitute for common sense, nor does it necessarily compensate for statistical naiveté. Always check your output to make sure that it makes sense, given what you know about your own data. Do some hand-calculator computations to get a feel for your data. And read the computer output line by line, especially if you have enlisted a consultant's help. Such technicians know less about your data than you do, and you must take responsibility for making sure that the appropriate analyses have been requested for whatever statistical software is being used. A user-friendly system, such as SPSS, can be particularly helpful in this regard.

EXERCISES

In the following exercises we refer to exercises in preceding chapters and ask you to use SPSS to conduct the appropriate analyses. These problems are all small enough to be easily done on personal computers or, interactively, with mainframes. Obviously, these exercises are intended only for those students who are using this text in conjunction with other materials (see the Selected Readings section) designed to develop a *working* familiarity with data processing and SPSS.

Revisit the following exercises, using SPSS to perform the relevant data analyses:

1. Use FREQUENCIES to analyze the data given in exercise 8, Chapter 2. (To analyze each group separately, use the SELECT IF command.)
2. Use PEARSON CORR to analyze the relationship between the two variables in exercise 7, Chapter 6.
3. Use REGRESSION to analyze the bivariate relationship in exercise 3, Chapter 8.
4. Use REGRESSION to analyze the multivariate relationship in exercise 9, Chapter 8.
5. Use T-TEST to test the mean difference for the data in exercise 4, Chapter 10.
6. Use T-TEST to test the mean difference for the data in exercise 7, Chapter 10.
7. Use ONEWAY to analyze the data in exercise 6, Chapter 12. Also, use a priori contrasts to test the specific comparisons called for in exercise 7, Chapter 12.
8. Use ONEWAY to analyze the data in exercise 9, Chapter 12. Also, use the Tukey post hoc comparison procedure to test the contrasts called for in exercise 10, Chapter 12.
9. Use ANOVA to analyze the two-way design in exercise 1, Chapter 14.
10. Use ANOVA to test for all main effects and interactions in the three-way design in exercise 3, Chapter 14.
11. Use ANOVA to perform an analysis of covariance on the data in the single-classification design given in exercise 1, Chapter 16.
12. Use ANOVA to perform an analysis of covariance on the data in the multiple-classification design given in exercise 2, Chapter 16.
13. Use CROSSTABS to perform a chi-square analysis on the data in exercise 3, Chapter 19.
14. Use NPAR TESTS to perform the indicated nonparametric test for each of the following exercises in Chapter 19:

	Exercise	Nonparametric Test
a.	5	WILCOXON
b.	6	SIGN
c.	7	M-W
d.	9	FRIEDMAN
e.	10	K-W

15. Use NPAR CORR to compute the rank-order correlation for the data in exercise 12, Chapter 19.

SELECTED READINGS

Norusis, Marija J. *The SPSS Guide to Data Analysis*. Chicago: SPSS, Inc., 1990.
SPSS, Inc. *SPSS Reference Guide*. Chicago: SPSS, Inc., 1989.

Answers to Exercises

Note: Minor differences in answers to numerical questions may occur because of differences in rounding procedures.

Chapter 2

1. $\mu = 38.40$

2. $\mu = 110.80$

3. (a) 99.5
   (b) 8.0
   (c) 25.5

4. (a) $\mu = 6.81$
   (b) $\mu = 26.75$
   (c) $\mu = 47.13$

5. Range = 28   Mode = 118

6. $\sigma = 2.81$

7. $\sigma^2 = 32.78$ $\sigma = 5.73$

8. (a) Group A: $\mu = 52.05$ Median = 54 $\sigma = 7.81$ Range = 30
       Group B: $\mu = 60.00$ Median = 61 $\sigma = 6.25$ Range = 21
   (b) Group B
   (c) Group A
   (d) Group B

9. Because of the truncated distribution, the median should be used.

10. Who can tell? We must determine precisely which measure of central tendency is being employed before attaching any interpretation to such phrases as "average citizen."

11. (a) Period 2 class.
    (b) Period 2 class.
    (c) Because of its greater heterogeneity, probably the period 4 class for both highest and lowest scores.

Chapter 3

1. Approximately 16 percent.

2. Positively skewed, or skewed to the right. (This assumes that low to high scores are represented, as is customary, from left to right.)

3. Matched centiles and z scores:

Percentile	z
84th	1.0
50th	0.0
16th	-1.0
98th	2.0
2nd	-2.0

4. (a) $z = 2.0$ (b) $z = -1.0$ (c) $z = 1.0$ (d) $z = 2.0$

5. (a) $z = -1.39$ (c) $z = -1.08$ (e) $z = 1.13$
   (b) $z = 0.02$ (d) $z = 1.06$ (f) $z = 0.36$

6. (a) 2 As; 7 Bs; 11 Cs; 7 Ds; 2 Fs
   (b) 9, 11, 13, 15

7. (a) $Z = 36.1$ (c) $Z = 39.2$ (e) $Z = 61.3$
   (b) $Z = 50.2$ (d) $Z = 60.6$ (f) $Z = 53.6$

8. (a) 50th   (b) 84th   (c) 98th   (d) 16th

9. The researcher could transform all of the achievement-test scores into normalized standard scores (NCEs) on the basis of the standardization data for each achievement test, then match on the basis of the normalized standard scores.

10. Nothing. No percentage interpretations should be made from standard scores in nonnormal distributions.

11. (a) 67th   (b) 80th   (c) 97th   (d) 14th

12. (a) 55.2   (b) 68.8   (c) 45.0   (d) 50.0

Chapter 4

1. Reject it.

2. Do not reject it.

3. No, a 0.05 level of significance signifies that what has been observed in these samples (in this instance, a difference between means) would occur *by chance alone* only five times in one hundred.

4. Reject it because of the extremely improbable (by chance alone) z value.

5. (a) Reject   (d) Reject only if p is less than 0.05, for example, 0.02
   (b) Do not reject   (e) Do not reject
   (c) Reject   (f) Reject

6. Yes.

7. One-tailed test.

8. 0.10

9. Type I

10. Because the psychologist is now more interested in the question "How much difference?" than the question "Is there a difference?" there should be more interest in estimation procedures.

11. (a) 95%: 19.4 to 21.8   99%: 19.1 to 22.1
    (b) 95%: 18.9 to 22.3   99%: 18.4 to 22.8
    The more data sampled, the more reliable the estimate and the tighter the interval of estimation.

Chapter 5

1. $r = -0.71$

2. (a) r should not be used, for the assumption of homoscedasticity cannot be satisfied.
   (b) r can be used, for the assumptions of homoscedasticity and linearity appear to be satisfied.
   (c) r should not be used, for the assumption of a linear relationship cannot be satisfied.

3. Remembering that in using Table C, $df =$ number of pairs minus 2:
   (a) Reject null hypothesis.
   (b) Do not reject null hypothesis.
   (c) Reject null hypothesis.
   (d) Reject null hypothesis.
   (e) Do not reject null hypothesis.

4. Product-moment correlation coefficient.

5. Point biserial coefficient (continuous variable *versus* dichotomous variable).

6. Correlation ratio.

7. Multiple correlation.

8. Partial correlation.

9. The psychologist should compute a 95 percent confidence interval for the r of 0.53. For example, a range of $0.40 - 0.66$ for r might indicate that by using a similar process, the population r can be assumed to fall within similar limits 95 percent of the time.

Chapter 6

1. $r = 0.86$

2. Yes.   From Table C, $p < 0.01$.

3. $r = 0.67$

4. No, although an r of 0.67 with 8 df is significant beyond the 0.05 level.

5. $r = 0.49$

6. Yes.

7. $r = 0.35$.   No, $p > 0.05$.

8. (a) $R_{x \cdot yx} = 0.22$ (b) $R_{y \cdot xz} = 0.18$ (c) $R_{z \cdot xy} = 0.19$

9. (a) $r_{xy \cdot z} = 0.16$ (b) $r_{yz \cdot x} = 0.12$ (c) $r_{xz \cdot y} = -0.17$

10. 0.76 to 0.83

11. 0.25 to 0.86

Chapter 7

1. Regression.

2. No, variables may serve as criteria in certain instances and as predictors in others. For example, while college academic achievement is usually a criterion variable, it might serve as a predictor variable for success in various post-college endeavors.

3. Because the whole scheme of regression prediction is predicated on the notion that the relationship between criterion and predictor in the sample can serve as a guide for making estimates in subsequent cases, if the individual for whom the prediction is to be made is markedly unlike those in the regression sample, the relationship between criterion and predictor will be less likely to hold for that individual.

4. Situation A.

5. 43.5

6. (a) $s_{y \cdot x} = 8.4$

7. Multiple regression.

Chapter 8

1. $a = -9.55$ $b = 0.585$

2. (a) 18.53   (c) 13.85   (e) 8.59
    (b) 15.02   (d) 12.68   (f) 6.83

3. $\tilde{Y} = 1.20 + 0.20 \, X$ $(r = 0.73)$

4. (a) 136.88   (c) 127.15   (e) 101.85
    (b) 134.93   (d) 113.53   (f) 97.96

5. $s_{y \cdot x} = 10.78$

6. Approximately 32 times in 100, because 68 percent of the time the actual score will fall within a range $\pm$ one standard error of estimate (10.78).

7. $\bar{Y} = 12.93 + 1.488X$

8. (a) 62.53   (c) 65.74   (e) 38.12
   (b) 63.68   (d) 59.79

9. $\bar{X} = 4.15 + 0.85Y - 0.21Z$ $(R = 0.83)$

Chapter 9

1. Investigator B.

2. Investigator A.

3. Investigator B.

4. $t = 2.25$ and $df = 30$.

5. No, because the mean difference represents only the numerator of the t model. Other factors such as sample size may produce a much larger t value for a smaller mean difference.

6. $t = -2.42$, for it is the absolute value of t that determines its probability level.

7. (1) A one-tailed t test with $t = 1.90$ and $df = 9$ allows one to reject the null hypothesis at the 0.05 probability level (which is indicated under the 0.10 column in Table E).

Chapter 10

1. (a) Use pooled-variance formula; $df = 37$.
   (b) Use either pooled-variance formula or separate-variance formula; $df = 13$.
   (c) Use pooled-variance formula; $df = 34$.
   (d) Use separate-variance formula; df is a special case involving interpolation. See discussion in the chapter. The t value needed for rejection of null hypothesis at 0.05 level is 2.00.

2. (a) $t = -3.23$.   Reject the null hypothesis.
   (b) $t = 2.52$.   Reject the null hypothesis.
   (c) $t = 1.10$.   Do not reject the null hypothesis.
   (d) $t = 2.11$.   Reject the null hypothesis.

3. (a) $F_{14,13} = 1.42$.   Consider groups homogeneous.
   (b) $F_{50,61} = 1.73$.   Consider groups heterogeneous.
   (c) $F_{9,9} = 1.55$.   Consider groups homogeneous.
   (d) $F_{99,50} = 3.25$.   Consider groups heterogeneous.
   (e) $F_{60,40} = 2.53$.   Consider groups heterogeneous.

4. Use pooled-variance t model. $df = 14$. $t = 1.45$.   Do not reject the null hypothesis.

5. Use pooled-variance t model. $df = 18$. $t = 1.01$.   Do not reject the null hypothesis.

6. $t = 11.15$.   Reject the null hypothesis.

7. $r = 0.845$. $t = 29.70$.   Reject the null hypothesis.

8. Null hypothesis should be rejected. When using t table, be sure to halve probability values for one-tailed tests.

9. Consistent with the one-tailed prediction test, the investigator must not reject the null hypothesis. Under the circumstances, the study should undoubtedly be replicated and the resulting data treated with a two-tailed significance test.

Chapter 11

1. The null hypothesis will not be rejected.

2. Analysis of variance. A priori or post hoc comparisons as appropriate, given the investigator's research design.

3. Analysis A.

4. No, the significant F indicates that such mean differences exist, but additional analyses (such as those described in Chapters 11 and 12) are required to locate the individual means that are significantly disparate.

5. Yes.

Chapter 12

1. $F = 13.33$.   Reject the null hypothesis.

2. (a) Yes   (b) Yes   (c) No

3. (a) Yes   (b) Yes   (c) Yes

4. Total SS $= 563.73$.   Within SS $= 446.00$.   Between SS $= 117.73$.

5. The largest variance is for group X, where $s_x^2 = 49.8$, while the smallest variance is for group Y, where $s_y^2 = 23.5$. Dividing the smaller variance into the larger variance, an F of 2.12 is produced. With 4 and 4 degrees of freedom, this F is not large enough to reject the null hypothesis, so the variances may be considered homogeneous.

6. Within MS $= 7.88$.   Between MS $= 77.62$. $F_{3,24} = 9.85$.

7. Contrast coefficients and F tests are:
   (a) 1, -1, 0, and 0; $F_{1,24} = 0.74$ (n.s.)
   (b) 0, 0, 1, and -1; $F_{1,24} = 23.60$ (p <0.01)
   (c) 1, 1, -1, and -1; $F_{1,24} = 5.25$ (p <0.05)

8. Yes; to within rounding error, the SS_c for each contrast (5.82, 186.00, and 41.33) add up to the between groups SS (232.86). Alternatively, calculating the quantity $\Sigma c_g d_g$ three times, once for each of the three pairs of contrast coefficients, verifies that the quantities equal 0.

9. $F_{2,27} = 9.12$ (p <0.05).

10. Using Tukey's method of honestly significant differences, $CV = 3.5 \sqrt{15.4/10} = 4.3$. Only the difference between the means of approaches 1 and 3 exceed this critical value, illustrating the conservative nature of this post hoc comparison procedure.

11. Between MS $= 215.76$.   Within MS $= 32.63$. $F_{2,42} = 9.85$.

Chapter 13

1. Single-classification analysis of variance.

2. Multiple-classification analysis of variance.

3. Yes.

4. Yes, because with each additional source of variation such as an independent variable, the error term in the denominator of all the F ratios in the problem is reduced, thereby increasing the probability of significant F values. This is why a multiple-classification analysis of variance model is such a powerful statistical technique.

5. Tenable, for all F values will be less than 1.

Chapter 14

1. Methods MS $= 0.05$. $F_{2,54} = 0.005$.   Do not reject the null hypothesis.
   Sex MS $= 2.4$. $F_{1,54} = 0.23$.   Do not reject the null hypothesis.
   Interaction MS $= 149.45$. $F_{2,54} = 14.09$.   Reject the null hypothesis.

2. (a) Instructional method $F_{2,72} = 22.61$, $p < 0.05$.
   (b) Aptitude level $F_{2,72} = 29.63$, $p < 0.05$.
   (c) Interaction $F_{4,72} = 0.99$, $p > 0.05$.

3.

Source	SS	df	MS	F
A	120.600	2	60.300	14.28
B	2.700	1	2.700	.64
C	.300	1	.300	.07
AB	13.400	2	6.700	1.59
AC	25.800	2	12.900	3.06
BC	24.300	1	24.300	5.76
ABC	1.400	2	.700	.17
Error	456.000	108	4.222	

Chapter 15

1. Analysis of covariance. By employing this model, the school psychologist can statistically compensate for the initial intellectual differences between the groups. Single-classification analysis of variance does not possess this analysis capacity.

2. Yes.

3. Group A.

4. Yes.

5. What does it mean to "statistically equate" groups on a variable, academic aptitude, that may be (for various reasons) related in fundamental ways to the differences between groups? Reconsider the example of "statistically equating" males and females on the variable "height" in an analysis of their differences on the variable "weight" which was mentioned in the chapter.

6. No adjustment would take place. The three ellipses would stack on top of one another with centers all on the same vertical line intersecting the X axis at the same value, namely the mean for all three groups. (Regression lines would all be parallel.)

Chapter 16

1. $F_{1,20} = 0.11$.   Do not reject the null hypothesis.

2. For A, $F = 149.39$.   Reject the null hypothesis.
   For B, $F = 8.77$.   Reject the null hypothesis.
   For A $\times$ B, $F = 2.43$.   Do not reject the null hypothesis.

Chapter 17

Exercise calls for an essay-type answer.

Chapter 18

1. Because of its greater power, the parametric test.

2. The Mann-Whitney U Test.

3. The Spearman rank-order correlation coefficient.

4. The chi-square test.

5. The sign test and the Wilcoxon matched-pairs signed-ranks test, with the latter being more powerful.

6. The chi-square test.

7. The Friedman two-way analysis of variance.

8. With nominal data, the chi-square test.
   With ordinal data, the Kruskal-Wallis one-way analysis of variance.

Chapter 19

1. $\chi^2 = 24.40$ $(df = 3)$, $p < 0.01$. This year's foreign language enrollment is indeed significantly different from the average distribution of previous years' enrollments.

2.

	13	14	15	16	17	18	19	20
Observed Frequencies	20	40	60	80	80	60	40	20
Expected Frequencies	19.8^a	34.5	62.2	83.5	83.5	62.2	34.5	19.8^a

   [a]Expected frequencies in the two extreme cells were calculated on the basis of the proportion of the normal curve that was not already covered by the other six cells, that is, 0.0495 in each cell.

   $\chi^2 = 2.21$ $(df = 5)$, $p > 0.80$. The distribution does not depart significantly from normality.

3. $\chi^2 = 39.71$ $(df = 3)$, $p < 0.01$.   Reject the null hypothesis.

4. Regrouping into a 2×4 table so that the categories are "50 and below, 51–60, 61–70, 71 and above," $\chi^2 = 0.60$ $(df = 3)$, $p > 0.80$. The two samples can be considered to have been drawn from the same population.

5. $T = 3.5$, $p < 0.05$ $(z = -2.5)$

6. With the number of less frequent signs (x) equaling 2, $p < 0.05$. Thus the difference between the two groups is significant at the required level.

7. $U = 4$, $p < 0.05$ (one-tailed). The performance of Group I can be judged significantly superior to that of Group II.

8. $U = 52.5$, $z = -3.73$, $p < 0.01$.   The null hypothesis should be rejected.

9. $\chi_r^2 = 7.5$, $p > 0.05$.   Do not reject the null hypothesis.

10. $H = 1.51$.   With samples of 5, 4, and 3, an H value of 5.66 is needed to reject the null hypothesis at the 0.05 level, so the three samples should be considered part of the same population.

11. $r_s = 0.25$

12. $r_s = 0.93$, $p < 0.05$

Chapter 20

No additional exercises.

Chapter 21

1. From exercise 8, Chapter 2.

INPUT

```
TITLE              EXAMPLE OF INDIVIDUAL GROUP FREQUENCIES
DATA LIST          FILE=INLINE RECORDS=1
                   /GROUP 1 SCORE 3-4

BEGIN DATA
1 62
1 60
1 60
    .
    .
    .
2 51
2 50
2 48
END DATA
TEMPORARY
SELECT IF          (GROUP EQ 1)
FREQUENCIES        VARIABLES=SCORE/
                   STATISTICS=MEAN,MEDIAN,MODE,STDDEV,VARIANCE,RANGE/

TEMPORARY
SELECT IF          (GROUP EQ 2)
FREQUENCIES        VARIABLES=SCORE/
                   STATISTICS=MEAN,MEDIAN,MODE,STDDEV,VARIANCE,RANGE/
```

OUTPUT

SCORE

VALUE LABEL	VALUE	FREQUENCY	PERCENT	VALID PERCENT	CUM PERCENT
	32	1	4.8	4.8	4.8
	37	1	4.8	4.8	9.5
	40	1	4.8	4.8	14.3
	47	1	4.8	4.8	19.0
	48	1	4.8	4.8	23.8
	50	2	9.5	9.5	33.3
	51	1	4.8	4.8	38.1
	52	1	4.8	4.8	42.9
	53	1	4.8	4.8	47.6
	54	1	4.8	4.8	52.4
	55	2	9.5	9.5	61.9
	56	1	4.8	4.8	66.7
	57	2	9.5	9.5	76.2
	58	1	4.8	4.8	81.0
	59	1	4.8	4.8	85.7
	60	2	9.5	9.5	95.2
	62	1	4.8	4.8	100.0
		-------	-------	-------	
	TOTAL	21	100.0	100.0	

MEAN	52.048	MEDIAN	54.000	MODE	50.000
STD DEV	7.813	VARIANCE	61.048	RANGE	30.000

VALID CASES   21   MISSING CASES   0

SCORE

VALUE LABEL	VALUE	FREQUENCY	PERCENT	VALID PERCENT	CUM PERCENT
	48	1	4.8	4.8	4.8
	50	1	4.8	4.8	9.5
	51	1	4.8	4.8	14.3
	54	2	9.5	9.5	23.8
	56	2	9.5	9.5	33.3
	58	2	9.5	9.5	42.9
	60	1	4.8	4.8	47.6
	61	1	4.8	4.8	52.4
	62	1	4.8	4.8	57.1
	63	1	4.8	4.8	61.9
	64	3	14.3	14.3	76.2
	65	1	4.8	4.8	81.0
	67	1	4.8	4.8	85.7
	68	2	9.5	9.5	95.2
	69	1	4.8	4.8	100.0
		-------	-------	-------	
	TOTAL	21	100.0	100.0	

MEAN	60.000	MEDIAN	61.000	MODE	64.000
STD DEV	6.253	VARIANCE	39.100	RANGE	21.000

VALID CASES   21   MISSING CASES   0

2. From exercise 7, Chapter 6.

INPUT

```
TITLE          EXAMPLE OF PEARSON CORRELATION
DATA LIST      FILE=INLINE RECORDS=1
               /QUIZ 1-2 FINAL 4-5
BEGIN DATA
23 82
20 90
15 78
   .
   .
   .
19 78
18 85
23 90
END DATA
PEARSON CORR   QUIZ WITH FINAL
```

OUTPUT

```
            FINAL

QUIZ         .3473
           (   19)
           P= .072
```

---

3. From exercise 3, Chapter 8.

INPUT

```
TITLE          REGRESSION EXAMPLE WITH 50 SUBJECTS
DATA LIST      FILE=INLINE RECORDS=1
               /X 1-2 Y 4-5
BEGIN DATA
62 150
61 151
61 143
   .
   .
   .
42 103
41 101
40 101
END DATA
REGRESSION     VARIABLES=X,Y/DEPENDENT=Y/TEST=(X)/
```

OUTPUT

VARIABLE(S) ENTERED ON STEP NUMBER 1..   X

HYPOTHESIS TESTS

DF	SUM OF SQUARES	RSQ CHG	F	SIG F	SOURCE
1	63.82847	.53827	55.95765	.0000	X
1	63.82847		55.95765	.0000	REGRESSION
48	54.75153				RESIDUAL
49	118.58000				TOTAL

		ANALYSIS OF VARIANCE			
MULTIPLE R	.73367				
R SQUARE	.53827		DF	SUM OF SQUARES	MEAN SQUARE
ADJUSTED R SQUARE	.52865	REGRESSION	1	63.82847	63.82847
STANDARD ERROR	1.06802	RESIDUAL	48	54.75153	1.14066

F =   55.95765   SIGNIF F =   .0000

----------------- VARIABLES IN THE EQUATION ------------------

VARIABLE	B	SE B	BETA	T	SIG T
X	.20293	.02713	.73367	7.480	.0000
(CONSTANT)	1.19942	1.42247		.843	.4033

4. From exercise 9, Chapter 8.

INPUT

```
TITLE         REGRESSION EXAMPLE WITH TWO PREDICTORS
DATA LIST     FILE=INLINE RECORDS=1
              /X 1 Y 3 Z 5
BEGIN DATA
6 3 2
7 3 2
8 5 4
6 4 3
5 2 4
END DATA
REGRESSION    VARIABLES=X,Y,Z/DEPENDENT=X/TEST=(Y)(Z)/
```

OUTPUT

```
VARIABLE(S) ENTERED ON STEP NUMBER  1..    Z
                                    2..    Y

HYPOTHESIS TESTS
```

DF	SUM OF SQUARES	RSQ CHG	F	SIG F	SOURCE
1	3.56364	.68531	4.35556	.1722	Y
1	.17133	.03295	.20940	.6921	Z
2	3.56364		2.17778	.3147	REGRESSION
2	1.63636				RESIDUAL
4	5.20000				TOTAL

```
MULTIPLE R          .82784       ANALYSIS OF VARIANCE
R SQUARE            .68531
ADJUSTED R SQUARE   .37063              DF   SUM OF SQUARES   MEAN SQUARE
STANDARD ERROR      .90453       REGRESSION    2      3.56364      1.78182
                                 RESIDUAL      2      1.63636       .81818

                                 F =    2.17778   SIGNIF F =   .3147
```

```
----------------- VARIABLES IN THE EQUATION ------------------
```

VARIABLE	B	SE B	BETA	T	SIG T
Z	-.21212	.46355	-.18604	-.458	.6921
Y	.84848	.40656	.84848	2.087	.1722
(CONSTANT)	4.15152	1.77913		2.333	.1448

---

5. From exercise 4, Chapter 10.

INPUT

```
TITLE           T-TEST FOR INDEPENDENT GROUPS
DATA LIST       FILE=INLINE RECORDS=1
                /GRP 1 SCORE 3-4
BEGIN DATA
0 42
0 69
0 48
  .
  .
  .
1 36
1 42
1 18
END DATA
T-TEST          GROUPS=GRP(0,1)/VARIABLES=SCORE/
```

OUTPUT

- T - T E S T -

						* POOLED VARIANCE ESTIMATE			* SEPARATE VARIANCE ESTIMATE		
VARIABLE	NUMBER OF CASES	MEAN	STANDARD DEVIATION	STANDARD ERROR	* F VALUE 2-TAIL PROB.	* T VALUE	DEGREES OF FREEDOM	2-TAIL PROB.	* T VALUE	DEGREES OF FREEDOM	2-TAIL PROB.
SCORE					*	*			*		
GROUP 1	8	48.8750	18.177	6.427	*	*			*		
					* 3.77 .101	* 1.45	14	.168	* 1.45	10.47	.176
GROUP 2	8	38.3750	9.365	3.311	*	*			*		

----

6. From exercise 7, Chapter 10.

INPUT

```
TITLE           T-TEST FOR PAIRED SCORES
DATA LIST       FILE=INLINE RECORDS=1
                /PSTTXA 1-2 PSTTXB 4-5
BEGIN DATA
94 62
92 60
91 63
  .
  .
  .
75 43
74 49
74 42
END DATA
T-TEST          PAIRS=PSTTXA,PSTTXB/
```

OUTPUT

- T - T E S T -

VARIABLE	NUMBER OF CASES	MEAN	STANDARD DEVIATION	STANDARD ERROR	*(DIFFERENCE) MEAN	STANDARD DEVIATION	STANDARD ERROR	* 2-TAIL * CORR. PROB. *	T VALUE	DEGREES OF FREEDOM	2-TAIL PROB.
PSTTXA		83.7500	6.640	1.485	*			*			
	20				* 28.8500	4.344	.971	* .845 .000 *	29.70	19	.000
PSTTXB		54.9000	8.104	1.812	*			*			

----

7. From exercises 6 and 7, Chapter 12.

INPUT

```
TITLE           ONE-WAY ANOVA EXAMPLE WITH TEACHING METHODS
DATA LIST       FILE=INLINE RECORDS=1
                /METHOD 1 FINAL 3-4
BEGIN DATA
1 14
1 12
1 10
   .
   .
   .
4  2
4  2
4  2
END DATA
ONEWAY          FINAL BY METHOD(1,4)/
                CONTRAST 1 -1  0  0/        0172
                CONTRAST 0  0  1 -1/
                CONTRAST 1  1 -1 -1/
```

OUTPUT

ANALYSIS OF VARIANCE

SOURCE	D.F.	SUM OF SQUARES	MEAN SQUARES	F RATIO	F PROB.
BETWEEN GROUPS	3	232.8571	77.6190	9.8489	.0002
WITHIN GROUPS	24	189.1429	7.8810		
TOTAL	27	422.0000			

CONTRAST COEFFICIENT MATRIX

	GRP 1	GRP 2	GRP 3	GRP 4
CONTRAST 1	1.0	-1.0	.0	.0
CONTRAST 2	.0	.0	1.0	-1.0
CONTRAST 3	1.0	1.0	-1.0	-1.0

	VALUE	S. ERROR	POOLED VARIANCE ESTIMATE T VALUE	D.F.	T PROB.	S. ERROR	SEPARATE VARIANCE ESTIMATE T VALUE	D.F.	T PROB.
CONTRAST 1	-1.2857	1.5006	-.857	24.0	.400	1.8553	-.693	11.1	.502
CONTRAST 2	7.2857	1.5006	4.855	24.0	.000	1.0302	7.072	9.8	.000
CONTRAST 3	4.8571	2.1221	2.289	24.0	.031	2.1221	2.289	17.2	.035

8. From exercises 9 and 10, Chapter 12.

INPUT

```
TITLE           ONE-WAY ANOVA EXAMPLE WITH 30 SOPHOMORES
DATA LIST       FILE=INLINE RECORDS=1
                /METHOD 1 ATSCALE 3-4
BEGIN DATA
1 38
1 37
1 37
  .
  .
  .
3 23
3 21
3 21
END DATA
ONEWAY          ATSCALE BY METHOD(1,3)/
                RANGES=TUKEY
```

OUTPUT

ANALYSIS OF VARIANCE

SOURCE	D.F.	SUM OF SQUARES	MEAN SQUARES	F RATIO	F PROB.
BETWEEN GROUPS	2	281.2667	140.6333	9.1233	.0009
WITHIN GROUPS	27	416.2000	15.4148		
TOTAL	29	697.4667			

```
TUKEY-HSD PROCEDURE
RANGES FOR THE   .050 LEVEL -

        3.50    3.50

THE RANGES ABOVE ARE TABLE RANGES.
THE VALUE ACTUALLY COMPARED WITH MEAN(J)-MEAN(I) IS..
        2.7762 * RANGE * SQRT(1/N(I) + 1/N(J))


  (*) DENOTES PAIRS OF GROUPS SIGNIFICANTLY DIFFERENT AT THE   .050 LEVEL


                              G G G
                              R R R
                              P P P

      MEAN        GROUP       3 2 1

    26.4000      GRP 3
    30.1000      GRP 2
    33.9000      GRP 1       *


  HOMOGENEOUS SUBSETS   (SUBSETS OF GROUPS, WHOSE HIGHEST AND LOWEST MEANS
                         DO NOT DIFFER BY MORE THAN THE SHORTEST
                         SIGNIFICANT RANGE FOR A SUBSET OF THAT SIZE)


  SUBSET   1

  GROUP       GRP 3        GRP 2
  MEAN       26.4000      30.1000
  - -

  SUBSET   2

  GROUP       GRP 2        GRP 1
  MEAN       30.1000      33.9000
  - -
```

---

9. From exercise 1, Chapter 14.

INPUT

```
TITLE          TWO-WAY ANOVA EXAMPLE
DATA LIST      FILE=INLINE RECORDS=1
               /SEX 1 METH 3 SCORE 5-6
BEGIN DATA
1  1   8
1  1   9
1  1   9
       .
       .
       .
2  3  11
2  3   4
2  3   5
END DATA
ANOVA          SCORE BY SEX(1,2) METH(1,3)/
```

OUTPUT

SOURCE OF VARIATION	SUM OF SQUARES	DF	MEAN SQUARE	F	SIGNIF. OF F
MAIN EFFECTS	2.500	3	.833	.079	.971
SEX	2.400	1	2.400	.226	.636
METH	.100	2	.050	.005	.995
2-WAY INTERACTIONS	298.900	2	149.450	14.084	.000
SEX METH	298.900	2	149.450	14.084	.000
EXPLAINED	301.400	5	60.280	5.681	.000
RESIDUAL	573.000	54	10.611		
TOTAL	874.400	59	14.820		

---

10. From exercise 3, Chapter 14.

INPUT

```
TITLE          THREE-WAY ANOVA EXAMPLE
DATA LIST      FILE=INLINE RECORDS=1
               /A 1 B 3 C 5 Y 7-8
BEGIN DATA
1  1  1   9
1  1  1   9
1  1  1   8
          .
          .
          .
3  2  2   7
3  2  2   6
3  2  2   6
END DATA
ANOVA          Y BY A,B,C(1,3)/
```

OUTPUT

SOURCE OF VARIATION	SUM OF SQUARES	DF	MEAN SQUARE	F	SIGNIF. OF F
MAIN EFFECTS	123.600	4	30.900	7.318	.000
A	120.600	2	60.300	14.282	.000
B	2.700	1	2.700	.639	.426
C	.300	1	.300	.071	.790
2-WAY INTERACTIONS	63.500	5	12.700	3.008	.014
A B	13.400	2	6.700	1.587	.209
A C	25.800	2	12.900	3.055	.051
B C	24.300	1	24.300	5.755	.018
3-WAY INTERACTIONS	1.400	2	.700	.166	.847
A B C	1.400	2	.700	.166	.847
EXPLAINED	188.500	11	17.136	4.059	.000
RESIDUAL	456.000	108	4.222		
TOTAL	644.500	119	5.416		

11. From exercise 1, Chapter 16.

INPUT

```
TITLE          ELEMENTARY SCHOOL ANALYSIS OF COVARIANCE EXAMPLE
DATA LIST      FILE=INLINE RECORDS=1
               /GROUP 1 ARITH 3-4(1) VA 6-7 GEOM 9-10
BEGIN DATA
1 71 83 82
1 49 77 45
1 58 75 19
        .
        .
        .
2 36 62 14
2 52 56 29
2 57 62 39
END DATA
ANOVA          GEOM BY GROUP(1,2) WITH ARITH,VA/
```

OUTPUT

SOURCE OF VARIATION	SUM OF SQUARES	DF	MEAN SQUARE	F	SIGNIF OF F
COVARIATES	3335.530	2	1667.765	6.234	.008
ARITH	2325.538	1	2325.538	8.692	.008
VA	139.085	1	139.085	.520	.479
MAIN EFFECTS	30.291	1	30.291	.113	.740
GROUP	30.291	1	30.291	.113	.740
EXPLAINED	3365.821	3	1121.940	4.194	.019
RESIDUAL	5350.804	20	267.540		
TOTAL	8716.625	23	378.984		

---

12. From exercise 2, Chapter 16.

INPUT

```
TITLE          ANALYSIS OF COVARIANCE WITH TWO PREDICTORS AND COVARIATES
DATA LIST      FILE=INLINE RECORDS=1
               /A 1 B 3 X1 5 X2 7 Y 9
BEGIN DATA
1 1 5 9 9
1 1 5 9 6
1 1 4 9 6
       .
       .
       .
2 2 4 2 7
2 2 4 4 7
2 2 4 3 6
END DATA
ANOVA          Y BY A(1,2) B(1,2) WITH X1,X2/
```

OUTPUT

SOURCE OF VARIATION	SUM OF SQUARES	DF	MEAN SQUARE	F	SIGNIF. OF F
COVARIATES	26.272	2	13.136	17.261	.000
X1	22.244	1	22.244	29.229	.000
X2	1.031	1	1.031	1.355	.253
MAIN EFFECTS	152.400	2	76.200	100.126	.000
A	113.694	1	113.694	149.393	.000
B	6.677	1	6.677	8.773	.006
2-WAY INTERACTIONS	1.853	1	1.853	2.434	.128
A B	1.853	1	1.853	2.434	.128
EXPLAINED	180.525	5	36.105	47.442	.000
RESIDUAL	25.875	34	.761		
TOTAL	206.400	39	5.292		

---

13. From exercise 3, Chapter 19.

INPUT

```
TITLE           CHI-SQUARE TWO-SAMPLE TEST
DATA LIST       FILE=INLINE RECORDS=1
                /GROUP 1 ITEM 3 FREQ 5-6
BEGIN DATA
1 1 60
1 2 50
1 3 40
    .
    .
    .
2 2 10
2 3 30
2 4 30
END DATA
WEIGHT          BY FREQ
CROSSTABS       TABLES=GROUP BY ITEM
OPTIONS         14
STATISTICS      1
```

OUTPUT

```
                    ITEM
           COUNT  I
           EXP VAL I
                  I                                      ROW
                  I                                      TOTAL
                  I     1I      2I      3I      4I
GROUP      --------+-------+-------+-------+-------+
              1  I   60  I   50  I   40  I   50  I   200
                 I 44.4  I 44.4  I 51.9  I 59.3  I  74.1P
                 +-------+-------+-------+-------+
              2  I    0  I   10  I   30  I   30  I    70
                 I 15.6  I 15.6  I 18.1  I 20.7  I  25.9P
                 +-------+-------+-------+-------+
           COLUMN     60      60      70      80     270
           TOTAL   22.2P   22.2P   25.9P   29.6P  100.0P


CHI-SQUARE    D.F.     SIGNIFICANCE      MIN E.F.    CELLS WITH E.F.< 5
----------    ----     ------------      --------    ------------------

 39.70791      3          .0000           15.556            NONE
```

14a. From exercise 5, Chapter 19.

INPUT

```
TITLE           ELEMENTARY SCHOOL WILCOXON EXAMPLE
DATA LIST       FILE=INLINE RECORDS=1
                /MATX 1-2 MATZ 4-5
BEGIN DATA
28 31
33 35
40 39
  .
  .
  .
21 26
32 30
43 56
END DATA
NONPAR TESTS    WILCOXON=MATX WITH MATZ
```

OUTPUT

```
MEAN RANK      CASES

    1.75         2  -  RANKS (MATZ LT MATX)
    6.44         8  +  RANKS (MATZ GT MATX)
                 0     TIES  (MATZ EQ MATX)
                --
                10     TOTAL

     Z =  -2.4463          2-TAILED P =   .0144
```

14b. From exercise 6, Chapter 19.

INPUT

```
TITLE          SIGN TEST EXAMPLE WITH READING GROUPS
DATA LIST      FILE=INLINE RECORDS=1
               /CON 1 AUG 3
BEGIN DATA
O 1
O 1
O 1
  .
  .
  .
O 1
1 O
1 O
END DATA
NONPAR TESTS   SIGN=CON WITH AUG
OPTION         6
```

OUTPUT

```
CASES

    2  -  DIFFS (AUG LT CON)
   10  +  DIFFS (AUG GT CON)        (BINOMIAL)
    O     TIES                      2-TAILED P =      .0386
   --
   12     TOTAL
```

14c. From exercise 7, Chapter 19.

INPUT

```
TITLE          MANN-WHITNEY EXAMPLE: ONE-TAILED TEST
DATA LIST      FILE=INLINE RECORDS=1
               /GROUP 1 SCORE 3-4
BEGIN DATA
1  2
1  3
1  5
   .
   .
   .
2  1
2  4
2  4
END DATA
NONPAR TESTS   M-W=SCORE BY GROUP(1,2)
```

OUTPUT

```
MEAN RANK     CASES

    7.43       7   GROUP = 1
    3.50       4   GROUP = 2
              --
              11   TOTAL

                        EXACT            CORRECTED FOR TIES
     U        W      2-TAILED P       Z       2-TAILED P
    4.0      14.0      .0727       -1.9028      .0571
```

14d. From exercise 9, Chapter 19.

INPUT

```
TITLE             FRIEDMAN EXAMPLE WITH INSTRUCTIONAL TECHNIQUES
DATA LIST         FILE=INLINE RECORDS=1
                  /IT1 1 IT2 3 IT3 5 IT4 7
BEGIN DATA
4  2  1  3
4  3  1  2
4  3  1  1
END DATA
NONPAR TESTS      FRIEDMAN=IT1 IT2 IT3 IT4
```

OUTPUT

```
MEAN RANK    VARIABLE

    4.00     IT1
    2.67     IT2
    1.17     IT3
    2.17     IT4

    CASES          CHI-SQUARE      D.F.    SIGNIFICANCE
      3             7.5000          3           .0576
```

14e. From exercise 10, Chapter 19.

INPUT

```
TITLE             SECONDARY TEACHER KRUSKAL-WALLIS EXAMPLE
DATA LIST         FILE=INLINE RECORDS=1
                  /MAJOR 1 SCORE 3-4
BEGIN DATA
1  64
1  63
1  58
  .
  .
  .
3  59
3  42
3  29
END DATA
NONPAR TESTS      K-W=SCORE BY MAJOR(1,3)
```

OUTPUT

```
MEAN RANK    CASES

    8.00        5     MAJOR = 1
    5.63        4     MAJOR = 2
    5.17        3     MAJOR = 3
               --
               12     TOTAL

                                        CORRECTED FOR TIES
    CASES    CHI-SQUARE   SIGNIFICANCE   CHI-SQUARE   SIGNIFICANCE
     12        1.5112        .4697         1.5165        .4685
```

15. From exercise 12, Chapter 19.

INPUT

```
TITLE           SPEARMAN CORRELATION: ESSAY RANKING
DATA LIST       FILE=INLINE RECORDS=1
                /T1RNK 1 T2RNK 3
BEGIN DATA
1 1
3 2
2 3
   .
   .
   .
4 5
6 6
7 7
END DATA
NONPAR CORR     T1RNK WITH T2RNK
OPTION          6
```

OUTPUT

```
                T2RNK

T1RNK            .9286
                N(   7)
                SIG .001
```

Appendix
Tables

Table A   **Areas and Ordinates of the Normal Curve in Terms of x/σ**

(1) z Standard Score $\left(\dfrac{x}{\sigma}\right)$	(2) A Area from Mean to $\dfrac{x}{\sigma}$	(3) B Area in Larger Portion	(4) C Area in Smaller Portion	(5) y Ordinate at $\dfrac{x}{\sigma}$
0.00	.0000	.5000	.5000	.3989
0.01	.0040	.5040	.4960	.3989
0.02	.0080	.5080	.4920	.3989
0.03	.0120	.5120	.4880	.3988
0.04	.0160	.5160	.4840	.3986
0.05	.0199	.5199	.4801	.3984
0.06	.0239	.5239	.4761	.3982
0.07	.0279	.5279	.4721	.3980
0.08	.0319	.5319	.4681	.3977
0.09	.0359	.5359	.4641	.3973
0.10	.0398	.5398	.4602	.3970
0.11	.0438	.5438	.4562	.3965
0.12	.0478	.5478	.4522	.3961
0.13	.0517	.5517	.4483	.3956
0.14	.0557	.5557	.4443	.3951
0.15	.0596	.5596	.4404	.3945
0.16	.0636	.5636	.4364	.3939
0.17	.0675	.5675	.4325	.3932
0.18	.0714	.5714	.4286	.3925
0.19	.0753	.5753	.4247	.3918
0.20	.0793	.5793	.4207	.3910
0.21	.0832	.5832	.4168	.3902
0.22	.0871	.5871	.4129	.3894
0.23	.0910	.5910	.4090	.3885
0.24	.0948	.5948	.4052	.3876
0.25	.0987	.5987	.4013	.3867
0.26	.1026	.6026	.3974	.3857
0.27	.1064	.6064	.3936	.3847
0.28	.1103	.6103	.3897	.3836
0.29	.1141	.6141	.3859	.3825
0.30	.1179	.6179	.3821	.3814
0.31	.1217	.6217	.3783	.3802
0.32	.1255	.6255	.3745	.3790
0.33	.1293	.6293	.3707	.3790
0.34	.1331	.6331	.3669	.3765
0.35	.1368	.6368	.3632	.3752
0.36	.1406	.6406	.3594	.3739
0.37	.1443	.6443	.3557	.3725
0.38	.1480	.6480	.3520	.3712
0.39	.1517	.6517	.3483	.3697
0.40	.1554	.6554	.3446	.3683
0.41	.1591	.6591	.3409	.3668
0.42	.1628	.6628	.3372	.3653
0.43	.1664	.6664	.3336	.3637
0.44	.1700	.6700	.3300	.3621

Source: A. L. Edwards, *Statistical Methods for the Behavioral Sciences,* Holt, Rinehart and Winston, Inc., ©1954, pp. 490–99.

Table A (continued)

(1) z Standard Score $\left(\frac{x}{\sigma}\right)$	(2) A Area from Mean to $\frac{x}{\sigma}$	(3) B Area in Larger Portion	(4) C Area in Smaller Portion	(5) y Ordinate at $\frac{x}{\sigma}$
0.45	.1736	.6736	.3264	.3605
0.46	.1772	.6772	.3228	.3589
0.47	.1808	.6808	.3192	.3572
0.48	.1844	.6844	.3156	.3555
0.49	.1879	.6879	.3121	.3538
0.50	.1915	.6915	.3085	.3521
0.51	.1950	.6950	.3050	.3503
0.52	.1985	.6985	.3015	.3485
0.53	.2019	.7019	.2981	.3467
0.54	.2054	.7054	.2946	.3448
0.55	.2088	.7088	.2912	.3429
0.56	.2123	.7123	.2877	.3410
0.57	.2157	.7157	.2843	.3391
0.58	.2190	.7190	.2810	.3372
0.59	.2224	.7224	.2776	.3352
0.60	.2257	.7257	.2743	.3332
0.61	.2291	.7291	.2709	.3312
0.62	.2324	.7324	.2676	.3292
0.63	.2357	.7357	.2643	.3271
0.64	.2389	.7389	.2611	.3251
0.65	.2422	.7422	.2578	.3230
0.66	.2454	.7454	.2546	.3209
0.67	.2486	.7486	.2514	.3187
0.68	.2517	.7517	.2483	.3166
0.69	.2549	.7549	.2451	.3144
0.70	.2580	.7580	.2420	.3123
0.71	.2611	.7611	.2389	.3101
0.72	.2642	.7642	.2358	.3079
0.73	.2673	.7673	.2327	.3056
0.74	.2704	.7704	.2296	.3034
0.75	.2734	.7734	.2266	.3011
0.76	.2764	.7764	.2236	.2989
0.77	.2794	.7794	.2206	.2966
0.78	.2823	.7823	.2177	.2943
0.79	.2852	.7852	.2148	.2920
0.80	.2881	.7881	.2119	.2897
0.81	.2910	.7910	.2090	.2874
0.82	.2939	.7939	.2061	.2850
0.83	.2967	.7967	.2033	.2827
0.84	.2995	.7995	.2005	.2803
0.85	.3023	.8023	.1977	.2780
0.86	.3051	.8051	.1949	.2756
0.87	.3078	.8078	.1922	.2732
0.88	.3106	.8106	.1894	.2709
0.89	.3133	.8133	.1867	.2685

Table A   (continued)

(1) z Standard Score $\left(\dfrac{x}{\sigma}\right)$	(2) A Area from Mean to $\dfrac{x}{\sigma}$	(3) B Area in Larger Portion	(4) C Area in Smaller Portion	(5) y Ordinate at $\dfrac{x}{\sigma}$
0.90	.3159	.8159	.1841	.2661
0.91	.3186	.8186	.1814	.2637
0.92	.3212	.8212	.1788	.2613
0.93	.3238	.8238	.1762	.2589
0.94	.3264	.8264	.1736	.2565
0.95	.3289	.8289	.1711	.2541
0.96	.3315	.8315	.1685	.2516
0.97	.3340	.8340	.1660	.2492
0.98	.3365	.8365	.1635	.2468
0.99	.3389	.8389	.1611	.2444
1.00	.3413	.8413	.1587	.2420
1.01	.3438	.8438	.1562	.2396
1.02	.3461	.8461	.1539	.2371
1.03	.3485	.8485	.1515	.2347
1.04	.3508	.8508	.1492	.2323
1.05	.3531	.8531	.1469	.2299
1.06	.3554	.8554	.1446	.2275
1.07	.3577	.8577	.1423	.2251
1.08	.3599	.8599	.1401	.2227
1.09	.3621	.8621	.1379	.2203
1.10	.3643	.8643	.1357	.2179
1.11	.3665	.8665	.1335	.2155
1.12	.3686	.8686	.1314	.2131
1.13	.3708	.8708	.1292	.2107
1.14	.3729	.8729	.1271	.2083
1.15	.3749	.8749	.1251	.2059
1.16	.3770	.8770	.1230	.2036
1.17	.3790	.8790	.1210	.2012
1.18	.3810	.8810	.1190	.1989
1.19	.3830	.8830	.1170	.1965
1.20	.3849	.8849	.1151	.1942
1.21	.3869	.8869	.1131	.1919
1.22	.3888	.8888	.1112	.1895
1.23	.3907	.8907	.1093	.1872
1.24	.3925	.8925	.1075	.1849
1.25	.3944	.8944	.1056	.1826
1.26	.3962	.8962	.1038	.1804
1.27	.3980	.8980	.1020	.1781
1.28	.3997	.8997	.1003	.1758
1.29	.4015	.9015	.0985	.1736
1.30	.4032	.9032	.0968	.1714
1.31	.4049	.9049	.0951	.1691
1.32	.4066	.9066	.0934	.1669
1.33	.4082	.9082	.0918	.1647
1.34	.4099	.9099	.0901	.1626

Table A (continued)

(1) z Standard Score $\left(\dfrac{x}{\sigma}\right)$	(2) A Area from Mean to $\dfrac{x}{\sigma}$	(3) B Area in Larger Portion	(4) C Area in Smaller Portion	(5) y Ordinate at $\dfrac{x}{\sigma}$
1.35	.4115	.9115	.0885	.1604
1.36	.4131	.9131	.0869	.1582
1.37	.4147	.9147	.0853	.1561
1.38	.4162	.9162	.0838	.1539
1.39	.4177	.9177	.0823	.1518
1.40	.4192	.9192	.0808	.1497
1.41	.4207	.9207	.0793	.1476
1.42	.4222	.9222	.0778	.1456
1.43	.4236	.9236	.0764	.1435
1.44	.4251	.9251	.0749	.1415
1.45	.4265	.9265	.0735	.1394
1.46	.4279	.9279	.0721	.1374
1.47	.4292	.9292	.0708	.1354
1.48	.4306	.9306	.0694	.1334
1.49	.4319	.9319	.0681	.1315
1.50	.4332	.9332	.0668	.1295
1.51	.4345	.9345	.0655	.1276
1.52	.4357	.9357	.0643	.1257
1.53	.4370	.9370	.0630	.1238
1.54	.4382	.9382	.0618	.1219
1.55	.4394	.9394	.0606	.1200
1.56	.4406	.9406	.0594	.1182
1.57	.4418	.9418	.0582	.1163
1.58	.4429	.9429	.0571	.1145
1.59	.4441	.9441	.0559	.1127
1.60	.4452	.9452	.0548	.1109
1.61	.4463	.9463	.0537	.1092
1.62	.4474	.9474	.0526	.1074
1.63	.4484	.9484	.0516	.1057
1.64	.4495	.9495	.0505	.1040
1.65	.4505	.9505	.0495	.1023
1.66	.4515	.9515	.0485	.1006
1.67	.4525	.9525	.0475	.0989
1.68	.4535	.9535	.0465	.0973
1.69	.4545	.9545	.0455	.0957
1.70	.4554	.9554	.0446	.0940
1.71	.4564	.9564	.0436	.0925
1.72	.4573	.9573	.0427	.0909
1.73	.4582	.9582	.0418	.0893
1.74	.4591	.9591	.0409	.0878
1.75	.4599	.9599	.0401	.0863
1.76	.4608	.9608	.0392	.0848
1.77	.4616	.9616	.0384	.0833
1.78	.4625	.9625	.0375	.0818
1.79	.4633	.9633	.0367	.0804

Table A   **(continued)**

(1) z Standard Score $\left(\dfrac{x}{\sigma}\right)$	(2) A Area from Mean to $\dfrac{x}{\sigma}$	(3) B Area in Larger Portion	(4) C Area in Smaller Portion	(5) y Ordinate at $\dfrac{x}{\sigma}$
1.80	.4641	.9641	.0359	.0790
1.81	.4649	.9649	.0351	.0775
1.82	.4656	.9656	.0344	.0761
1.83	.4664	.9664	.0336	.0748
1.84	.4671	.9671	.0329	.0734
1.85	.4678	.9678	.0322	.0721
1.86	.4686	.9686	.0314	.0707
1.87	.4693	.9693	.0307	.0694
1.88	.4699	.9699	.0301	.0681
1.89	.4706	.9706	.0294	.0669
1.90	.4713	.9713	.0287	.0656
1.91	.4719	.9719	.0281	.0644
1.92	.4726	.9726	.0274	.0632
1.93	.4732	.9732	.0268	.0620
1.94	.4738	.9738	.0262	.0608
1.95	.4744	.9744	.0256	.0596
1.96	.4750	.9750	.0250	.0584
1.97	.4756	.9756	.0244	.0573
1.98	.4761	.9761	.0239	.0562
1.99	.4767	.9767	.0233	.0551
2.00	.4772	.9772	.0228	.0540
2.01	.4778	.9778	.0222	.0529
2.02	.4783	.9783	.0217	.0519
2.03	.4788	.9788	.0212	.0508
2.04	.4793	.9793	.0207	.0498
2.05	.4798	.9798	.0202	.0488
2.06	.4803	.9803	.0197	.0478
2.07	.4808	.9808	.0192	.0468
2.08	.4812	.9812	.0188	.0459
2.09	.4817	.9817	.0183	.0449
2.10	.4821	.9821	.0179	.0440
2.11	.4826	.9826	.0174	.0431
2.12	.4830	.9830	.0170	.0422
2.13	.4834	.9834	.0166	.0413
2.14	.4838	.9838	.0162	.0404
2.15	.4842	.9842	.0158	.0396
2.16	.4846	.9846	.0154	.0387
2.17	.4850	.9850	.0150	.0379
2.18	.4854	.9854	.0146	.0371
2.19	.4857	.9857	.0143	.0363
2.20	.4861	.9861	.0139	.0355
2.21	.4864	.9864	.0136	.0347
2.22	.4868	.9868	.0132	.0339
2.23	.4871	.9871	.0129	.0332
2.24	.4875	.9875	.0125	.0325

Table A   **(continued)**

(1) z Standard Score $\left(\dfrac{x}{\sigma}\right)$	(2) A Area from Mean to $\dfrac{x}{\sigma}$	(3) B Area in Larger Portion	(4) C Area in Smaller Portion	(5) y Ordinate at $\dfrac{x}{\sigma}$
2.25	.4878	.9878	.0122	.0317
2.26	.4881	.9881	.0119	.0310
2.27	.4884	.9884	.0116	.0303
2.28	.4887	.9887	.0113	.0297
2.29	.4890	.9890	.0110	.0290
2.30	.4893	.9893	.0107	.0283
2.31	.4896	.9896	.0104	.0277
2.32	.4898	.9898	.0102	.0270
2.33	.4901	.9901	.0099	.0264
2.34	.4904	.9904	.0096	.0258
2.35	.4906	.9906	.0094	.0252
2.36	.4909	.9909	.0091	.0246
2.37	.4911	.9911	.0089	.0241
2.38	.4913	.9913	.0087	.0235
2.39	.4916	.9916	.0084	.0229
2.40	.4918	.9918	.0082	.0224
2.41	.4920	.9920	.0080	.0219
2.42	.4922	.9922	.0078	.0213
2.43	.4925	.9925	.0075	.0208
2.44	.4927	.9927	.0073	.0203
2.45	.4929	.9929	.0071	.0198
2.46	.4931	.9931	.0069	.0194
2.47	.4932	.9932	.0068	.0189
2.48	.4934	.9934	.0066	.0184
2.49	.4936	.9936	.0064	.0180
2.50	.4938	.9938	.0062	.0175
2.51	.4940	.9940	.0060	.0171
2.52	.4941	.9941	.0059	.0167
2.53	.4943	.9943	.0057	.0163
2.54	.4945	.9945	.0055	.0158
2.55	.4946	.9946	.0054	.0154
2.56	.4948	.9948	.0052	.0151
2.57	.4949	.9949	.0051	.0147
2.58	.4951	.9951	.0049	.0143
2.59	.4952	.9952	.0048	.0139
2.60	.4953	.9953	.0047	.0136
2.61	.4955	.9955	.0045	.0132
2.62	.4956	.9956	.0044	.0129
2.63	.4957	.9957	.0043	.0126
2.64	.4959	.9959	.0041	.0122
2.65	.4960	.9960	.0040	.0119
2.66	.4961	.9961	.0039	.0116
2.67	.4962	.9962	.0038	.0113
2.68	.4963	.9963	.0037	.0110
2.69	.4964	.9964	.0036	.0107

Table A **(continued)**

(1) z Standard Score $\left(\dfrac{x}{\sigma}\right)$	(2) A Area from Mean to $\dfrac{x}{\sigma}$	(3) B Area in Larger Portion	(4) C Area in Smaller Portion	(5) y Ordinate at $\dfrac{x}{\sigma}$
2.70	.4965	.9965	.0035	.0104
2.71	.4966	.9966	.0034	.0101
2.72	.4967	.9967	.0033	.0099
2.73	.4968	.9968	.0032	.0096
2.74	.4969	.9969	.0031	.0093
2.75	.4970	.9970	.0030	.0091
2.76	.4971	.9971	.0029	.0088
2.77	.4972	.9972	.0028	.0086
2.78	.4973	.9973	.0027	.0084
2.79	.4974	.9974	.0026	.0081
2.80	.4974	.9974	.0026	.0079
2.81	.4975	.9975	.0025	.0077
2.82	.4976	.9976	.0024	.0075
2.83	.4977	.9977	.0023	.0073
2.84	.4977	.9977	.0023	.0071
2.85	.4978	.9978	.0022	.0069
2.86	.4979	.9979	.0021	.0067
2.87	.4979	.9979	.0021	.0065
2.88	.4980	.9980	.0020	.0063
2.89	.4981	.9981	.0019	.0061
2.90	.4981	.9981	.0019	.0060
2.91	.4982	.9982	.0018	.0058
2.92	.4982	.9982	.0018	.0056
2.93	.4983	.9983	.0017	.0055
2.94	.4984	.9984	.0016	.0053
2.95	.4984	.9984	.0016	.0051
2.96	.4985	.9985	.0015	.0050
2.97	.4985	.9985	.0015	.0048
2.98	.4986	.9986	.0014	.0047
2.99	.4986	.9986	.0014	.0046
3.00	.4987	.9987	.0013	.0044
3.01	.4987	.9987	.0013	.0043
3.02	.4987	.9987	.0013	.0042
3.03	.4988	.9988	.0012	.0040
3.04	.4988	.9988	.0012	.0039
3.05	.4989	.9989	.0011	.0038
3.06	.4989	.9989	.0011	.0037
3.07	.4989	.9989	.0011	.0036
3.08	.4990	.9990	.0010	.0035
3.09	.4990	.9990	.0010	.0034
3.10	.4990	.9990	.0010	.0033
3.11	.4991	.9991	.0009	.0032
3.12	.4991	.9991	.0009	.0031
3.13	.4991	.9991	.0009	.0030
3.14	.4992	.9992	.0008	.0029

Table A   **(continued)**

(1) z Standard Score $\left(\frac{x}{\sigma}\right)$	(2) A Area from Mean to $\frac{x}{\sigma}$	(3) B Area in Larger Portion	(4) C Area in Smaller Portion	(5) y Ordinate at $\frac{x}{\sigma}$
3.15	.4992	.9992	.0008	.0028
3.16	.4992	.9992	.0008	.0027
3.17	.4992	.9992	.0008	.0026
3.18	.4993	.9993	.0007	.0025
3.19	.4993	.9993	.0007	.0025
3.20	.4993	.9993	.0007	.0024
3.21	.4993	.9993	.0007	.0023
3.22	.4994	.9994	.0006	.0022
3.23	.4994	.9994	.0006	.0022
3.24	.4994	.9994	.0006	.0021
3.30	.4995	.9995	.0005	.0017
3.40	.4997	.9997	.0003	.0012
3.50	.4998	.9998	.0002	.0009
3.60	.4998	.9998	.0002	.0006
3.70	.4999	.9999	.0001	.0004

Table B   **Table of Random Numbers**

Row	COLUMN NUMBER							
	00000 01234	00000 56789	11111 01234	11111 56789	22222 01234	22222 56789	33333 01234	33333 56789
				1st Thousand				
00	23157	54859	01837	25993	76249	70886	95230	36744
01	05545	55043	10537	43508	90611	83744	10962	21343
02	14871	60350	32404	36223	50051	00322	11543	80834
03	38976	74951	94051	75853	78805	90194	32428	71695
04	97312	61718	99755	30870	94251	25841	54882	10513
05	11742	69381	44339	30872	32797	33118	22647	06850
06	43361	28859	11016	45623	93009	00499	43640	74036
07	93806	20478	38268	04491	55751	18932	58475	52571
08	49540	13181	08429	84187	69538	29661	77738	09527
09	36768	72633	37948	21569	41959	68670	45274	83880
10	07092	52392	24627	12067	06558	45344	67338	45320
11	43310	01081	44863	80307	52555	16148	89742	94647
12	61570	06360	06173	63775	63148	95123	35017	46993
13	31352	83799	10779	18941	31579	76448	62584	86919
14	57048	86526	27795	93692	90529	56546	35065	32254
15	09243	44200	68721	07137	30729	75756	09298	27650
16	97957	35018	40894	88329	52230	82521	22532	61587
17	93732	59570	43781	98885	56671	66826	95996	44569
18	72621	11225	00922	68264	35666	59434	71687	58167
19	61020	74418	45371	20794	95917	37866	99536	19378
20	97839	85474	33055	91718	45473	54144	22034	23000
21	89160	97192	22232	90637	35055	45489	88438	16361
22	25966	88220	62871	79265	02823	52862	84919	54883
23	81443	31719	05049	54806	74690	07567	65017	16543
24	11322	54931	42362	34386	08624	97687	46245	23245
				2nd Thousand				
00	64755	83885	84122	25920	17696	15655	95045	95947
01	10302	52289	77436	34430	38112	49067	07348	23328
02	71017	98495	51308	50374	66591	02887	53765	69149
03	60012	55605	88410	34879	79655	90169	78800	03666
04	37330	94656	49161	42802	48274	54755	44553	65090
05	47869	87001	31591	12273	60626	12822	34691	61212
06	38040	42737	64167	89578	39323	49324	88434	38706
07	73508	30908	83054	80078	86669	30295	56460	45336
08	32623	46474	84061	04324	20628	37319	32356	43969
09	97591	99549	36630	35106	62069	92975	95320	57734
10	74012	31955	59790	96982	66224	24015	96749	07589
11	56754	26457	13351	05014	90966	33674	69096	33488
12	49800	49908	54831	21998	08528	26372	92923	65026
13	43584	89647	24878	56670	00221	50193	99591	62377
14	16653	79664	60325	71301	35742	83636	73058	87229
15	48502	69055	65322	58748	31446	80237	31252	96367
16	96765	54692	36316	86230	48296	38352	23816	64094
17	38923	61550	80357	81784	23444	12463	33992	28128
18	77958	81694	25225	05587	51073	01070	60218	61961
19	17928	28065	25586	08771	02641	85064	65796	48170
20	94036	85978	02318	04499	41054	10531	87431	21596
21	47460	60479	56230	48417	14372	85167	27558	00368
22	47856	56088	51992	82439	40644	17170	13463	18288
23	57616	34653	92298	62018	10375	76515	62986	90756
24	08300	92704	66752	66610	57188	79107	54222	22013

Source: M. G. Kendall and B. B. Smith, "Randomness and Random Sampling Numbers," *Journal of the Royal Statistical Society,* vol. 101 (1938), pp. 147–66. By permission of the Royal Statistical Society.

Table B   (continued)

Row	COLUMN NUMBER							
	00000 01234	00000 56789	11111 01234	11111 56789	22222 01234	22222 56789	33333 01234	33333 56789

3rd Thousand

Row								
00	89221	02362	65787	74733	51272	30213	92441	39651
01	04005	99818	63918	29032	94012	42363	01261	10650
02	98546	38066	50856	75045	40645	22841	53254	44125
03	41719	84401	59226	01314	54581	40398	49988	65579
04	28733	72489	00785	25843	24613	49797	85567	84471
05	65213	83927	77762	03086	80742	24395	68476	83792
06	65553	12678	90906	90466	43670	26217	69900	31205
07	05668	69080	73029	85746	58332	78231	45986	92998
08	39302	99718	49757	79519	27387	76373	47262	91612
09	64592	32254	45879	29431	38320	05981	18067	87137
10	07513	48792	47314	83660	68907	05336	82579	91582
11	86593	68501	56638	99800	82839	35148	56541	07232
12	83735	22599	97977	81248	36838	99560	32410	67614
13	08595	21826	54655	08204	87990	17033	56258	05384
14	41273	27149	44293	69458	16828	63962	15864	35431
15	00473	75908	56238	12242	72631	76314	47252	06347
16	86131	53789	81383	07868	89132	96182	07009	86432
17	33849	78359	08402	03586	03176	88663	08018	22546
18	61870	41657	07468	08612	98083	97349	20775	45091
19	43898	65923	25078	86129	78491	97653	91500	80786
20	29939	39123	04548	45985	60952	06641	28726	46473
21	38505	85555	14388	55077	18657	94887	67831	70819
22	31824	38431	67125	25511	72044	11562	53279	82268
23	91430	03767	13561	15597	06750	92552	02391	38753
24	38635	68976	25498	97526	96458	03805	04116	63514

4th Thousand

Row								
00	02490	54122	27944	39364	94239	72074	11679	54082
01	11967	36469	60627	83701	09253	30208	01385	37482
02	48256	83465	49699	24079	05403	35154	39613	03136
03	27246	73080	21481	23536	04881	89977	49484	93071
04	32532	77265	72430	70722	86529	18457	92657	10011
05	66757	98955	92375	93431	43204	55825	45443	69265
06	11266	34545	76505	97746	34668	26999	26742	97516
07	17872	39142	45561	80146	93137	48924	64257	59284
08	62561	30365	03408	14754	51798	08133	61010	97730
09	62796	30779	35497	70501	30105	08133	00997	91970
10	75510	21771	04339	33660	42757	62223	87565	48468
11	87439	01691	63517	26590	44437	07217	98706	39032
12	97742	02621	10748	78803	38337	65226	92149	59051
13	98811	06001	21571	02875	21828	83912	85188	61624
14	51264	01852	64607	92553	29004	26695	78583	62998
15	40239	93376	10419	68610	49120	02941	80035	99317
16	26936	59186	51667	27645	46329	44681	94190	66647
17	88502	11716	98299	40974	42394	62200	69094	81646
18	63499	38093	25593	61995	79867	80569	01023	38374
19	36379	81206	03317	78710	73828	31083	60509	44091
20	93801	22322	47479	57017	59334	30647	43061	26660
21	29856	87120	56311	50053	25365	81265	22414	02431
22	97720	87931	88265	13050	71017	15177	06957	92919
23	85237	09105	74601	46377	59938	15647	34177	92753
24	75746	75268	31727	95773	72364	87324	36879	06802

Table B   (continued)

Row	COLUMN NUMBER							
	00000 01234	00000 56789	11111 01234	11111 56789	22222 01234	22222 56789	33333 01234	33333 56789
				5th Thousand				
00	29935	06971	63175	52579	10478	89379	61428	21363
01	15114	07126	51890	77787	75510	13103	42942	48111
02	03870	43225	10589	87629	22039	94124	38127	65022
03	79390	39188	40756	45269	65959	20640	14284	22960
04	30035	06915	79196	54428	64819	52314	48721	81594
05	29039	99861	28759	79802	68531	39198	38137	24373
06	78196	08108	24107	49777	09599	43569	84820	94956
07	15847	85493	91442	91351	80130	73752	21539	10986
08	36614	62248	49194	97209	92587	92053	41021	80064
09	40549	54884	91465	43862	35541	44466	88894	74180
10	40878	08997	14286	09982	90308	78007	51587	16658
11	10229	49282	41173	31468	59455	18756	08908	06660
12	15918	76787	30624	25928	44124	25088	31137	71614
13	13403	18796	49909	94404	64979	41462	18155	98335
14	66523	94596	74908	90271	10009	98648	17640	68909
15	91665	36469	68343	17870	25975	04662	21272	50620
16	67415	87515	08207	73729	73201	57593	96917	69699
17	76527	96996	23724	33448	63392	32394	60887	90617
18	19815	47789	74348	17147	10954	34355	81194	54407
19	25592	53587	76384	72575	84347	68918	05739	57222
20	55902	45539	63646	31609	95999	82887	40666	66692
21	02470	58376	79794	22482	42423	96162	47491	17264
22	18630	53263	13319	97619	35859	12350	14632	87659
23	89673	38230	16063	92007	59503	38402	76450	33333
24	62986	67364	06595	17427	84623	14565	82860	57300

Table C **Values of the Correlation Coefficient (Pearson's *r*) for Different Levels of Significance**

df	p = .10	.05	.02	.01
1	.988	.997	.9995	.9999
2	.900	.950	.980	.990
3	.805	.878	.934	.959
4	.729	.811	.882	.917
5	.669	.754	.833	.874
6	.622	.707	.789	.834
7	.582	.666	.750	.798
8	.549	.632	.716	.765
9	.521	.602	.685	.735
10	.497	.576	.658	.708
11	.476	.553	.634	.684
12	.458	.532	.612	.661
13	.441	.514	.592	.641
14	.426	.497	.574	.623
15	.412	.482	.558	.606
16	.400	.468	.542	.590
17	.389	.456	.528	.575
18	.378	.444	.516	.561
19	.369	.433	.503	.549
20	.360	.423	.492	.537
21	.352	.413	.482	.526
22	.344	.404	.472	.515
23	.337	.396	.462	.505
24	.330	.388	.453	.496
25	.323	.381	.445	.487
26	.317	.374	.437	.479
27	.311	.367	.430	.471
28	.306	.361	.423	.463
29	.301	.355	.416	.456
30	.296	.349	.409	.449
35	.275	.325	.381	.418
40	.257	.304	.358	.393
45	.243	.288	.338	.372
50	.231	.273	.322	.354
60	.211	.250	.295	.325
70	.195	.232	.274	.302
80	.183	.217	.256	.283
90	.173	.205	.242	.267
100	.164	.195	.230	.254

Additional values of *r* at the 5 and 1 percent levels of significance

df	.05	.01	df	.05	.01	df	.05	.01
32	.339	.436	48	.279	.361	150	.159	.208
34	.329	.424	55	.261	.338	175	.148	.193
36	.320	.413	65	.241	.313	200	.138	.181
38	.312	.403	75	.224	.292	300	.113	.148
42	.297	.384	85	.211	.275	400	.098	.128
44	.291	.376	95	.200	.260	500	.088	.115
46	.284	.368	125	.174	.228	1,000	.062	.081

Source: Table C is reprinted from Table VA in Fisher & Yates, *Statistical Methods for Research Workers*, published by Oliver and Boyd Ltd., Edinburgh, and by permission of the author and publishers.

Note: The probabilities given are for a two-tailed test of significance, that is with the sign of *r* ignored. For a one-tailed test of significance, the tabled probabilities should be halved.

Table D   **Conversion of a Pearson's *r* into a Corresponding Fisher's z_r Coefficient**

r	*z*	*r*	*z*	*r*	*z*	*r*	*z*	*r*	*z*	*r*	*z*
.25	.26	.40	.42	.55	.62	.70	.87	.85	1.26	.950	1.83
.26	.27	.41	.44	.56	.63	.71	.89	.86	1.29	.955	1.89
.27	.28	.42	.45	.57	.65	.72	.91	.87	1.33	.960	1.95
.28	.29	.43	.46	.58	.66	.73	.93	.88	1.38	.965	2.01
.29	.30	.44	.47	.59	.68	.74	.95	.89	1.42	.970	2.09
.30	.31	.45	.48	.60	.69	.75	.97	.90	1.47	.975	2.18
.31	.32	.46	.50	.61	.71	.76	1.00	.905	1.50	.980	2.30
.32	.33	.47	.51	.62	.73	.77	1.02	.910	1.53	.985	2.44
.33	.34	.48	.52	.63	.74	.78	1.05	.915	1.56	.990	2.65
.34	.35	.49	.54	.64	.76	.79	1.07	.920	1.59	.995	2.99
.35	.37	.50	.55	.65	.78	.80	1.10	.925	1.62		
.36	.38	.51	.56	.66	.79	.81	1.13	.930	1.66		
.37	.39	.52	.58	.67	.81	.82	1.16	.935	1.70		
.38	.40	.53	.59	.68	.83	.83	1.19	.940	1.74		
.39	.41	.54	.60	.69	.85	.84	1.22	.945	1.78		

Source: The values in this table were derived from Table VB in Fisher & Yates, *Statistical Methods for Research Workers,* published by Oliver & Boyd Ltd., Edinburgh, and by permission of the authors and publishers.

Note: For all values of *r* below 0.25, *r* = *z* to two decimal places.

Table E   Distribution of *t*

	Level of significance for two-tailed test					
	.10	.05	.025	.01	.005	.0005
df	Level of significance for two-tailed test					
	.20	.10	.05	.02	.01	.001
1	3.078	6.314	12.706	31.821	63.657	636.619
2	1.886	2.920	4.303	6.965	9.925	31.598
3	1.638	2.353	3.182	4.541	5.841	12.941
4	1.533	2.132	2.776	3.747	4.604	8.610
5	1.476	2.015	2.571	3.365	4.032	6.859
6	1.440	1.943	2.447	3.143	3.707	5.959
7	1.415	1.895	2.365	2.998	3.499	5.405
8	1.397	1.860	2.306	2.896	3.355	5.041
9	1.383	1.833	2.262	2.821	3.250	4.781
10	1.372	1.812	2.228	2.764	3.169	4.587
11	1.363	1.796	2.201	2.718	3.106	4.437
12	1.356	1.782	2.179	2.681	3.055	4.318
13	1.350	1.771	2.160	2.650	3.012	4.221
14	1.345	1.761	2.145	2.624	2.977	4.140
15	1.341	1.753	2.131	2.602	2.947	4.073
16	1.337	1.746	2.120	2.583	2.921	4.015
17	1.333	1.740	2.110	2.567	2.898	3.965
18	1.330	1.734	2.101	2.552	2.878	3.922
19	1.328	1.729	2.093	2.539	2.861	3.883
20	1.325	1.725	2.086	2.528	2.845	3.850
21	1.323	1.721	2.080	2.518	2.831	3.819
22	1.321	1.717	2.074	2.508	2.819	3.792
23	1.319	1.714	2.069	2.500	2.807	3.767
24	1.318	1.711	2.064	2.492	2.797	3.745
25	1.316	1.708	2.060	2.485	2.787	3.725
26	1.315	1.706	2.056	2.479	2.779	3.707
27	1.314	1.703	2.052	2.473	2.771	3.690
28	1.313	1.701	2.048	2.467	2.763	3.674
29	1.311	1.699	2.045	2.462	2.756	3.659
30	1.310	1.697	2.042	2.457	2.750	3.646
40	1.303	1.684	2.021	2.423	2.704	3.551
60	1.296	1.671	2.000	2.390	2.660	3.460
120	1.289	1.658	1.980	2.358	2.617	3.373
∞	1.282	1.645	1.960	2.326	2.576	3.291

Source: Table E is taken from Table III of Fisher & Yates: *Statistical Tables for Biological, Agricultural and Medical Research* published by Longman Group UK Ltd. London (previously published by Oliver and Boyd Ltd, Edinburgh) and by permission of the authors and publishers.

Table F   The 5 percent (Lightface Type) and 1 percent (Boldface Type) Points for the Distribution of F

n_1 degrees of freedom (for greater mean square)

n_2	1	2	3	4	5	6	7	8	9	10	11	12	14	16	20	24	30	40	50	75	100	200	500	∞
1	161 **4,052**	200 **4,999**	216 **5,403**	225 **5,625**	230 **5,764**	234 **5,859**	237 **5,928**	239 **5,981**	241 **6,022**	242 **6,056**	243 **6,082**	244 **6,106**	245 **6,142**	246 **6,169**	248 **6,208**	249 **6,234**	250 **6,258**	251 **6,286**	252 **6,302**	253 **6,323**	253 **6,334**	254 **6,352**	254 **6,361**	254 **6,366**
2	18.51 **98.49**	19.00 **99.00**	19.16 **99.17**	19.25 **99.25**	19.30 **99.30**	19.33 **99.33**	19.36 **99.34**	19.37 **99.36**	19.38 **99.38**	19.39 **99.40**	19.40 **99.41**	19.41 **99.42**	19.42 **99.43**	19.43 **99.44**	19.44 **99.45**	19.45 **99.46**	19.46 **99.47**	19.47 **99.48**	19.47 **99.48**	19.48 **99.49**	19.49 **99.49**	19.49 **99.49**	19.50 **99.50**	19.50 **99.50**
3	10.13 **34.12**	9.55 **30.82**	9.28 **29.46**	9.12 **28.71**	9.01 **28.24**	8.94 **27.91**	8.88 **27.67**	8.84 **27.49**	8.81 **27.34**	8.78 **27.23**	8.76 **27.13**	8.74 **27.05**	8.71 **26.92**	8.69 **26.83**	8.66 **26.69**	8.64 **26.60**	8.62 **26.50**	8.60 **26.41**	8.58 **26.35**	8.57 **26.27**	8.56 **26.23**	8.54 **26.18**	8.54 **26.14**	8.53 **26.12**
4	7.71 **21.20**	6.94 **18.00**	6.59 **16.69**	6.39 **15.98**	6.26 **15.52**	6.16 **15.21**	6.09 **14.98**	6.04 **14.80**	6.00 **14.66**	5.96 **14.54**	5.93 **14.45**	5.91 **14.37**	5.87 **14.24**	5.84 **14.15**	5.80 **14.02**	5.77 **13.93**	5.74 **13.83**	5.71 **13.74**	5.70 **13.69**	5.68 **13.61**	5.66 **13.57**	5.65 **13.52**	5.64 **13.48**	5.63 **13.46**
5	6.61 **16.26**	5.79 **13.27**	5.41 **12.06**	5.19 **11.39**	5.05 **10.97**	4.95 **10.67**	4.88 **10.45**	4.82 **10.27**	4.78 **10.15**	4.74 **10.05**	4.70 **9.96**	4.68 **9.89**	4.64 **9.77**	4.60 **9.68**	4.56 **9.55**	4.53 **9.47**	4.50 **9.38**	4.46 **9.29**	4.44 **9.24**	4.42 **9.17**	4.40 **9.13**	4.38 **9.07**	4.37 **9.04**	4.36 **9.02**
6	5.99 **13.74**	5.14 **10.92**	4.76 **9.78**	4.53 **9.15**	4.39 **8.75**	4.28 **8.47**	4.21 **8.26**	4.15 **8.10**	4.10 **7.98**	4.06 **7.87**	4.03 **7.79**	4.00 **7.72**	3.96 **7.60**	3.92 **7.52**	3.87 **7.39**	3.84 **7.31**	3.81 **7.23**	3.77 **7.14**	3.75 **7.09**	3.72 **7.02**	3.71 **6.99**	3.69 **6.94**	3.68 **6.90**	3.67 **6.88**
7	5.59 **12.25**	4.74 **9.55**	4.35 **8.45**	4.12 **7.85**	3.97 **7.46**	3.87 **7.19**	3.79 **7.00**	3.73 **6.84**	3.68 **6.71**	3.63 **6.62**	3.60 **6.54**	3.57 **6.47**	3.52 **6.35**	3.49 **6.27**	3.44 **6.15**	3.41 **6.07**	3.38 **5.98**	3.34 **5.90**	3.32 **5.85**	3.29 **5.78**	3.28 **5.75**	3.25 **5.70**	3.24 **5.67**	3.23 **5.65**
8	5.32 **11.26**	4.46 **8.65**	4.07 **7.59**	3.84 **7.01**	3.69 **6.63**	3.58 **6.37**	3.50 **6.19**	3.44 **6.03**	3.39 **5.91**	3.34 **5.82**	3.31 **5.74**	3.28 **5.67**	3.23 **5.56**	3.20 **5.48**	3.15 **5.36**	3.12 **5.28**	3.08 **5.20**	3.05 **5.11**	3.03 **5.06**	3.00 **5.00**	2.98 **4.96**	2.96 **4.91**	2.94 **4.88**	2.93 **4.86**
9	5.12 **10.56**	4.26 **8.02**	3.86 **6.99**	3.63 **6.42**	3.48 **6.06**	3.37 **5.80**	3.29 **5.62**	3.23 **5.47**	3.18 **5.35**	3.13 **5.26**	3.10 **5.18**	3.07 **5.11**	3.02 **5.00**	2.98 **4.92**	2.93 **4.80**	2.90 **4.73**	2.86 **4.64**	2.82 **4.56**	2.80 **4.51**	2.77 **4.45**	2.76 **4.41**	2.73 **4.36**	2.72 **4.33**	2.71 **4.31**
10	4.96 **10.04**	4.10 **7.56**	3.71 **6.55**	3.48 **5.99**	3.33 **5.64**	3.22 **5.39**	3.14 **5.21**	3.07 **5.06**	3.02 **4.95**	2.97 **4.85**	2.94 **4.78**	2.91 **4.71**	2.86 **4.60**	2.82 **4.52**	2.77 **4.41**	2.74 **4.33**	2.70 **4.25**	2.67 **4.17**	2.64 **4.12**	2.61 **4.05**	2.59 **4.01**	2.56 **3.96**	2.55 **3.93**	2.54 **3.91**
11	4.84 **9.65**	3.98 **7.20**	3.59 **6.22**	3.36 **5.67**	3.20 **5.32**	3.09 **5.07**	3.01 **4.88**	2.95 **4.74**	2.90 **4.63**	2.86 **4.54**	2.82 **4.46**	2.79 **4.40**	2.74 **4.29**	2.70 **4.21**	2.65 **4.10**	2.61 **4.02**	2.57 **3.94**	2.53 **3.86**	2.50 **3.80**	2.47 **3.74**	2.45 **3.70**	2.42 **3.66**	2.41 **3.62**	2.40 **3.60**
12	4.75 **9.33**	3.88 **6.93**	3.49 **5.95**	3.26 **5.41**	3.11 **5.06**	3.00 **4.82**	2.92 **4.65**	2.85 **4.50**	2.80 **4.39**	2.76 **4.30**	2.72 **4.22**	2.69 **4.16**	2.64 **4.05**	2.60 **3.98**	2.54 **3.86**	2.50 **3.78**	2.46 **3.70**	2.42 **3.61**	2.40 **3.56**	2.36 **3.49**	2.35 **3.46**	2.32 **3.41**	2.31 **3.38**	2.30 **3.36**
13	4.67 **9.07**	3.80 **6.70**	3.41 **5.74**	3.18 **5.20**	3.02 **4.86**	2.92 **4.62**	2.84 **4.44**	2.77 **4.30**	2.72 **4.19**	2.67 **4.10**	2.63 **4.02**	2.60 **3.96**	2.55 **3.85**	2.51 **3.78**	2.46 **3.67**	2.42 **3.59**	2.38 **3.51**	2.34 **3.42**	2.32 **3.37**	2.28 **3.30**	2.26 **3.27**	2.24 **3.21**	2.22 **3.18**	2.21 **3.16**

Source: Table F is reproduced from G. W. Snedecor, *Statistical Methods*, 5th ed., Iowa State University Press, Ames, Iowa, by permission of the author and publisher.

Table F   (continued)

n_1 degrees of freedom (for greater mean square)

n_2	1	2	3	4	5	6	7	8	9	10	11	12	14	16	20	24	30	40	50	75	100	200	500	∞
14	4.60 **8.86**	3.74 **6.51**	3.34 **5.56**	3.11 **5.03**	2.96 **4.69**	2.85 **4.46**	2.77 **4.28**	2.70 **4.14**	2.65 **4.03**	2.60 **3.94**	2.56 **3.86**	2.53 **3.80**	2.48 **3.70**	2.44 **3.62**	2.39 **3.51**	2.35 **3.43**	2.31 **3.34**	2.27 **3.26**	2.24 **3.21**	2.21 **3.14**	2.19 **3.11**	2.16 **3.06**	2.14 **3.02**	2.13 **3.00**
15	4.54 **8.68**	3.68 **6.36**	3.29 **5.42**	3.06 **4.89**	2.90 **4.56**	2.79 **4.32**	2.70 **4.14**	2.64 **4.00**	2.59 **3.89**	2.55 **3.80**	2.51 **3.73**	2.48 **3.67**	2.43 **3.56**	2.39 **3.48**	2.33 **3.36**	2.29 **3.29**	2.25 **3.20**	2.21 **3.12**	2.18 **3.07**	2.15 **3.00**	2.12 **2.97**	2.10 **2.92**	2.08 **2.89**	2.07 **2.87**
16	4.49 **8.53**	3.63 **6.23**	3.24 **5.29**	3.01 **4.77**	2.85 **4.44**	2.74 **4.20**	2.66 **4.03**	2.59 **3.89**	2.54 **3.78**	2.49 **3.69**	2.45 **3.61**	2.42 **3.55**	2.37 **3.45**	2.33 **3.37**	2.28 **3.25**	2.24 **3.18**	2.20 **3.10**	2.16 **3.01**	2.13 **2.96**	2.09 **2.89**	2.07 **2.86**	2.04 **2.80**	2.02 **2.77**	2.01 **2.75**
17	4.45 **8.40**	3.59 **6.11**	3.20 **5.18**	2.96 **4.67**	2.81 **4.34**	2.70 **4.10**	2.62 **3.93**	2.55 **3.79**	2.50 **3.68**	2.45 **3.59**	2.41 **3.52**	2.38 **3.45**	2.33 **3.35**	2.29 **3.27**	2.23 **3.16**	2.19 **3.08**	2.15 **3.00**	2.11 **2.92**	2.08 **2.86**	2.04 **2.79**	2.02 **2.76**	1.99 **2.70**	1.97 **2.67**	1.96 **2.65**
18	4.41 **8.28**	3.55 **6.01**	3.16 **5.09**	2.93 **4.58**	2.77 **4.25**	2.66 **4.01**	2.58 **3.85**	2.51 **3.71**	2.46 **3.60**	2.41 **3.51**	2.37 **3.44**	2.34 **3.37**	2.29 **3.27**	2.25 **3.19**	2.19 **3.07**	2.15 **3.00**	2.11 **2.91**	2.07 **2.83**	2.04 **2.78**	2.00 **2.71**	1.98 **2.68**	1.95 **2.62**	1.93 **2.59**	1.92 **2.57**
19	4.38 **8.18**	3.52 **5.93**	3.13 **5.01**	2.90 **4.50**	2.74 **4.17**	2.63 **3.94**	2.55 **3.77**	2.48 **3.63**	2.43 **3.52**	2.38 **3.43**	2.34 **3.36**	2.31 **3.30**	2.26 **3.19**	2.21 **3.12**	2.15 **3.00**	2.11 **2.92**	2.07 **2.84**	2.02 **2.76**	2.00 **2.70**	1.96 **2.63**	1.94 **2.60**	1.91 **2.54**	1.90 **2.51**	1.88 **2.49**
20	4.35 **8.10**	3.49 **5.85**	3.10 **4.94**	2.87 **4.43**	2.71 **4.10**	2.60 **3.87**	2.52 **3.71**	2.45 **3.56**	2.40 **3.45**	2.35 **3.37**	2.31 **3.30**	2.28 **3.23**	2.23 **3.13**	2.18 **3.05**	2.12 **2.94**	2.08 **2.86**	2.04 **2.77**	1.99 **2.69**	1.96 **2.63**	1.92 **2.56**	1.90 **2.53**	1.87 **2.47**	1.85 **2.44**	1.84 **2.42**
21	4.32 **8.02**	3.47 **5.78**	3.07 **4.87**	2.84 **4.37**	2.68 **4.04**	2.57 **3.81**	2.49 **3.65**	2.42 **3.51**	2.37 **3.40**	2.32 **3.31**	2.28 **3.24**	2.25 **3.17**	2.20 **3.07**	2.15 **2.99**	2.09 **2.88**	2.05 **2.80**	2.00 **2.72**	1.96 **2.63**	1.93 **2.58**	1.89 **2.51**	1.87 **2.47**	1.84 **2.42**	1.82 **2.38**	1.81 **2.36**
22	4.30 **7.94**	3.44 **5.72**	3.05 **4.82**	2.82 **4.31**	2.66 **3.99**	2.55 **3.76**	2.47 **3.59**	2.40 **3.45**	2.35 **3.35**	2.30 **3.26**	2.26 **3.18**	2.23 **3.12**	2.18 **3.02**	2.13 **2.94**	2.07 **2.83**	2.03 **2.75**	1.98 **2.67**	1.93 **2.58**	1.91 **2.53**	1.87 **2.46**	1.84 **2.42**	1.81 **2.37**	1.80 **2.33**	1.78 **2.31**
23	4.28 **7.88**	3.42 **5.66**	3.03 **4.76**	2.80 **4.26**	2.64 **3.94**	2.53 **3.71**	2.45 **3.54**	2.38 **3.41**	2.32 **3.30**	2.28 **3.21**	2.24 **3.14**	2.20 **3.07**	2.14 **2.97**	2.10 **2.89**	2.04 **2.78**	2.00 **2.70**	1.96 **2.62**	1.91 **2.53**	1.88 **2.48**	1.84 **2.41**	1.82 **2.37**	1.79 **2.32**	1.77 **2.28**	1.76 **2.26**
24	4.26 **7.82**	3.40 **5.61**	3.01 **4.72**	2.78 **4.22**	2.62 **3.90**	2.51 **3.67**	2.43 **3.50**	2.36 **3.36**	2.30 **3.25**	2.26 **3.17**	2.22 **3.09**	2.18 **3.03**	2.13 **2.93**	2.09 **2.85**	2.02 **2.74**	1.98 **2.66**	1.94 **2.58**	1.89 **2.49**	1.86 **2.44**	1.82 **2.36**	1.80 **2.33**	1.76 **2.27**	1.74 **2.23**	1.73 **2.21**
25	4.24 **7.77**	3.38 **5.57**	2.99 **4.68**	2.76 **4.18**	2.60 **3.86**	2.49 **3.63**	2.41 **3.46**	2.34 **3.32**	2.28 **3.21**	2.24 **3.13**	2.20 **3.05**	2.16 **2.99**	2.11 **2.89**	2.06 **2.81**	2.00 **2.70**	1.96 **2.62**	1.92 **2.54**	1.87 **2.45**	1.84 **2.40**	1.80 **2.32**	1.77 **2.29**	1.74 **2.23**	1.72 **2.19**	1.71 **2.17**
26	4.22 **7.72**	3.37 **5.53**	2.98 **4.64**	2.74 **4.14**	2.59 **3.82**	2.47 **3.59**	2.39 **3.42**	2.32 **3.29**	2.27 **3.17**	2.22 **3.09**	2.18 **3.02**	2.15 **2.96**	2.10 **2.86**	2.05 **2.77**	1.99 **2.66**	1.95 **2.58**	1.90 **2.50**	1.85 **2.41**	1.82 **2.36**	1.78 **2.28**	1.76 **2.25**	1.72 **2.19**	1.70 **2.15**	1.69 **2.13**

Table F (continued)

n_1 degrees of freedom (for greater mean square)

n_2	1	2	3	4	5	6	7	8	9	10	11	12	14	16	20	24	30	40	50	75	100	200	500	∞
27	4.21 **7.68**	3.35 **5.49**	2.96 **4.60**	2.73 **4.11**	2.57 **3.79**	2.46 **3.56**	2.37 **3.39**	2.30 **3.26**	2.25 **3.14**	2.20 **3.06**	2.16 **2.98**	2.13 **2.93**	2.08 **2.83**	2.03 **2.74**	1.97 **2.63**	1.93 **2.55**	1.88 **2.47**	1.84 **2.38**	1.80 **2.33**	1.76 **2.25**	1.74 **2.21**	1.71 **2.16**	1.68 **2.12**	1.67 **2.10**
28	4.20 **7.64**	3.34 **5.45**	2.95 **4.57**	2.71 **4.07**	2.56 **3.76**	2.44 **3.53**	2.36 **3.36**	2.29 **3.23**	2.24 **3.11**	2.19 **3.03**	2.15 **2.95**	2.12 **2.90**	2.06 **2.80**	2.02 **2.71**	1.96 **2.60**	1.91 **2.52**	1.87 **2.44**	1.81 **2.35**	1.78 **2.30**	1.75 **2.22**	1.72 **2.18**	1.69 **2.13**	1.67 **2.09**	1.65 **2.06**
29	4.18 **7.60**	3.33 **5.42**	2.93 **4.54**	2.70 **4.04**	2.54 **3.73**	2.43 **3.50**	2.35 **3.33**	2.28 **3.20**	2.22 **3.08**	2.18 **3.00**	2.14 **2.92**	2.10 **2.87**	2.05 **2.77**	2.00 **2.68**	1.94 **2.57**	1.90 **2.49**	1.85 **2.41**	1.80 **2.32**	1.77 **2.27**	1.73 **2.19**	1.71 **2.15**	1.68 **2.10**	1.65 **2.06**	1.64 **2.03**
30	4.17 **7.56**	3.32 **5.39**	2.92 **4.51**	2.69 **4.02**	2.53 **3.70**	2.42 **3.47**	2.34 **3.30**	2.27 **3.17**	2.21 **3.06**	2.16 **2.98**	2.12 **2.90**	2.09 **2.84**	2.04 **2.74**	1.99 **2.66**	1.93 **2.55**	1.89 **2.47**	1.84 **2.38**	1.79 **2.29**	1.76 **2.24**	1.72 **2.16**	1.69 **2.13**	1.66 **2.07**	1.64 **2.03**	1.62 **2.01**
32	4.15 **7.50**	3.30 **5.34**	2.90 **4.46**	2.67 **3.97**	2.51 **3.66**	2.40 **3.42**	2.32 **3.25**	2.25 **3.12**	2.19 **3.01**	2.14 **2.94**	2.10 **2.86**	2.07 **2.80**	2.02 **2.70**	1.97 **2.62**	1.91 **2.51**	1.86 **2.42**	1.82 **2.34**	1.76 **2.25**	1.74 **2.20**	1.69 **2.12**	1.67 **2.08**	1.64 **2.02**	1.61 **1.98**	1.59 **1.96**
34	4.13 **7.44**	3.28 **5.29**	2.88 **4.42**	2.65 **3.93**	2.49 **3.61**	2.38 **3.38**	2.30 **3.21**	2.23 **3.08**	2.17 **2.97**	2.12 **2.89**	2.08 **2.82**	2.05 **2.76**	2.00 **2.66**	1.95 **2.58**	1.89 **2.47**	1.84 **2.38**	1.80 **2.30**	1.74 **2.21**	1.71 **2.15**	1.67 **2.08**	1.64 **2.04**	1.61 **1.98**	1.59 **1.94**	1.57 **1.91**
36	4.11 **7.39**	3.26 **5.25**	2.86 **4.38**	2.63 **3.89**	2.48 **3.58**	2.36 **3.35**	2.28 **3.18**	2.21 **3.04**	2.15 **2.94**	2.10 **2.86**	2.06 **2.78**	2.03 **2.72**	1.98 **2.62**	1.93 **2.54**	1.87 **2.43**	1.82 **2.35**	1.78 **2.26**	1.72 **2.17**	1.69 **2.12**	1.65 **2.04**	1.62 **2.00**	1.59 **1.94**	1.56 **1.90**	1.55 **1.87**
38	4.10 **7.35**	3.25 **5.21**	2.85 **4.34**	2.62 **3.86**	2.46 **3.54**	2.35 **3.32**	2.26 **3.15**	2.19 **3.02**	2.14 **2.91**	2.09 **2.82**	2.05 **2.75**	2.02 **2.69**	1.96 **2.59**	1.92 **2.51**	1.85 **2.40**	1.80 **2.32**	1.76 **2.22**	1.71 **2.14**	1.67 **2.08**	1.63 **2.00**	1.60 **1.97**	1.57 **1.90**	1.54 **1.86**	1.53 **1.84**
40	4.08 **7.31**	3.23 **5.18**	2.84 **4.31**	2.61 **3.83**	2.45 **3.51**	2.34 **3.29**	2.25 **3.12**	2.18 **2.99**	2.12 **2.88**	2.07 **2.80**	2.04 **2.73**	2.00 **2.66**	1.95 **2.56**	1.90 **2.49**	1.84 **2.37**	1.79 **2.29**	1.74 **2.20**	1.69 **2.11**	1.66 **2.05**	1.61 **1.97**	1.59 **1.94**	1.55 **1.88**	1.53 **1.84**	1.51 **1.81**
42	4.07 **7.27**	3.22 **5.15**	2.83 **4.29**	2.59 **3.80**	2.44 **3.49**	2.32 **3.26**	2.24 **3.10**	2.17 **2.96**	2.11 **2.86**	2.06 **2.77**	2.02 **2.70**	1.99 **2.64**	1.94 **2.54**	1.89 **2.46**	1.82 **2.35**	1.78 **2.26**	1.73 **2.17**	1.68 **2.08**	1.64 **2.02**	1.60 **1.94**	1.57 **1.91**	1.54 **1.85**	1.51 **1.80**	1.49 **1.78**
44	4.06 **7.24**	3.21 **5.12**	2.82 **4.26**	2.58 **3.78**	2.43 **3.46**	2.31 **3.24**	2.23 **3.07**	2.16 **2.94**	2.10 **2.84**	2.05 **2.75**	2.01 **2.68**	1.98 **2.62**	1.92 **2.52**	1.88 **2.44**	1.81 **2.32**	1.76 **2.24**	1.72 **2.15**	1.66 **2.06**	1.63 **2.00**	1.58 **1.92**	1.56 **1.88**	1.52 **1.82**	1.50 **1.78**	1.48 **1.75**
46	4.05 **7.21**	3.20 **5.10**	2.81 **4.24**	2.57 **3.76**	2.42 **3.44**	2.30 **3.22**	2.22 **3.05**	2.14 **2.92**	2.09 **2.82**	2.04 **2.73**	2.00 **2.66**	1.97 **2.60**	1.91 **2.50**	1.87 **2.42**	1.80 **2.30**	1.75 **2.22**	1.71 **2.13**	1.65 **2.04**	1.62 **1.98**	1.57 **1.90**	1.54 **1.86**	1.51 **1.80**	1.48 **1.76**	1.46 **1.72**
48	4.04 **7.19**	3.19 **5.08**	2.80 **4.22**	2.56 **3.74**	2.41 **3.42**	2.30 **3.20**	2.21 **3.04**	2.14 **2.90**	2.08 **2.80**	2.03 **2.71**	1.99 **2.64**	1.96 **2.58**	1.90 **2.48**	1.86 **2.40**	1.79 **2.28**	1.74 **2.20**	1.70 **2.11**	1.64 **2.02**	1.61 **1.96**	1.56 **1.88**	1.53 **1.84**	1.50 **1.78**	1.47 **1.73**	1.45 **1.70**

Table F   (continued)

n_1 degrees of freedom (for greater mean square)

n_2	1	2	3	4	5	6	7	8	9	10	11	12	14	16	20	24	30	40	50	75	100	200	500	∞
50	4.03 / 7.17	3.18 / 5.06	2.79 / 4.20	2.56 / 3.72	2.40 / 3.41	2.29 / 3.18	2.20 / 3.02	2.13 / 2.88	2.07 / 2.78	2.02 / 2.70	1.98 / 2.62	1.95 / 2.56	1.90 / 2.46	1.85 / 2.39	1.78 / 2.26	1.74 / 2.18	1.69 / 2.10	1.63 / 2.00	1.60 / 1.94	1.55 / 1.86	1.52 / 1.82	1.48 / 1.76	1.46 / 1.71	1.44 / 1.68
55	4.02 / 7.12	3.17 / 5.01	2.78 / 4.16	2.54 / 3.68	2.38 / 3.37	2.27 / 3.15	2.18 / 2.98	2.11 / 2.85	2.05 / 2.75	2.00 / 2.66	1.97 / 2.59	1.93 / 2.53	1.88 / 2.43	1.83 / 2.35	1.76 / 2.23	1.72 / 2.15	1.67 / 2.06	1.61 / 1.96	1.58 / 1.90	1.52 / 1.82	1.50 / 1.78	1.46 / 1.71	1.43 / 1.66	1.41 / 1.64
60	4.00 / 7.08	3.15 / 4.98	2.76 / 4.13	2.52 / 3.65	2.37 / 3.34	2.25 / 3.12	2.17 / 2.95	2.10 / 2.82	2.04 / 2.72	1.99 / 2.63	1.95 / 2.56	1.92 / 2.50	1.86 / 2.40	1.81 / 2.32	1.75 / 2.20	1.70 / 2.12	1.65 / 2.03	1.59 / 1.93	1.56 / 1.87	1.50 / 1.79	1.48 / 1.74	1.44 / 1.68	1.41 / 1.63	1.39 / 1.60
65	3.99 / 7.04	3.14 / 4.95	2.75 / 4.10	2.51 / 3.62	2.36 / 3.31	2.24 / 3.09	2.15 / 2.93	2.08 / 2.79	2.02 / 2.70	1.98 / 2.61	1.94 / 2.54	1.90 / 2.47	1.85 / 2.37	1.80 / 2.30	1.73 / 2.18	1.68 / 2.09	1.63 / 2.00	1.57 / 1.90	1.54 / 1.84	1.49 / 1.76	1.46 / 1.71	1.42 / 1.64	1.39 / 1.60	1.37 / 1.56
70	3.98 / 7.01	3.13 / 4.92	2.74 / 4.08	2.50 / 3.60	2.35 / 3.29	2.23 / 3.07	2.14 / 2.91	2.07 / 2.77	2.01 / 2.67	1.97 / 2.59	1.93 / 2.51	1.89 / 2.45	1.84 / 2.35	1.79 / 2.28	1.72 / 2.15	1.67 / 2.07	1.62 / 1.98	1.56 / 1.88	1.53 / 1.82	1.47 / 1.74	1.45 / 1.69	1.40 / 1.62	1.37 / 1.56	1.35 / 1.53
80	3.96 / 6.96	3.11 / 4.88	2.72 / 4.04	2.48 / 3.56	2.33 / 3.25	2.21 / 3.04	2.12 / 2.87	2.05 / 2.74	1.99 / 2.64	1.95 / 2.55	1.91 / 2.48	1.88 / 2.41	1.82 / 2.32	1.77 / 2.24	1.70 / 2.11	1.65 / 2.03	1.60 / 1.94	1.54 / 1.84	1.51 / 1.78	1.45 / 1.70	1.42 / 1.65	1.38 / 1.57	1.35 / 1.52	1.32 / 1.49
100	3.94 / 6.90	3.09 / 4.82	2.70 / 3.98	2.46 / 3.51	2.30 / 3.20	2.19 / 2.99	2.10 / 2.82	2.03 / 2.69	1.97 / 2.59	1.92 / 2.51	1.88 / 2.43	1.85 / 2.36	1.79 / 2.26	1.75 / 2.19	1.68 / 2.06	1.63 / 1.98	1.57 / 1.89	1.51 / 1.79	1.48 / 1.73	1.42 / 1.64	1.39 / 1.59	1.34 / 1.51	1.30 / 1.46	1.28 / 1.43
125	3.92 / 6.84	3.07 / 4.78	2.68 / 3.94	2.44 / 3.47	2.29 / 3.17	2.17 / 2.95	2.08 / 2.79	2.01 / 2.65	1.95 / 2.56	1.90 / 2.47	1.86 / 2.40	1.83 / 2.33	1.77 / 2.23	1.72 / 2.15	1.65 / 2.03	1.60 / 1.94	1.55 / 1.85	1.49 / 1.75	1.45 / 1.68	1.39 / 1.59	1.36 / 1.54	1.31 / 1.46	1.27 / 1.40	1.25 / 1.37
150	3.91 / 6.81	3.06 / 4.75	2.67 / 3.91	2.43 / 3.44	2.27 / 3.14	2.16 / 2.92	2.07 / 2.76	2.00 / 2.62	1.94 / 2.53	1.89 / 2.44	1.85 / 2.37	1.82 / 2.30	1.76 / 2.20	1.71 / 2.12	1.64 / 2.00	1.59 / 1.91	1.54 / 1.83	1.47 / 1.72	1.44 / 1.66	1.37 / 1.56	1.34 / 1.51	1.29 / 1.43	1.25 / 1.37	1.22 / 1.33
200	3.89 / 6.76	3.04 / 4.71	2.65 / 3.88	2.41 / 3.41	2.26 / 3.11	2.14 / 2.90	2.05 / 2.73	1.98 / 2.60	1.92 / 2.50	1.87 / 2.41	1.83 / 2.34	1.80 / 2.28	1.74 / 2.17	1.69 / 2.09	1.62 / 1.97	1.57 / 1.88	1.52 / 1.79	1.45 / 1.69	1.42 / 1.62	1.35 / 1.53	1.32 / 1.48	1.26 / 1.39	1.22 / 1.33	1.19 / 1.28
400	3.86 / 6.70	3.02 / 4.66	2.62 / 3.83	2.39 / 3.36	2.23 / 3.06	2.12 / 2.85	2.03 / 2.69	1.96 / 2.55	1.90 / 2.46	1.85 / 2.37	1.81 / 2.29	1.78 / 2.23	1.72 / 2.12	1.67 / 2.04	1.60 / 1.92	1.54 / 1.84	1.49 / 1.74	1.42 / 1.64	1.38 / 1.57	1.32 / 1.47	1.28 / 1.42	1.22 / 1.32	1.16 / 1.24	1.13 / 1.19
1000	3.85 / 6.66	3.00 / 4.62	2.61 / 3.80	2.38 / 3.34	2.22 / 3.04	2.10 / 2.82	2.02 / 2.66	1.95 / 2.53	1.89 / 2.43	1.84 / 2.34	1.80 / 2.26	1.76 / 2.20	1.70 / 2.09	1.65 / 2.01	1.58 / 1.89	1.53 / 1.81	1.47 / 1.71	1.41 / 1.61	1.36 / 1.54	1.30 / 1.44	1.26 / 1.38	1.19 / 1.28	1.13 / 1.19	1.08 / 1.11
∞	3.84 / 6.64	2.99 / 4.60	2.60 / 3.78	2.37 / 3.32	2.21 / 3.02	2.09 / 2.80	2.01 / 2.64	1.94 / 2.51	1.88 / 2.41	1.83 / 2.32	1.79 / 2.24	1.75 / 2.18	1.69 / 2.07	1.64 / 1.99	1.57 / 1.87	1.52 / 1.79	1.46 / 1.69	1.40 / 1.59	1.35 / 1.52	1.28 / 1.41	1.24 / 1.36	1.17 / 1.25	1.11 / 1.15	1.00 / 1.00

Table G   Distribution of the Studentized Range Statistic

df for within mean square	1 − α	\\(k\\) = number of groups													
		2	3	4	5	6	7	8	9	10	11	12	13	14	15
1	.95	18.0	27.0	32.8	37.1	40.4	43.1	45.4	47.4	49.1	50.6	52.0	53.2	54.3	55.4
	.99	90.0	135	164	186	202	216	227	237	246	253	260	266	272	277
2	.95	6.09	8.3	9.8	10.9	11.7	12.4	13.0	13.5	14.0	14.4	14.7	15.1	15.4	15.7
	.99	14.0	19.0	22.3	24.7	26.6	28.2	29.5	30.7	31.7	32.6	33.4	34.1	34.8	35.4
3	.95	4.50	5.91	6.82	7.50	8.04	8.48	8.85	9.18	9.46	9.72	9.95	10.2	10.4	10.5
	.99	8.26	10.6	12.2	13.3	14.2	15.0	15.6	16.2	16.7	17.1	17.5	17.9	18.2	18.5
4	.95	3.93	5.04	5.76	6.29	6.71	7.05	7.35	7.60	7.83	8.03	8.21	8.37	8.52	8.66
	.99	6.51	8.12	9.17	9.96	10.6	11.1	11.5	11.9	12.3	12.6	12.8	13.1	13.3	13.5
5	.95	3.64	4.60	5.22	5.67	6.03	6.33	6.58	6.80	6.99	7.17	7.32	7.47	7.60	7.72
	.99	5.70	6.97	7.80	8.42	8.91	9.32	9.67	9.97	10.2	10.5	10.7	10.9	11.1	11.2
6	.95	3.46	4.34	4.90	5.31	5.63	5.89	6.12	6.32	6.49	6.65	6.79	6.92	7.03	7.14
	.99	5.24	6.33	7.03	7.56	7.97	8.32	8.61	8.87	9.10	9.30	9.49	9.65	9.81	9.95
7	.95	3.34	4.16	4.69	5.06	5.36	5.61	5.82	6.00	6.16	6.30	6.43	6.55	6.66	6.76
	.99	4.95	5.92	6.54	7.01	7.37	7.68	7.94	8.17	8.37	8.55	8.71	8.86	9.00	9.12
8	.95	3.26	4.04	4.53	4.89	5.17	5.40	5.60	5.77	5.92	6.05	6.18	6.29	6.39	6.48
	.99	4.74	5.63	6.20	6.63	6.96	7.24	7.47	7.68	7.87	8.03	8.18	8.31	8.44	8.55
9	.95	3.20	3.95	4.42	4.76	5.02	5.24	5.43	5.60	5.74	5.87	5.98	6.09	6.19	6.28
	.99	4.60	5.43	5.96	6.35	6.66	6.91	7.13	7.32	7.49	7.65	7.78	7.91	8.03	8.13
10	.95	3.15	3.88	4.33	4.65	4.91	5.12	5.30	5.46	5.60	5.72	5.83	5.93	6.03	6.11
	.99	4.48	5.27	5.77	6.14	6.43	6.67	6.87	7.05	7.21	7.36	7.48	7.60	7.71	7.81

Source: Reprinted from September 1, 1971, issue of *Business Week* by special permission, copyright © 1971 by McGraw-Hill, Inc.
Table adapted from Table 11.2 in *The Probability Integrals of the Range and of the Studentized Range*, prepared by H. Leon Harter, Donald S. Clemm, and Eugene H. Guthrie, published in WADEC Tech. Rep. 58-484, vol. 2, 1959, Wright Air Development Center.

Table G (continued)

df for within mean square	$1-\alpha$	2	3	4	5	6	7	8	9	10	11	12	13	14	15
11	.95	3.11	3.82	4.26	4.57	4.82	5.03	5.20	5.35	5.49	5.61	5.71	5.81	5.90	5.99
	.99	4.39	5.14	5.62	5.97	6.25	6.48	6.67	6.84	6.99	7.13	7.26	7.36	7.46	7.56
12	.95	3.08	3.77	4.20	4.51	4.75	4.95	5.12	5.27	5.40	5.51	5.62	5.71	5.80	5.88
	.99	4.32	5.04	5.50	5.84	6.10	6.32	6.51	6.67	6.81	6.94	7.06	7.17	7.26	7.36
13	.95	3.06	3.73	4.15	4.45	4.69	4.88	5.05	5.19	5.32	5.43	5.53	5.63	5.71	5.79
	.99	4.26	4.96	5.40	5.73	5.98	6.19	6.37	6.53	6.67	6.79	6.90	7.01	7.10	7.19
14	.95	3.03	3.70	4.11	4.41	4.64	4.83	4.99	5.13	5.25	5.36	5.46	5.55	5.64	5.72
	.99	4.21	4.89	5.32	5.63	5.88	6.08	6.26	6.41	6.54	6.66	6.77	6.87	6.96	7.05
16	.95	3.00	3.65	4.05	4.33	4.56	4.74	4.90	5.03	5.15	5.26	5.35	5.44	5.52	5.59
	.99	4.13	4.78	5.19	5.49	5.72	5.92	6.08	6.22	6.35	6.46	6.56	6.66	6.74	6.82
18	.95	2.97	3.61	4.00	4.28	4.49	4.67	4.82	4.96	5.07	5.17	5.27	5.35	5.43	5.50
	.99	4.07	4.70	5.09	5.38	5.60	5.79	5.94	6.08	6.20	6.31	6.41	6.50	6.58	6.65
20	.95	2.95	3.58	3.96	4.23	4.45	4.62	4.77	4.90	5.01	5.11	5.20	5.28	5.36	5.43
	.99	4.02	4.64	5.02	5.29	5.51	5.69	5.84	5.97	6.09	6.19	6.29	6.37	6.45	6.52
24	.95	2.92	3.53	3.90	4.17	4.37	4.54	4.68	4.81	4.92	5.01	5.10	5.18	5.25	5.32
	.99	3.96	4.54	4.91	5.17	5.37	5.54	5.69	5.81	5.92	6.02	6.11	6.19	6.26	6.33
30	.95	2.89	3.49	3.84	4.10	4.30	4.46	4.60	4.72	4.83	4.92	5.00	5.08	5.15	5.21
	.99	3.89	4.45	4.80	5.05	5.24	5.40	5.54	5.56	5.76	5.85	5.93	6.01	6.08	6.14
40	.95	2.86	3.44	3.79	4.04	4.23	4.39	4.52	4.63	4.74	4.82	4.91	4.98	5.05	5.11
	.99	3.82	4.37	4.70	4.93	5.11	5.27	5.39	5.50	5.60	5.69	5.77	5.84	5.90	5.96
60	.95	2.83	3.40	3.74	3.98	4.16	4.31	4.44	4.55	4.65	4.73	4.81	4.88	4.94	5.00
	.99	3.76	4.28	4.60	4.82	4.99	5.13	5.25	5.36	5.45	5.53	5.60	5.67	5.73	5.79
120	.95	2.80	3.36	3.69	3.92	4.10	4.24	4.36	4.48	4.56	4.64	4.72	4.78	4.84	4.90
	.99	3.70	4.20	4.50	4.71	4.87	5.01	5.12	5.21	5.30	5.38	5.44	5.51	5.56	5.61
∞	.95	2.77	3.31	3.63	3.86	4.03	4.17	4.29	4.39	4.47	4.55	4.62	4.68	4.74	4.80
	.99	3.64	4.12	4.40	4.60	4.76	4.88	4.99	5.08	5.16	5.23	5.29	5.35	5.40	5.45

k = number of groups

Table H   Distribution of Chi Square

df	.99	.98	.95	.90	.80	.70	.50	.30	.20	.10	.05	.02	.01	.001
1	$.0^3157$	$.0^3628$	.00393	.0158	.0642	.148	.455	1.074	1.642	2.706	3.841	5.412	6.635	10.827
2	.0201	.0404	.103	.211	.446	.713	1.386	2.408	3.219	4.605	5.991	7.824	9.210	13.815
3	.115	.185	.352	.584	1.005	1.424	2.366	3.665	4.642	6.251	7.815	9.837	11.341	16.268
4	.297	.429	.711	1.064	1.649	2.195	3.357	4.878	5.989	7.779	9.488	11.668	13.277	18.465
5	.554	.752	1.145	1.610	2.343	3.000	4.351	6.064	7.289	9.236	11.070	13.388	15.086	20.517
6	.872	1.134	1.635	2.204	3.070	3.828	5.348	7.231	8.558	10.645	12.592	15.033	16.812	22.457
7	1.239	1.564	2.167	2.833	3.822	4.671	6.346	8.383	9.803	12.017	14.067	16.622	18.475	24.322
8	1.646	2.032	2.733	3.490	4.594	5.527	7.344	9.524	11.030	13.362	15.507	18.168	20.090	26.125
9	2.088	2.532	3.325	4.168	5.380	6.393	8.343	10.656	12.242	14.684	16.919	19.679	21.666	27.877
10	2.558	3.059	3.940	4.865	6.179	7.267	9.342	11.781	13.442	15.987	18.307	21.161	23.209	29.588
11	3.053	3.609	4.575	5.578	6.989	8.148	10.341	12.899	14.631	17.275	19.675	22.618	24.725	31.264
12	3.571	4.178	5.226	6.304	7.807	9.034	11.340	14.011	15.812	18.549	21.026	24.054	26.217	32.909
13	4.107	4.765	5.892	7.042	8.634	9.926	12.340	15.119	16.985	19.812	22.362	25.472	27.688	34.528
14	4.660	5.368	6.571	7.790	9.467	10.821	13.339	16.222	18.151	21.064	23.685	26.873	29.141	36.123
15	5.229	5.985	7.261	8.547	10.307	11.721	14.339	17.322	19.311	22.307	24.996	28.259	30.578	37.697
16	5.812	6.614	7.962	9.312	11.152	12.624	15.338	18.418	20.465	23.542	26.296	29.633	32.000	39.252
17	6.408	7.255	8.672	10.085	12.002	13.531	16.338	19.511	21.615	24.769	27.587	30.995	33.409	40.790
18	7.015	7.906	9.390	10.865	12.857	14.440	17.338	20.601	22.760	25.989	28.869	32.346	34.805	42.312
19	7.633	8.567	10.117	11.651	13.716	15.352	18.338	21.689	23.900	27.204	30.144	33.687	36.191	43.820
20	8.260	9.237	10.851	12.443	14.578	16.266	19.337	22.775	25.038	28.412	31.410	35.020	37.566	45.315
21	8.897	9.915	11.591	13.240	15.445	17.182	20.337	23.858	26.171	29.615	32.671	36.343	38.932	46.797
22	9.542	10.600	12.338	14.041	16.314	18.101	21.337	24.939	27.301	30.813	33.924	37.659	40.289	48.268
23	10.196	11.293	13.091	14.848	17.187	19.021	22.337	26.018	28.429	32.007	35.172	38.968	41.638	49.728
24	10.856	11.992	13.848	15.659	18.062	19.943	23.337	27.096	29.553	33.196	36.415	40.270	42.980	51.179
25	11.524	12.697	14.611	16.473	18.940	20.867	24.337	28.172	30.675	34.382	37.652	41.566	44.314	52.620
26	12.198	13.409	15.379	17.292	19.820	21.792	25.336	29.246	31.795	35.563	38.885	42.856	45.642	54.052
27	12.879	14.125	16.151	18.114	20.703	22.719	26.336	30.319	32.912	36.741	40.113	44.140	46.963	55.476
28	13.565	14.847	16.928	18.939	21.588	23.647	27.336	31.391	34.027	37.916	41.337	45.419	48.278	56.893
29	14.256	15.574	17.708	19.768	22.475	24.577	28.336	32.461	35.139	39.087	42.557	46.693	49.588	58.302
30	14.953	16.306	18.493	20.599	23.364	25.508	29.336	33.530	36.250	40.256	43.773	47.962	50.892	59.703

Source: Table H is taken from Table IV of Fisher & Yates: *Statistical Tables for Biological, Agricultural and Medical Research* published by Longman Group UK Ltd., London (previously published by Oliver and Boyd Ltd., Edinburgh) and by permission of the authors and publishers.

Note: For larger values of *df*, the expression $\sqrt{2\chi^2} - \sqrt{2df-1}$ may be used as a normal deviate with unit variance, remembering that the probability for χ^2 corresponds with that of a single tail of the normal curve.

Table I   **Critical Values of *T* in the Wilcoxon Matched-Pairs Signed-Ranks Test**

N	Level of significance, direction predicted (one-tailed test)		
	.025	.01	.005
	Level of significance, direction not predicted (two-tailed test)		
	.05	.02	.01
6	0	—	—
7	2	0	—
8	4	2	0
9	6	3	2
10	8	5	3
11	11	7	5
12	14	10	7
13	17	13	10
14	21	16	13
15	25	20	16
16	30	24	20
17	35	28	23
18	40	33	28
19	46	38	32
20	52	43	38
21	59	49	43
22	66	56	49
23	73	62	55
24	81	69	61
25	89	77	68

Source: F. Wilcoxon, *Some Rapid Approximate Statistical Procedures,* American Cyanamid Company, New York, 1949, table I, p. 13, with the kind permission of the author and publisher.

Table J   Probabilities Associated with Values as Small as Observed Values of x in the Binomial Test

One-tailed probabilities under H_0 for the binomial test when $P = Q = \frac{1}{2}$. To save space, decimal points are omitted in the p's.

N \ x	0	1	2	3	4	5	6	7	8	9	10	11	12	13	14	15
5	031	188	500	812	969	†										
6	016	109	344	656	891	984	†									
7	008	062	227	500	773	938	992	†								
8	004	035	145	363	637	855	965	996	†							
9	002	020	090	254	500	746	910	980	998	†						
10	001	011	055	172	377	623	828	945	989	999	†					
11		006	033	113	274	500	726	887	967	994	†	†				
12		003	019	073	194	387	613	806	927	981	997	†	†			
13		002	011	046	133	291	500	709	867	954	989	998	†	†		
14		001	006	029	090	212	395	605	788	910	971	994	999	†	†	
15			004	018	059	151	304	500	696	849	941	982	996	†	†	†
16			002	011	038	105	227	402	598	773	895	962	989	998	†	†
17			001	006	025	072	166	315	500	685	834	928	975	994	999	†
18			001	004	015	048	119	240	407	593	760	881	952	985	996	999
19				002	010	032	084	180	324	500	676	820	916	968	990	998
20				001	006	021	058	132	252	412	588	748	868	942	979	994
21				001	004	013	039	095	192	332	500	668	808	905	961	987
22					002	008	026	067	143	262	416	584	738	857	933	974
23					001	005	017	047	105	202	339	500	661	798	895	953
24					001	003	011	032	076	154	271	419	581	729	846	924
25						002	007	022	054	115	212	345	500	655	788	885

Source: Table IV B, of Helen Walker and J. Lev, *Statistical Inference*, New York, Holt, Rinehart and Winston, Inc., 1953, p. 458, with the kind permission of the authors and publisher.

†1.0 or approximately 1.0.

Table K   **Probabilities Associated with Values as Small as Observed Values of U in the Mann-Whitney Test**

$n_2 = 3$

U \ n_1	1	2	3
0	.250	.100	.050
1	.500	.200	.100
2	.750	.400	.200
3		.600	.350
4			.500
5			.650

$n_2 = 4$

U \ n_1	1	2	3	4
0	.200	.067	.028	.014
1	.400	.133	.057	.029
2	.600	.267	.114	.057
3		.400	.200	.100
4		.600	.314	.171
5			.429	.243
6			.571	.343
7				.443
8				.557

$n_2 = 5$

U \ n_1	1	2	3	4	5
0	.167	.047	.018	.008	.004
1	.333	.095	.036	.016	.008
2	.500	.190	.071	.032	.016
3	.667	.286	.125	.056	.028
4		.429	.196	.095	.048
5		.571	.286	.143	.075
6			.393	.206	.111
7			.500	.278	.155
8			.607	.365	.210
9				.452	.274
10				.548	.345
11					.421
12					.500
13					.579

$n_2 = 6$

U \ n_1	1	2	3	4	5	6
0	.143	.036	.012	.005	.002	.001
1	.286	.071	.024	.010	.004	.002
2	.428	.143	.048	.019	.009	.004
3	.571	.214	.083	.033	.015	.008
4		.321	.131	.057	.026	.013
5		.429	.190	.086	.041	.021
6		.571	.274	.129	.063	.032
7			.357	.176	.089	.047
8			.452	.238	.123	.066
9			.548	.305	.165	.090
10				.381	.214	.120
11				.457	.268	.155
12				.545	.331	.197
13					.396	.242
14					.465	.294
15					.535	.350
16						.409
17						.469
18						.531

Source: H. B. Mann, and D. R. Whitney, "On a Test of Whether One of Two Random Variables Is Stochastically Larger Than the Other," *Annals of Mathematical Statistics,* vol 18 (1947), pp. 52-54, with the kind permissions of the authors and the publisher, the Institute of Mathematical Statistics.

Table K   (continued)

	$n_2 = 7$						
n_1 U	1	2	3	4	5	6	7
0	.125	.028	.008	.003	.001	.001	.000
1	.250	.056	.017	.006	.003	.001	.001
2	.375	.111	.033	.012	.005	.002	.001
3	.500	.167	.058	.021	.009	.004	.002
4	.625	.250	.092	.036	.015	.007	.003
5		.333	.133	.055	.024	.011	.006
6		.444	.192	.082	.037	.017	.009
7		.556	.258	.115	.053	.026	.013
8			.333	.158	.074	.037	.019
9			.417	.206	.101	.051	.027
10			.500	.264	.134	.069	.036
11			.583	.324	.172	.090	.049
12				.394	.216	.117	.064
13				.464	.265	.147	.082
14				.538	.319	.183	.104
15					.378	.223	.130
16					.438	.267	.159
17					.500	.314	.191
18					.562	.365	.228
19						.418	.267
20						.473	.310
21						.527	.355
22							.402
23							.451
24							.500
25							.549

(Continued next page)

Table K   (continued)

$n_2 = 8$

U \ n_1	1	2	3	4	5	6	7	8	t	Normal
0	.111	.022	.006	.002	.001	.000	.000	.000	3.308	.001
1	.222	.044	.012	.004	.002	.001	.000	.000	3.203	.001
2	.333	.089	.024	.008	.003	.001	.001	.000	3.098	.001
3	.444	.133	.042	.014	.005	.002	.001	.001	2.993	.001
4	.556	.200	.067	.024	.009	.004	.002	.001	2.888	.002
5		.267	.097	.036	.015	.006	.003	.001	2.783	.003
6		.356	.139	.055	.023	.010	.005	.002	2.678	.004
7		.444	.188	.077	.033	.015	.007	.003	2.573	.005
8		.556	.248	.107	.047	.021	.010	.005	2.468	.007
9			.315	.141	.064	.030	.014	.007	2.363	.009
10			.387	.184	.085	.041	.020	.010	2.258	.012
11			.461	.230	.111	.054	.027	.014	2.153	.016
12			.539	.285	.142	.071	.036	.019	2.048	.020
13				.341	.177	.091	.047	.025	1.943	.026
14				.404	.217	.114	.060	.032	1.838	.033
15				.467	.262	.141	.076	.041	1.733	.041
16				.533	.311	.172	.095	.052	1.628	.052
17					.362	.207	.116	.065	1.523	.064
18					.416	.245	.140	.080	1.418	.078
19					.472	.286	.168	.097	1.313	.094
20					.528	.331	.198	.117	1.208	.113
21						.377	.232	.139	1.102	.135
22						.426	.268	.164	.998	.159
23						.475	.306	.191	.893	.185
24						.525	.347	.221	.788	.215
25							.389	.253	.683	.247
26							.433	.287	.578	.282
27							.478	.323	.473	.318
28							.522	.360	.368	.356
29								.399	.263	.396
30								.439	.158	.437
31								.480	.052	.481
32								.520		

Table L **411**

Table L   Critical Values of *U* in the Mann-Whitney Test

Critical values of *U* for a one-tailed test at $\alpha = 0.001$
or a two-tailed test at $\alpha = 0.002$

n_1 \ n_2	9	10	11	12	13	14	15	16	17	18	19	20
1												
2												
3									0	0	0	0
4		0	0	0	1	1	1	2	2	3	3	3
5	1	1	2	2	3	3	4	5	5	6	7	7
6	2	3	4	4	5	6	7	8	9	10	11	12
7	3	5	6	7	8	9	10	11	13	14	15	16
8	5	6	8	9	11	12	14	15	17	18	20	21
9	7	8	10	12	14	15	17	19	21	23	25	26
10	8	10	12	14	17	19	21	23	25	27	29	32
11	10	12	15	17	20	22	24	27	29	32	34	37
12	12	14	17	20	23	25	28	31	34	37	40	42
13	14	17	20	23	26	29	32	35	38	42	45	48
14	15	19	22	25	29	32	36	39	43	46	50	54
15	17	21	24	28	32	36	40	43	47	51	55	59
16	19	23	27	31	35	39	43	48	52	56	60	65
17	21	25	29	34	38	43	47	52	57	61	66	70
18	23	27	32	37	42	46	51	56	61	66	71	76
19	25	29	34	40	45	50	55	60	66	71	77	82
20	26	32	37	42	48	54	59	65	70	76	82	88

Critical values of *U* for a one-tailed test at $\alpha = .001$
or a two-tailed test at $\alpha = 0.02$

n_1 \ n_2	9	10	11	12	13	14	15	16	17	18	19	20
1												
2					0	0	0	0	0	0	1	1
3	1	1	1	2	2	2	3	3	4	4	4	5
4	3	3	4	5	5	6	7	7	8	9	9	10
5	5	6	7	8	9	10	11	12	13	14	15	16
6	7	8	9	11	12	13	15	16	18	19	20	22
7	9	11	12	14	16	17	19	21	23	24	26	28
8	11	13	15	17	20	22	24	26	28	30	32	34
9	14	16	18	21	23	26	28	31	33	36	38	40
10	16	19	22	24	27	30	33	36	38	41	44	47
11	18	22	25	28	31	34	37	41	44	47	50	53
12	21	24	28	31	35	38	42	46	49	53	56	60
13	23	27	31	35	39	43	47	51	55	59	63	67
14	26	30	34	38	43	47	51	56	60	65	69	73
15	28	33	37	42	47	51	56	61	66	70	75	80
16	31	36	41	46	51	56	61	66	71	76	82	87
17	33	38	44	49	55	60	66	71	77	82	88	93
18	36	41	47	53	59	65	70	76	82	88	94	100
19	38	44	50	56	63	69	75	82	88	94	101	107
20	40	47	53	60	67	73	80	87	93	100	107	114

Source: Tables 1, 3, 5, and 7 of D. Auble, "Extended Tables for the Mann-Whitney Statistic," *Bulletin of the Institute for Educational Research, Indiana University,* vol. 1, no. 2 (1953), with the kind permission of the author and the publisher.

Table L   (continued)

Critical values of U for a one-tailed test at $\alpha = 0.025$ or a two-tailed test at $\alpha = 0.05$

n_1 \ n_2	9	10	11	12	13	14	15	16	17	18	19	20
1												
2	0	0	0	1	1	1	1	1	2	2	2	2
3	2	3	3	4	4	5	5	6	6	7	7	8
4	4	5	6	7	8	9	10	11	11	12	13	13
5	7	8	9	11	12	13	14	15	17	18	19	20
6	10	11	13	14	16	17	19	21	22	24	25	27
7	12	14	16	18	20	22	24	26	28	30	32	34
8	15	17	19	22	24	26	29	31	34	36	38	41
9	17	20	23	26	28	31	34	37	39	42	45	48
10	20	23	26	29	33	36	39	42	45	48	52	55
11	23	26	30	33	37	40	44	47	51	55	58	62
12	26	29	33	37	41	45	49	53	57	61	65	69
13	28	33	37	41	45	50	54	59	63	67	72	76
14	31	36	40	45	50	55	59	64	67	74	78	83
15	34	39	44	49	54	59	64	70	75	80	85	90
16	37	42	47	53	59	64	70	75	81	86	92	98
17	39	45	51	57	63	67	75	81	87	93	99	105
18	42	48	55	61	67	74	80	86	93	99	106	112
19	45	52	58	65	72	78	85	92	99	106	113	119
20	48	55	62	69	76	83	90	98	105	112	119	127

Critical values of U for a one-tailed test at $\alpha = 0.05$ or for a two-tailed test at $\alpha = 0.10$

n_1 \ n_2	9	10	11	12	13	14	15	16	17	18	19	20
1											0	0
2	1	1	1	2	2	2	3	3	3	4	4	4
3	3	4	5	5	6	7	7	8	9	9	10	11
4	6	7	8	9	10	11	12	14	15	16	17	18
5	9	11	12	13	15	16	18	19	20	22	23	25
6	12	14	16	17	19	21	23	25	26	28	30	32
7	15	17	19	21	24	26	28	30	33	35	37	39
8	18	20	23	26	28	31	33	36	39	41	44	47
9	21	24	27	30	33	36	39	42	45	48	51	54
10	24	27	31	34	37	41	44	48	51	55	58	62
11	27	31	34	38	42	46	50	54	57	61	65	69
12	30	34	38	42	47	51	55	60	64	68	72	77
13	33	37	42	47	51	56	61	65	70	75	80	84
14	36	41	46	51	56	61	66	71	77	82	87	92
15	39	44	50	55	61	66	72	77	83	88	94	100
16	42	48	54	60	65	71	77	83	89	95	101	107
17	45	51	57	64	70	77	83	89	96	102	109	115
18	48	55	61	68	75	82	88	95	102	109	116	123
19	51	58	65	72	80	87	94	101	109	116	123	130
20	54	62	69	77	84	92	100	107	115	123	130	138

Table M **Probabilities Associated with Values as Large as Observed Values of** χ_r^2 **in the Friedman Two-Way Analysis of Variance by Ranks**

$k = 2$

χ_r^2	p	χ_r^2	p	χ_r^2	p	χ_r^2	p
$N=2$		**$N=3$**		**$N=4$**		**$N=5$**	
0	1.000	.000	1.000	.0	1.000	.0	1.000
1	.833	.667	.944	.5	.931	.4	.954
3	.500	2.000	.528	1.5	.653	1.2	.691
4	.167	2.667	.361	2.0	.431	1.6	.522
		4.667	.194	3.5	.273	2.8	.367
		6.000	.028	4.5	.125	3.6	.182
				6.0	.069	4.8	.124
				6.5	.042	5.2	.093
				8.0	.0046	6.4	.039
						7.6	.024
						8.4	.0085
						10.0	.00077

$k = 3$

χ_r^2	p	χ_r^2	p	χ_r^2	p	χ_r^2	p
$N=6$		**$N=7$**		**$N=8$**		**$N=9$**	
.00	1.000	.000	1.000	.00	1.000	.000	1.000
.33	.956	.286	.964	.25	.967	.222	.971
1.00	.740	.857	.768	.75	.794	.667	.814
1.33	.570	1.143	.620	1.00	.654	.889	.865
2.33	.430	2.000	.486	1.75	.531	1.556	.569
3.00	.252	2.571	.305	2.25	.355	2.000	.398
4.00	.184	3.429	.237	3.00	.285	2.667	.328
4.33	.142	3.714	.192	3.25	.236	2.889	.278
5.33	.072	4.571	.112	4.00	.149	3.556	.187
6.33	.052	5.429	.085	4.75	.120	4.222	.154
7.00	.029	6.000	.052	5.25	.079	4.667	.107
8.33	.012	7.143	.027	6.25	.047	5.556	.069
9.00	.0081	7.714	.021	6.75	.038	6.000	.057
9.33	.0055	8.000	.016	7.00	.030	6.222	.048
10.33	.0017	8.857	.0084	7.75	.018	6.889	.031
12.00	.00013	10.286	.0036	9.00	.0099	8.000	.019
		10.571	.0027	9.25	.0080	8.222	.016
		11.143	.0012	9.75	.0048	8.667	.010
		12.286	.00032	10.75	.0024	9.556	.0060
		14.000	.000021	12.00	.0011	10.667	.0035
				12.25	.00086	10.889	.0029
				13.00	.00026	11.556	.0013
				14.25	.000061	12.667	.00066
				16.00	.0000036	13.556	.00035
						14.000	.00020
						14.222	.000097
						14.889	.000054
						16.222	.000011
						18.000	.0000006

Source: M. Friedman, "The Use of Ranks to Avoid the Assumption of Normality Implicit in the Analysis of Variance," *Journal of the American Statistical Association,* vol. 32 (1937), pp. 688–89. Reprinted with the permission of the American Statistical Association.

(Continued next page)

Table M (continued)

$k = 4$

$N=2$		$N=3$		$N=4$			
χ_r^2	p	χ_r^2	p	χ_r^2	p	χ_r^2	p
.0	1.000	.2	1.000	.0	1.000	5.7	.141
.6	.958	.6	.958	.3	.992	6.0	.105
1.2	.834	1.0	.910	.6	.928	6.3	.094
1.8	.792	1.8	.727	.9	.900	6.6	.077
2.4	.625	2.2	.608	1.2	.800	6.9	.068
3.0	.542	2.6	.524	1.5	.754	7.2	.054
3.6	.458	3.4	.446	1.8	.677	7.5	.052
4.2	.375	3.8	.342	2.1	.649	7.8	.036
4.8	.208	4.2	.300	2.4	.524	8.1	.033
5.4	.167	5.0	.207	2.7	.508	8.4	.019
6.0	.042	5.4	.175	3.0	.432	8.7	.014
		5.8	.148	3.3	.389	9.3	.012
		6.6	.075	3.6	.355	9.6	.0069
		7.0	.054	3.9	.324	9.9	.0062
		7.4	.033	4.5	.242	10.2	.0027
		8.2	.017	4.8	.200	10.8	.0016
		9.0	.0017	5.1	.190	11.1	.00094
				5.4	.158	12.0	.000072

Table N   Probabilities Associated with Values as Large as Observed Values of H in the Kruskal-Wallis One-Way Analysis of Variance by Ranks

Sample sizes			H	p	Sample sizes			H	p
n_1	n_2	n_3			n_1	n_2	n_3		
2	1	1	2.7000	.500	4	3	2	6.4444	.008
								6.3000	.011
2	2	1	3.6000	.200				5.4444	.046
								5.4000	.051
2	2	2	4.5714	.067				4.5111	.098
			3.7143	.200				4.4444	.102
3	1	1	3.2000	.300	4	3	3	6.7455	.010
								6.7091	.013
3	2	1	4.2857	.100				5.7909	.046
			3.8571	.133				5.7273	.050
3	2	2	5.3572	.029				4.7091	.092
			4.7143	.048				4.7000	.101
			4.5000	.067					
			4.4643	.105	4	4	1	6.6667	.010
								6.1667	.022
3	3	1	5.1429	.043				4.9667	.048
			4.5714	.100				4.8667	.054
			4.0000	.129				4.1667	.082
								4.0667	.102
3	3	2	6.2500	.011	4	4	2	7.0364	.006
			5.3611	.032				6.8727	.011
			5.1389	.061				5.4545	.046
			4.5556	.100				5.2364	.052
			4.2500	.121				4.5545	.098
								4.4455	.103
3	3	3	7.2000	.004					
			6.4889	.011	4	4	3	7.1439	.010
			5.6889	.029				7.1364	.011
			5.6000	.050				5.5985	.049
			5.0667	.086				5.5758	.051
			4.6222	.100				4.5455	.099
								4.4773	.102
4	1	1	3.5714	.200					
					4	4	4	7.6538	.008
4	2	1	4.8214	.057				7.5385	.011
			4.5000	.076				5.6923	.049
			4.0179	.114				5.6538	.054
								4.6539	.097
4	2	2	6.0000	.014				4.5001	.104
			5.3333	.033					
			5.1250	.052	5	1	1	3.8571	.143
			4.4583	.100					
			4.1667	.105	5	2	1	5.2500	.036
								5.0000	.048
4	3	1	5.8333	.021				4.4500	.071
			5.2083	.050				4.2000	.095
			5.0000	.057				4.0500	.119
			4.0556	.093					
			3.8889	.129					

Source: W. H. Kruskal and W. A. Wallis, "Use of Ranks in One-Criterion Variance Analysis," *Journal of the American Statistical Association,* vol. 47 (1952), pp. 614–17. Reprinted with the permission of the American Statistical Association.

(Continued next page)

Table N **(continued)**

Sample sizes			H	p	Sample sizes			H	p
n_1	n_2	n_3			n_1	n_2	n_3		
5	2	2	6.5333	.008	5	4	4	7.7604	.009
			6.1333	.013				7.7440	.011
			5.1600	.034					
			5.0400	.056				5.6176	.050
			4.3733	.090				4.6187	.100
			4.2933	.122				4.5527	.102
			5.6571	.049					
					5	5	1	7.3091	.009
5	3	1	6.4000	.012				6.8364	.011
			4.9600	.048				5.1273	.046
			4.8711	.052				4.9091	.053
			4.0178	.095				4.1091	.086
			3.8400	.123				4.0364	.105
5	3	2	6.9091	.009	5	5	2	7.3385	.010
			6.8218	.010				7.2692	.010
			5.2509	.049				5.3385	.047
			5.1055	.052				5.2462	.051
			4.6509	.091				4.6231	.097
			4.4945	.101				4.5077	.100
5	3	3	7.0788	.009	5	5	3	7.5780	.010
			6.9818	.011				7.5429	.010
			5.6485	.049				5.7055	.046
			5.5152	.051				5.6264	.051
			4.5333	.097				4.5451	.100
			4.4121	.109				4.5363	.102
5	4	1	6.9545	.008	5	5	4	7.8229	.010
			6.8400	.011				7.7914	.010
			4.9855	.044				5.6657	.049
			4.8600	.056				5.6429	.050
			3.9873	.098				4.5229	.099
			3.9600	.102				4.5200	.101
5	4	2	7.2045	.009	5	5	5	8.0000	.009
			7.1182	.010				7.9800	.010
			5.2727	.049				5.7800	.049
			5.2682	.050				5.6600	.051
			4.5409	.098				4.5600	.100
			4.5182	.101				4.5000	.102
5	4	3	7.4449	.010					
			7.3949	.011					
			5.6564	.049					
			5.6308	.050					
			4.5487	.099					
			4.5231	.103					

Table O   **Critical Values of the Spearman Rank-Order Correlation Coefficient (r_s)**

N	Significance level (one-tailed test)	
	.05	.01
4	1.000	
5	.900	1.000
6	.829	.943
7	.714	.893
8	.643	.833
9	.600	.783
10	.564	.746
12	.506	.712
14	.456	.645
16	.425	.601
18	.399	.564
20	.377	.534
22	.359	.508
24	.343	.485
26	.329	.465
28	.317	.448
30	.306	.432

Source: E. G. Olds, "Distributions of Sums of Squares of Rank Differences for Small Numbers of Individuals," *Annals of Mathematical Statistics,* vol. 9 (1938), pp. 133–48. Reprinted with the permission of the Institute of Mathematical Statistics.

Index

UNDERSTANDING STATISTICS IN EDUCATION

Designed by Willis Proudfoot, Mt. Prospect, Illinois
Edited by Gloria Reardon, Belvidere, Illinois
Production supervision by Robert H. Grigg, Chicago, Illinois
Composition by Point West, Inc., Carol Stream, Illinois
Printed and bound by Braun-Brumfield, Inc., Ann Arbor, Michigan
Paper, 50 lb Springhill® Offset, by International Paper Co.
The text is set in English Times; display in Triumvirate